A Contractor's Guide

Remodeling Kitchens & Baths

Jack P. Jones

Craftsman Book Company
6058 Corte del Cedro, Carlsbad, CA 92009

acknowledgments

The author wishes to express his appreciation to the following companies and organizations for furnishing materials used in the preparation of various portions of this book:

American Olean Tile Co., Lansdale, Pennsylvania
American Woodmark Corp., Berryville, Virginia
Ceramic Tile Institute of America, Los Angeles, California
Dal-Tile Corp., Dallas, Texas
DuPont Co., Wilmington, Delaware
KitchenAid, Inc., St. Joseph, Michigan
Kohler Co., Kohler, Wisconsin
McKone & Co., (Ralph Wilson Plastics Co.), Irving, Texas
Merillat Industries, Inc., Adrian, Michigan
NuTone Inc., Cincinnati, Ohio
Philips Industries, Inc., Anaheim, California
Tub-Master Corp., Tuscaloosa, Alabama
Wood-Metal Industries, Inc., Kreamer, Pennsylvania

DEDICATION

This book is dedicated to Jessica, Ryan, and Rebecca

Library of Congress Cataloging-in-Publication Data

Jones, Jack Payne, 1928-
  Remodeling kitchens & baths.
  Includes index.

  1. Kitchens--Remodeling. 2. Bathrooms--Remodeling.
I. Title. II. Title: Remodeling kitchens and baths.
TH4816.3.K58J66 1989   643'.3   89-15901
ISBN 0-934041-44-X

contents

1

**Do You Want to Be a Remodeling Success?
Try Kitchens and Baths!   5**

What's in This Book for You? 6
Who Gets into the Remodeling Business? .. 7

2

Getting Started   8

Plan Your Success 8
Effective Advertising 11
Making the Sale 13
Keeping Up with the Latest Trends 31

3

Kitchen Design and Layout   32

Design for Efficiency 33
The Four Basic Kitchen Layouts 33
The Work Centers 36
Choosing the Right Colors for Your
 Design 41
Standard Design Dimensions 42
Planning Exercises 47

4

Installing Kitchen Cabinets   49

Cabinet Types and Specifications 52
Eurostyle or European Cabinetry 59
The Cabinet Layout 59
Preparations for Installing Kitchen
 Cabinets 64
The Installation 69
Estimating Manhours 74

5

Countertops and How to Install Them   84

Countertop Materials 84
How to Install Ceramic Tile Countertops ... 88
Solid-Material Countertops 105
Cross Sections of Tile Installation
 Methods 106
Installing a Corian Countertop 110
Estimating Manhours 119

6

Kitchen Sinks, Appliances, and Hoods   121

The Kitchen Sink 121
Built-in Cooktops .123
Range Hoods 125
Built-in Ovens 127
Dishwashers 130
The Ironing Center 138
Estimating Manhours 141

7

Bathroom Design and Layout   143

Bathroom Design .144
Remodeling the Modern Bathroom 146
Bathroom Layout .160
Bathroom Plans and Specifications 165

8

Installing Bathroom Fixtures   170

Installing the Tub 171
Installing a Fiberglass Shower Cove 181
Fiberglass Tub and Shower Units 187
Installing the Toilet 189
Installing the Lavatory 192
Electric Wall Heaters 199
Installing the Exhaust Fan 202
Wall Mounted Hair Dryer 207
Estimating Manhours 210

9

Installing Tub and Shower Surrounds **211**
Installing a Bathtub Wall Kit 212
Installing a Shower Wall 221
Installing a Tub Surround
   Over Ceramic Tile 230
Estimating Manhours 233

10

**Ceramic Tile Tub and Shower Wall
Installations** **235**
Installation Details 237
Bathtub Walls 237
Shower Walls and Receptors 241
Estimating Tile Manhours 244

11

Residential Wiring **249**
The Residential Electrical System 249
Adding on to the Household Electrical
   System 252
Manhours for Electrical Wiring 265

12

Suspended and Luminous Ceilings **267**
Determine Your Client's Lighting Needs . 267
The Room Layout 268
Material Requirements 273
Installation 274
Estimating Manhours 280

13

Redoing Floors **281**
Know Your Floors 281
Removing Existing Flooring 283
Use the Right Underlayment 285
Sheet Vinyl Floor Installation 286
Installing Vinyl-Composition Tile 294
Estimating Manhours 297

14

Redoing Walls and Ceilings **298**
Working with Interior Walls 298
Interior Wall Finishes 305

Working with Drywall 306
Plywood and Hardboard 314
Estimating Wallboard Costs 315
Plaster 321
The Trim 323
Wallpaper 326

15

How to Install Skylights **327**
Choose the Appropriate Skylight 327
Curb-Mounted Skylights 328
Self-Flashing Skylights 332
The Bubble Skylight 334
The Light Shaft 335
Estimating Manhours 337

16

The Use of Paint **338**
Texture and Color Sense 338
How Color Affects Us 340
Paint Materials 341
Surface Preparation 344
Now You're Ready to Paint 348
Paint Estimating 350

17

You Need a Business Plan **355**
How to Use This 355
The Business Plan Worksheet 356
How Will I Market My Business? 358
Planning Effective Advertising 360
What Personnel and Equipment Do
   You Need? 362
Put Your Plan Into Dollars 363
Put Your Plan Into Action 365
Planning the Work 366

18

Managing for Profits **368**
The Function of Management 368
How to Build Your Management Ability ..370
Record Keeping 371
Compare Operating Ratios 373
Overhead 378

Index **380**

Do You Want To Be a Remodeling Success?

Try Kitchens & Baths!

Remodeling homes is big business. If projected estimates are correct, there will be $65 to $70 billion dollars spent next year on remodeling owner-occupied homes, and another $30 to $40 billion spent on fixing up rental homes. A large slice of that remodeling money will go towards updating and improving kitchens and bathrooms. In fact, these are the most popular home remodeling projects.

As a remodeling contractor, you can carve yourself out a share of this lucrative market. Remodeling offers you a higher return on your time and investment than most building and construction projects, including new construction. Kitchen and bathroom reconstruction is especially attractive because there's a steady demand for the services of good contractors. Every home has a kitchen and a bath. They're the most intensely used rooms in a house, and the first ones homeowners want to modernize when they're ready for a change.

Remodeling isn't the place to begin learning the basics of construction, however. If you don't have the skills, or the money to hire people who do, don't even think about getting into the business. Depending on your area of the country, a basic kitchen remodeling job will cost at least $12,000.

Redoing a bathroom will run a minimum of $5,000. When people spend that kind of money on their kitchens and bathrooms, they expect to get what they want. If you're going to be successful, you'd better be able to give them *more* than what they want. After all, you're the professional!

Sometimes you'll have to wreck a kitchen or bath before you can remodel it. Wrecking someone's home is very touchy business. You must know exactly what to remove, and how to remove it. This isn't the demolition derby. If you don't know what you're doing, look out! You can lose your assets.

As in any business, survival in remodeling depends on recognizing the pitfalls of the profession and learning how to avoid them. This book will help you increase your opportunities— and your profits— in the competitive business of kitchen and bathroom remodeling.

In the 25 years I've spent building, remodeling, and repairing homes, I've learned what it takes to make a good living in kitchen and bath work. I know the business inside and out. Between the covers of this book I'm going to explain everything I've learned in those 25 years.

But be forewarned. I'm not a wheeler-dealer, razzle-dazzle blue suede shoe remodeling sharpie. I'm not a paper contractor with no crews and no payroll. I don't sub out all the work once a job is sold. I've seen lots of remodelers like that come and go in the last 25 years. From my standpoint, the secret of success is quality workmanship. If you can produce quality work at a fair price, you'll always have work to do and will always earn a fair profit — even when others close up shop and drift off to some other line of work.

Anyone who doesn't deliver a good job time after time will be pushed aside by those who do. The competition in remodeling is keen. If you want to succeed, you'd better learn the guiding rule now: Those who do good work, do good.

What's in This Book for You?

Let's get down to the nuts and bolts of remodeling kitchens and baths. I'll advise you on everything you need to know about the profession, from how to get the job, to producing a project that both you and your customers are proud of. Every chapter in this book is packed with information and illustrations to help you on your way to success.

First we'll talk about getting started, and how to keep new work rolling in — with the accent on advertising and sales. But the real concern of this book is how to get the job done. I'll give you pointers on designing new kitchens and baths; step-by-step instruction on installing cabinets, countertops, tile, appliances, fixtures, wiring and even skylights; we'll go over all the details you need to know to redo walls, ceilings, and floors; and finally, how to provide the finishing touches that will please the homeowner and guarantee you a profit.

A major concern on every job is how to inspect the site and make accurate estimates of materials and labor. This is the first, and probably the worst place you're going to make a mistake. Each chapter in this book deals with estimating a particular area of kitchen and bath work. I'll also explain how to incorporate your overhead expenses, job costs, taxes, insurance and even your profit into every estimate.

Accurate estimates are crucial to the job. If you underestimate a couple of items, you can kiss your profits goodbye. If you overestimate, someone who's better at figuring costs will probably get the job.

Kitchen and bathroom remodeling is hard to estimate accurately. There's one thing you can count on though; everything you do in remodeling takes *at least* twice as long as it would in new construction. For instance, it may take thirty minutes to install a window in a new home. It can take you as long as four hours to enlarge an opening for a similar window in an older home. Who pays for this extra work? You do — in the form of lost profits — if your manhour estimates aren't correct.

Many people have asked me, "What's the leading cause of failure in the kitchen and bath remodeling business?" If you've ever done a remodeling project, you probably know the answer. It's forgetting to crawl under the house to look at the joists and floor under the kitchen and bathroom. It's failing to check the plumbing and wiring, and forgetting to allow for what has to be repaired or replaced. It's not allowing enough manhours for tearing out old floors, walls, and ceilings, and hauling off the debris.

It's forgetting to figure in the time needed to work around appliances, fixtures, furniture *and occupants*. In short . . . it's bad estimating. The "hiders" are the things that can really bury your chances of success in this business.

When you're estimating remodeling, you can't assume *anything* unless it's this: Nothing will fit, nothing will match, and everything you can't see will have to be replaced.

Who Gets into the Remodeling Business?

Many contractors end up in the remodeling business purely by accident. They may have started by remodeling their own home or building a weekend cottage. Then a neighbor or friend, seeing what they had done, hired them to do a small remodeling or room addition project. Soon, word-of-mouth had them in business.

Some contractors began remodeling kitchens and baths as a sideline while working full time on larger projects. They discovered that they prefer smaller, quicker jobs. Many tradespeople, tired of working for others, decide to try business on their own. Kitchen and bath work seems like the logical starting point for them.

It's not important where or how you learned construction skills. It's only important that you be competent at the job you've chosen to do. You don't have to be a master of every trade to manage your own company. It's essential, though, that you be able to recognize professional quality workmanship.

Most remodelers start out small, working with a one- or two-man crew. They work one job at a time until they have enough business to hire additional crews and handle several jobs at once. Some remodelers keep on expanding like this until they've built a large company. A growing remodeling business, like any business, requires good management skills, hard work, and long hours. It also involves risk. That's not for everyone. Some remodelers prefer to stay small and more easily manageable. They concentrate on profits, quality, and building a professional reputation. There's nothing wrong with that. One of the nice things about the remodeling business is that you can have it either way. It's your choice.

Whether you remain a one-crew outfit or decide to expand and grow, one fact is certain. Before you succeed at running a large remodeling business, you have to succeed in running a small one.

It's amazing how many mistakes you can make when you're learning anything as complex as running a remodeling project. And the lessons are usually expensive! It's one thing to make expensive mistakes remodeling your own bathroom. It's devastating when it happens on a job you're being paid for. That can cost you both your profit *and* your pride. The purpose of this book is to help you steer clear of the most common mistakes and save you a bundle in the process.

Remodeling is like building a ship out on the open ocean. Once you start, you've got to finish. There's no other choice. One mistake and the darn thing can sink, taking you down with it. Fortunately, staying out of trouble is fairly easy if you know the fundamentals: *how to, why to, where to, when to, how much*, and *how long*. You need to understand the key parts of a job and how they fit together. Those who do make a good living in the kitchen and bathroom business. If that's what you want, go on to Chapter 2.

Getting Started

It takes a lot of hard work to earn success in any field. Kitchen and bathroom remodeling is no exception. While there are many successful remodelers earning excellent profits for their know-how and performance, there are many who fail every year and go back to working for others. The successful ones are those who did their homework and planned for their success.

Plan Your Success

It's fairly easy to sell something when buyers have few choices in who they buy from. However, kitchen and bath remodeling isn't that kind of business. It's very competitive, and unless you live in a small town, it'll take time for you to build a reputation.

When new home construction is up, your competition will be down. But when general housing construction bottoms out, contractors looking for work invariably enter the remodeling field. It may be the only type of residential construction being done. When that happens, it may seem like there are a hundred contractors competing for every job.

Success in the remodeling business is built on satisfied customers. When you do it right, every job should sell two or three more. Figures 2-1 and 2-2 are examples of the kind of work that speaks volumes about your skill and professionalism. But even if every job you do looks this great, you'll still need to advertise and keep your name in front of the public. Until you've completed a few successful jobs, advertising is the only way you have to find new business.

Bringing in Prospective Customers

When I say you need to advertise, you may start thinking, "Oh no, there goes my budget. If I do that, I'll have to have an office and someone to

Figure 2-1
An attractive and efficient kitchen design
Courtesy: Merrillat Industries, Inc.

answer the phone." That's not necessarily the case. Many small businesses are run out of the contractor's home, with family members helping out with calls and bookkeeping. If that won't work for you, you can have your office in the cab of your pickup and have an answering service take your calls. You need to keep your expenses down at first, but you still have to advertise or you won't have enough work to keep your crew busy.

Business will seldom hunt you down. At least not until you're well established and you've edged out some of the competition. You have to be aggressive, and you have to *sell* your services. You have to look for the good business — the kind where you get not only the kitchen job but the bathroom remodeling work as well. The high-margin work is found by those who go after it. You can't survive in remodeling by always being the lowest bidder. All businesses need to make a

Figure 2-2
Space and comfort in a remodeled bathroom
Courtesy: Merrillat Industries, Inc.

profit. The trick is to keep your company name before likely prospects, and then convince those people that you can do the best work at the best price.

You can do that through advertising. You have to help people associate your company's name with remodeling — and with quality. Word-of-mouth is one form of advertising. That may be all you need in a small town, but even then you should back it up with an ad in the Yellow Pages or your local telephone directory. In larger towns and cities, word-of-mouth helps, but it's never enough to bring in a constant flow of prospects. You can't rely on your reputation alone to build up your bank account.

The first step in promoting your business through advertising is to plan your market area. How large an area do you live in? How far can you realistically travel to a job? If you have more than one job at a time, how much time can you afford to spend commuting between them? Be careful when you think about these questions. You want a large enough market to bring in a steady business, but you don't want to get yourself strung out. The larger the population in your community, the smaller your area can be. The smaller the population, the larger your service area should be.

Your goal is to be sure that every potential client in your targeted area associates your name with remodeling kitchens and bathrooms. If your last name happens to be Kitchens, you have a ready-made association. If your full name is Tubs N. Kitchens, you surely wouldn't need an advertising specialist to capitalize on that!

Effective Advertising

Invest your advertising dollars wisely. Advertising can make your personal sales efforts more productive, and create public goodwill. It brings in inquiries and starts people thinking about a "new" kitchen or bathroom. It's also an effective way to keep in touch with former clients. You want them to think of you for their future remodeling work and for referrals.

If you're just starting out in business, you probably can't afford to use every form of advertising that's available. Select what best suits your community and your budget. You want to reach the largest number of potential clients for the least amount of money. Here are some of the possibilities:

- The Yellow Pages
- Flyers and doorknob hangers
- Job signs
- Direct mail letters
- Newspapers
- Billboards and posters
- Bus stop benches
- Local radio and TV

Every home has a kitchen and a bathroom. Most have a TV set. Why not advertise on television and cover the whole market in one blast? Because that doesn't work. One-shot TV spots are just that. They're a shot in the dark. They aren't cost-effective because they only hit the audience one time. You need consistency in your advertising program. People need to see your company name over and over again until your company and remodeling become a natural association, like bacon and eggs or Laurel and Hardy.

Most kitchen and bath remodelers spend the majority of their advertising dollars on ads in the Yellow Pages and newspapers. The Yellow Pages get into almost every home and office. So you have a ready-made audience. A nice ad will pay for itself in the business it attracts. People automatically turn to the Yellow Pages when they need to locate a service.

Local newspapers are also a good advertising bet. You don't need to run an ad every day of the week. Think about the Sunday "Home" section, or the service directory in a biweekly local paper. You want your advertising where you'll get your best local exposure. Check with the newspapers in your area. They'll not only give you advice, they'll probably help you design your ad.

There are other good and inexpensive ways to advertise. You can have circulars professionally printed and then distribute them in selected areas where people are likely to need remodeling services. Figure 2-3 is an example of a flyer designed to fit over a doorknob. Put them out in neighborhoods where you're working and briefly describe the kind of remodeling work you do.

I've found that a sign advertising my company brings good results when placed in the front yard of the homes where I'm doing a job. Most homeowners don't object to a sign if it's tastefully done and not too large. A 24 by 36 inch sign is about the right size. Make it professional and attractive. Your name and phone number should be featured. Add a logo or slogan if you have one.

Homeowners who are looking for a remodeling contractor often contact lumber yards, builder's supply houses, or cabinet shops for referrals. Get

Figure 2-3
Doorhangers can bring in additional neighborhood business

some attractive business cards and pass them out to as many businesses as you can find. Put your business card on bulletin boards in supermarkets, laundries, hardware stores and anywhere prospective customers are likely to see them.

Use your pickup or van to advertise your business. A vehicle with your company name and telephone number painted on the sides helps to establish you as a professional. Remember, you'll often be judged by the truck you drive, so make sure it's kept up. A remodeler in a dirty, beat-up truck doesn't present a very good image. You don't need a new truck every year. Just keep the one you drive painted and in good repair, and most important, *keep it clean!*

Other forms of advertising are available. But they're usually more expensive. When you have a medium-to-large business or you're ready to expand to that size, then look into broadcast advertising or display advertising that can reach a larger audience. Remember that attracting more business than you can handle is almost as bad as not attracting enough. It's very easy to get in over your head and lose control. That's why careful planning is important.

Build a Prospect List

Your advertising will bring inquiries — nothing more. But every sale begins with an inquiry from a prospective customer. That's the source of your future business. Even if you don't make an immediate sale, keep prospect names on file. Use the list for direct-mail marketing.

Also keep a list of your past customers. If they're happy with the kitchen you modernized for them last year, they might be thinking about having you redo their old bathroom. And those who hired you to remodel their bathroom could be likely prospects for a kitchen update. Keep your eye on future business and include your past clients on your holiday greetings list.

Remember, if you want the job, you have to go after it, work for it, and earn it. Every community is unique. Use your imagination to find the best way to turn each prospect into a customer.

Making the Sale

Once your advertising starts bringing in prospects, you can begin to sell your product. What you're selling is quality workmanship and remodeling design. But you have to be sold on yourself before you can sell to someone else. You have to be confident that your product is one that you're proud of.

Kitchen and bath remodeling requires a great deal of skill. It's a high-prestige occupation. Always remember when you approach a prospect that you have something worthwhile to sell. Ask yourself this question: "Why am I the best one for this job?" Review all your positive attributes. When you feel sure that you're the best in the business, it's time to go in and make the sale.

What Is Selling?

Your skill as a salesperson turns prospects into clients. Enthusiasm is contagious. Selling is just a matter of making the client feel as excited about your proposition as you are. When you have a sincere desire to solve your prospects' problems, your honesty and good common sense will win their agreement. Successful selling requires knowledge and a sensitivity to what your prospects want and can afford. It doesn't require a highly persuasive personality.

While there may be some "natural-born salesmen," anyone can learn to sell. It's no mystery. Anyone can learn the basics of selling. But if you don't feel comfortable selling, it may be better to hire someone who likes this type of work.

But if you do enjoy selling and want to hone your skills, there are several books you can read to help you develop your techniques. There are even some available which deal specifically with selling remodeling. One is *How to Sell Remodeling*. You can order a copy using the order form in the back of this book. Or a phone call to the number given will get you the book in a matter of days.

What's the difference between an average salesperson and a really good salesperson? Creativity. Sometimes one remodeler may lose out on a job, only to have a second contractor make the sale a week later. And not only did the other contractor get the job, but it turned out to be a bigger and better project than the first remodeler had bid on! What happened? The first contractor simply bid the job the homeowner requested: new kitchen cabinets, flooring and tile. The second bidder developed an imaginative new kitchen design . . . and the homeowners loved what they saw.

Routine salesmanship is giving the customer simply what he asks for and nothing more. Creative salesmanship is showing the possibilities, educating your customers on want can be done. Your prospects know they need something new. They may not know exactly what they want. Maybe they liked a picture they saw in a magazine. But they probably don't know whether their home is suited for the changes they have in mind. They need someone to show them the possibilities and to help them through their choices. A good salesperson can *create* a desire that's so compelling that it overcomes any hesitancy that the homeowner feels about remodeling.

As a creative and effective salesperson you need to approach each situation with a plan. At the first meeting, listen carefully, make notes, suggest a few alternatives, show some pictures (either out of a remodeling magazine or of work you've done) and then offer to come back with a specific proposal.

At the second meeting, bring rough sketches for a remodeled kitchen *and* bathroom that are suited to their home. Then point out how the changes would add to the comfort and appearance of the house, as well as increasing its market value. People don't buy *remodeling*, they buy the *benefits* that remodeling provides.

Selling is part product and part psychology. A farmer doesn't just buy a tractor — he buys convenience, lower labor costs, increased horsepower, and ease of operation. And when we buy a house, we don't buy a shelter, we buy a home. We buy the freedom to do our own decorating, to have a garden, to create a private and comfortable world of our own. We buy with both our intellect and our emotions. A good salesperson knows this and uses this knowledge in selling.

Prepare a Presentation Kit

A presentation kit is a valuable tool for turning prospects into customers. Gather together photographs, drawings, sketches, charts, and manufacturers' brochures to show your customers. These are visual aids. When you use visual aids in a presentation, your customers know exactly what you're talking about. You help them visualize what you can do for them.

Any homeowner can appreciate the beauty of the kitchen and bath shown in Figures 2-1 and 2-2. The rooms are spacious, well-designed and functional. Visual aids can help turn curiosity into reality for your prospect. People rarely want what they can't see. But if you produce a picture or a sketch of someone's dream kitchen and you can make the design work for them, you've got a sale.

Include an assortment of kitchen and bathroom photos in your presentation kit. You'll want to be able to show prospects pictures of rooms similar in size and shape to what you'll have to work with. You can't show someone pictures of a large, elaborate custom kitchen and expect them to believe you can make their 8 x 12 cubicle look like that. You have to have a variety of examples to suit a variety of customers.

Cabinet makers such as *Merillat Industries, Inc.* and *Wood-Metal Industries, Inc.* supply their trade customers with kitchen design and planning kits.

They also have color photographs of kitchen and bathroom jobs that include their products.

Wood-Metal Industries are manufacturers of the *Wood-Mode* line of custom cabinets shown in Figures 2-4 and 2-5. They'll custom-design cabinets for odd shaped or otherwise unique projects. Many remodelers of expensive projects prefer to offer custom-designed cabinets rather than modular units. Photographs like these will be a helpful addition to the cabinetry section of your kit.

Kohler Company makes and distributes a wide range of plumbing products. They can furnish sales aids for your presentation kit.

Your presentation kit won't be complete without tile and marble information. Ceramic tile is a good choice for kitchen and bathroom countertops and floors, as well as bathroom walls and showers. *American Olean Tile Company*, like many other companies, has excellent tile material you can include.

Make your portfolio as complete as possible. Visit the kitchen and bathroom displays at retail stores and contractor's supply companies in your area. They're an excellent source for kit materials and ideas. Include catalogs and brochures for every item that might be included in a kitchen or bath remodel. If your clients want to know what type of kitchen or bathroom exhaust fan you plan to install, be ready to show them.

The following list of manufacturers will be helpful in starting your presentation kit. But don't stop with these, there are a lot more sources and many more companies that will be happy to provide you with information on their products.

Kitchen and Bathroom Cabinetry:

Merillat Industries, Inc.
Corporate Headquarters
P.O. Box 1946
Adrian, Michigan 49221
(517) 263-0771

Wood-Metal Industries, Inc.
Kreamer, Snyder County, PA 17833
(717) 374-2711

Figure 2-4
Custom designed cabinets and work island
Courtesy: Wood-Mode Cabinetry

American Woodmark Corporation
P.O. Box 514
Berryville, VA 22611
(703) 955-3174

Ceramic Tile:

American Olean Tile Company
Executive Offices
Lansdale, PA 19446-0271
(215) 855-1111

Dal-Tile Corporation
P.O. Box 17130
Dallas, Texas 75217
(214) 398-1411

Corian, Countertops and Tub and Shower Enclosures:

DuPont Company, Inc.
External Affairs Dept.
Wilmington, DE 19898
(302) 774-3830

Figure 2-5
Customized cabinets can fit into odd-shaped areas
Courtesy: Wood-Mode Cabinetry

Bath and Kitchen Fixtures:

> Kohler Company
> Kohler, WI 53044
> (414) 457-4441

Ventilating Fans, Heat Lamps, Medicine Cabinets, Lighting Fixtures:

> NuTone Inc.
> Madison & Red Bank Roads
> Cincinnati, OH 45227
> (513) 527-5100

Selling Steps

Once you've organized an effective presentation kit, it's time to take it on the road and use it. There are four elements to the sales process:

1) The preparation
2) The approach
3) The interview or presentation
4) The closing

The Preparation: Before you approach the prospect, you'd better be prepared for the meeting. Get as much information about the prospect as you can before your visit. Try to avoid going to see prospects "cold" — that is, without knowing anything about them. You can get most of the information you need about prospects by careful screening during your initial phone call.

Find out about the family's circumstances. Inquire about the type of kitchen or bathroom they want. Find out how many people will be involved in the buying decision. You'll want them all there when you make your presentation. Make sure you're familiar with the area where the prospects live, and the kind of housing you'll find there. You'll need to know how old the home is. If it's in a tract, you might be able to get a copy of the floor plan before you visit the site.

The preparation includes knowing your proposal in detail. Be ready to modify your arguments, meet objections, and maneuver around a cold turn-down.

The Approach: Your first approach to a prospective customer is a sale in itself. You have to sell your prospect on the idea of letting you have enough time to present your ideas completely. Many people automatically resist any sales attempt. Your approach will have to overcome that resistance. There are five steps to turning prospects into clients.

1) Get the prospects' attention

2) Arouse their interest in your proposition

3) Show the real value in what you're offering

4) Make the prospects want it

5) Be sure they want it enough to buy it

First, give the prospects some idea of what you want to do for them. Arouse their curiosity. If you've done your homework, you'll know something about what they want. Show how your proposal will be the perfect solution for them.

Think about how they'll react to what you say. What would be *your* reaction to a salesman who wants to sell you the cabinets for a kitchen you're remodeling? Suppose he says, "I'd like to sell you the cabinets you'll need on this job." That probably won't do anything for you. You don't hear any extra coins going into your pocket, or see any reason to change from your present supplier.

But what if that salesman said instead: "I can save you twenty-five percent on the cabinet cost and guarantee they're a better quality than what you've been getting." You'll probably put down your hammer and look him over. "Yeah? Tell me more." He caught your attention. You're willing to listen. He's taken a successful first step in making a sale.

Base your approach on the customer's self-interest. Make them think about what your proposal will do for them. To approach your prospects most effectively, ask yourself this question: "Why should these people give me fifteen minutes of their time?" Your honest answer will give you the key to your approach.

Why would anyone want their kitchen remodeled? Because very often the kitchen is the center of the house. A nice kitchen makes the home more comfortable, attractive, and efficient. It also increases the resale value of the property far more than the cost of the remodeling job.

That's a good opening approach. You're talking about benefits to the customer. You're going to make their property more useful, attractive and valuable. Get them interested by explaining it in a way they can believe. Stay away from technical jargon. Use familiar phrases and descriptions that work quickly and effectively on the imagination.

The Presentation: Now move on into your presentation. There are two avenues of appeal you can use. One is through logic and intellect, the other through imagination and emotions. Few people decide a matter by logic alone. What's surprising is that many sales *are* made on the basis of emotional appeal alone. Most often however, people make decisions based on a mixture of logic and emotion.

People respond better to pictures than words or verbal descriptions. Now is the time to take out your presentation kit. Show your customers what you can do for them. Help them build mental images which include them as the central figure. If you don't have an actual photograph or draw-

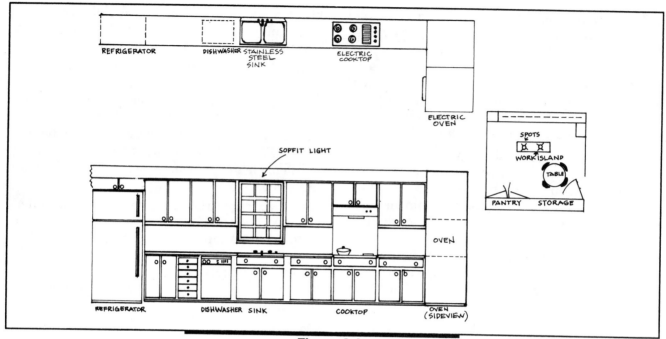

Figure 2-6
Floor plan and elevation

ing of what the finished project will look like, make your own drawing or sketch and describe in detail what you'd like to do for them.

A kitchen with windows shaded by trees needs more lighting. You might say, "We'll install an energy-saving skylight in the ceiling to throw natural light over the work areas. You'll be amazed at how much electricity can be saved by not having to burn your kitchen lights all the time. The skylight will soon pay for itself and you'll have a brighter kitchen."

With every new client you have to develop trust and confidence. You have to show them you're a professional with creative ideas and the skill to turn those ideas into reality. Your remodeling plan is the key step in developing this confidence. You're not charging for this initial session. You're establishing yourself, in the eyes of your prospect, as someone who is honest and capable, and who can get the job done.

Use your plan to claim your prospect's attention and hold it. It will give them something def-

inite to focus on and keep their mind from wandering away from your presentation. While you draw, discuss costs and financing. You can give your clients an idea of the price range they're getting into and find out if they plan to obtain a home improvement loan or pay cash.

Another advantage of including a plan in your presentation is to give prospects the opportunity to show you what they like and dislike. Each decision they make on your plan puts you one step closer to making a sale. Throughout your presentation, you'll be making suggestions, countering objections, offering reassurances, and skillfully closing your sale.

The plan as a sales tool— Figure 2-6 is a floor plan and elevation of a kitchen. Designing a detailed layout of a kitchen or bathroom takes a lot of thought and work. The plan or sketch you make and describe during your presentation is a preliminary drawing which you can use as a sales tool. Don't spend too much time and effort on this plan. More than one remodeler has developed a complete and detailed plan at no cost to the po-

---

Memorandum of Agreement

The undersigned agree to have _____

prepare a floor plan, elevation view, construction cost estimate and outline specifications for a pro-

posed remodeling of the _____in the

residence located at _____

at a cost of _____. The sum of _____

is hereby acknowledged as received and the balance is due upon completion of the plans, estimate

and specifications. If_____

is authorized to complete all or a substantial portion of the work proposed, the fee for preparing the

plan, estimate and specifications will be credited in full against the cost of construction.

Owner _____   Builder _____

Owner _____   Date _____

Figure 2-7
Memorandum of agreement

tential client, only to have the client hire a carpenter to do the work shown in the free plan!

If your prospects want more than a freehand sketch on the spot, tell them you'll be happy to design a personalized kitchen or bathroom — for a fee. Explain that if you do the job, the fee will be applied to the remodeling contract. If your prospects are sincere about the remodeling job, the fee won't scare them off.

Your fee depends on what you're going to produce. A complete work-up includes a floor plan, elevation, drawings, specifications, and a detailed estimate. You should charge enough to pay you for your time plus a decent profit.

Sometimes people will come up with their own plans and ask you to give them an estimate. Beware of designs a relative or friend did for your prospect. Check them over carefully; they're often loaded with errors. You don't want to be footing the bill for someone else's mistakes.

Closing the Sale: Chances are, if your prospects are pleased with your preliminary drawing, they'll ask you to work up a detailed plan and an estimate. It's now time to bring out a copy of the Memorandum of Agreement shown in Figure 2-7. This is a formal agreement for the design and layout services that you can provide independent of the remodeling work. Again, the cost of this service will be included in the construction contract if they approve your plan. It's possible that they may already be sold on your company, and you may be able to write up the contract at this point. If not, be sure that you have an agreement in writing before providing your design services.

Your next planning step is to have your customers complete a Kitchen Preference Form and/or Bathroom Preference Form. These are questionnaires that will help you create designs suited to the taste of your clients. Figures 2-8 and 2-9 are sample preference forms that you can use. Create your own forms if you prefer and include your own special design ideas.

When you have all the information you need, set up a date for a follow-up appointment. You can now draw a detailed "before" and "after" floor plan of the kitchen or bathroom with all the measurements. This will be your sales clincher, so make it as appealing as possible. How much "designing" you do depends on your method of operation. But you'll need to give your clients enough material so they can make a decision. Pictures, floor plans, elevation drawings, specs, color charts, material samples and fixture brochures are all an effective part of the design package.

Next, you'll work up your cost figures in a format similar to Figure 2-10. Then prepare a contract for signature. Keep in mind that you'll need to make a complete inspection of wiring, plumbing, structural soundness of floors, walls and any other areas that you'll be involved with before agreeing to a dollar amount. Figure 2-11 is a sample Proposal and Contract form. You must include the federally required notice that describes the customer's right to cancel the contract, shown in Figure 2-12.

Be sure you have with you all the paperwork and information you need to close the sale when you make your presentation. If you *can* complete the sale, you'll be ready. If the prospects sign the contract, the job is yours. Don't stay and visit. Leave before you talk yourself out of the job. Conversation after the fact always leads to new questions by the homeowner and your off-the-cuff answers may not be what the owner wants to hear.

Often, after your presentation or even after you return with your design, the prospects are still reluctant to sign the contract. Search out their objections and get around them. If you're well prepared, this shouldn't be hard to do. Remember, if you don't get the job now, you probably never will. It's important that you be prepared to offer reasons why it's to their advantage to sign now. You might come up with some ideas similar to these:

1) You're working in the neighborhood and you can start your crew on the job without delay. This will result in a lower cost to them.

2) Materials and labor costs will be going up soon. You can't guarantee you can do the job at the same price at a later date.

3) The job is estimated at bottom dollar because you have a slack period before your next scheduled project and need "fill-in" work to keep your crew busy.

4) Or, you might say, "I'd like to get on this project as soon possible. We've hired on some new craftsmen and we're running ahead of schedule. In order to keep the crew busy, I'm prepared to add that skylight (or cooktop, exhaust fan, etc.) at no charge. All you have to do is OK the job right now. I hate to lay off good craftsmen. I might not be able to get them back." Then hand the prospect a pen and the contract to sign. Often, they'll sign right away. Everyone likes to think they're getting a deal.

Persistence pays off when closing. If your prospects are reluctant to sign, there's a reason. Go over the highlights of your presentation, emphasizing the advantages of having the work done. Feel them out. Find out what the reasons are for not signing, counter them, then close the sale.

The "Other" Room

The "other" room is the second half of the kitchen and bath remodeler's business. Once you close the sale on kitchen remodeling, direct the homeowner's interest to redoing their old bathroom. If you've just closed a bathroom remodeling job, lead into remodeling the kitchen. Explain there's a 3 to 5 percent savings when they have

Kitchen Preference Form

Name _____

Address _____ Phone _____ Date _____

To design a kitchen to an individual's personal preference, it is essential to know what that individual desires in a kitchen. In order for us to personalize your kitchen, please check the following:

1. My personal kitchen should have:
☐ A quiet corner where I can relax while alone or with a friend over a cup of coffee.
☐ Soft lighting for a "meal for two" or a quiet moment.
☐ A radio.
☐ A television set.
☐ An intercom system to the rest of the house.
☐ A view of my garden or the outside.
☐ A telephone extension.
☐ Access to a convenience bath.
☐ Open view to the family room.

_____

_____

2. My favorite kitchen colors are:
☐ Bright tones   ☐ Soft tones   ☐ Medium tones
☐ A mixture of colors for soft contrast.
☐ A mixture of colors for bright contrast.
☐ White   ☐ green   ☐ yellow   ☐ orange
　　　☐ red   ☐ blue   ☐ purple

_____

_____

3. I want my kitchen to have the following:
☐ Refrigerator with freezer compartment in the:
　　　☐ top   ☐ bottom   ☐ side by side
☐ Refrigerator with ☐ ice maker   ☐ ice and water dispenser in the door
☐ A double sink
☐ A single sink
☐ Breakfast nook
☐ Breakfast bar
☐ Dishwasher
☐ Garbage disposal unit
☐ Trash compactor
☐ Ceiling fan
☐ Built-in oven
☐ Built-in mixer
☐ Range top
☐ Lazy Susan shelves
☐ Range hood
☐ Molded countertop

☐ Cabinets
　　type _____
　　style _____
☐ Air conditioning
☐ Cabinets extended to ceiling
☐ Lowered ceilings
☐ Microwave oven
☐ More wall outlets
☐ Separate freezer
☐ New floor covering
☐ Chopping block
☐ New wall covering
☐ Built-in ironing board
☐ Repainted
☐ Broom closet
☐ Pantry
☐ Multiple lighting for:
　　bright _____
　　soft _____
☐ Conventional lighting

4. I prefer a kitchen with:
☐ More window space   ☐ Less window space
☐ Same window space   ☐ More floor space
☐ Less floor space   ☐ Same floor space

5. Of the four basic kitchen plans I like the following best:
☐ U-shaped   ☐ L-shaped   ☐ Corridor   ☐ One-wall

6. The worst points about my present kitchen are:

_____

_____

7. My favorite color for appliances is:_____

_____

8. My favorite theme is:
☐ Contemporary (clean lines, bold colors, natural wood)
☐ Early American (pewter, copper utensils, traditional woods)
☐ Traditional (flexible style, simple, informal)
☐ Spanish/Mediterranean (wrought iron, massive wood)

9. My choice of floor covering is:
☐ Vinyl   ☐ Carpet   ☐ Inlaid style   ☐ Tile
☐ Resilient tile   ☐ Other _____

Figure 2-8
Kitchen preference form

10. My wall choice is:
☐ Paint ☐ Wallpaper
☐ Paneling ☐ Brick ☐ Stone

11. My ceiling choice is:
☐ Luminous ☐ Beamed ☐ Textured
☐ Drop ☐ Paneling ☐ Paint

12. I will consider:
☐ Changing location of windows.
☐ Changing location of doors.
☐ Opening new doorway or closing existing one.
☐ Opening new window or closing existing one.
☐ Extending kitchen beyond house walls (addition).
☐ Changing location of
☐ sink ☐ range ☐ refrigerator.
☐ Adding new cabinets.
☐ Replacing old cabinets with new.
☐ Redoing existing cabinets.

13. I would like my kitchen to look like:
☐ The attached picture.
☐ My friend's, whose address is _____

_____

☐ My own creation.

14. If I am unable to completely redo my kitchen at this time, the following may be put off until later:
☐ New appliances ☐ New cabinets
☐ New countertops
☐ Flooring ☐ Walls ☐ Ceiling

15. How many in your family: adults _____,
children _____? Ages of children _____?

16. The height of the person who will use the kitchen most is _____

17. The kitchen will be used to prepare meals for:
☐ Breakfast ☐ Lunch ☐ Dinner
on a ☐ regular ☐ irregular basis

18. I entertain adult guests ☐ seldom ☐ often,
about _____ times a month.

19. I would like to have the following in the kitchen:
☐ Laundry area ☐ Eating area ☐ Desk/art area
☐ Bar ☐ Children's play area

20. If I had to put a dollar limit on a personalized kitchen, that limit would be $ _____

21. The kitchen layout I like would look something like this:

Figure 2-8
Kitchen preference form (continued)

Bathroom Preference Form

Name_____

Address _____ Phone _____ Date _____

In order to design a personalized bathroom for you, it is essential to know what your preferences are. Please review this form and make selections from each of the following choices:

1. My personal bathroom should have the following fixtures:

☐ Tub/shower combination
☐ Tub   ☐ cast iron   ☐ steel   ☐ fiberglass
☐ Separate shower cove
☐ Whirlpool tub
☐ Close-coupled toilet   (2-piece)
☐ Low profile toilet   (1-piece)
☐ Bidet
☐ Vanity with   ☐ 1 lavatory   ☐ 2 lavatories
☐ Pedestal lavatory
☐ Tub enclosure   ☐ mirrored glass
   ☐ obscure glass   ☐ curtain

2. I prefer the following type medicine cabinet:

☐ Standard size (16 x 26 overall dimension)
☐ Large "mirrored wall"
☐ Top lighted   ☐ Side lighted
☐ Modern   ☐ Antique
☐ Brass frame   ☐ Wood frame
☐ Other _____

3. I prefer my bathroom have:

☐ Full height mirror   ☐ Wide wall mirror
☐ Decorator mirror   ☐ Antique frame mirror
☐ Brass frame mirror   ☐ Frameless mirror

4. I would like for my bathroom to have:

☐ Built-in hair dryer
☐ Telephone   ☐ Intercom
☐ Live plants   ☐ Decorator plants
☐ Built-in wall niche (magazine rack, storage)
☐ Built-in (revolving) concealed lavatory unit
   for toothbrush, soap and tumbler
☐ Recessed tissue holder

5. I want my bathroom to have the following finish/accessories:

☐ Solid brass   ☐ Antique
☐ Polished   ☐ Crystal
☐ Other _____
☐ Soap holder
☐ Recessed soap/tumbler holder
   with removable tray
☐ Toothbrush and tumbler holder
☐ Recessed soap and bar with removable tray
☐ Surface-mounted paper holder
☐ Recessed paper holder   ☐ with hood
☐ Towel ring   ☐ Towel tree   ☐ Towel bar
☐ Other _____

6. I enjoy plenty of closet space and prefer to have a design that includes extra storage space for:

☐ Towels/washcloths   ☐ Cosmetics
☐ Toiletries   ☐ Robe
☐ Hair dryer   ☐ Curling iron
☐ Other _____

7. Lighting is so important in a bathroom. I prefer:

☐ A luminous ceiling
☐ Supplemental soft ornamental lighting
☐ Theater-style lighting at mirror

8. For my bathroom floor I choose:

☐ Carpet   ☐ Ceramic tile   ☐ Marble
☐ Quarry tile   ☐ Sheet vinyl
☐ Stone   ☐ Vinyl tile
☐ Other _____

Figure 2-9
Bathroom preference form

9. **For my bathroom walls I prefer:**

   ☐ Wallpaper   ☐ Ceramic tile   ☐ Marble
   ☐ Wood panel   ☐ Stone   ☐ Brick
   ☐ Plaster   ☐ Gypsum board   ☐ Glass block
   ☐ Mirrors   ☐ A combination of the above

10. **My bathroom ceiling should be:**

    ☐ Drop
    ☐ Luminous panels
       ☐ ornamental   ☐ plain   ☐ pebbled
    ☐ Gypsum board   ☐ Textured
    ☐ Wood   ☐ Plaster   ☐ Painted
    ☐ Other _____

11. **Below are some of the things my present bathroom does not have that I wish to have added during remodeling:**

    ☐ Adequate wall receptacles
    ☐ Skylight   ☐ Overhead lights
    ☐ Adequate heating   ☐ Overhead heat lamps
    ☐ Exhaust fan   ☐ Other _____

12. **I prefer a bathroom with:**

    ☐ More floor space   ☐ Same floor space
    ☐ More window space   ☐ Same window space
    ☐ Skylight   ☐ Other _____

13. **My favorite colors are:**

    ☐ Bright tones
    ☐ Soft tones
    ☐ Medium tones
    ☐ A mixture of colors for soft contrast
    ☐ A mixture of colors for bright contrast
    ☐ White   ☐ green   ☐ yellow
    ☐ orange   ☐ red   ☐ blue
    ☐ purple   ☐ pink   ☐ _____

14. **I prefer a bathroom styled:**

    ☐ Early traditional
    ☐ Contemporary
    ☐ Elegant, in the Kohler or American Standard tradition

15. **I will consider:**

    ☐ Changing or eliminating window
    ☐ Changing location of door
    ☐ Opening new doorway
    ☐ Extending bathroom beyond interior partition(s)
    ☐ Partially remodeling bathroom
    ☐ Completely remodeling bathroom
    ☐ Installing skylight

16. **I would like my bathroom to look like:**

    ☐ The attached picture
    ☐ My friend's, whose address is _____
    _____
    ☐ My own creation

17. **How many bathrooms do you have?**

    ☐ One   ☐ Two   ☐ Three or more

18. **How many in your family?**

    _____ Adults   _____ Children

19. **I have overnight guests**

    ☐ seldom   ☐ often,
       about_____ times a month

20. **If you had to put a dollar limit on a personalized bathroom, what would be the limit?**

    $_____

21. **Comments** _____
    _____
    _____
    _____

Figure 2-9
Bathroom preference form (continued)

Job Specifications

Contractor's Name _____
Address _____
City _____ State _____ Zip_____
Phone _____
Prepared by _____

Owners's Name_____
Address _____
City _____ State _____ Zip_____
Job Address _____
Phone _____
Date _____ Job No. _____

Contractor proposes to provide the building permit, labor, materials and equipment necessary to complete installation of the following:

Const. Requirements   Descr.
Removal_____ $ _____
Replacement _____ $ _____
Addition_____ $ _____
Relocate _____ $ _____
Floor _____ $ _____
Wall_____ $ _____
Ceiling _____ $ _____
Doors/windows _____ $ _____
           Total cost $ _____

Plumbing Requirements   Descr.
Removal_____ $ _____
Supply _____ $ _____
Waste_____ $ _____
Vent_____ $ _____
Gas _____ $ _____
Steam_____ $ _____
           Total cost $ _____

Floor
Removal _____
Underlayment _____
Cove _____
Finish _____
Sill_____
Other _____
Replacement _____
Total area _____
Type _____
Color_____
           Total cost $ _____

Walls
Removal _____
Tub area _____
Finish _____
Other areas_____
Finish _____
Wainscot_____
Finish _____
Other _____
Replacement _____
Size _____
Color_____
Size _____
Color_____
Size _____
Color_____
           Total cost $ _____

Ceilings
Removal _____
Description_____
Finish _____
Other _____
Replacement _____
Size _____
Color_____
           Total cost $ _____

Ventilation
Fan _____
Venting _____
Switch _____
Other _____
Type _____
Timer _____
Humidistat _____
Other _____
           Total cost $ _____

Figure 2-10
Job specifications and cost estimate

Access.   **Finish   No.   Descr.   Cost**
Matched tile _____
Tub trim _____
Grab bars _____
Bar soap dish _____
Soap dishes _____
Towel bars _____
Tumbler holder _____
Paper holder _____
Tissue dispenser _____
Mirrors _____
Hooks _____
Decorative items _____
Folding stools _____
                    Total cost $ _____

Medicine Cabinet(s)
Quantity _____
Mount _____
Color _____
Lights _____
Manufacturer's no. _____
Style _____
Mirror size _____
Type _____
                    Total cost $ _____

Fixtures & Fittings   Color   Descr.   Cost
Tub _____ $ _____
Whirlpool _____ $ _____
Shower cabinet _____ $ _____
Shower cove _____ $ _____
Toilet & seat _____ $ _____
Lavatory _____ $ _____
Bidet _____ $ _____
Lavatory faucets _____ $ _____
Lavatory fittings _____ $ _____
Lavatory valve _____ $ _____
Bath valve _____ $ _____
Shower head _____ $ _____
Diverter _____ $ _____
Tub fittings & overflow _____ $ _____
                    Total cost $ _____

Vanity   **No. 1**   **No. 2**
Cabinet style _____
Cabinet color _____

Manufacturer _____
Knob and pull no. _____
Hinge no. _____
Back plate no. _____
Doors _____
Shelves _____
        Total cost $ _____   Total cost $ _____

Enclosures
Description _____
Color _____
Door size _____
Rod length _____
Replacement _____
Size _____
Glass type _____
                    Total cost $ _____

Storage
Type _____
Doors _____
Shelves _____
Finish _____
Size _____
Drawer _____
Number _____
Hardware _____
                    Total cost $ _____

Heating/Cooling
Heating _____
Size _____
Manufacturer _____
Type _____
Cooling _____
Size _____
Manufacturer _____
Type _____
Duct _____
Registers _____
Size _____
Size/Color _____
                    Total cost $ _____

Figure 2-10
Job specifications and cost estimate (continued)

Electrical & Lighting
Removal _____
Service entrance _____
Wire outlets _____
Electrical heater _____
Wire lighting _____
Switches _____
Lighting _____
Replacement _____
New service _____
Wire switches _____
Electrical cooling _____
Wire fan _____
Outlets_____
Heat lamps_____
Total cost $ _____

Tops ( ) as per drawing attached
Material _____
Style _____
Color_____
Number of cutouts _____
Edge treatment _____
Splash height_____
Splash type_____
Total cost $ _____

Lavatories
Quantity _____
Mount _____
Style _____
Manufacturer & no. _____
Color_____
Material _____
Total cost $ _____

Contractor will do the following demolition and dispose of items removed:

☐ Vanity   ☐ Top   ☐ Lavatory   ☐ Tub
☐ Toilet   ☐ Shower enclosure
☐ Radiator   ☐ Medicine cabinet

☐ Bath fittings   ☐ Deteriorated pipe
☐ Partition _____   ☐ Electric
☐ Doors   ☐ Windows
☐ Heating equipment   ☐ Cooling equipment
☐ Ducting
☐ Flooring   (_____ sq. ft.)
☐ Wall covering   (_____ sq. ft.)
☐ Ceiling cover   (_____ sq. ft.)
Total cost $_____

Contractor will make the following repairs:

Item	Description	Cost
_____	_____	_____
_____	_____	_____
_____	_____	_____

Total cost $_____

Total costs above $ _____

Tax $ _____

Total $ _____

Owner will furnish labor and material as follows:

Item	Description
_____	_____
_____	_____

These are the total and complete specifications for this job. Only the items checked or for which a cost is indicated are included in this job.

Contractor _____

Owner _____

Date _____

Figure 2-10
Job specifications and cost estimate (continued)

Proposal and Contract

Date _____ 19 _____

To _____

Dear Sir/Madam:

We propose to furnish all materials and perform all labor necessary to complete the following:

_____

_____

_____

Job location: _____ _____

All of the above work to be completed according to the floor plan, job specifications, and terms and conditions on the back of this form, for the sum of:

Dollars ($ _____)

Payments to be made as the work progresses as follows:_____

_____

_____

the entire amount of the contract to be paid within _____ days after substantial completion and acceptance by the owner. The price quoted is for immediate acceptance only. Delay in acceptance will require a verification of prevailing labor and material costs. This offer becomes a contract upon acceptance by contractor but shall be null and void if not executed within 5 days from the date above.

By _____

"YOU, THE BUYER, MAY CANCEL THIS TRANSACTION AT ANY TIME PRIOR TO MIDNIGHT OF THE THIRD BUSINESS DAY AFTER THE DATE OF THIS TRANSACTION. SEE THE ATTACHED NOTICE OF CANCELLATION FORM FOR AN EXPLANATION OF THIS RIGHT."

You are hereby authorized to furnish all materials and labor required to complete the work according to the plans, job specifications, and terms and conditions on the back of this proposal, for which we agree to pay the amounts itemized above.

Owner _____

Owner _____

Accepted by Contractor _____ Date _____

Figure 2-11
Proposal and contract

1. The Contractor agrees to commence work within (10) days after the last to occur of the following, (1) receipt of written notice from the Lien Holder, if any, to the effect that all documents required to be recorded prior to the commencement of construction have been properly recorded; (2) the materials required are available and on hand, and (3) a building permit has been issued. Contractor agrees to prosecute work thereafter to completion, and to complete the work within a reasonable time, subject to such delays as are permissible under this contract. If no first Lien Holder exists, all references to Lien Holder are to be disregarded.

2. Contractor shall pay all valid bills and charge for material and labor arising out of the construction of the structure and will hold Owner of the property free and harmless against all liens and claims of lien for labor and material filed against the property.

3. No payment under this contract shall be construed as an acceptance of any work done up to the time of such payment, except as to such items as are plainly evident to anyone not experienced in construction work, but the entire work is to be subject to the inspection and approval of the inspector for the Public Authority at the time when it shall be claimed by the Contractor that the work has been completed. At the completion of the work, acceptance by the Public Authority shall entitle Contractor to receive all progress payments according to the schedule set forth.

4. The plan and job specification are intended to supplement each other, so that any works exhibited in either and not mentioned in the other are to be executed the same as if they were mentioned and set forth in both. In the event that any conflict exists between any estimate of costs of construction and the terms of this Contract, this Contract shall be controlling. The Contractor may substitute materials that are equal in quality to those specified if the Contractor deems it advisable to do so. All dimensions and designations on the plan or job specification are subject to adjustment as required by job conditions.

5. Owner agrees to pay Contractor its normal selling price for all additions, alterations or deviations. No additional work shall be done without the prior written authorization of Owner. Any such authorization shall be on a change-order form, approved by both parties, which shall become a part of this Contract. Where such additional work is added to this Contract, it is agreed that all terms and conditions of this Contract shall apply equally to such additional work. Any change in specifications or construction necessary to conform to existing or future building codes, zoning laws, or regulations of inspecting Public Authorities shall be considered additional work to be paid for by Owner as additional work.

6. The Contractor shall not be responsible for any damage occasioned by the Owner or Owner's agent, Acts of God, earthquake, or other causes beyond the control of Contractor, unless otherwise provided or unless he is obligated to provide insurance against such hazards, Contractor shall not be liable for damages or defects resulting from work done by subcontractors. In the event Owner authorizes access through adjacent properties for Contractor's use during construction. Owner is required to obtain permission from the owner(s) of the adjacent properties for such. Owner agrees to be responsible and to hold Contractor harmless and accept any risks resulting from access through adjacent properties.

7. The time during which the Contractor is delayed in this work by (a) the acts of Owner or his agents or employees or those claiming under agreement with or grant from Owner, including any notice to the Lien Holder to withhold progress payments, or by (b) any acts or delays occasioned by the Lien Holder, or by (c) the Acts of God which Contractor could not have reasonably foreseen and provided against, or by (d) stormy or inclement weather which necessarily delays the work, or by (e) any strikes, boycotts or like obstructive actions by employees or labor organizations and which are beyond the control of Contractor and which he cannot reasonably overcome, or by (f) extra work requested by the Owner, or by (g) failure of Owner to promptly pay for any extra work as authorized, shall be added to the time for completion by a fair and reasonable allowance. Should work be stopped for more than 30 days by any or all of (a) through (g) above, the Contractor may terminate this Contract and collect for all work completed plus a reasonable profit.

8. Contractor shall at his own expense carry all workers' compensation insurance and public liability insurance necessary for the full protection of Contractor and Owner during the progress of the work. Certificates of insurance shall be filed with Owner and Lien Holder if Owner and Lien Holder require. Owner agrees to procure at his own expense, prior to the commencement of any work, fire insurance with Course of Construction. All Physical Loss and Vandalism and Malicious Mischief clauses attached in a sum equal to the total cost of the improvements. Such insurance shall be written to protect the Owner and Contractor, and Lien Holder, as their interests may appear. Should Owner fail so to do, Contractor may procure such insurance, as agent for Owner, but is not required to do so, and Owner agrees in demand to reimburse Contractor in cash for the cost thereof.

9. Where materials are to be matched, Contractor shall make every reasonable effort to do so using standard materials, but does not guarantee a perfect match.

10. Owner agrees to sign and file for record within five days after substantial completion and acceptance of work a notice of completion. Contractor agrees upon receipt of final payment to release the property from any and all claims that may have accrued by reason of the construction.

11. Any controversy or claim arising out of or relating to this contract shall be settled by arbitration in accordance with the Rules of the American Arbitration Association, and judgment upon the award rendered by the Arbitrator(s) may be entered in any Court having jurisdiction.

12. Should either party bring suit in court to enforce the terms of this agreement, any judgment awarded shall include court costs and reasonable attorney's fees to the successful party plus interest at the legal rate.

13. Unless otherwise specified, the contract price is based upon Owner's representation that there are no conditions preventing Contractor from proceeding with usual construction procedures and that all existing electrical and plumbing facilities are capable of carrying the extra load caused by the work to be performed by Contractor. Any electrical meter charges required by Public Authorities or utility companies are not included in the price of this Contract, unless included in the job specifications. If existing conditions are not as represented,

thereby necessitating additional plumbing, electrical, or other work, these shall be paid for by Owner as additional work.

14. The Owner is solely responsible for providing Contractor prior to the commencing of construction with any water, electricity and refuse removal service at the job site as may be required by Contractor to effect the improvement covered by this contract. Owner shall provide a toilet during the course of construction when required by law.

15. The Contractor shall not be responsible for damage to existing walks, curbs, driveways, cesspools, septic tanks, sewer lines, water or gas lines, arches, shrubs, lawn, trees, clotheslines, telephone and electric lines, etc., by the Contractor, subcontractor, or supplier incurred in the performance of work or in the delivery of materials for the job. Owner hereby warrants and represents that he shall be solely responsible for the condition of the building with respect to moisture, drainage, slippage and sinking or any other condition that may exist over which the Contractor has no control and subsequently results in damage to the building.

16. The Owner is solely responsible for the location of all lot lines and shall if requested, identify all corner posts of his lot for the Contractor. If any doubt exists as to the location of lot lines, the Owner shall at his own cost, order and pay for a survey. If the Owner wrongly identifies the location of the lot lines of the property, any changes required by the Contractor shall be at Owner's expense. This cost shall be paid by Owner to Contractor in cash prior to continuation of work.

17. Contractor has the right to subcontract any part, or all, of the work agreed to be performed.

18. Owner agrees to install and connect at Owner's expense, such utilities and make such improvements in addition to work covered by this Contract as may be required by Lien Holder or Public Authority prior to completion of work of Contractor. Correction of existing building code violations, damaged pipes, inadequate wiring, deteriorated structural parts, and the relocation or alteration of concealed obstructions will be an addition to this agreement and will be billed to Owner at Contractor's usual selling price.

19. Contractor shall not be responsible for any damages occasioned by plumbing leaks unless water service is connected to the plumbing facilities prior to the time of rough inspection.

20. Title to equipment and materials purchased shall pass to the Owner upon delivery to the job. The risk of loss of the said materials and equipment shall be borne by the Owner.

21. Owner hereby grants to Contractor the right to display signs and advertise at the job site.

22. Contractor shall have the right to stop work and keep the job idle if payments are not made to him when due. If any payments are not made to Contractor when due, Owner shall pay to Contractor an additional charge of 10% of the amount of such payment. If the work shall be stopped by the Owner for a period of sixty days, then the Contractor may, at Contractor's option, upon five days written notice, demand and receive payment for all work executed and materials ordered or supplied and any other loss sustained, including a profit of 10% of the contract price. In the event of work stoppage for any reason, Owner shall provide for protection of, and be responsible for any damage, warpage, racking, or loss of material on the premises.

23. Within ten days after execution of this Contract, Contractor shall have the right to cancel this Contract should it be determined that there is any uncertainty that all payments due under this Contract will be made when due or that any error has been made in computing the cost of completing the work.

24. This agreement constitutes the entire Contract and the parties are not bound by oral expression or representation by any party or agent of either party.

25. The price quoted for completion of the structure is subject to change to the extent of any difference in the cost of labor and material as of the date and the actual cost to Contractor at the time materials are purchased and work is done.

26. The Contractor is not responsible for labor or materials furnished by Owner or anyone working under the direction of the Owner and any loss or additional work that results therefrom shall be the responsibility of the Owner. Removal or use of equipment or materials not furnished by Contractor is at Owner's risk, and Contractor will not be responsible for the condition and operation of these items, or service for them.

27. No action arising from or related to the contract, or the performance thereof, shall be commenced by either party against the other more than two years after the completion or cessation of work under this contract. This limitation applies to all actions of any character, whether at law or in equity, and whether sounding in contract, tort, or otherwise. This limitation shall not be extended by any negligent misrepresentation or unintentional concealment, but shall be extended as provided by law for willful fraud, concealment, or misrepresentation.

28. All taxes and special assessments levied against the property shall be paid by the Owner.

29. Contractor agrees to complete the work in a substantial and workmanlike manner but is not responsible for failures or defects that result from work done by others prior, at the time of or subsequent to work done under this agreement.

30. Contractor makes no warranty, express or implied (including warranty of fitness for purpose and merchantability). Any warranty or limited warranty shall be as provided by the manufacturer of the products and materials used in construction.

31. Contractor agrees to perform this Contract in conformity with accepted industry practices and commercially accepted tolerances. Any claim for adjustment shall not be construed as reason to delay payment of the purchase price as shown on the payment schedule. The manufacturers' specifications are the final authority on questions about any factory produced item. Exposed interior surfaces, except factory finished items, will not be covered or finished unless otherwise specified herein. Any specially designed, custom built or special ordered item may not be changed or cancelled after five days from the acceptance of this Contract by Contractor.

Figure 2-11
Proposal and contract (continued)

Notice To Customer Required By Federal Law

You have entered into a transaction on _____ which may result in a lien, mortgage, or other security interest on your home. You have a legal right under federal law to cancel this transaction without any penalty or obligation if you desire to do so within three business days from the above date, or any later date on which all material disclosures required under the Truth in Lending Act have been given to you. If you so cancel the transaction, any lien, mortgage, or other security interest on your home arising from this transaction is automatically void. You are also entitled to receive a refund of any down payment or other consideration if you cancel. If you decide to cancel this transaction, you may do so by notifying:

_____
(Name of Creditor)

at_____
(Address of Creditor's Place of Business)

by mail or telegram sent not later than midnight of _____ . You may also use any other form of written notice identifying the transaction as long as it is delivered to the above address no later than the stipulated time. This notice may be used for the purpose of cancelling transaction by dating and signing below.

I hereby cancel this transaction.

_____
(Date)   (Customer's Signature)

Effect of rescission. When a customer exercises his right to rescind, he is not liable for any finance or other charge, and any security interest becomes void upon such a rescission. Within 10 days after receipt of a notice of rescission, the creditor shall return to the customer any money or property given as earnest money, down payment, or otherwise, and shall take any action necessary or appropriate to reflect the termination of any security interest created under the transaction. If the creditor has delivered any property to the customer, the customer may retain possession of it. Upon the performance of the creditor's obligations under this section, the customer shall tender the property to the creditor, except that if return of the property in kind would be impracticable or inequitable, the customer shall tender its reasonable value. Tender shall be made at the location of the property or at the residence of the customer, at the option of the customer. If the creditor does not take possession of the property within 10 days after tender by the customer, ownership of the property vests in the customer without obligation on his part to pay for it.

Figure 2-12
Customer's cancellation notice

the kitchen *and* bathroom redone at the same time. If you can't get the other room included in the contract, you've at least planted the thought. Often, when your clients see what a beautiful job you're doing on the kitchen (or bathroom), they'll be anxious for you to do the other room too.

Always make an effort to sell the prospect on remodeling that second room. For most people, the kitchen and bathroom are the rooms with the greatest potential character or personality. Those rooms lend themselves to a variety of designs and styles that can catch the eye of visitors. And when the owners decide to sell, these rooms can be an important selling point.

Keep Up With the Latest Trends and Requirements

As a successful remodeler, you'll not only be expected to sell your product effectively, but you'll also need to know all the latest information on designing, estimating, and building. You must keep up with all the changes in the industry, especially changes in the laws, building codes, and building permit requirements.

Read everything you can relating to the building industry in general and remodeling in particular. You've got to assume that your competition is keeping abreast of the interesting events and changes affecting your business.

Subscribe to industry magazines and newsletters. That's one way to keep up-to-date with what's happening in the kitchen and bathroom remodeling business. You'll also learn about the latest products and home fashion trends.

Builder, the magazine of the National Association of Home Builders (NAHB), is an excellent publication. It's published each month and will

inform you of industry events and new products. The magazine offers a reader service card you can use to order free product information from advertisers. You can order the magazine by contacting:

National Association of Home Builders
P.O. Box 2029
Marion, OH 43306-2029

Keep Up Your Professional Attitude

You don't need to take a three-month positive attitude or self-image course in order to show your confidence and your enthusiasm for your work. Once you begin work on a project, always remain positive and professional. Save the jokes for after work. Your client's real interest is in your performance on the job, so be friendly but businesslike.

Every client is unique. For the most part they'll be hardworking people just like you. Some will watch your every move, paying close attention to every nail you drive. A few will know absolutely nothing about what you're doing and only care about having a professional job completed on time. Others will always be underfoot. Many will be friendly. Some won't. And occasionally you'll come across some you can't please even if you plaster their bathroom with gold dust.

But you're not in the business of earning personality awards. Do a professional job as contracted, using quality materials, and your problems will be minimal. Stick to your schedule. Whatever you do, don't spread yourself so thin that you're trying to keep several jobs going by spending just a few hours at each. The remodeler most recommended to friends and neighbors is the one who goes in, does the work, and finishes in the shortest time, with the least inconvenience to the homeowners.

Kitchen Design and Layout

The kitchen is probably the most used room in the house. It's the family "hangout." Guests and family members spend a great deal of time socializing and working in the kitchen. The kitchen table has traditionally been the center of activity in the average home. It's the work bench for Mr. Fix-it, the desk for home management, and the study and play table for the children. Yet in spite of its important role in family life, the kitchen hasn't had the design attention it deserves.

The main reason homeowners want their kitchen remodeled is because it's poorly laid out and designed. In many older homes (and even some of the newer ones), the builder's main concern was cost. The sink was installed against a common wall with the bathroom to save on plumbing costs; appliances were located where they fit, not where they were convenient; cabinet space was inadequate; and traffic flowed through the middle of the work area. You could say these kitchens weren't designed at all — they were just built.

The result is countless unnecessary steps and wasted effort by the homeowners who have to use those kitchens. Is it any wonder that people are anxious to have their kitchens remodeled? A well-designed kitchen saves time and energy. And it creates a pleasant and comfortable atmosphere in the home.

There's a lot to learn about kitchen layout. You need to gather as much information as you can, memorize standard measurements, know your products and their best uses, and keep all these facts at your fingertips. Without a good working knowledge of layout and design concepts, you'll be at a serious disadvantage in the remodeling business. You can never know too much!

Of course, not every job will involve a complete renovation, but there are high profits in those that do. You can be a successful remodeler, and make people's lives easier, by creating comfortable and efficient kitchens for them.

Design for Efficiency

If the cook has to walk 30 feet to make the circuit from the sink to the refrigerator to the stove and back to the sink — something's wrong. That's just too far. While walking is good exercise, few people care to combine their aerobic workout with fixing dinner. They want efficiency. And the key to an efficient kitchen is the *work triangle*.

The Work Triangle

Figure 3-1 shows a *work triangle*, the length between the center of each of the three major work areas in every kitchen.

- Food preparation (cooking)

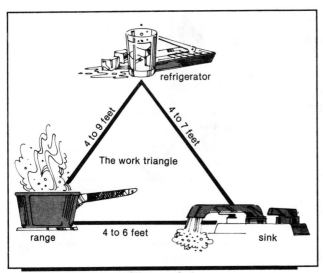

Figure 3-1
The work triangle

- Food storage (refrigeration)

- Clean-up (sink)

When designing a kitchen, allow 4 to 9 feet from the stove to the refrigerator, 4 to 7 feet from the refrigerator to the sink, and 4 to 6 feet from the sink to the stove.

The total distance around the triangle shouldn't be more than 22 feet, or less than 14 feet. The normal work pattern is from the refrigerator to the sink to the range, usually in a counter-clockwise direction.

The Four Basic Kitchen Layouts

There are four common layouts for kitchens. They are:

1) L-shaped

2) U-shaped

3) Corridor

4) Straight or single wall

Study the L-shape and U-shape kitchen designs you see. Decide what you like and what you don't like about each. If you can't discuss the basics of kitchen layout with your clients, you're sure to lose sales. Of course, there are variations in any of these designs, such as the broken L or the broken U, but these are just the basic layouts with a second path or opening into the kitchen.

You can include an island in any of the designs as long as there's enough space. A comfortable kitchen should have between 100 and 150 square feet of floor space. As a remodeler, you'll normally design and build within the existing walls, so the floor space in the kitchen is already decided for you. However, if the homeowner wants you to remove or relocate a partition wall, then you can reach for the optimum in floor space.

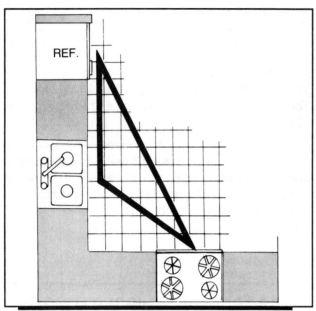

Figure 3-2
The L-shaped kitchen

The L-Shaped Kitchen

An L-shaped kitchen is one of the most popular designs. You can form a work triangle that won't be interrupted by traffic through the kitchen. As you can see in Figure 3-2, the legs of the L provide convenient placement of the appliances for both cooking and clean-up. Figure 3-3 shows a basic L-shape with an added bar, which provides an eating area as well as increased counter space.

The U-Shaped Kitchen

The U-shaped kitchen shown in Figure 3-4 is another favorite layout. Like the L-shaped kitchen, it provides an excellent work triangle with no traffic cutting through it. One leg of the U is often designed as a peninsula separating the kitchen area from the eating area.

Figure 3-3
An L-shaped kitchen with counter leg
Courtesy: Merillat Industries, Inc.

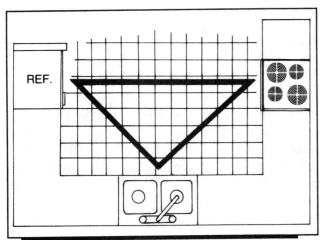

Figure 3-4
The U-shaped kitchen

Figure 3-5 shows a basic U-shaped kitchen with a work island. When you're remodeling a kitchen, you can always modify any of the basic designs to make the kitchen more efficient, even if you can't make it larger.

The Corridor Kitchen

Figure 3-6 shows a corridor kitchen. Corridor kitchens make efficient use of small spaces. They can be as narrow as 8 feet from wall to wall. With cabinets and appliances on both sides, you need a minimum of 4 feet for the "corridor," measured from the face of the cabinets on each side. The work triangle in a corridor, unless it's quite long,

Figure 3-5
A U-shaped kitchen with work island
Courtesy: Merillat Industries, Inc.

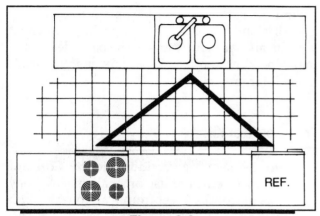

Figure 3-6
A corridor kitchen

is usually small. By closing off one end of the corridor with a bar or counter space, you can eliminate traffic through the work area.

The Straight or Single-Wall Kitchen

The straight or single-wall kitchen is usually found in smaller homes, apartments, or vacation homes with limited space. The design lends itself to open plan arrangements.

If you have to locate two or more appliances on the same wall, as you would in a single-wall kitchen, you should make sure they're at least 4 feet apart. Measure the distance from the center of each appliance. A one-wall kitchen shouldn't be more than 22 feet long. Otherwise, the distance between appliances becomes too great for the efficiency you hope to achieve.

Figure 3-7 is a straight-wall kitchen in an open plan apartment. A work counter has been added to separate the kitchen and living areas.

The Island

As you can see in Figures 3-5 and 3-7, a kitchen work island can take a variety of shapes and sizes. It can be an eating counter, a room divider, or it can be used as part of the work triangle, holding a sink or cooktop. You might have a sec-

ond sink located in an island to ease congestion and allow more than one cook to work at once. Figure 3-8 shows an island that's part of the work triangle and doubles as an eating area.

If an island is located in the center of the kitchen, as in Figure 3-5, you need to allow at least 36 inches of aisle space on each side. A 42-inch aisle is even better. If the island is used as a work center, don't forget to include the cost of installing plumbing or electrical lines. An island that includes a cooktop also needs an exhaust hood and appropriate lighting.

The Work Centers

There are three main work centers forming the work triangle in every kitchen: food storage, food preparation, and clean-up. But they're not the only work centers possible in a kitchen. You can also include in your design a hobby or homework center, or a desk with space for cookbooks for meal planning. These are accessories, and pleasant additions to the kitchen. But the primary emphasis in a good functional layout will always be your three central work areas.

The Food Storage Center

The refrigerator is the main component of the food storage center. It should be located near the kitchen entrance, preferably close to the back door. You want it near the shortest route from the car, to make bringing in the groceries as easy as possible. You'll also need counter space next to the refrigerator; at least 15 inches of countertop is desirable, 24 inches is better.

Try to arrange for nonperishables to be stored in an adjacent cabinet or pantry area. When all the food is stored in one area, the cook doesn't have to chase all over the kitchen to put things away or to gather the ingredients for a meal. If there's

Figure 3-7
A straight-wall kitchen
Courtesy: Wood-Mode Cabinetry

room for a walk-in or closet-type pantry, it should also be near the refrigerator.

A refrigerator at the end of the cabinets gives the kitchen balance. Figure 3-9 shows a well-placed refrigerator. The door handle of the refrigerator should be next to the counter so the refrigerator opens *into* the kitchen. On the other side of the refrigerator in this picture is the entry door to the kitchen.

The Food Preparation Center

When you lay out the cooking and serving center, you'll include the range, oven, microwave oven and all other small electric appliances used for cooking. You'll need to include enough storage space for pots, pans, and other utensils nearby. Don't forget to include space for special items needed for microwave cooking.

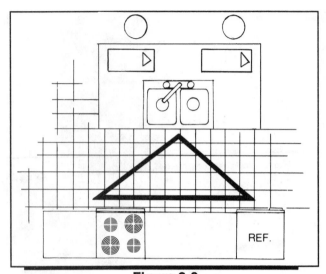

Figure 3-8
An island work center and eating area

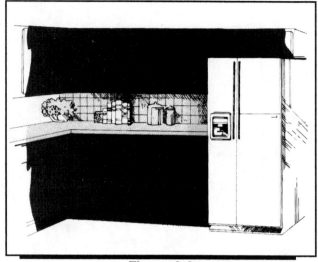

Figure 3-9
Locate refrigerator near door

Your client might want to store some food items such as coffee, tea or soups in this area as well. Everyone does things a little differently. Remember, you're designing the kitchen for *your client*. Be sure you know what *they* want.

Locate the cooking and serving center near the eating area to cut down the distance hot food must be carried. A heat-resistant countertop area on both sides of the range and oven is a must. Often, the cook must get rid of a hot dish or pan in a hurry. Create a convenient landing place.

Your client's choice of cooking appliances affects your overall plan for counters and cabinets. Try to avoid placing a built-in oven next to the range. Two hot appliances in a small area can create a fire hazard. Figure 3-10 shows an efficient preparation center that includes a range, built-in microwave oven, and plenty of adjacent counter space.

The Clean-Up Center

Skimp elsewhere if you have to, but make sure you allow for a minimum of 30 inches of counter space on each side of the sink. The sink is a high traffic area. Don't put it too close to the range or oven. Plan carefully to reduce the potential for accidents between the cook, who's often carrying a hot pot or pan, and someone else who might be walking through the work area.

If the dishwasher is built in, put it next to the sink. The person cleaning up shouldn't have to take more than one step from the sink to the dishwasher. Allow a 24-inch space for the dishwasher. If the dishwasher is located in a corner, you'll have to allow a minimum of 3 inches between the dishwasher and the corner cabinet for clearance of the door and drawer in the adjacent cabinet. If space is limited, you might suggest using an 18-inch dishwasher. The dishwasher in Figure 3-10 is ideally located immediately to the right of the sink.

A lot of work goes on here, so if there's space, a swing-out stool at the sink is a nice added feature. When it's not needed, it can swing back under the cabinet.

A garbage disposal will be essential in most sinks. But check your local code first. Some communities require them and others prohibit them. Usually it's a matter of choice. If you're not installing a disposal, you'll probably want to make some arrangement for garbage storage under the sink. Line the inside of the garbage pail storage compartment with the same material as the countertops for easy cleanup of spatters and spills.

Figure 3-10
An efficient food preparation center
Courtesy: Merillat Industries, Inc.

Provide some sort of ventilation for the compartment. A decorative screen or air holes can improve air circulation.

If you plan to include a trash compactor, put it near the clean-up center. Allow 15 inches in width for most compactors. Be sure you double-check the specifications on all the appliance models you plan to install to avoid problems.

In Figure 3-11 the clean-up center is used as a divider between the kitchen and living area. If you study this design, you'll see it's a basic corridor kitchen even though there's only one "wall." You'll also notice that there's a second island or room divider with a second sink, which provides additional counter space and work area. In this design there wasn't room for countertop space

Figure 3-11
Island clean-up center
Courtesy: Merillat Industries, Inc.

next to the refrigerator. However, the location of the table solves that problem.

Kitchen design requires imagination and study. There's a right plan for every homeowner. Chances are that you'll find it among the many designs and layouts available. However, don't hesitate to change any design to meet your client's wishes. There's no rule that dictates how a kitchen must look. The important thing is that it's functional, efficient, and it works for your client. As a kitchen remodeler, you're expected to be both competent and creative in your designs.

The Other Kitchen Centers

If there's room for more than the basics in a kitchen, most homeowners will choose the convenience of a *planning center*. It doesn't have to take much space, if space is a problem, but it provides a special touch your clients will really appreciate. Include space for a telephone, recipe files, and cookbooks. Desk units are available from many cabinet dealers. They're 21 inches deep and can be inserted into your cabinet design.

The kitchens in Figures 3-10 and 3-12 both include a planning center. In Figure 3-10, the desk is in an alcove right off the kitchen. And in Figure

Figure 3-12
A meal planning center

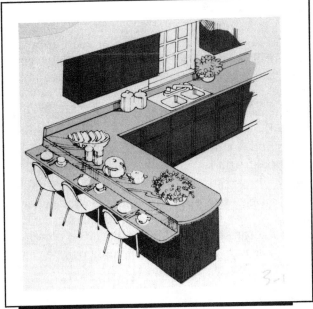

Figure 3-13
An eating or serving center

3-12, the center is an extension of the kitchen counter. As you can see, there are many ways to incorporate a meal planning center into your design.

If a planning center doesn't appeal to your clients, have them consider an informal eating area. Many families enjoy having a table or counter arrangement in the kitchen for eating, snacking, or just taking a break. Sometimes you can have one area double as a planning center and an informal eating center.

Figure 3-13 shows a kitchen serving bar. The eating counter is a lip extended off the countertop, and lowered to accommodate chairs of average height. It could easily have been designed at standard countertop height, but then you'd have to use bar stools rather than standard chairs for seating. A serving bar opposite the cooking center makes serving easy.

If you use a table arrangement in your design, allow at least 36 inches in all directions around the table and chairs for adequate clearance.

Choosing the Right Colors for Your Design

Color sets the mood of a room. Your clients may want to make a design statement in their kitchen by using a favorite color. Or you may have to help them decide on a color scheme. Take special care in color selection. They'll have to live with their choices for a long time.

The Kitchen Preference Form mentioned in Chapter 2 is an extremely useful design tool. Go through the form carefully with your clients while they make their color selections. If they're keeping the existing kitchen appliances or fixtures, you must work these into the color scheme. And what about the rest of the house? You want to make sure that the colors used in the new kitchen don't conflict with the colors in adjoining rooms, especially if they're open to view from the kitchen.

Color Schemes

If you've studied color design or read enough to be familiar with how decorators use color, you know the three fundamental color schemes they rely on.

A *monochromatic* scheme uses one color as a base with variations of hues or tints. The different shades and textures set off the basic color. Neighboring colors on the color wheel, such as red and orange, are used to create a related color scheme.

Or you can use opposite colors on the wheel, such as yellow and red, for *contrasting* or *complementary* color schemes. Most often, in a complementary scheme, one dominant color will be used with other colors as accents.

How to Use Color

Does your client want an open, airy effect? Light colors will give the impression of a spacious, open room. If a more intimate, cozy feeling is preferred, dark colors would be a good choice. Don't go to extremes. Red walls with a black ceiling will make the room feel like a tunnel. You'll want to stoop over every time you enter the room, even though the ceiling is 10 feet high. Painting a tall ceiling darker than the walls makes it appear lower.

In a long, narrow room, dark paint or wallpaper on one end will "shrink" the distance. Warm (dark) colors appear close, while cool (light) colors appear farther away. Warm and bright colors usually look best in small amounts set against large areas of cool color.

When choosing colors, the homeowners should select the color of the cabinets first. These set the style of the decor. Then select the colors of the countertop, floor, walls, and ceiling. The last choices are the accent colors. Everything that will be exposed in the room will have to be considered when deciding on colors. Kitchen items, collections, appliances — all play a part in the color scheme. And lighting must be considered along with the color.

Lighting

Consider the effect of light on any colors your clients choose. When they're selecting colors, remind them that the lighting in the kitchen changes throughout the day.

Natural light gives the truest reading of a color. But no room is always illuminated by the sun. Check the colors under electric light. Incandescent light is most like sunlight. Warm colors seem brighter, while cool colors may appear to be duller.

Fluorescent light can present problems. Each of the several types of fluorescent bulbs affects color differently. The ones that distort color the least also give the least light. If you're installing fluorescent lighting, have your clients choose the type of illumination they prefer, then check their color choices under that light. Advise them to replace the fluorescent bulbs with the same type to avoid distorting the color scheme.

Be sure you consider the amount of natural light the room receives as well as the type of artificial light you use. If the window faces north or is heavily shaded, light colors and light wood tones will maximize the available light.

A narrow room with little natural light can seem more like a cave than a kitchen. Adding a skylight will help lighten and brighten it.

Standard Design Dimensions

Anyone with enough cash or borrowing power available to remodel isn't going to be interested in a purely utilitarian kitchen of the past. They want more: Designs that offer more space and a warm atmosphere — a pleasant place to live and work. The sterile kitchens found in many older homes don't offer much room for improvement. You'll see cramped, outdated kitchens in every older neighborhood. In many of these you're better off replacing everything down to the bare walls. Starting over is better and cheaper than trying to

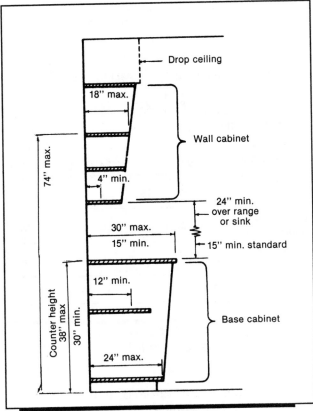

Figure 3-14
Kitchen cabinet dimensions

fit new pieces into an old puzzle. So let's look at the standard dimensions for kitchen cabinets, fixtures, countertops, and storage space.

Cabinet Space

Every kitchen has to have space for a range, oven, refrigerator, sink, and at least a minimum of countertop and cabinet storage space. There are generally accepted standards for the amount of cabinet and storage space needed in the average kitchen.

The space you provide should suit the potential occupant load of the house, not the current occupant load. Even if your client is a widow living alone, plan around the existing house, not the existing owner. Some day the house will be sold,

probably to an owner who needs all the space available.

To determine the amount of space needed in a kitchen, count the number of bedrooms. You can assume that there will be two occupants for most master bedrooms. Other bedrooms will have one resident each. For each potential permanent resident of the house, you need to plan 6 square feet of storage space in *wall* cabinets. An additional 12 square feet of wall cabinet space is required for the overflow of overnight guests.

So in a three-bedroom house (one master bedroom and two standard bedrooms, with a potential capacity of four people) there would be 6 square feet of wall cabinet space for each person, or a total of 24 square feet. Adding the 12 square feet for entertaining makes a total of 36 square feet of required kitchen wall-cabinet space. In a five-bedroom house you'd need 48 square feet of wall cabinet space.

The standard dimensions for kitchen cabinets are shown in Figure 3-14. When you know how many square feet you need, you can figure out what size cabinets it will take to provide the space. Standard wall cabinets come in depths ranging from 4 inches to 18 inches. They can begin 15 inches above the countertops (24 inches minimum over ranges and sinks) and go as high up as you want.

Storage Area

Usually, base cabinets occupy the space under the wall cabinets except where the stove, refrigerator, and dishwasher are located. The base cabinets should provide one-third of the storage required for the kitchen. And at least 60 percent of the storage area should be enclosed by cabinet doors.

Figure 3-15 shows the minimum shelf and drawer area needed for storage, based on the number of bedrooms in the house. A two-bedroom house needs at least 38 square feet of shelf area and 8 square feet of drawer area.

	Number of Bedrooms				
	0	1	2	3	4
Minimum shelf area (square feet)	24	30	38	44	50
Minimum drawer area (square feet)	4	6	8	10	12

Figure 3-15
Kitchen storage area dimensions

A dishwasher can be counted as 4 square feet of base cabinet storage. But you can't include wall cabinets located over refrigerators, or any shelf area located 74 inches (or higher) above the finish floor, as part of the required storage space. Inside corner cabinets generally have only 50 percent usable space unless you install revolving shelves. With revolving shelves you can count the entire shelf area as storage area.

If drawers are more than 6 inches deep, include the excess drawer capacity as additional shelf area.

Fixture and Countertop Space

The fixture and countertop space is also determined by the number of bedrooms in the home, as shown in Figure 3-16. Measure the frontage requirements for appliances in linear inches. These are minimums, so be sure the particular appliances selected by the homeowners fit into the spaces you're planning. There are also other considerations to keep in mind when arranging space for fixtures.

- Sink— If you're installing a dishwasher, a 24-inch sink is acceptable even for three- and four-bedroom homes.

- Range— Don't locate range burners under a window or within 12 inches of a window. If there's a cabinet above a range, you must have a clearance of at least 30 inches from

	Number of Bedrooms				
	0	1	2	3	4
Minimum Frontage (Linear inches)					
Sink	18	24	24	32	32
Countertop, one side	15	18	21	24	30
Range space	21	21	24	30	30
Countertop, one side	15	18	21	24	30
Refrigerator space	30	30	36	36	36
Countertop, one side	15	15	15	15	18
Mixing countertop	21	30	36	36	42

Figure 3-16
Kitchen countertop and fixture dimensions

the range to the bottom of an unprotected cabinet (or a 24-inch clearance to the bottom of a protected cabinet). If you aren't installing the range, provide a minimum frontage space of 30 inches. There should be a clearance of 48 inches between the range and door to the kitchen.

- Range countertop— You should provide at least 9 inches of counter space between the edge of the range and the adjacent corner cabinet. Where there's a built-in wall oven, make sure you have an 18-inch countertop adjacent to the oven. You'll need at least 3 feet, but not more than 4 feet of counter space between the range and the sink.

- Refrigerator— If a refrigerator door opens within its own width, the refrigerator space can be 30 inches wide. Be sure you install the refrigerator away from the oven or range. The cost of operating a refrigerator is high enough without having a hot oven heating it up.

- Refrigerator countertop— Provide a 15-inch countertop between the side of the

Figure 3-17
A nicely designed cabinet corner
Courtesy: Merillat Industries, Inc.

refrigerator and an adjacent cabinet. Between the refrigerator and sink, you should plan between 4-1/2 and 5-1/2 feet of counter space.

- Cabinets— When you're hanging cabinet doors, make sure they don't open against the front of an appliance, especially the oven.

In most cases, countertops should be 24 inches deep and 36 inches above the floor. Allow at least 48 inches of clearance between base cabinet fronts in the food preparation (cooking) center.

The Cabinet Corner Treatment

In some homes, the cabinet corners are as bland as the inside of a closet. Some remodelers think that corners are just a place to take up slack in the layout. Corners can be attractive — and should be — since the corner is usually where the eye strays when you enter a kitchen. Look at Figure 3-17. This corner is very attractive. The lines are clean

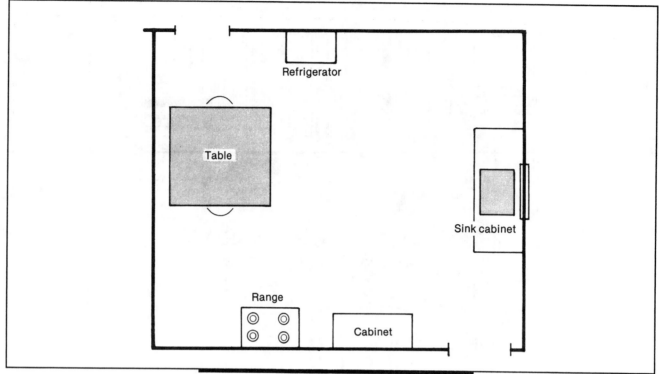

Figure 3-18
Old kitchen

and simple. There's a good balance created by the tall utility cabinet and the location of the oven. This is good design.

Ventilation

An effective ventilation system can make any kitchen a more enjoyable place to work, and it's often required by the building code.

It isn't the size of the range hood or stove that determines the amount of ventilation you need — it's the size of the kitchen. A 160-square foot kitchen with an 8-foot ceiling requires a 320 c.f.m.(cubic foot per minute) size fan. Try to use the quietest exhaust fan you can find. Your clients will appreciate your professionalism every time they flip on the fan switch. Little irritations like a noisy fan can spoil an otherwise perfect job.

Windows are also part of the kitchen ventilation system. They add both fresh air and light to the room. Most people like to have a window

located above the sink. If you're going to install a window, don't put it too close to the corner of the room. Allow at least 15 inches from the window to the corner so there will be space on each side for a wall cabinet. The rough opening for the window should be about 44 inches from the floor. This will provide space for a 4-inch backsplash below the window.

Other Design Considerations

When you remodel a kitchen, you have two priorities. First, comply with the building code. Second, make sure your clients get what they want. Remember, it's their home and their money. Even if what they want violates some general design rule, as long it's legal, give them what they want. You should always explain why you think their way may not be the best way, and how it differs from the standard or recommended design. It's important that you know what goes into

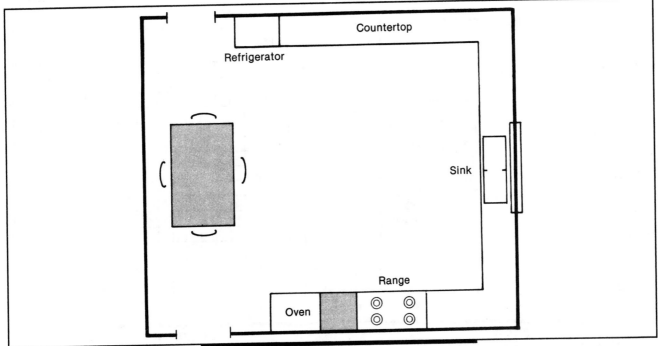

Figure 3-19
Recommended layout of old kitchen

planning a kitchen, and that you're totally familiar with the codes and rules that affect your work. But don't try to talk a client out of something he or she really wants. You may both be sorry later.

What do you do when the work triangle exceeds 22 feet — the distance beyond which kitchen efficiency declines? A modern kitchen can have space exceeding the standards and still be efficient. The triangle concept is sound logic, but it isn't law. Many cooks favor a large, spacious kitchen, even if the work triangle is greater than it should be.

If you're working in a small kitchen with limited space, consider installing space-saving appliances. Appliances like an over-the-range microwave oven with built-in ventilating unit allow you to design efficiency and convenience into a small area.

Drop ceilings, luminous ceilings, floor and wall treatments are also key elements in your kitchen design. We'll cover these subjects in detail in the chapters ahead.

Planning Exercises

I'm sure you've seen a kitchen layout like the one shown in Figure 3-18. It's very poorly designed. There's a severe shortage of cabinet space, and traffic moves right through the middle of the work triangle.

How would you redesign this kitchen? Would you move the interior door to change the traffic flow? If you would, you've grasped the concept of kitchen planning. Study Figure 3-19 and compare it to Figure 3-18.

Now try handling a design problem of your own. Figure 3-20 is an old kitchen that a potential client is thinking about remodeling. How would you do it? Use the graph scale in Figure 3-21. Each block represents one square foot.

Designing efficient and comfortable kitchens is an exercise in common sense using the information you have available. With all the material

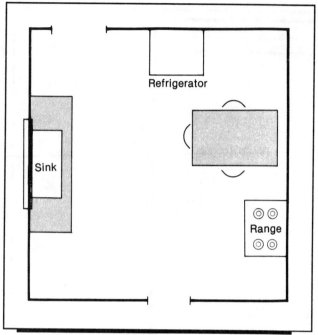

Figure 3-20
An old kitchen you will redesign

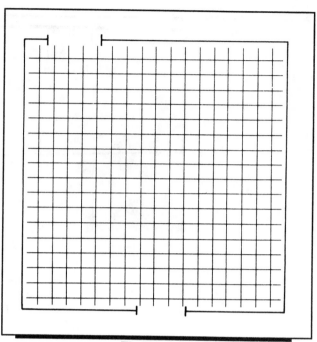

Figure 3-21
Your recommended layout of Figure 3-20

available today, there's unlimited opportunity for innovative and creative design in kitchen remodeling. Every kitchen job you have comes with the potential to create a real showcase! This is exciting work. Ingenuity and creativity can turn what was a drab eyesore into an enduring source of pride, admiration and increased resale value. The opportunity is yours to command.

Installing Kitchen Cabinets

An experienced remodeler knows it's never safe to assume any room is square, any wall plumb, or any floor or ceiling level. Buildings go through a settling process as they age which causes them to fall out of square. In some cases, the house or building may not have been built square, plumb, or level to begin with. These are just a few of the many problems you'll be confronted with when you're installing new cabinets in an old kitchen. In this chapter I'll show you how to solve these remodeling headaches.

Types of Cabinets

Unless you're a cabinetmaker, you'll let the experts build your cabinets. Few carpenters have the necessary skills and tools to build the high-quality cabinets demanded by homeowners today. The wood cabinets you find in some of the better-built older homes were handcrafted like furniture. A few of us old timers have built those kinds of kitchen cabinets, but it's a losing proposition. It just takes too much time. It's far more profitable for the average remodeler to let the cabinet shop do the manufacturing. Some remodelers even leave the installation to the cabinetmaker. That way, if there's a problem with the fit, it's not yours. This is worth something.

Good quality stock cabinets and custom designed cabinets are available in most areas. *Never* install second-rate cabinets in one of your projects. By second-rate, I mean cabinets that are poorly built. Quality cabinets have solid construction, doors that fit properly, and drawers that work smoothly, sliding on guides and rollers. This isn't the place to do any cost-cutting.

Many styles of kitchen and bathroom cabinets are available. You can select matching wall and base cabinets in various combinations of heights, widths, and depths to provide exactly the right grouping for your design.

Figure 4-1 shows the standard dimensions for kitchen cabinetry. You might want to make a copy of this figure and include it in your notebook or presentation kit for ready reference.

Wall Cabinets

You can choose wall cabinets in single-door models with adjustable shelves, or double-door models with two fixed shelves. Most single-door wall cabinets can be hung with either end up. This feature allows you to install the cabinet with the doors hinged on either the left or the right side.

Standard wall cabinets are 12 inches deep from back to front, not including the thickness of the door. Wall cabinets come in a variety of heights, but the most common sizes are between 30 and 40 inches high. You can get them in widths of 9 to 48 inches, with the widths increasing in 3-inch increments.

The standard height of cabinets installed over refrigerators is 15 inches, although this obviously depends on the height of the appliance. Over the range, you would normally install an 18-inch cabinet. Use 24-inch wall cabinets if you have additional space over appliances.

This range of heights provides many design choices. If you're not building a soffit, you can choose 42-inch-high wall cabinets. Or you can stack cabinets of two different heights over the counter to reach the ceiling. A 24-inch cabinet paired with an 18-inch cabinet could start at the customary 54-inch line above the floor and reach up to an 8-foot ceiling. You can also stack a 12-inch cabinet on top of a 30-inch cabinet to reach the 8-foot height with a different effect.

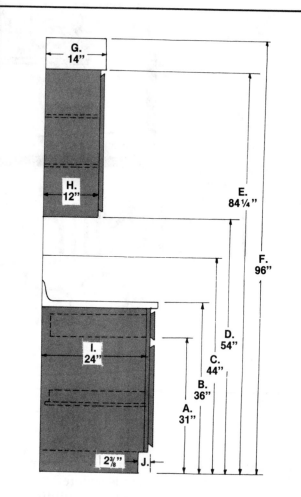

A. Counter height for planning area or sit-down area, 31" from floor.

B. Standard countertop, 36" from floor.

C. Wall switches and outlets, 44" from floor

D. Bottom of 30" wall cabinet, 54" from floor

E. Top of wall cabinet, 84¼" from floor.

F. Ceiling, 96" from floor.

G. Depth of soffit, 14".

H. Depth of wall cabinet, 12" (not including doors).

I. Depth of base cabinet, 24" (not including doors).

J. Depth of toe space, 2⅜".

Figure 4-1
Standard cabinet dimensions

Base Cabinets

Kitchen base cabinets are all 34-1/2 inches high and 24 inches deep from front to back, not including the thickness of the door. Single-door base cabinets can be hinged on either side. You can get them in widths from 9 to 24 inches, with the widths increasing in 3-inch increments. Most base cabinets include one drawer at the top.

Many cabinet manufacturers offer a 36-inch-wide single-drawer base cabinet. It has one wide drawer, two doors, and two roll-out trays instead of shelves.

Consider a lazy susan base cabinet in corners where you'll have cabinets on adjoining walls. They require 36 inches of wall space, 18 inches in each direction from the corner. A lazy susan usually has two revolving shelves, giving easy access to everything in the cabinet.

Special Cabinets

Angled corner wall cabinets with two adjustable shelves are available in two styles, single or double faced. The single-faced cabinet fits neatly into the corner and has one door opening into the kitchen. The double-faced corner cabinet was designed for use between the kitchen and dining area. It has doors on each side, one opening into the dining room and one opening into the kitchen. Some cabinetmakers offer an optional revolving shelf kit for either model.

Many homeowners like the convenience of utility cabinets. You can get them 18 or 24 inches wide and 12 or 24 inches deep. They're 66 inches high and can be converted into pantry cabinets with shelf kits which are available through most dealers.

Built-in oven cabinets also come in 66-inch heights. The widths are 27, 30, or 33 inches, so be sure you know the appliance manufacturer's cut-out dimensions when you order the oven cabinet. A matching 18-inch-high wall cabinet is usually mounted on top of utility and oven cabinets to provide storage up to the standard 84-inch cabinet height.

Many manufacturers offer several other types of standard cabinets. Microwave oven cabinets are available for both front-venting and built-in models. One manufacturer I know of offers decorative range hoods to match cabinets. They come complete with a metal liner, a 350 c.f.m. double squirrel cage blower unit and a light.

Other special features you can order include cabinets with bread drawers, cutlery trays, cutting boards, and even stained glass doors. These features can give a customized look to your cabinet design.

Cabinet Dimension Abbreviations

Manufacturers usually abbreviate the descriptions used in their catalogs. Sometimes these abbreviations can be a little confusing. Although abbreviations vary slightly within the industry, most manufacturer and dealer abbreviations are fairly similar. Once you're familiar with the abbreviations one manufacturer uses, you'll have little trouble ordering the right cabinet from any catalog.

Wall Cabinet Abbreviations

Figure 4-2 is a Merrillat catalog showing the specifications for their cabinets. The first item in the catalog is a single-door wall cabinet. The abbreviation for the dimensions of this cabinet is W 930. The W stands for *wall* cabinet. The first number (9) designates the *width* of the cabinet, and the second number (30) designates its *height*.

For example:

W 930 equals   W = Wall cabinet

9 = Width inches

30 = Height inches

W 1824 would designate a wall cabinet 18 inches wide and 24 inches high.

WALL CABINETS

WALL CABINETS 30″ HIGH

Merillat offers a wide selection of popular cabinet sizes to fit any kitchen or bath plan.

This mark ● next to the model number designates popular large volume units.

All single door wall cabinets and wall blind corner cabinets, are invertible for left or right hinging except Omni and Cathedral designs; for these specify L or R.

SINGLE DOOR

W 930
● W 1230
● W 1530
● W 1830
● W 2130
● W 2430S

2 Adjustable shelves
Invertible for L or R Hinging Except Omni and Cathedral lines

DOUBLE DOOR

● W 2430D●
● W 2730
● W 3030
● W 3330
● W 3630
● W 3930
● W 4230
W 4530
● W 4830

2 Fixed Shelves
*Not available in Omni Horizon and Nouveau lines

WALL CABINETS 24″ HIGH

SINGLE DOOR

W 1824
W 2424

DOUBLE DOOR

W 2724
W 3024
W 3324
W 3624
W 3924
W 4224
W 4524
W 4824

1 Fixed shelf
Invertible for L or R hinging Except Omni and Cathedral lines

1 Fixed Shelf

WALL CABINETS 18″ HIGH

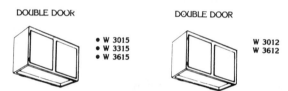

SINGLE DOOR

W 1818
●W 2418

DOUBLE DOOR

W 2718
●W 3018
W 3318
●W 3618
W 3918
W 4218
W 4518
W 4818

Invertible for L or R hinging Except Omni and Cathedral lines

NOT RECOMMENDED FOR RECESSED OR "STEP-BACK" USE OVER 24″ DEEP UTILITY OR OVEN CABINETS IN OMNI LINE

WALL CABINETS 18″ HIGH x 24″ DEEP

FOR USE OVER 24″ DEEP UTILITY AND OVEN CABINETS

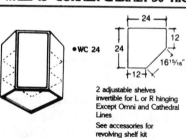

SINGLE DOOR

W 182418
W 242418

DOUBLE DOOR

W 272418
W 302418
W 332418

Invertible for L or R hinging except Omni and Cathedral lines.
Do not hang these 24″ deep cabinets by the hang-rail alone. These cabinets must also be supported through the front frames of adjacent cabinets.

WALL CABINETS 15″ HIGH

DOUBLE DOOR

● W 3015
● W 3315
● W 3615

WALL CABINETS 12″ HIGH

DOUBLE DOOR

W 3012
W 3612

WALL 45° CORNER CABINET 30″ HIGH

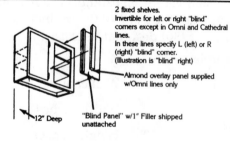

● WC 24

2 adjustable shelves invertible for L or R hinging Except Omni and Cathedral Lines

See accessories for revolving shelf kit

WALL 45° DOUBLE FACED CORNER CABINET 30″ HIGH

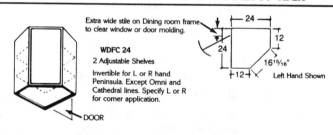

Extra wide stile on Dining room frame to clear window or door molding.

WDFC 24
2 Adjustable Shelves

Invertible for L or R hand Peninsula. Except Omni and Cathedral lines. Specify L or R for corner application.

DOOR

Left Hand Shown

WALL BLIND CORNER CABINETS 30″ HIGH

2 fixed shelves.
Invertible for left or right "blind" corners except in Omni and Cathedral lines.
In these lines specify L (left) or R (right) "blind" corner.
(Illustration is "blind" right)

Almond overlay panel supplied w/Omni lines only

12″ Deep

"Blind Panel" w/1″ Filler shipped unattached

SINGLE DOOR ON "BLIND" SIDE

	A	B
WBC 24/27	24	27
WBC 27/30	27	30
WBC 30/33	30	33
WBC 33/36	33	36
●WBC 36/39	36	39

DOUBLE DOOR ON "BLIND" SIDE

	A	B
WBC 42/45*	42	45
WBC 48/51*	48	51

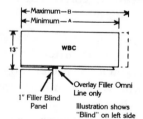

WBC

1″ Filler Blind Panel

Overlay Filler Omni Line only

Illustration shows "Blind" on left side

*Double door blind corner cabinets have two different size doors on blind side, the smaller door is located next to the blind panel, for door sizes consult cabinet door size charts M8409, M8410 and M8412.

Figure 4-2
Cabinet types and specifications
Courtesy: Merillat Industries Inc.

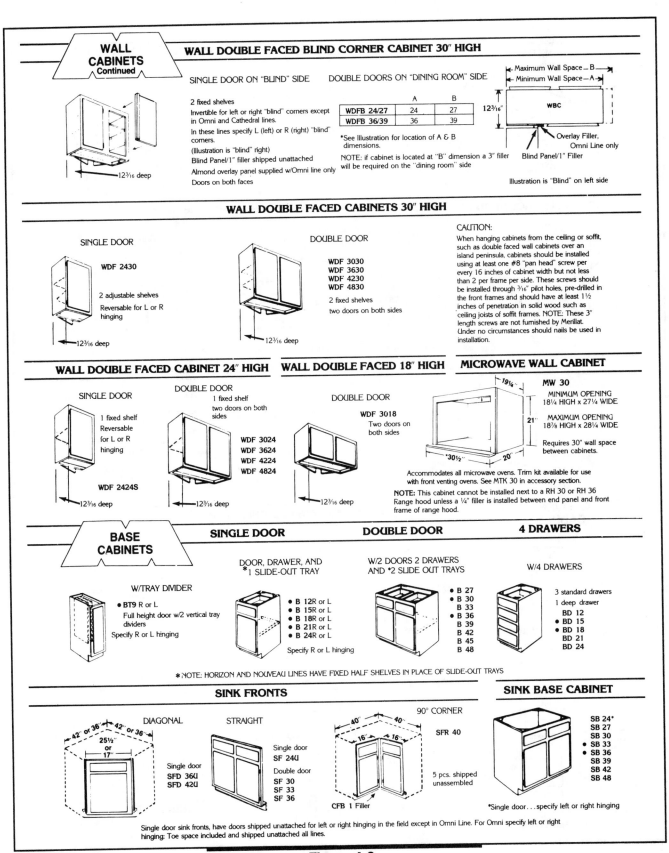

WALL CABINETS Continued

WALL DOUBLE FACED BLIND CORNER CABINET 30" HIGH

SINGLE DOOR ON "BLIND" SIDE   DOUBLE DOORS ON "DINING ROOM" SIDE

2 fixed shelves
Invertible for left or right "blind" corners except in Omni and Cathedral lines.
In these lines specify L (left) or R (right) "blind" corners.
(Illustration is "blind" right)
Blind Panel/1" filler shipped unattached
Almond overlay panel supplied w/Omni line only
Doors on both faces

	A	B
WDFB 24/27	24	27
WDFB 36/39	36	39

*See Illustration for location of A & B dimensions.

NOTE: if cabinet is located at "B" dimension a 3" filler will be required on the "dining room" side

Maximum Wall Space – B
Minimum Wall Space – A

12³⁄₁₆   WBC

Overlay Filler, Omni Line only
Blind Panel/1" Filler

Illustration is "Blind" on left side

12³⁄₁₆ deep

WALL DOUBLE FACED CABINETS 30" HIGH

SINGLE DOOR

WDF 2430

2 adjustable shelves
Reversable for L or R hinging

12³⁄₁₆ deep

DOUBLE DOOR

WDF 3030
WDF 3630
WDF 4230
WDF 4830

2 fixed shelves
two doors on both sides

12³⁄₁₆ deep

CAUTION:
When hanging cabinets from the ceiling or soffit, such as double faced wall cabinets over an island peninsula, cabinets should be installed using at least one #8 "pan head" screw per every 16 inches of cabinet width but not less than 2 per frame per side. These screws should be installed through ³⁄₁₆" pilot holes, pre-drilled in the front frames and should have at least 1½ inches of penetration in solid wood such as ceiling joists or soffit frames. NOTE: These 3" length screws are not furnished by Merillat. Under no circumstances should nails be used in installation.

WALL DOUBLE FACED CABINET 24" HIGH

SINGLE DOOR

1 fixed shelf
Reversable for L or R hinging

WDF 2424S

12³⁄₁₆ deep

DOUBLE DOOR

1 fixed shelf
two doors on both sides

WDF 3024
WDF 3624
WDF 4224
WDF 4824

12³⁄₁₆ deep

WALL DOUBLE FACED CABINET 18" HIGH

DOUBLE DOOR

WDF 3018
Two doors on both sides

12³⁄₁₆ deep

MICROWAVE WALL CABINET

19¼
21"
30½"   20"

MW 30
MINIMUM OPENING
18¼ HIGH x 27¼ WIDE

MAXIMUM OPENING
18⅞ HIGH x 28¼ WIDE

Requires 30" wall space between cabinets.

Accommodates all microwave ovens. Trim kit available for use with front venting ovens. See MTK 30 in accessory section.
NOTE: This cabinet cannot be installed next to a RH 30 or RH 36 Range hood unless a ¼" filler is installed between end panel and front frame of range hood.

BASE CABINETS

SINGLE DOOR

W/TRAY DIVIDER

● BT9 R or L
Full height door w/2 vertical tray dividers
Specify R or L hinging

DOOR, DRAWER, AND
*1 SLIDE-OUT TRAY

● B 12R or L
● B 15R or L
● B 18R or L
● B 21R or L
● B 24R or L

Specify R or L hinging

DOUBLE DOOR

W/2 DOORS 2 DRAWERS
AND *2 SLIDE OUT TRAYS

● B 27
● B 30
● B 33
● B 36
● B 39
● B 42
● B 45
● B 48

4 DRAWERS

W/4 DRAWERS

3 standard drawers
1 deep drawer

BD 12
● **BD 15**
● **BD 18**
BD 21
BD 24

*NOTE: HORIZON AND NOUVEAU LINES HAVE FIXED HALF SHELVES IN PLACE OF SLIDE-OUT TRAYS

SINK FRONTS

DIAGONAL

42" or 36"   42" or 36"
25½" or 17"

Single door
SFD 36U
SFD 42U

STRAIGHT

Single door
SF 24U

Double door
SF 30
SF 33
SF 36

90° CORNER

40'   40'
16"   16"

SFR 40

5 pcs. shipped unassembled

CFB 1 Filler

SINK BASE CABINET

SB 24*
SB 27
SB 30
● **SB 33**
● **SB 36**
SB 39
SB 42
SB 48

*Single door...specify left or right hinging

Single door sink fronts, have doors shipped unattached for left or right hinging in the field except in Omni Line. For Omni specify left or right hinging; Toe space included and shipped unattached all lines.

Figure 4-2
Cabinet types and specifications (continued)
Courtesy: Merillat Industries Inc.

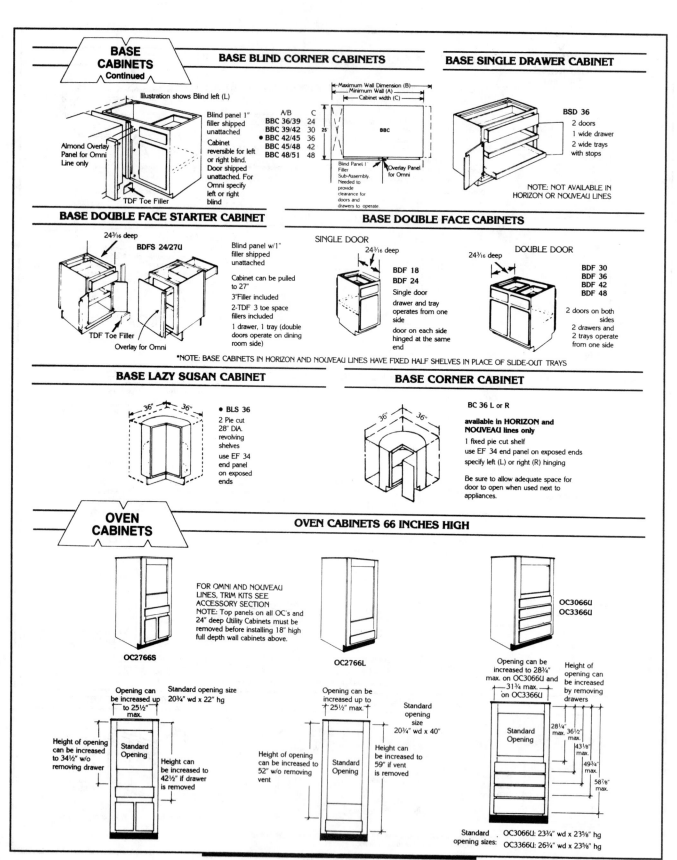

BASE CABINETS
Continued

BASE BLIND CORNER CABINETS

Illustration shows Blind left (L)

Almond Overlay Panel for Omni Line only

Blind panel 1" filler shipped unattached

Cabinet reversible for left or right blind. Door shipped unattached. For Omni specify left or right blind

TDF Toe Filler

Maximum Wall Dimension (B)
Minimum Wall (A)
Cabinet width (C)

BBC

	A/B	C
BBC 36/39		24
BBC 39/42		30
● BBC 42/45		36
BBC 45/48		42
BBC 48/51		48

25

Blind Panel 1 Filler Sub-Assembly. Needed to provide clearance for doors and drawers to operate.

Overlay Panel for Omni

BASE SINGLE DRAWER CABINET

BSD 36

2 doors
1 wide drawer
2 wide trays with stops

NOTE: NOT AVAILABLE IN HORIZON OR NOUVEAU LINES

BASE DOUBLE FACE STARTER CABINET

24³⁄₁₆ deep

BDFS 24/27U

TDF Toe Filler
Overlay for Omni

Blind panel w/1" filler shipped unattached

Cabinet can be pulled to 27"

3"Filler included

2-TDF 3 toe space fillers included

1 drawer, 1 tray (double doors operate on dining room side)

BASE DOUBLE FACE CABINETS

SINGLE DOOR

24³⁄₁₆ deep

BDF 18
BDF 24

Single door drawer and tray operates from one side

door on each side hinged at the same end

DOUBLE DOOR

24³⁄₁₆ deep

BDF 30
BDF 36
BDF 42
BDF 48

2 doors on both sides
2 drawers and 2 trays operate from one side

*NOTE: BASE CABINETS IN HORIZON AND NOUVEAU LINES HAVE FIXED HALF SHELVES IN PLACE OF SLIDE-OUT TRAYS

BASE LAZY SUSAN CABINET

36" 36"

● BLS 36
2 Pie cut
28" DIA. revolving shelves
use EF 34 end panel on exposed ends

BASE CORNER CABINET

36" 36"

BC 36 L or R

available in HORIZON and NOUVEAU lines only

1 fixed pie cut shelf
use EF 34 end panel on exposed ends
specify left (L) or right (R) hinging

Be sure to allow adequate space for door to open when used next to appliances.

OVEN CABINETS

OVEN CABINETS 66 INCHES HIGH

FOR OMNI AND NOUVEAU LINES, TRIM KITS SEE ACCESSORY SECTION
NOTE: Top panels on all OC's and 24" deep Utility Cabinets must be removed before installing 18" high full depth wall cabinets above.

OC2766S

OC2766L

OC3066U
OC3366U

Opening can be increased up to 25½" max.

Standard opening size 20¾" wd x 22" hg

Height of opening can be increased to 34½" w/o removing drawer

Standard Opening

Height can be increased to 42½" if drawer is removed

Opening can be increased up to 25½" max.

Standard opening size 20¾" wd x 40"

Height of opening can be increased to 52" w/o removing vent

Standard Opening

Height can be increased to 59" if vent is removed

Opening can be increased to 28¼" max. on OC3066U and 31¾" max. on OC3366U

Height of opening can be increased by removing drawers

Standard Opening

28¼" max. 36½" max.

43⅛" max.

49¼" max.

58⅞" max.

Standard opening sizes: OC3066U: 23¾" wd x 23⅜" hg
OC3366U: 26¾" wd x 23⅜" hg

Figure 4-2
Cabinet types and specifications (continued)
Courtesy: Merillat Industries Inc.

UTILITY CABINETS 66 INCHES HIGH   Doors Shipped Unattached

OMNI UTILITY CABINETS

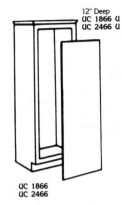

12" Deep
UC 1866 U
UC 2466 U

24"Deep
UC 182466 U
UC 242466 U

UC 1866
UC 2466

UC 182466
UC 242466

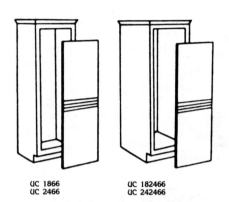

UC 1866
UC 2466

UC 182466
UC 242466

Shelf kits, revolving shelf kits and pantry door shelf kits available. see Accessory Section

OMNI CAUTION: Due to the location of the full width oak pull on 12" deep Omni wall cabinets, they are not recommended for recessed or set-back use above 24" deep utility or oven cabinets, use 24" deep wall cabinets. On Omni utility cabinets the front frame is "dimpled" for drilling and door hinge location on both sides for L or R hinging.

ACCESSORIES
(Factory orders in carton quantities only)

REVOLVING PANTRY SHELF KITS

DOOR SHELF KITS

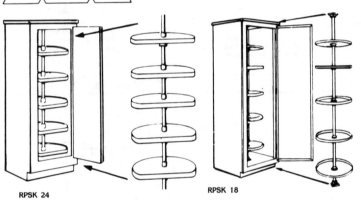

RPSK 24

RPSK 18

5 revolving shelves with center rod and brackets for use in 18" and 24" wide utility cabinets.
Includes mounting hardware and "support" foot. 1/ctn.

DSK 18
DSK 24
5 storage units, 2 door uprights, "snap-in" clips, mounting hardware and an extra set of two hinges (shipped in 2 cartons)

DSK

NOTE: This unit can be used with the RPSK24 and RPSK18

REVOLVING SHELF KIT

OVEN TRIM KITS

UTILITY CABINET SHELF KITS

For 24" deep Utility Cabinets

For 12" deep Utility Cabinets

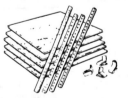

LS 3
Fits 30" high wall 45° diagonal corner cabinets, 3 plastic revolving shelves with center post, hardware and mounting instructions.

OMNI & NOUVEAU trim kit used on face of oven cabinet to give flush contemporary look. Must be trimmed to proper height and opening cut for oven. Includes instructions and mounting screws.

OTK 27 Fits 27" oven cabinet ¾" thick x 26 ⅝" x 60 ⅝"

OTK 30 Fits 30" oven cabinet ¾" thick x 29 ⅝" x 60 ⅝"

OTK 33 Fits 33" oven cabinet ¾" thick x 32 "⅝" x 60⅝"

FDSK 18 or 24 Five shelves, four metal standards and 20 metal clips (two cartons). Ease of storage, plus convenience DSK can be used with this accessory if if shevles are cut down.

PSK 18 or 24 Five shelves and 20 supports per package. Makes storage of high or low items convenient

DSK cannot be used with this accessory

Figure 4-2
Cabinet types and specifications (continued)
Courtesy: Merillat Industries Inc.

MODULAR SHELVING SYSTEM

This is an R.T.A. (ready to assemble) furniture system. All assembly hardware is included. These units are not to be used as a freestanding unit.

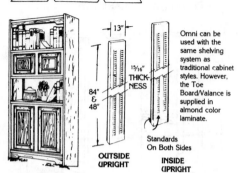

Omni can be used with the same shelving system as traditional cabinet styles. However, the Toe Board/Valance is supplied in almond color laminate.

THICKNESS 1⁵/₁₆″

84″ & 48″

OUTSIDE UPRIGHT

INSIDE UPRIGHT

Standards On Both Sides

Outside Uprights w/metal standards		
ITEM	LGTH.	CTN. QTY.
OU 48	48″	2
OU 84	84″	2
Inside Uprights w/metal standards 2 sides		
IU 48	48″	1
IU 84	84″	1

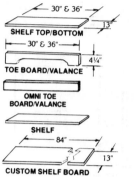

SHELF TOP/BOTTOM — 30″ & 36″ — 13″

TOE BOARD/VALANCE — 30″ & 36″ — 4¼″

OMNI TOE BOARD/VALANCE

SHELF

CUSTOM SHELF BOARD — 84″ — 13″

SEE: Merillat Modular Shelving literature P8105 for ideas on various shelving layouts

MODULAR SHELFING SYSTEM (Cont'd.)

TOE BOARD/VALANCES w/hardware		
ITEM	CTN. LGTH.	QTY.
TBV 30	30″	1
TBV 36	36″	1
SHELF KIT w/clips		
SK 30	30″	3
SK 36	36″	3

SHELF TOP/ BOTTOM w/hardware		
CTN. ITEM	LGTH.	QTY.
STB 30	30″	2
STB 36	36″	2
CUSTOM SHELF BOARD		
CSK 84	84″	1

OAK ROLL TOP DESKS

Specify L (light) D (dark)
RTD 30 & 36

16⁷/₈″

30 & 36″

23³/₁₆″

Oak Roll top desk unit can be used with AD (Apron Drawer Unit) and all the modular shelving systems.

OAK DESK LEG

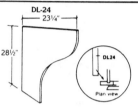

DL-24

23¼″

28½″

DL24

Plan view

¾″ thick solid oak panel 23¼″ deep X 28½″ high. Used to support apron drawer unit. (Specify light or dark oak)

OAK RANGE HOODS

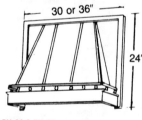

30 or 36″

24″

RH 30 & RH 36

30″ and 36″ wide decorative oak range hood comes complete with metal liner which mounts between two 30″ high wall cabinets. Gallery plate rail furnished unattached.

Metal Liner

NOTE: Liner is 30½″ wide and fits behind frame of adjacent cabinet. Do not install microwave cabinet next to hood without ¼″ filler.

OMNI RANGE HOODS

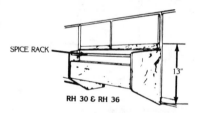

SPICE RACK

13″

RH 30 & RH 36

30″ or 36″ wide decorative almond color/wood range hood. Comes complete with metal liner which mounts between 2 adjacent 30″ high wall cabinets. A W 3015 or W 3615 wall cabinet is required above the Omni range hood

RANGE HOOD BLOWER UNIT

RHB Blower Unit
Double squirrel cage Blower Unit 350 CFM W/Lights and infinite speed solid state controls. Complete w/3¼″ x 10″ Transition Damper Unit.

Blower Unit

Transition Damper

RANGE HOOD LITE UNIT

RHL (1/ctn.)
2-40 watt lights (bulbs not included) fits RH 30 or 36 metal liner. For use where down-draft stove or where no ventilation is required.

MICROWAVE TRIM KITS

For front venting "built in" microwaves only. Oak frame kit to use with MW 30 microwave cabinet w/instruction, hardware

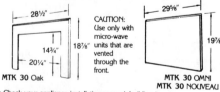

28½″

14¾″

20¼″

18½″

MTK 30 Oak

CAUTION: Use only with micro-wave units that are vented through the front.

29⅝″

19⅞″

MTK 30 OMNI
MTK 30 NOUVEAU

NOTE: Check your appliance installation manual, building-in some microwaves will void the warranty.

Figure 4-2
Cabinet types and specifications (continued)
Courtesy: Merillat Industries Inc.

ACCESSORIES
(Continued)

CUTTING BOARD KNIFE TRAY KITS

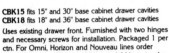

CBK 15,
CBK 18

CBK15 fits 15″ and 30″ base cabinet drawer cavities
CBK18 fits 18″ and 36″ base cabinet drawer cavities
Uses existing drawer front. Furnished with two hinges and necessary screws for installation. Packaged 1 per ctn. For Omni, Horizon and Nouveau lines order "Omni" type kit which contains special hinges and a finger pull.

WIRE BASKETS

Fits all 18″ and 36″
Base Cabinets

Pot Lid Kit
w/2 Tray Guides

ITEM	CTN. QTY.
UBK 18	1/CTN.
PLK 18	1/CTN.

Utility Basket Kit w/2
Tray Guides

BREAD BOX

BB 18 4/ctn.
Bright tin w/sliding top...keeps bread and bakery goods fresher. For lower drawer in BD 18 only. 4 per master carton.

CUTLERY TRAY

Cut here to
fit B 15

CT 18 12/ctn.

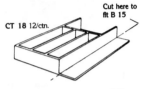

Drawer cutlery organizer for any 18″ or 36″ base cabinet (May be cut to fit drawers in 15″ or 30″ cabinet. Individually cartoned 12 per carton.

DECORATIVE HARDWARE*

HBA
Decorative antique brass finish.

HCK
Ceramic handle with stamped brass finish backplate and two nails.

HRC
Flattened half round raised center and ball ends. Brass finished.

The ideal way to give Merillat kitchens that custom look, Merillat Decorative Hardware will be packed one per cellobag with screws for installing. 100 pulls per box, with drilling templates (except HCK) no templates.

HCV
Chalet vanity pull w/blackplate (2 pcs.)

HDB Flat with ball ends.

HWP Wire style pull.
Antique brass finish.

HWG
Brass finish with woodgrained insert.

*Factory orders in carton quantities only.

APPLIANCE GARAGE STRAIGHT

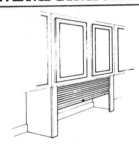

AGS 36   **AGS 24**

Fits under W 2430 or W. 3630 wall cabinets. Provides countertop out-of-sight storage for toaster, mixers and other small appliances. Features a roll-up (tambour) door in Oak, or Omni and Nouveau styles.
AGS 24 can be cut to fit 12″-21″ wall cabinets
AGS 36 can be cut to fit 27″-33″ wall cabinets.

APPLIANCE GARAGE DIAGONAL

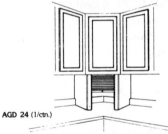

AGD 24 (1/ctn.)

Fits under a WC corner wall cabinet. Provides countertop out-of-sight storage for toaster, mixers and other small appliances. Features a roll-up (tambour) door in Oak, Omni or Nouveau. Oak handles with an 13 ¾″ wide x 15¼″ high opening.
Cabinet is furnished flat with two end panels for easy field assembly. End panels must be notched to fit back splash of countertop and bottom of wall cabinet.

BASE OPEN SHELVES

BOSE 9

OAK
24 ³⁄₁₆″ wide,
34 ½″ high,
6 ½″ radius,
9 ⅝″ deep.

WALL WHAT-NOT-SHELF

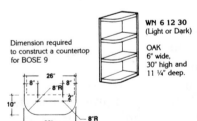

WN 6 12 30
(Light or Dark)

OAK
6″ wide,
30″ high and
11 ¼″ deep.

Dimension required to construct a countertop for BOSE 9

STAINED GLASS DOORS

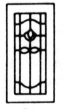 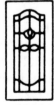

Square   Cathedral

GD-S & GD-C   1/CTN.
14½″ x 28″ leaded stained glass door, hand made in square or cathedral style. For WC or WDFC 24 OR W3330 wall cabinets. Shipped without hinges. 1/ctn. Order S (square) or C (cathedral)

Figure 4-2
Cabinet types and specifications (continued)
Courtesy: Merillat Industries Inc.

Note:

All standard wall cabinets are 12 inches deep and all standard base cabinets are 24 inches deep, measuring back to front, not including the door thickness. All standard base cabinets are 34-1/2 inches high, not counting the countertop. Unless otherwise specified, you can assume that these standard measurements apply to all cabinets.

Base Cabinet Abbreviations

Single-door base cabinets are available in left- or right-hinged models. So you use L to specify left hinging and R to specify right hinging when abbreviating the dimensions for a base cabinet. Remember, all standard base cabinets are 34-1/2 inches high and 24 inches deep, so you only need to know the width dimension and which way the door hinges. Example:

B 12L equals = Base cabinet

12 = 12 inches in width

L = Left side hinging of door

So B 12L is read as a base cabinet (B), 12 inches wide (12), with a door which hinges on the left (L).

All wall and base cabinets over 24 inches wide have two doors (with the exception of corner cabinets and lazy susan cabinets). If you see a dimension given as B 27, you should recognize that it designates a base (B) cabinet, 27 inches wide (27) with double doors. Notice that with double doors, you don't need to show L or R for the hinge side. W 3030 designates a wall cabinet, 30 inches wide and 30 inches high, with double doors.

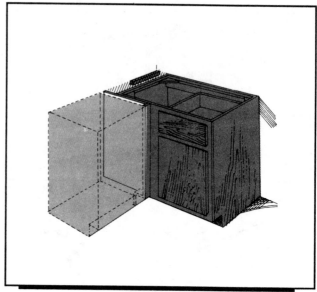

Figure 4-3
Blind corner arrangement

Blind Corner Cabinet Abbreviations

Base blind corner cabinets are designated as BBC's, followed by two numbers separated by a slash. The numbers represent its minimum and maximum dimensions. For example, BBC 36/39 is a base blind corner cabinet which can be used in a space that's a minimum of 36 inches to a maximum of 39 inches. This flexibility in a corner cabinet allows you to expand the length on one wall up to 3 inches to get an exact fit for all the cabinets on that wall. See Figure 4-3. Wall blind corner cabinets are used in the same way. These are called WBC's. A WBC 42/45 uses a minimum of 42 inches and a maximum of 45 inches of wall space.

Other Abbreviations

Figure 4-2 also shows most of the other cabinet abbreviations you should recognize, including oven and utility cabinets and modular shelving. Use this figure to become familiar with the abbreviations and how they're used.

Eurostyle or European Cabinetry

So far we've been discussing standard wood cabinetry. Wood cabinets are generally face-frame construction, made with various kinds of soft and hard woods. A fairly recent innovation in cabinetry is the *Eurostyle* or *European* cabinet. This is a frameless style cabinet made of particleboard or plywood, which is covered with plastic laminate. These come in a variety of colors.

Check with a cabinet shop or dealer in your area to compare prices for Eurostyle cabinets. A smooth board surface is used to achieve the right look. You'll want cabinets made with a 45-pound medium density particleboard or a smooth surface plywood such as A-face. The plywood cabinets will probably cost a little more. The cabinets are designed with matching laminate edges or contrasting PVC edges. Figures 4-4 and 4-5 show how these frameless cabinets are put together.

1) The cabinet hanging rails let you install the cabinet straight.

2) With the cabinet suspension fittings, you can adjust the cabinet three ways: side to side, up and down, and in and out.

3) Cover caps match the color of the cabinet's interior. Also use them to cover extra holes that are drilled.

4) The assembly fittings allow for most installation methods.

5) Shelf supports, in metal or nylon, come in all shapes and sizes. You can choose locking features in vertical and horizontal positions, or select completely concealed shelf supports.

6) The clip hinge lets you mount doors to cabinets quickly, without tools.

7) Connecting screws that join single cabinets together through holes drilled through the side panels.

8) The drawer front adjusters work well with all four-sided drawer box and drawer front applications. You can apply them to the front of the drawer box with a press type fitting.

9) Drawer runners feature an epoxy coating for silent, smooth rolling.

10) The cabinet levelers are 4 to 6 inches high and are adjustable from the inside or outside of the cabinet. After all the cabinets are permanently set, you clip on a continuous toekick rail at the base.

11) The surface mount assembly fittings are suited for rails, stretchers, and blind fronts, without requiring any machining.

12) Door bumpers provide for soft door closing and protect the cabinet surfaces.

Figure 4-6 is a remodeled kitchen using Eurostyle cabinets. The sleek European look is shown in Figure 4-7.

The Cabinet Layout

Think carefully about cabinet layout. Many remodelers have discovered a major flaw in their layout *after* installation is complete. That's too late. Take the time to plan carefully.

Kitchens cabinets should be laid out symmetrically to give the room balance. If the window isn't in the center of the wall, you won't be able to install exactly the same size cabinets on both sides of the window. However, you can achieve the proper balance by placing the same width cabinets on the wall as the base cabinets you use below them. See Figure 4-8.

Consider what the homeowner will store in each cabinet when choosing the cabinet widths. Make sure you allow enough clearance for placing and removing items on the shelves. Double-door cabinets have a center post which limits their width capacity. This is something you have to keep in mind.

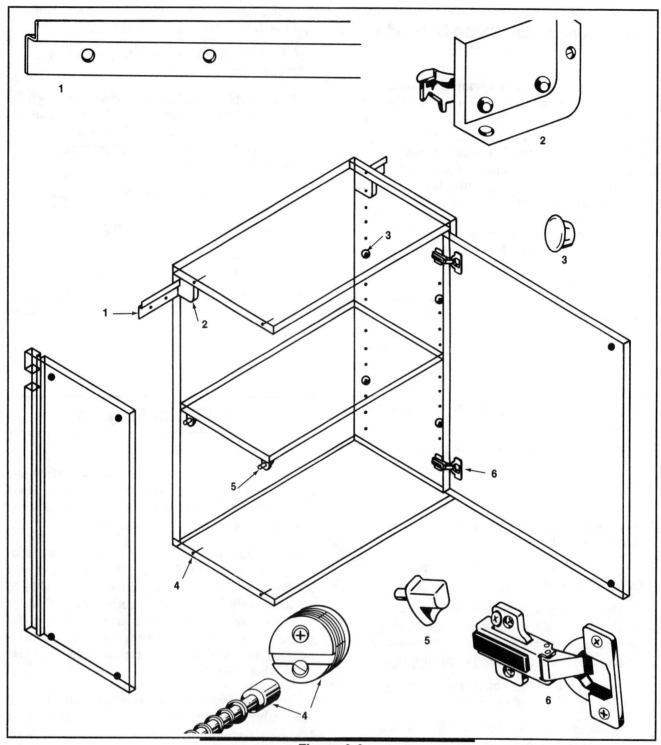

Figure 4-4
Assembly parts for Eurostyle cabinets
Courtesy: McKone and Company, Inc.

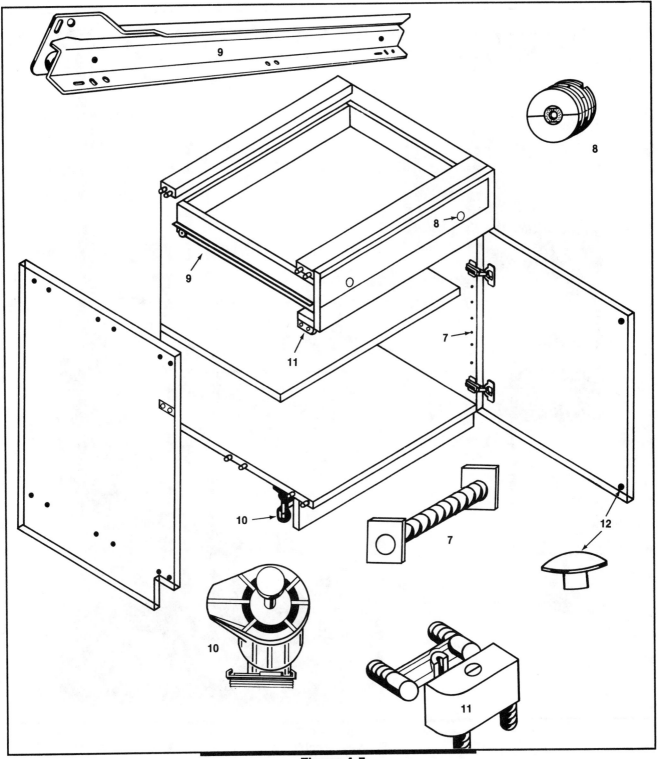

Figure 4-5
Note frameless construction
Courtesy: McKone and Company, Inc.

Figure 4-6
Eurostyle cabinets
Courtesy: McKone and Co., Inc.

Figure 4-7

Modern European style cabinet design
Courtesy: Merillat Industries, Inc.

Figure 4-8
Use wall and base cabinets of the same width

When you're redesigning cabinets for a small kitchen, plan the aisle space carefully. Consider cabinets with narrow doors that don't project so far into the room when open. For example, if you have a 72-inch space, you could use three 24-inch cabinets. However, opening the doors would take up considerable aisle space. The better choice would be two 36-inch-wide cabinets. These have four 16-inch doors, which would look better and present less of a safety hazard if left open.

Utility cabinets or pantries look best when they're placed at the end of the cabinet run rather than in the center. You don't want to break up the horizontal line of the countertop. You can see in Figure 4-9 how poorly-placed cabinets can close in the kitchen work areas and limit the function of the counter space.

Ceiling Height Problems

Do ceilings higher than 8 feet present a design problem for you? Do you always go for a drop ceiling in such cases? A ceiling-to-cabinet soffit may not be the best answer.

The imaginative kitchen and bath remodeler isn't hindered by either customary or unusual designs. An experienced remodeler knows that the more space there is available, the better the opportunity for adding creative design and beauty to the kitchen.

High ceilings shouldn't be a problem. Look again at Figure 4-7. This is a kitchen many homeowners would consider the ultimate in function and design. The high skylights, the "beam" shelf over the cabinets, and the molded soffit show how an accomplished designer can use high ceilings to enhance the room's design. Symmetrically, it's a perfect utilization of space, and few could argue the aesthetics.

Preparations for Installing Kitchen Cabinets

If you've ever remodeled a kitchen that had level floors, square corners, and plumb walls, consider yourself lucky. Play it safe when you're estimating any kitchen remodeling job. Assume that extra manhours and materials will be re-

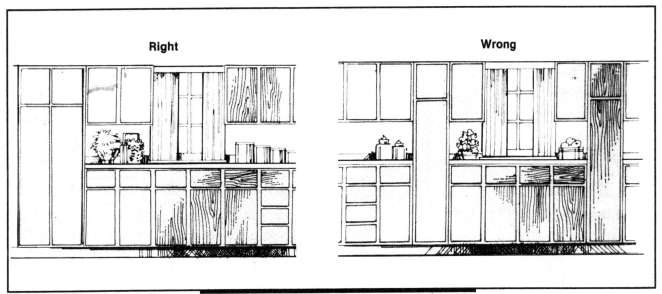

Right   **Wrong**

Figure 4-9
Place tall cabinets at the end of cabinet "run"

quired for just about every part of the job, including cabinet installation.

Measuring the Room

Measure each wall in the room in both directions as shown in Figure 4-10. Record the measurements in inches and fractions on your sketch or in your work notes. Take very careful measurements; your accuracy will save you time and money. Always measure wall to wall, not base molding to base molding.

Start in one corner and measure to the windows or doors (to the outside edge of the trim molding). Next, measure the width and height of the windows and doors to include the trim molding. When measuring window to door, your measurement will be trim to trim. See Figure 4-11. You'll also need the measurement from the floor to the bottom of the window stool and from the bottom of the stool to the top of the window trim molding.

Measure room heights from the floor to the ceiling, or floor to soffit if there is one. Measure the wall height in several locations, and measure each wall diagonally in both directions. This will sometimes reveal floor unevenness.

Few kitchen walls are exactly vertical and at exactly a right angle to adjoining walls. To get correct width measurements, measure the wall at the height and depth where you'll be hanging each cabinet. If the cabinets are to be 14 inches deep, you would measure up to the proposed height and then out 14 inches on each wall. Measure the width of the room between those two points, as shown in Figure 4-12. Never use a midroom or base measurement for your cabinet installation. It could throw you off an inch or more and create unnecessary problems.

If you'll be installing cabinets around the homeowner's existing appliances, measure their width, height, and depth and record the measurements on your sketch. If you're installing new appliances, be sure you know their exact dimensions before drawing your plans.

Show the location of all appliances, sink plumbing, water pipes, grills, heating ducts, lighting fixtures, wall receptacles and wall switches on your sketch.

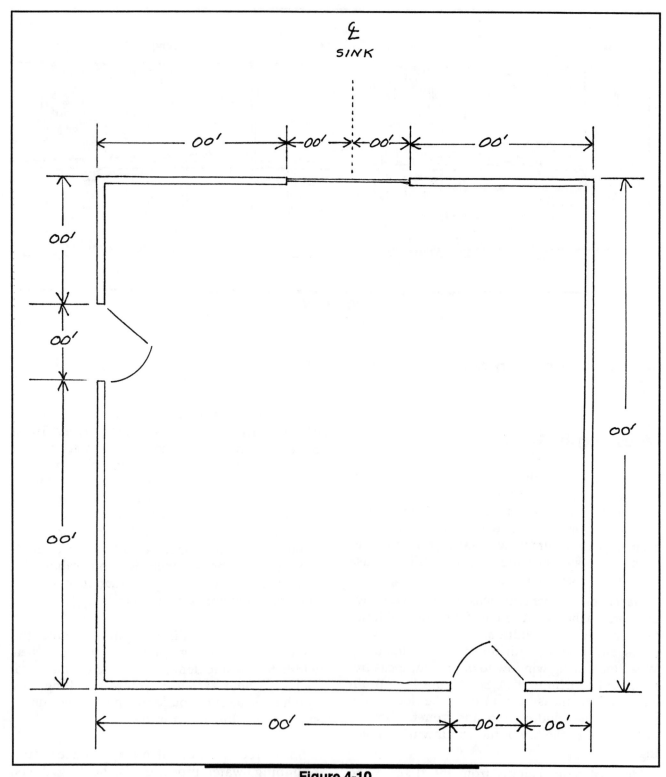

Figure 4-10
Measure the room wall-to-wall in both directions from doors, windows and sink

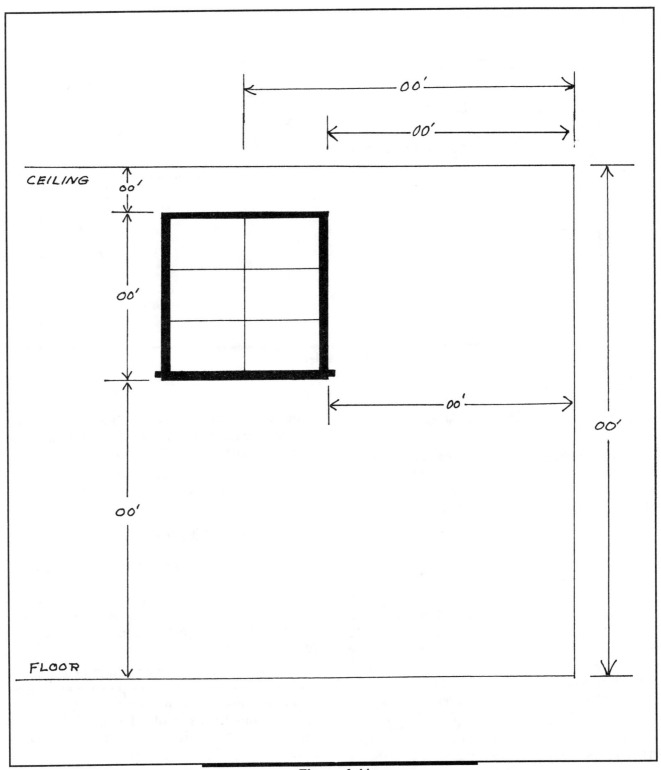

Figure 4-11
Measure windows and doors from corner to outside of trim molding

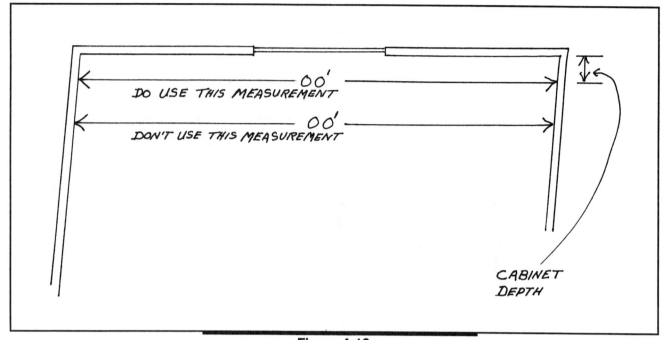

Figure 4-12
Proper procedure for measuring a room that is not square

Compensating for Uneven Areas

Because floors and walls often have uneven spots that affect the installation of cabinets, you have to locate these uneven areas. You'll need to shim or cut the cabinets to hang them plumb, true and square.

An uneven floor will affect installation of your base cabinets. Check the floor for high spots with a straight 2 x 4 and a level. Check all around the room within 22 inches of the walls where your base cabinets are to be installed. Find the highest point on the floor. Then strike a level line on the wall all around the room from this point, using your level and chalkline. See Figure 4-13. This is your *base level line*. You'll have to brace up the cabinets to make sure they're level with this line.

Mark the outline of all wall cabinets on the wall to verify the accuracy of your cabinet layout. Then check for uneven spots, using a straight 2 x 4 as shown in Figure 4-13. An uneven wall can cause misaligned cabinets, resulting in the racking or twisting of doors and drawer fronts. Where

uneven spots interfere, remove the high spots by scraping or sanding the wall. Fill in or shim the low spots with thin pieces of wood.

Then locate the wall studs and mark the locations where you'll secure the cabinets.

Wall Cabinets With a Soffit

If the wall cabinets butt against a ceiling soffit, install the soffit first. Soffits in a room with 8-foot ceilings are normally 12 inches high and 14 inches wide. This allows a 1-1/4-inch overhang for cabinets that are 12-3/4 inches deep from door face to the back of the cabinet.

If a soffit is used over an island peninsula, it should be 16-1/4 inches deep. This will allow approximately 1-1/4 inch of overhang on each side for double-face wall cabinets. They're normally 13-11/16 inches deep from door face to door face.

Design the bottom of the soffit to be 84-1/4 inches from the floor if you plan to use upper cabinets over broom or utility cabinets.

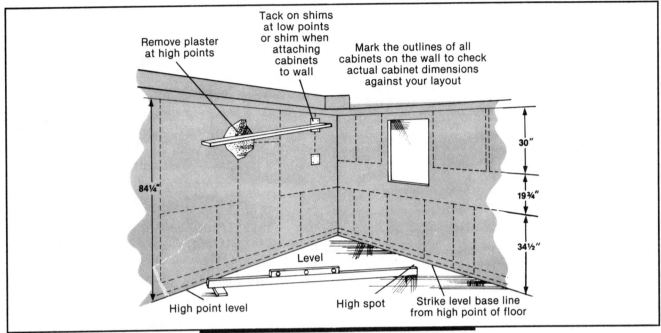

Remove plaster at high points

Tack on shims at low points or shim when attaching cabinets to wall

Mark the outlines of all cabinets on the wall to check actual cabinet dimensions against your layout

84¼"

30"

19¾"

34½"

Level

High point level

High spot

Strike level base line from high point of floor

Figure 4-13
Finding unevenness in floors and walls

Wall Cabinets Without a Soffit

Measure up from the base level reference line 54 inches. Place a mark on the wall. Do this at several points on each wall. With a level and straightedge, draw a level line around the room parallel to the base line. This 54-inch-high line will be your bottom line for installing 30-inch-high standard wall cabinets.

The Installation

Shut off the water lines to the sink and refrigerator and cut off the gas and electricity to the appliances. Disconnect and remove the stove, refrigerator, dishwasher, and other appliances. It's best to move these out of the kitchen so you'll have more working space.

Now, take out the sink and remove the old countertops and cabinets. You'll also need to remove the baseboard and any chair rail or moldings which would interfere with your cabinet installation. If you're going to replace the floor covering, remove the old covering unless the new floor can be installed directly over the old floor cover. There's more about this in Chapter 13.

Installing Standard Cabinets

Plan carefully the location of kitchen cabinets, fixtures, countertops and storage space. Remember, the efficient kitchen has a work triangle of no more than 22 feet. After choosing the best layout for your kitchen, draw up a complete floor plan of the kitchen.

Tips:

- Allow 2 feet of counter space on each side of the range and sink.

- Allow 15 inches of counter space next to the refrigerator.

- Refrigerator doors should swing away from the adjoining work surface. Be sure there's enough space to open the refrigerator door and pull out the shelves without the shelves hitting the door.

- Use a sink cabinet that's at least 3 inches wider than the actual sink dimension.

- Locate tall utility cabinets at the end of a row of lower cabinets.

Tools:

- Chalkline

- Countersink

- Electric drill with several bits

- A 4-foot level

- A 10- or 12-foot wood extension rule

- A 2-foot carpenter's square

- Stepladder

- Screwdriver

- Wood screws

- Wood shims (made from shingles or scrap wood)

- Two 4-inch C-clamps

Installation steps:

Follow these step-by-step instructions for installing cabinets. See Figure 4-14.

1) *Prepare the walls*— Cabinets must be mounted perfectly level and square. To prepare the walls for cabinet installation, first remove all the moldings, baseboards, and other protruding objects. Use a level to locate the high point on the floor. Then mark this point on the wall. This is your base level.

2) *Measure and mark the walls*— To measure and mark cabinet locations, begin at the floor base level mark you just made on the wall. From this point, measure 34-1/2 inches up the wall and draw a horizontal line. This will be the top line of your base cabinets. Starting again at the floor base level mark, measure 84 inches up the wall and draw another horizontal line. This will be the top line of your wall cabinets. These measurements are for a standard 8-foot ceiling.

3) *Locate the wall studs*— Cabinets must be attached to studs. To locate the studs, you can use a magnetic stud finder, tap the wall with a hammer, or test the wall with a nail. Use a nail only if the nail holes will later be hidden from view. Studs are usually spaced 16 inches on center.

4) *Wall cabinet installation*— It's important that you always start with the corner wall cabinets. After locating the wall studs, place the top of your wall cabinet along the 84-inch line. Use a 3/16-inch twist bit to drill installation holes through the hanging strips built into the back of the cabinet. Then use a 3/32-inch twist bit to drill (through the hanging-strip holes) 1-3/4 inches into the studs. Use two 2-1/2-inch flat-head wood screws to fasten the cabinet to the wall. To make stronger fasteners that have a nicer appearance, install chrome-head grommets behind the screw heads. All screws must penetrate the studs at least 1 inch. Do not tighten down screws until all the wall cabinets have been installed. When all the wall cabinets are installed, make the final leveling and shim adjustments. Then tighten all the screws down. *Warning: If you don't use shims when tightening the back rails against a crooked wall, you can break the joint between the rail and the cabinet. This can cause the cabinet to fall off the wall.*

5) *Blind corner wall cabinets*— Blind corner cabinets can be pulled up to 4-1/2 inches out from the wall. Use the normal cabinet-hanging procedure, but add a 3-inch wall filler. To attach the filler to the cabinet, use the same procedure you use for joining front frames. The procedure is explained in step 7.

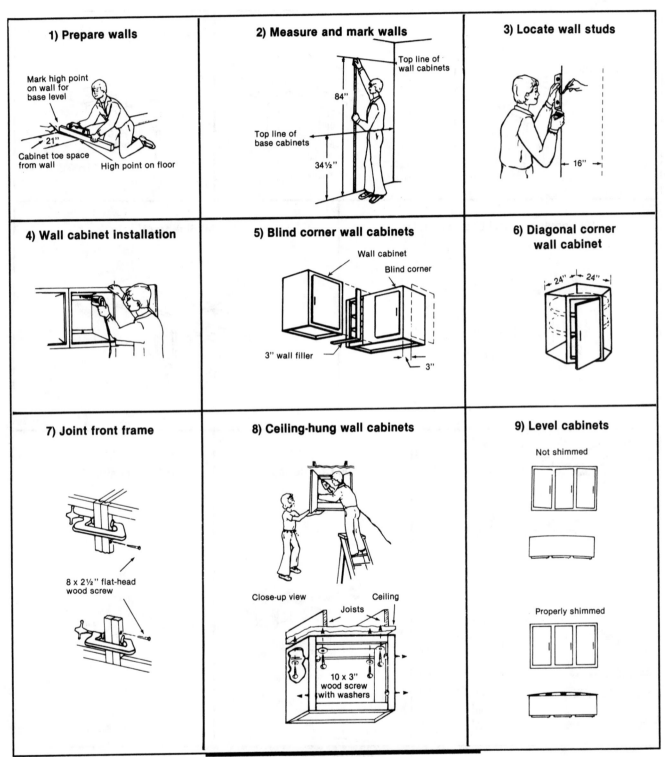

Figure 4-14
Cabinet installation details

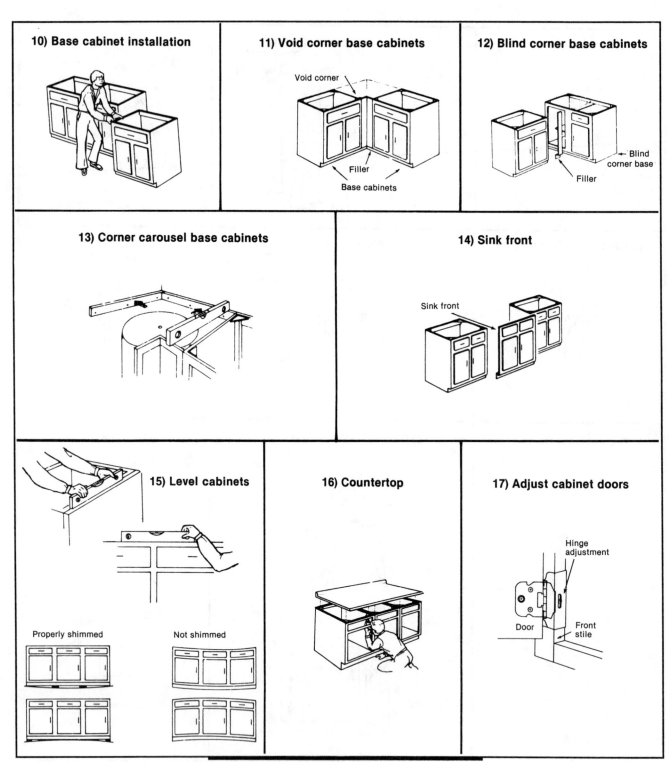

Figure 4-14
Cabinet installation details (continued)

6) *Diagonal corner wall cabinets*— Diagonal cabinets extend out from the corner 24 inches along each wall. Be sure the cabinets are perfectly plumb on both sides and front. Use your carpenter's level to make sure they're level, both horizontally and vertically. It's especially important that the corner cabinets are plumb and level — the correct positioning of the other cabinets depends on it!

7) *Joining the front frames*— Frames must be flush at the top and bottom. Use C-clamps to secure the cabinets together while drilling and fastening. Use an 11/64-inch twist bit to drill a hole in the cabinet stile. Then use a 7/64-inch bit to drill a pilot hole approximately 1 inch deep in the adjoining cabinet stile. Fasten the cabinets together with No. 8 x 2-1/2-inch flat-head wood screws. Countersink for the screw heads. Trim fillers to fit and fasten them to the cabinet with wood glue or color-matched panel nails.

8) *Ceiling-hung wall cabinets*— Locate the ceiling joists above the wall cabinets. Use a 3/16-inch twist bit to drill four holes through the top frame of the cabinet. Use a 3/32-inch twist bit to drill (through the existing holes) about 1-1/2 inches into the ceiling and joists. Use No. 10 x 3-inch round-head wood screws with washers. Attach the cabinet to the front frame as described in step 7.

9) *Level the wall cabinets*— After all the cabinets have been hung, use your carpenter's level to make sure they're plumb and level on front, sides, and bottom. To correct uneven walls, shim behind the cabinets. After the cabinets and doors are perfectly aligned, tighten all the screws.

10) *Base cabinets*— After all the wall cabinets have been installed, begin your base cabinet installation. *Again, start with the corner base cabinets.* Drill small (1/8-inch) holes through the top rail at the back of the cabinet and into the studs. Insert No. 10 x 2-1/2-inch screws. Assemble the base corner unit by adding one cabinet on each side of the corner cabinet. Before fastening the cabinets together, remove the cabinet doors and hinges. Between the hinge holes, drill holes for the screws you're using to fasten the cabinets together. Insert the screws. When the door is replaced, these screws will be hidden. Join the front frames as described in step 7.

11) *Void corner base cabinets*— Use a filler when installing base cabinets with a void corner. A properly used filler can give you a void corner of 27 by 27 inches. Attach the filler as described in step 7.

12) *Blind corner base cabinets*— To determine the proper distance between the wall and the cabinet, check the layout drawing. The distance will vary, depending on the size of each unit. Position and fasten the cabinets in the usual way, but always use a filler. Attach the filler as described in step 7.

13) *Corner carousel base cabinets*— This unit must be perfectly plumb or the carousel won't operate properly. To provide support for the countertop, secure two 36-inch wood strips (1 x 2's) to the wall. Make sure the strips are level with the front rails.

14) *Sink fronts*— Align the sink front flush with the adjacent cabinets. Attach the front frames as described in step 7.

15) *Level base cabinets*— As you install each cabinet, use a level to check it across the front edge and from front to back. Make sure the front frame is plumb. Use shims if necessary.

16) *Countertops*— Attach the countertop to the corner blocks of the cabinet. To insure proper installation, follow the countertop manufacturer's instructions.

17) *Adjust the cabinet doors*— Loosen the adjustment screw on each hinge. Align the door in the frame, then tighten the screws. If the hinge is bent, use a screwdriver to ease the hinge into the correct position.

Installing Appliance Units

Figure 4-15 shows details for installing a 30-inch slide-in range. It's supported by the countertop and the cabinets. The countertop should extend over the edge of the cabinet 1-1/4 inches. Complete the gas or electrical hook-up before installing the range. Slide the unit into place with the top trim of the range resting on the countertop. Figures 4-16 through 4-22 illustrate cabinet details for various range, oven, and cooktop units.

You can provide the kitchen appliances for your remodeling projects, or you can have your clients pick out and purchase their appliances separately. If you supply the appliances, you should make a little extra on the transaction. You buy from the supplier at discount and sell at retail. However, before you start jingling the money in your pocket, think about whether the mark-up is worth the extra trouble.

Some appliances don't work right, or are noisy, or leak, or whatever. If you're the one who sold them the appliance, who do you think your clients will call? You guessed it! But you're not an appliance manufacturer or repairman. Nor should your reputation be tarnished by a defective appliance. Some of us learned this lesson the hard way. Now I prefer to let my clients buy their own appliances. If there's a problem with the unit, it isn't my problem.

Estimating Manhours

Cabinets are a key element in the design of the kitchen. Make sure you install them properly. Study what I've recommended in this chapter. Use the correct tools and the right size screws to hang the cabinets. *Never use nails.* Nails can eventually work loose and provide inadequate anchoring.

Estimate cabinets and their installation carefully. Use your own manhour records if you have them available. The best estimate is the one based on your own experience. Be sure you include the incidental costs for each cabinet you install, such as the shims and the extra time required for working with uneven floors, off-square rooms, and out-of-plumb walls. You didn't cause this extra work. You shouldn't have to pay for it out of your profit.

Figure 4-23 shows my manhour estimates for installing cabinets, including time for removing old cabinets, preparation, and clean-up.

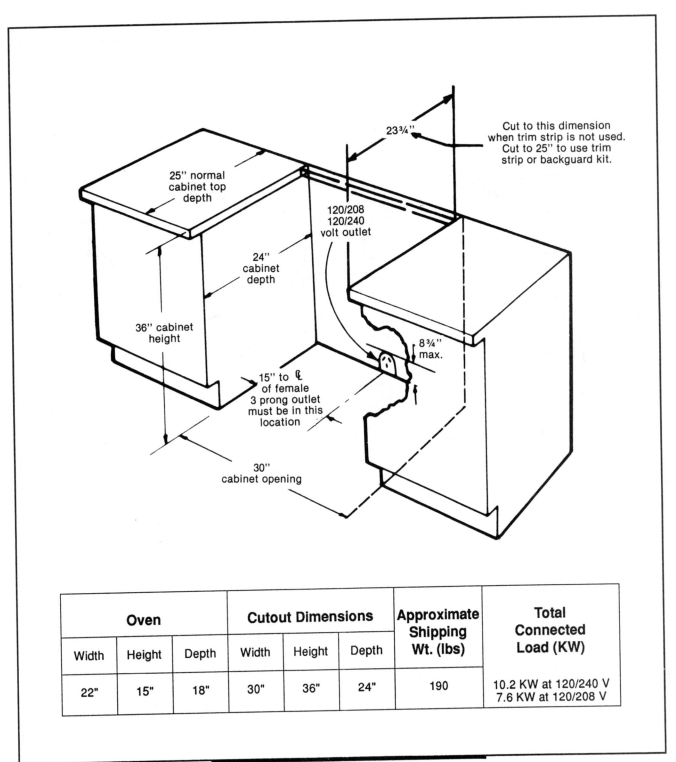

Figure 4-15
Electric slide-in ranges

Oven			Cutout Dimensions			Approximate Shipping Wt. (lbs)	Total Connected Load (KW)
Width	Height	Depth	Width	Height	Depth		
22"	15"	18"	30"	36"	24"	190	10.2 KW at 120/240 V 7.6 KW at 120/208 V

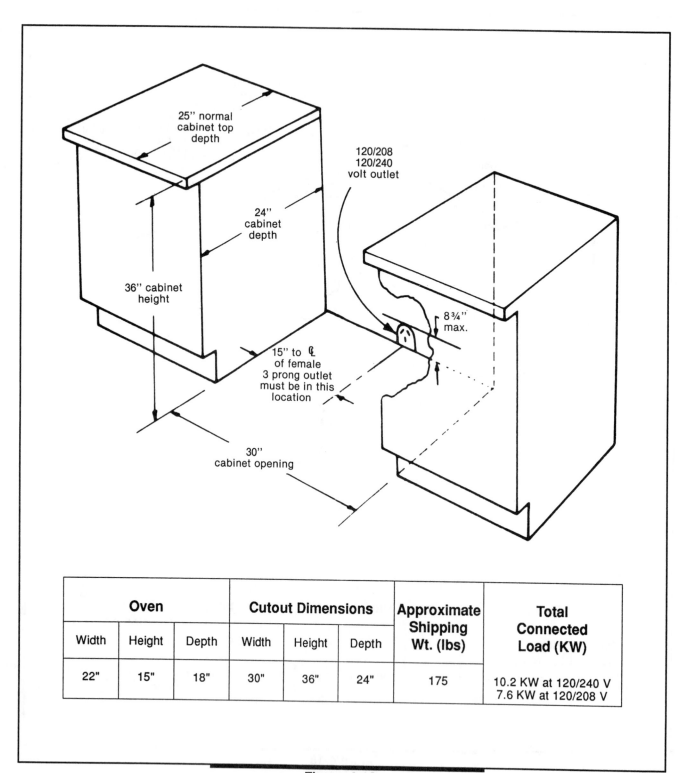

Oven			Cutout Dimensions			Approximate Shipping Wt. (lbs)	Total Connected Load (KW)
Width	Height	Depth	Width	Height	Depth		
22"	15"	18"	30"	36"	24"	175	10.2 KW at 120/240 V 7.6 KW at 120/208 V

Figure 4-16
Electric freestanding ranges

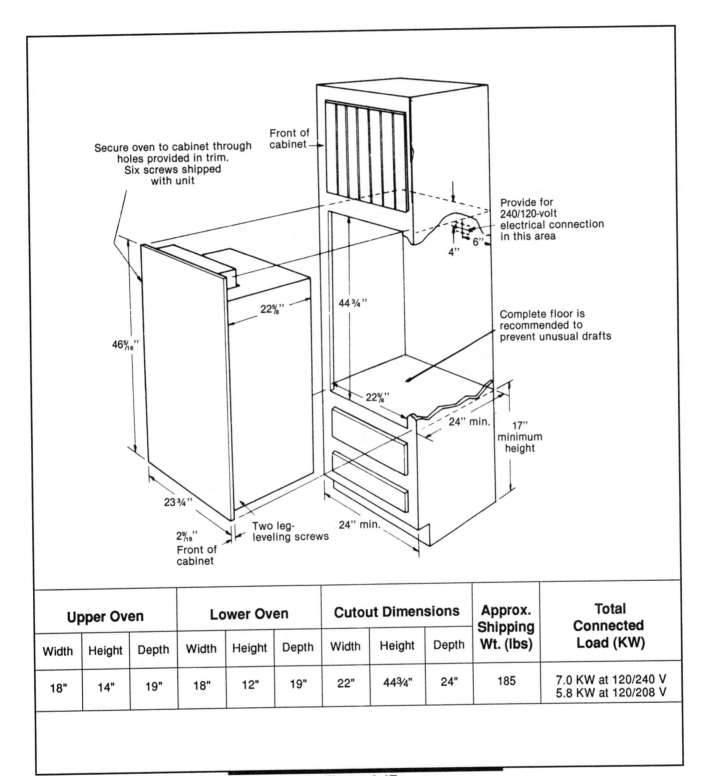

Figure 4-17
Electric wall ovens

Upper Oven			Lower Oven			Cutout Dimensions			Approx. Shipping Wt. (lbs)	Total Connected Load (KW)
Width	Height	Depth	Width	Height	Depth	Width	Height	Depth		
18"	14"	19"	18"	12"	19"	22"	44¾"	24"	185	7.0 KW at 120/240 V 5.8 KW at 120/208 V

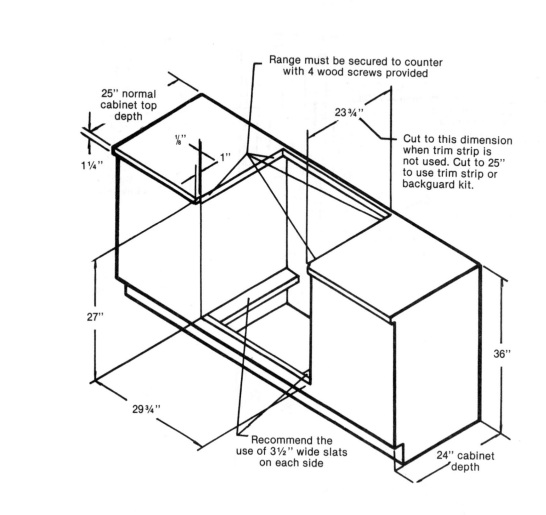

Figure 4-18
Electric drop-in ranges

Oven			Cutout Dimensions			Approximate Shipping Wt. (lbs)	Total Connected Load (KW)
Width	Height	Depth	Width	Height	Depth		
22"	15"	18"	29¾"	27"	23¾"	170	10.2 KW at 120/240 V 7.6 KW at 120/208 V

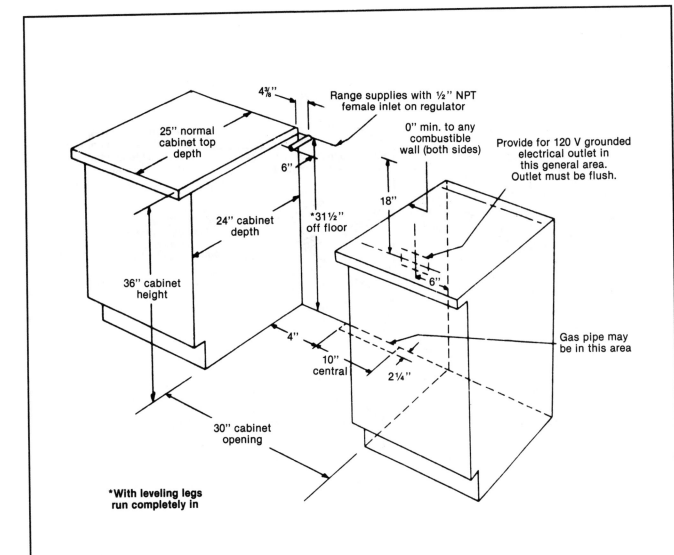

Figure 4-19
Gas freestanding ranges

Oven			Broiler			Cutout Dimensions			Approx. Shipping Wt. (lbs)
Width	Height	Depth	Width	Height	Depth	Width	Height	Depth	
22"	15"	18"	13½"	3½"	15"	30"	36"	24"	195

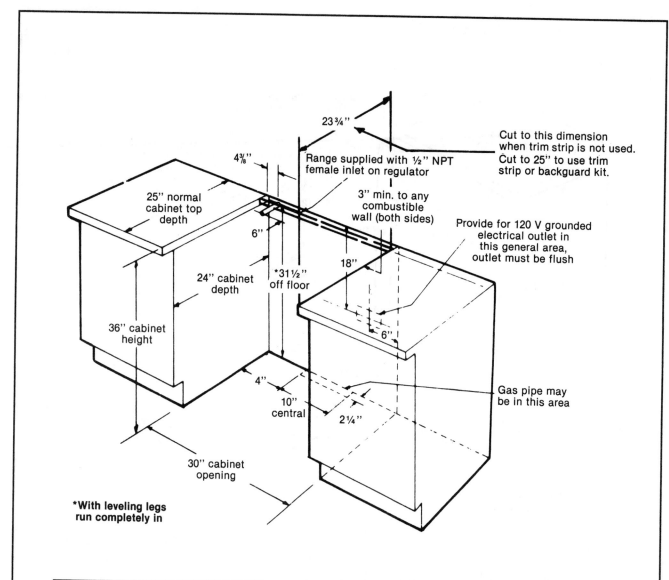

Oven			Broiler			Cutout Dimensions			Approx. Shipping Wt. (lbs)
Width	Height	Depth	Width	Height	Depth	Width	Height	Depth	
22"	15"	18"	13½"	3½"	15"	30"	36"	24"	195

Figure 4-20
Gas slide-in ranges

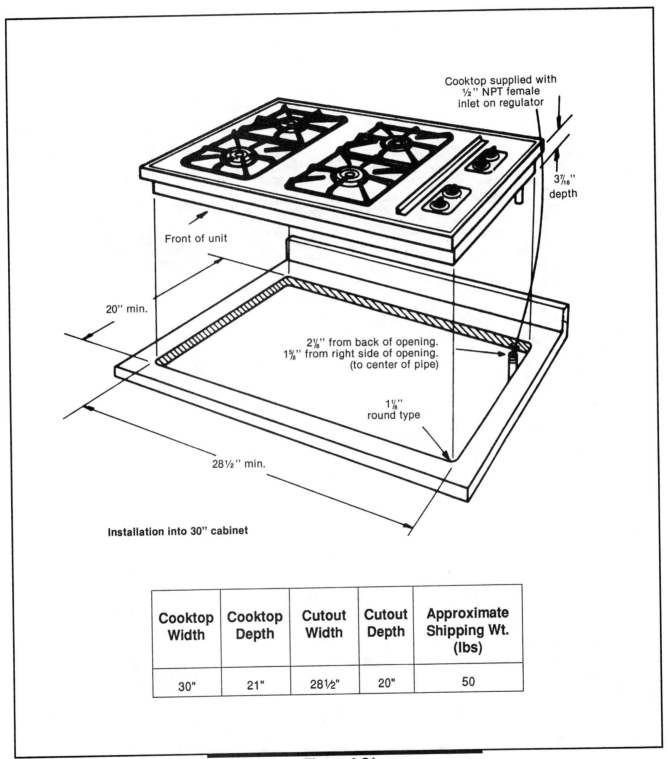

Figure 4-21
Gas cooktops

Cooktop Width	Cooktop Depth	Cutout Width	Cutout Depth	Approximate Shipping Wt. (lbs)
30"	21"	28½"	20"	50

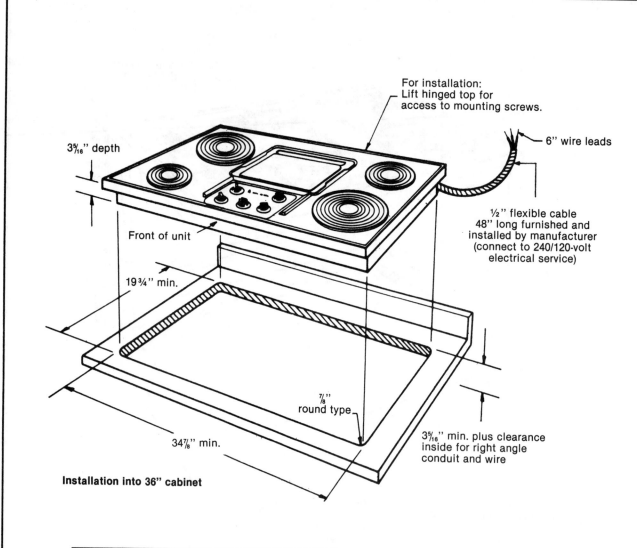

Figure 4-22
Electric cooktops

Cooktop Width	Cooktop Depth	Cutout Width	Cutout Depth	Approximate Shipping Wt. (lbs)	Total Connected Load (KW)
36"	21"	34⅞"	19¾"	50	7.6 KW at 120/240V 5.7 KW at 120/208 V

Work element	Unit	Manhours per unit
Base cabinets, 34½" high		
24" wide	each	2.0
36" wide	each	2.4
Base corner cabinets, 36" wide	each	5.5
Wall cabinets, 12" deep		
12" x 18"	each	1.7
18" x 18"	each	1.9
18" x 36"	each	2.0
24" x 36"	each	2.6
Cabinet stain finish	100 SF	1.0
Cabinet paint finish	100 SF	1.2
Cabinet vinyl finish	100 SF	1.4
Suggested Crew: 1 carpenter and 1 laborer; 1 painter for finishing.		

Figure 4-23
Manhours for installing cabinets

Countertops and How to Install Them

An attractive, clean and spacious countertop sets off the rest of the kitchen. It's as important for its design as it is for its function. There are a variety of materials to choose from. You can design a countertop that's simple and efficient, or one that's elaborate and personalizes your client's kitchen.

When you design a kitchen, give as much attention to the countertop as you do to the cabinets, floor, walls, and ceiling. Think about convenience, style, clean lines, and durability. Advise your client concerning the best choices for their particular style of living. How much cooking do they do? How much time and energy will it take to maintain their choice of countertop? How durable should it be? Remember, whatever they choose, it will be in view and in use for a long time. Take care to do some of your best work here. If there are flaws in workmanship, they too will be in view for a long time.

Countertop Materials

There are advantages and disadvantages to all the countertop materials available. Discuss these with your clients so they can make a selection based on sound information.

Plastic Laminate

Plastic laminates are made with layers of impregnated paper, cloth, or wood bonded together under high temperature with plastic resin. A melamine overlay gives the desired finish. Laminates have several advantages. They're reasonably priced, durable and have excellent impact and water resistance. And there are many patterns and colors available. The disadvantage is that it cuts and nicks easily, and has only fair resistance to heat.

Ceramic Tile

Ceramic tile is made of clay fired at high temperatures. What are the advantages? It's durable, impervious to water, and can be installed over an existing countertop. It has excellent heat and abrasion resistance. The disadvantage is that the grout joints are hard to clean and may have to be replaced after a few years. It's also noisy, and can be cracked or chipped by a sharp blow.

Corian

Corian is a solid sheet material made of methyl methacrylate binder. It has good heat, stain, water, abrasion, and impact resistance. It's easy to maintain and the color goes all the way through the material. It's nonporous and extremely durable. The disadvantage is that Corian is expensive and requires skilled installation.

Butcher Block Maple

Butcher block is made of hardwood layers laminated together. It has an extremely durable and excellent cutting surface. Minor damage to the surface is easily corrected. The disadvantage is poor water resistance. The top has to be oiled or sealed occasionally to maintain its attractive appearance.

Marble

Marble comes in a variety of shades. It has the advantage of a fine, smooth, and cool surface. The disadvantage is that it scratches easily and can crack. It's also slightly porous. Repairs on marble are difficult. You'll see it more often on bathroom or vanity countertops than kitchen counters. Besides being very expensive, it takes special tools and skills for installation.

Molded or Factory Prefabricated Countertops

The molded countertop has the edge and backsplash molded in one piece. It's usually a plastic laminate on a particleboard substrate. You can buy molded tops at most cabinet shops and builder supply companies. Prefabricated countertops are excellent for most kitchen and bathroom remodeling jobs as well as for new construction. There's no seam between the backsplash and top surface or between the edge and top surface. The molded countertop, sometimes called a formed top, gives a neat, professional finish to your kitchen job. As long as it's properly installed, it will give your customers years of service.

Many kitchen and bathroom remodelers find it more economical to install molded countertops than to fabricate laminate countertops on the job. Figure 5-1 shows three types of molded or postformed edge treatments.

Many grades and types of laminate countertop material are available. Solicor is a high pressure

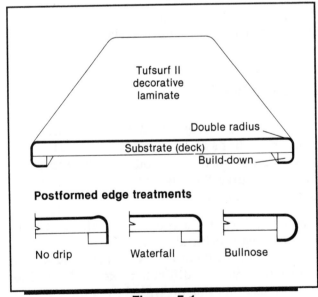

Figure 5-1
Typical postformed countertop

Figure 5-2
Countertop without trim shapes

Figure 5-3
Countertop with trim shapes

decorative laminate with a single color throughout both face and core. It's a registered trademark of Ralph Wilson Plastics Company, which manufactures decorative laminate products under the *Wilsonart* brand. *Formica* is a trade name of American Cyanamide Corporation.

If your client wants plastic laminate countertops, they're available in many colors and designs, in grades ranging from standard to the extremely heat and chemical resistant.

Ceramic Tile Countertops

Ceramic tile makes an attractive and durable countertop. If it's installed right, that is. The tiles must align perfectly, and you need the appropriate trim to give the edge and backsplash a finished appearance.

Figure 5-2 shows a ceramic mosaic tile countertop which was installed without trim tiles. The front edge of the counter has an unsightly rough edge which is also difficult to keep clean. The joint edges don't line up with the counter surface lines for design uniformity. In short, it has an unfinished look.

Compare Figure 5-2 with the countertop in Figure 5-3. You can clearly see the difference in quality. Figure 5-3 has the professional look you want. The flat and trim tiles align perfectly. The back of the counter slopes into the backsplash using a cove trim tile, the front edge is rounded, smooth and neat. The decor tile sets the countertop off nicely and ties into the kitchen's color scheme.

Ceramic tile comes in glazed and unglazed surfaces. A glazed tile surface is made with a glasslike substance fused to the body of the tile when it's fired. You can get glazed tile runners or stretchers in many sizes. The 4-1/4-inch square is the most popular size for kitchens and bathrooms, but the 6-inch square tile is also good for countertops. You can use glazed ceramic tile for walls as well, especially in bathroom and shower areas. The extra-duty glazed tile is recommended for countertop or floor installation because it's more wear-resistant. Figure 5-4 shows glazed ceramic tile trim pieces and where to use them.

Unglazed tile ceramic mosaics are manufactured in small 1 x 1 and 2 x 2-inch squares, 2 x 1-inch rectangles, and 2-inch hexagonal shapes. They're used for floors, walls, countertops, window sills, fireplaces, and as decor pieces.

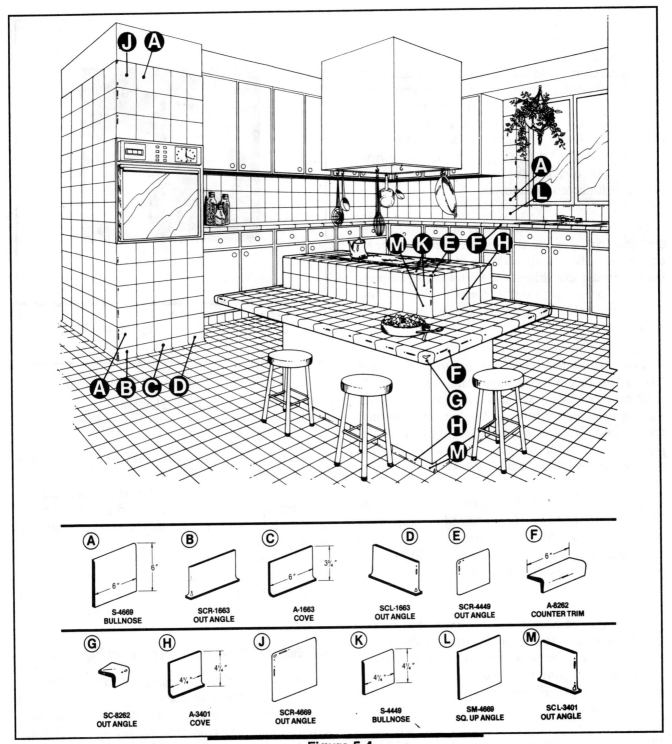

Figure 5-4
Glazed tile trim installation usage
Courtesy: American Olean Tile

Be careful when selecting the tile design for your project. Ceramic tile manufacturers have produced tiles for specific types of installation. American Olean Tile Company offers a complete line of glazed tile (including trim) designed specifically for conventional mortar or thin-set installation methods. Conventional tile is designated by an A prefix in the catalog. The bullnose tile labeled A in Figure 5-5 is an example of an A type tile. The A tile is installed primarily with portland cement mortar.

Thin-set tile installation uses an organic adhesive (mastic), dry-set mortar, epoxy mortar, or an epoxy adhesive. Most ceramic tile jobs being installed today are thin-set, usually using organic adhesive or dry-set mortar. American Olean designates their thin-set tile with the prefix S in their catalogs.

Look at the tiles labeled A in Figure 5-5. They have more pronounced shape and curve. The A-4402 bullnose has a 3/4-inch radius. This allows the tile to fit better into the thicker conventional mortar bed. The A shapes are useful for remodeling jobs when your're installing new ceramic tile over old tile because of their thickness.

The S tiles have a flat back similar to the regular tiles, but with a less pronounced radius. This makes them best for installation in a thinner setting bed. The S-4449 bullnose has a radius of 1/4 inch compared to the 3/4-inch radius of the A-4402 bullnose.

The angles of both A and S shapes follow the same design configuration. Figure 5-6 shows the specifications of bullnose and cap tiles in conventional runners and trim. Figure 5-7 shows the specifications of bullnose and cap tiles in thin-set runners and trim.

Figure 5-8 shows ceramic mosaic trim tiles appropriate for use on a countertop like the one pictured in Figure 5-3. The S-832 cap and related angles, as well as the C-833 cove, were used in the installation of that countertop.

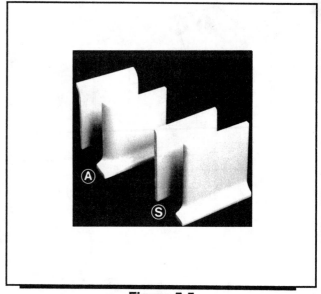

Figure 5-5
Conventional (A) trim and thin-set (S) trim

How to Install Ceramic Tile Countertops

A ceramic tile countertop might be just the idea that sells the job and boosts your profits. Given the choice, many people will elect to have ceramic countertops in their kitchens and baths. If you're a skilled tilesetter, no doubt you'll try to convince your prospects to go with ceramic tile. If you're not a tilesetter, you should know what's involved in the task so you'll recognize a job that's poorly done. Remember, your subcontractor's quality is *your* quality when he's working on your project.

Installing Tile with Adhesive on Plywood

Let's say you're remodeling a kitchen. You've finished all the new construction and installed new cabinets. It's now time to install the new countertop. Your client has chosen 6 x 6-inch thin-set American Olean tile. The kitchen is looking really good, so keep it that way! *Always* protect the base cabinets while installing the countertop. Hang a dropcloth or blanket over the cabinets until the counter is finished.

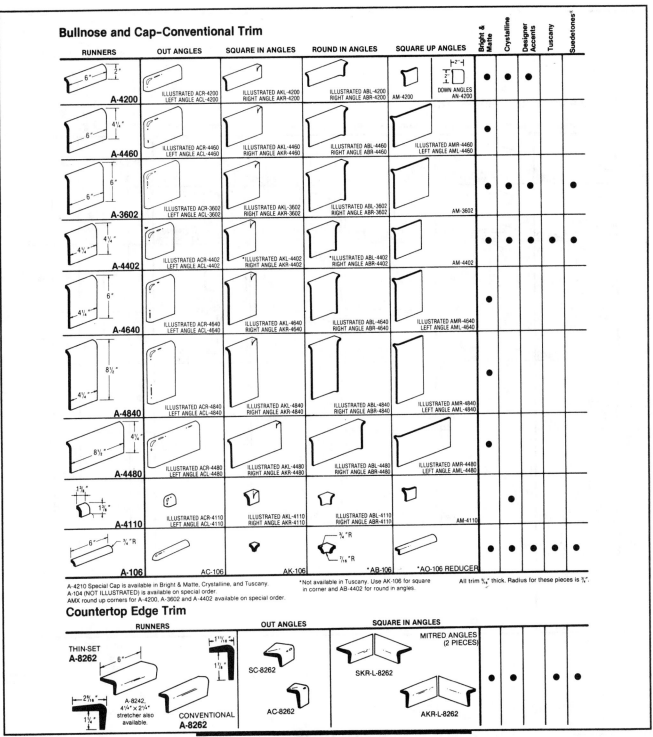

Figure 5-6
Glazed A-type trim
Courtesy: American Olean Tile

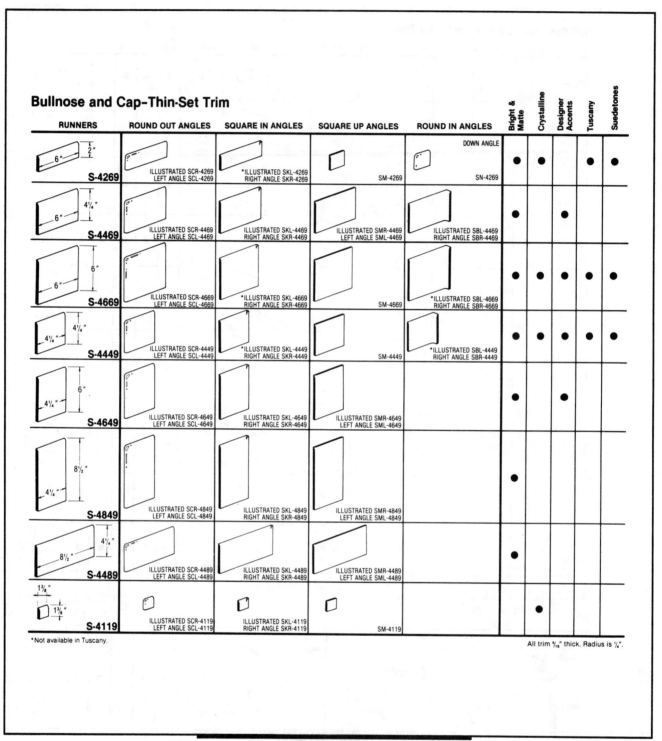

Bullnose and Cap-Thin-Set Trim

RUNNERS	ROUND OUT ANGLES	SQUARE IN ANGLES	SQUARE UP ANGLES	ROUND IN ANGLES	Bright & Matte	Crystalline	Designer Accents	Tuscany	Suedetones
S-4269	ILLUSTRATED SCR-4269 LEFT ANGLE SCL-4269	*ILLUSTRATED SKL-4269 RIGHT ANGLE SKR-4269	SM-4269	DOWN ANGLE SN-4269	●	●		●	●
S-4469	ILLUSTRATED SCR-4469 LEFT ANGLE SCL-4469	ILLUSTRATED SKL-4469 RIGHT ANGLE SKR-4469	ILLUSTRATED SMR-4469 LEFT ANGLE SML-4469	ILLUSTRATED SBL-4469 RIGHT ANGLE SBR-4469	●		●		
S-4669	ILLUSTRATED SCR-4669 LEFT ANGLE SCL-4669	*ILLUSTRATED SKL-4669 RIGHT ANGLE SKR-4669	SM-4669	*ILLUSTRATED SBL-4669 RIGHT ANGLE SBR-4669	●	●	●	●	●
S-4449	ILLUSTRATED SCR-4449 LEFT ANGLE SCL-4449	*ILLUSTRATED SKL-4449 RIGHT ANGLE SKR-4449	SM-4449	*ILLUSTRATED SBL-4449 RIGHT ANGLE SBR-4449	●	●	●	●	●
S-4649	ILLUSTRATED SCR-4649 LEFT ANGLE SCL-4649	ILLUSTRATED SKL-4649 RIGHT ANGLE SKR-4649	ILLUSTRATED SMR-4649 LEFT ANGLE SML-4649		●		●		
S-4849	ILLUSTRATED SCR-4849 LEFT ANGLE SCL-4849	ILLUSTRATED SKL-4849 RIGHT ANGLE SKR-4849	ILLUSTRATED SMR-4849 LEFT ANGLE SML-4849		●				
S-4489	ILLUSTRATED SCR-4489 LEFT ANGLE SCL-4489	ILLUSTRATED SKL-4489 RIGHT ANGLE SKR-4489	ILLUSTRATED SMR-4489 LEFT ANGLE SML-4489		●				
S-4119	ILLUSTRATED SCR-4119 LEFT ANGLE SCL-4119	ILLUSTRATED SKL-4119 RIGHT ANGLE SKR-4119	SM-4119			●			

*Not available in Tuscany.

All trim ⁵⁄₁₆″ thick. Radius is ¼″.

Figure 5-7
Bullnose and cap thin-set trim
Courtesy: American Olean Tile

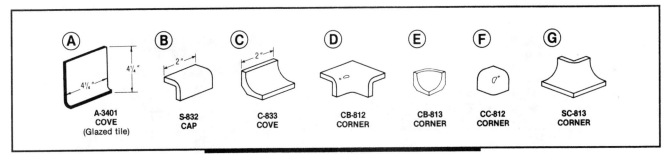

Figure 5-8
Ceramic mosaic trim
Courtesy: American Olean Tile

Step 1: Exterior grade 3/4-inch plywood (not flakeboard or interior plywood) should be your counter base. First, plan out the height of countertop so that the bottom edge of the front tile allows clearance for the dishwasher or trash compactor door. Make your cutouts for the sink and appliances in the plywood as shown in Figure 5-9, Step 1. (Figure 5-9 shows each step in the installation process.)

Step 2: Place an A-8262 (like the one shown in Figure 5-4, F) trim piece on the front edge. Lay out a trial row or two of tile, from the front to the back of counter, allowing for the desired joint width. You'll need to mark the exact location of the necessary cut on the last tile back. I recommend making your cuts before setting begins, but you may decide to do the cutting as you lay tile.

Step 3: Clean off all the dust from the counter base. Apply A0 1700 adhesive to the base with a 3/16-inch V-notched trowel, as recommended by the adhesive manufacturer. Use enough adhesive to assure you'll have complete contact with each tile, but not so much that it will squeeze up into the joints.

Step 4: Starting with the front counter trim, press the tiles firmly into the adhesive. Be sure to maintain *uniform* joint spacing and *straight* joint lines as you install the tiles. Use a damp sponge to clean off any adhesive smudges before you go on to the next area.

Step 5: When you come to the opening for the sink or an appliance, make a corner cut in tile with tile nippers or a Remington rod saw (a special carbide grit, round blade which fits into a standard hacksaw). Smooth the sharp edges of the cut with a carborundum stone to reduce the chance of cutting yourself.

Step 6: Spread adhesive on the backsplash and set the tile just as you did with the countertop. If you need to cut the tile for the backsplash, cut the top row. You want the cut edge up against the bottom of the wall cabinet so it won't show.

Step 7: Trim the edge of the backsplash with S-4269 surface bullnose tile (Figure 5-7). Cut it to fit the contour of the countertop trim. Use a damp sponge to remove any excess adhesive from the adjacent wall surface.

Step 8: Wait at least one day for the adhesive to dry and firm up before you fill the joints between tile. I use American Olean drywall grout. Mix the amount you need for the job, following the instructions on the bag. Press the grout into the joints using a Groutmaster or similar trowel. Clean the excess grout off the tile surface.

Step 9: Pack all the joints with a narrow tool like a tongue depressor so they're firm, smooth, and uniform. This makes the joints more water resistant and easier to keep clean.

Step 10: Use a damp sponge to remove the grout film. Rinse your sponge frequently in clean water for best results. The small pigment particles of colored grouts require a thorough cleaning.

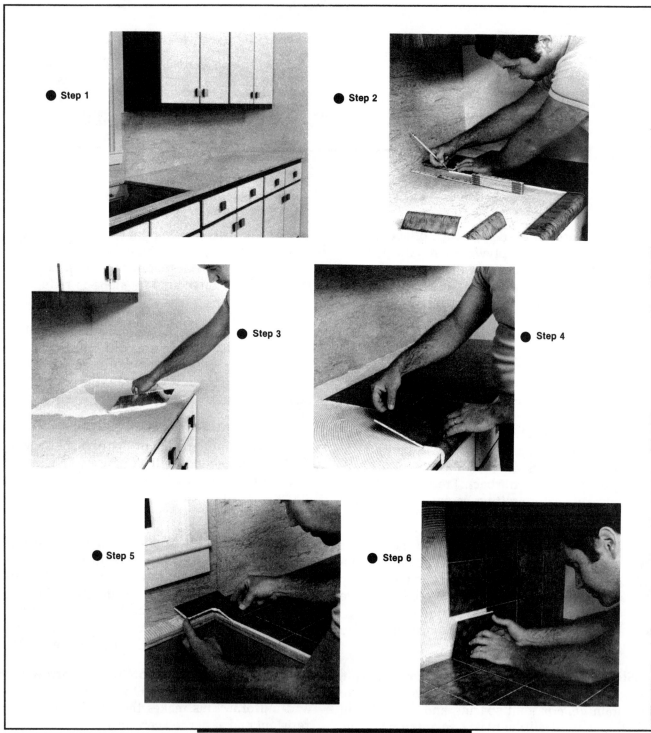

Figure 5-9
Tile installation with adhesive on plywood
Courtesy: American Olean Tile

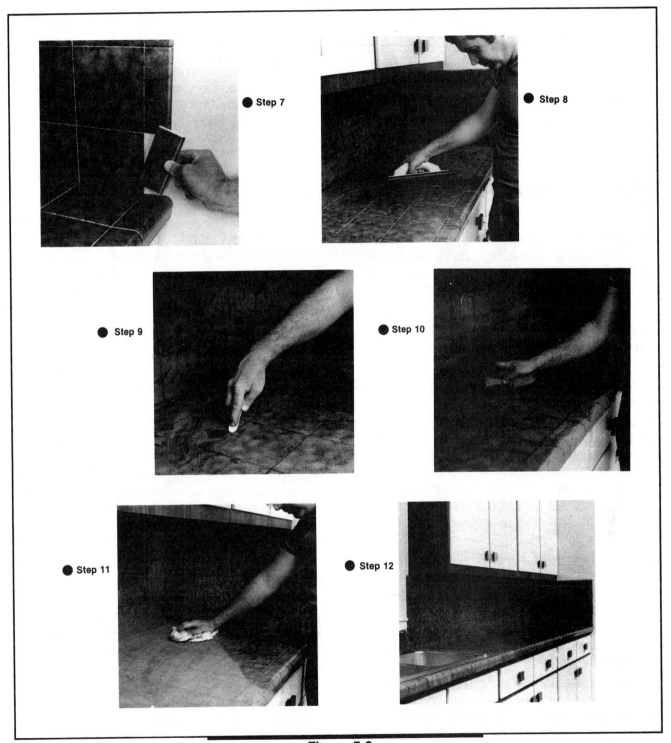

Figure 5-9
Tile installation with adhesive on plywood (continued)
Courtesy: American Olean Tile

Step 11: After the first cleaning, wait until the surface dries. There will still be a grout haze on the tile. Clean it off with a soft, dry cloth. Be sure the surface of each tile is completely clean.

Step 12: Examine the finished countertop. When it's flawless, stand back and admire your work. Your client will appreciate it too.

Installing Tile with Adhesive on Laminate

If your client wants ceramic tile installed over an old laminate countertop, that's no problem. Figure 5-10 shows all the steps involved in installing a new tile surface on a worn laminate top.

Step 1: Begin by removing any metal trim that may protrude and interfere with a smooth flat surface.

Step 2: Lightly sand the laminate surface with coarse sandpaper. Remove all the dust. This will ensure a reliable adhesive bond.

Step 3: Before you spread the adhesive, decide where you will have to cut the tiles. Place the A-8262 counter trim on the front edge, then lay one or two rows of tiles front-to-back, allowing for your desired joint width. Mark the exact location for the cut on the last tile back. You can make the cuts either before you set the tile or as you go along.

Step 4: American Olean recommends that you use A0 1700 adhesive with a laminate surface. Apply it with a 3/16-inch V-shaped trowel. Use enough adhesive to assure complete contact with each tile, but not so much that it will squeeze up into the joints. Clean off the excess adhesive with a damp sponge.

Step 5: Starting with the front counter trim, press the tiles firmly into the adhesive. Make sure you maintain *uniform* spacing for the joints and *straight* joint lines. Use a damp sponge to clean off adhesive smudges before you go on to the next row.

Step 6: At the sink and appliance openings, make corner cuts in the tile with tile nippers or a

Remington rod saw. Smooth the sharp edges with carborundum stone so you won't cut yourself while working with the tile.

Step 7: You can continue laying the tile using the same procedures outlined in Steps 6 through 12 for the installation of tile with adhesives on plywood. (See Figure 5-9 also).

Tile Using Conventional Mortar on a Wood Base

The first two examples of tile installation we covered involved the use of thin-set tiles. Now suppose you have a job where you'll need to use a thicker mortar bed. You'll use an A type tile and conventional mortar methods for installation. Follow along in Figure 5-11.

Step 1: You begin by installing a 3/4-inch exterior grade plywood top on the counter area. Since the bottom edge of the plywood will also be the bottom of the tile trim in front, be sure the height from the floor allows enough clearance for the dishwasher or trash compactor. Make cutouts for the sink and any appliances.

Step 2: Cover the plywood surface, including the counter edge, with a waterproof membrane. Either 15-pound roofing felt or 4-mil polyethylene works well. Lap the edges at least 2 inches up the adjacent drywall backsplash and sidewall to guard against moisture from the mortar. Staple or tack the membrane into place.

Step 3: Cover the entire surface with 3.4-pound metal lath or 2-inch by 2-inch wire, allowing a 1/16 inch to 1/8 inch clearance from the adjacent walls and front edge. Lap the metal reinforcing at least one full mesh, then staple or nail it in place.

Step 4: Nail and level the special punched metal trim strip through the vertical nailing slots in the reinforcing. You want the lower edge of the metal strip to be flush with the bottom of the plywood. This strip makes your tile installation faster and easier. It's available from dealers that sell American Olean tile.

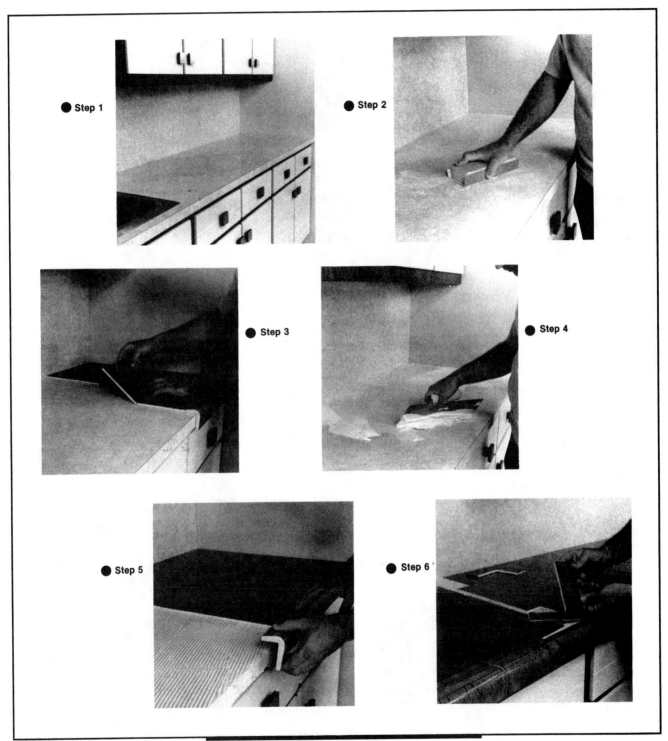

Figure 5-10
Tile installation with adhesive on laminate
Courtesy: American Olean Tile

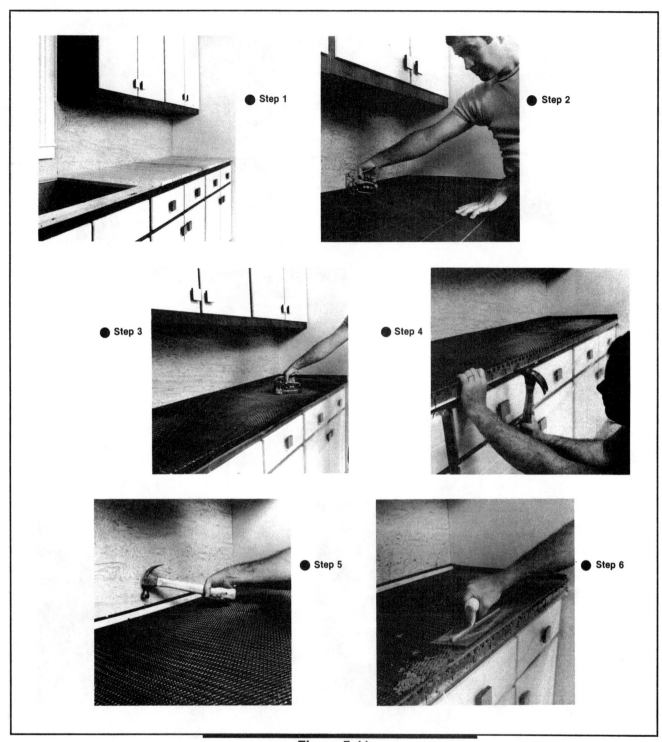

Figure 5-11
Tile installation with conventional mortar on wood base
Courtesy: American Olean Tile

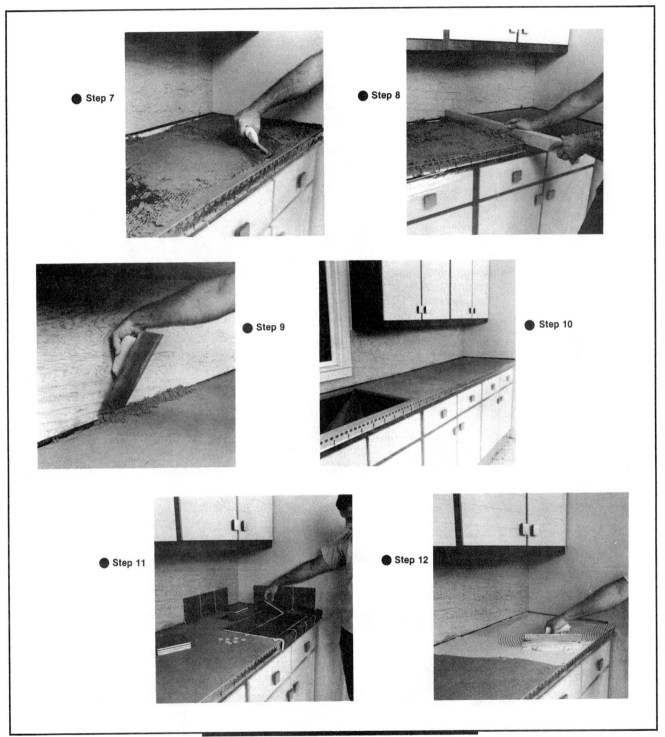

Figure 5-11
Tile installation with conventional mortar on wood base (continued)
Courtesy: American Olean Tile

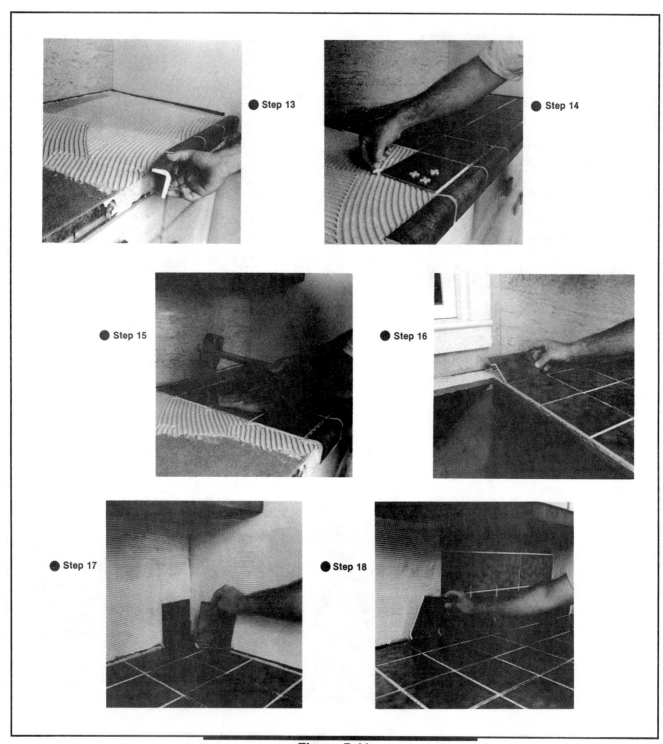

Figure 5-11
Tile installation with conventional mortar on wood base (continued)
Courtesy: American Olean Tile

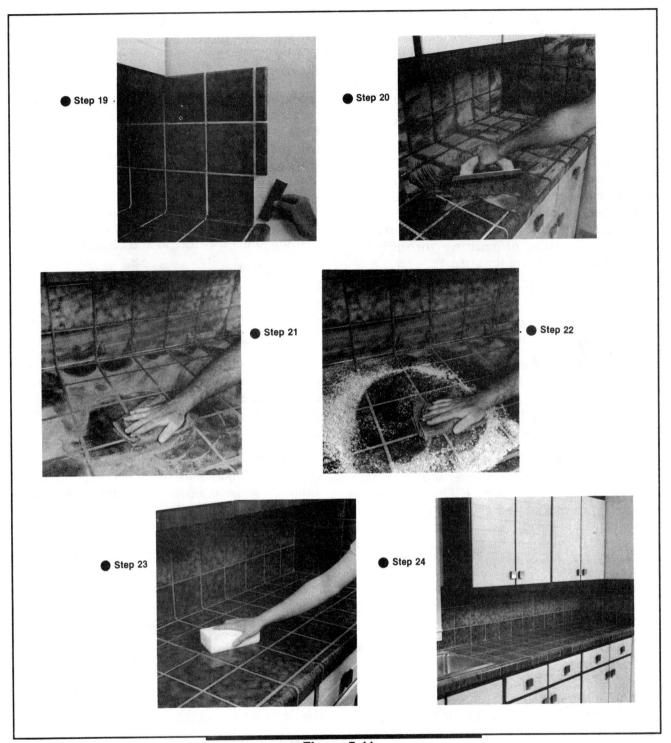

Figure 5-11
Tile installation with conventional mortar on wood base (continued)
Courtesy: American Olean Tile

Step 5: Nail a temporary wood screed strip along the back of the counter, one inch away from back wall. Level and shim this strip to the same elevation as the metal trim strip along the front. You should also install screed strips around sink and appliance openings, about one inch from the opening, and leveled to the same elevation as the front strip.

Step 6: Mix your cement mortar (1 part portland cement to 6 parts damp sand by volume) and densely compact it behind the metal strip. The mortar bed should be at least 3/4 inch, but no more than 1-1/2 inches thick. The fresh mortar should be visible, protruding through the punched round holes of the strip.

Step 7: Place mortar all over the surface of the counter and spread it evenly. It should be approximately 1/4 inch higher than the screed. Tamp it so the entire bed is firm and level.

Step 8: Use the front and back strips to guide a wood or metal straightedge over the surface and screed off the excess mortar. Move the straightedge back and forth over the surface until you fill up all the low spots.

Step 9: Remove the temporary wood strips from along the back of the counter and around the sink and appliance openings. Fill in the resulting crevices with mortar and compact it into place. Use a trowel to smooth off and plane those surface areas as evenly as the adjacent mortar bed surfaces.

Step 10: The finished mortar bed should be flat, level, and smooth before you proceed with laying out and setting the tile.

Step 11: Lay the tile out to determine the best location for cuts. You'll be using A-8262 trim, A-3601 cove, and 6-inch by 6-inch flat tile. For easy, uniform joint spacing, use 1/4-inch plastic joint spacers made especially for this purpose. Leave the spacers in place. Draw cutting lines on the tiles that need to be trimmed.

Step 12: Mix white sanded wall mortar with water to a thick, creamy consistency. If the mortar bed is still soft and damp, apply the mortar in a

uniform 1/16-inch thickness using a smooth trowel. If the mortar bed is hard and dry, use a 1/4 by 1/4-inch square notched trowel to apply the mortar.

Step 13: Apply the mortar firmly into the recesses of the punched metal trim strip along the front of the counter. Press the A-8262 countertop trim pieces firmly into the fresh mortar. Position them to rest directly on top of the metal trim strip.

Step 14: Press each tile into the fresh wet mortar. Set in the 1/4-inch permanent plastic joint spacers and adjust the tile and counter trim so that the joints are straight and uniform in width.

Step 15: Use a standard tile cutter to cut the back row of tile to the desired size. Smooth the sharp cut edges with a carborundum stone. Press the cut tiles firmly into place with a wooden block and rubber mallet.

Step 16: Cut the tile and trim pieces around the sink and appliance openings and tap them firmly into the mortar. Use nippers or a carbide grit saw for making angle cuts. Always smooth all exposed cut edges.

Step 17: Use a 3/16-inch V-notched trowel to spread A0 1700 adhesive on the backsplash and sidewall. Miter the cove lips of two A-3601 cove trim pieces with a tile cutting saw to make a square in-corner. Tap the tile into the adhesive.

Step 18: Continue setting the cove trim. Then set the flat tile on the backsplash and sidewall areas. Use plastic joint spacers and adjust the tiles for straight, uniform joint lines. Cut the top row of tile to fit under the cabinet.

Step 19: Finish the top and front of the tilework on the sidewall with an S-4269 bullnose trim (shown in Figure 5-7). Cut the S-4269 so that the vertical strip at the right front conforms with the line contours of the counter trim piece.

Step 20: When your tile joints are 1/4 inch or wider, use American Olean sanded floor grout. Mix it according to the instructions on the bag. Use a floor trowel to spread grout over the tiled areas and press it firmly into the joints.

Step 21: After you trowel the joints full, take dry grout powder directly from the grout bag and dust it evenly over the tiled areas until the dust is about 1/32 inch thick all over. Take a burlap pad and rub dry grout into the joints using a circular motion. This will thicken the grout in the joints and bring them up flush with tile surface.

Step 22: Sprinkle dry sawdust over the countertop and use the same burlap pad to rub the sawdust vigorously over the damp grout film. Sawdust absorbs the colored grout pigment and cleans the tile surface.

Step 23: Remove any remaining grout haze with the light touch of a damp sponge. Install the sink and any drop-in appliances. Caulk the joints between the sink rim and tile with silicone rubber sealant.

Step 24: Now step back and admire a job well done!

Tile in Dry-Set Mortar on Wonder-Board

Wonder-Board is a registered trademark of Modulars, Inc. It has a lightweight concrete core reinforced with fiberglass mesh. Bonded to each side is a coating of high density portland cement. That gives you a solid, masonry-type base for your dry-set installation. You'll usually lay 2-inch by 2-inch thin-set ceramic mosaic tiles on Wonder-Board.

Step 1: Install 3/4-inch exterior grade plywood as a base for the countertop. See Figure 5-12. Make sure the bottom of the plywood base is high enough to clear the dishwasher and trash compactor door. Make cutouts for the sink and any appliances.

Step 2: Cut the Wonder-Board to fit the counter. You'll need to use a mason-cutting blade in your power saw. Be sure you wear safety goggles while cutting this board.

Step 3: You'll need a 4-mil polyethylene film or 15-pound roofing felt between the plywood and the Wonder-Board. Place it on the plywood, covering the entire counter area. Then nail the Wonder-Board in place using 1-1/2-inch galvanized nails every 12 inches along all the edges of the counter surface. Where two Wonder-Board sheets abut, allow a 3/16-inch gap which you'll fill in with mortar.

Step 4: Lay out the mosaics with a thin-set bullnose along the front and a cove in back. Determine the location of the cuts you'll need to make and mark the tiles to be cut. The flat tile is back-mounted *Master-Set*. Each tile is joined to the next in 2-foot by 1-foot sheets. The trim tile is paper face-mounted in strips.

Step 5: Mix up dry-set mortar following the instructions on the mortar bag. Use the smooth end of a trowel to spread a thin band of mortar over the joint sections of Wonder-Board. Press 2-inch wide fiberglass reinforcing tape into the mortared joint and smooth it to a level plane.

Step 6: Spread mortar onto the surface of the Wonder-Board. Use a 1/4-inch square-notched trowel to comb the mortar into a uniform square-ribbed pattern. Slant the trowel to provide just enough mortar to squeeze up into the tile joints. The mortar ribs should be about 1/3 the tile thickness when tiles are pressed into them.

Step 7: Using the smooth side of the trowel, spread the mortar about 1/8 inch thick along the front edge of the counter. Press the front edge trim strip into this mortar. Then press the front edge bullnose strip into the mortar ribs on the top surface. Adjust both strips, so the front edge of the bullnose is flush with the front surface edge trim tile. Leave the paper facing on the trim tiles while you finish laying out the tiles.

Step 8: Lay the 2-foot by 1-foot sheets of tile in place on top of the mortar ribs. Cut the back row of tile on the lines previously marked, using tile cutters, wet tile saw, or nippers.

Step 9: Cut the tile around the sink and appliances. Press the cut tile firmly into the mortar ribs to assure a firm bond.

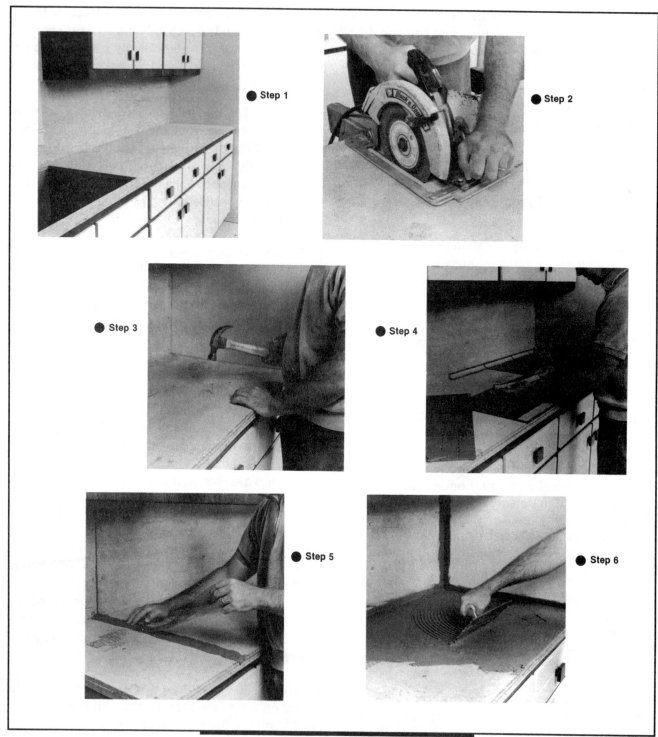

Figure 5-12
Installing tile with dry-set mortar on Wonder-Board over plywood
Courtesy: American Olean Tile

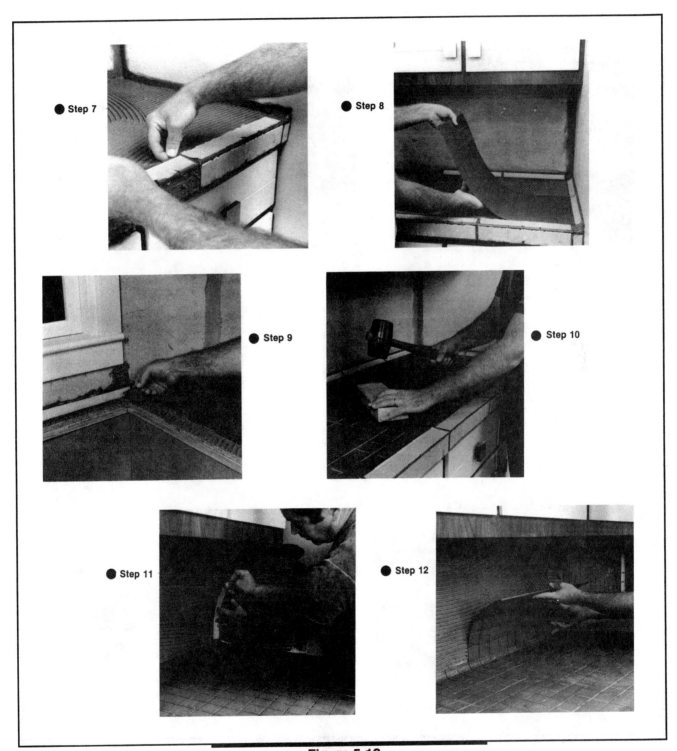

Figure 5-12
Installing tile with dry-set mortar on Wonder-Board over plywood (continued)
Courtesy: American Olean Tile

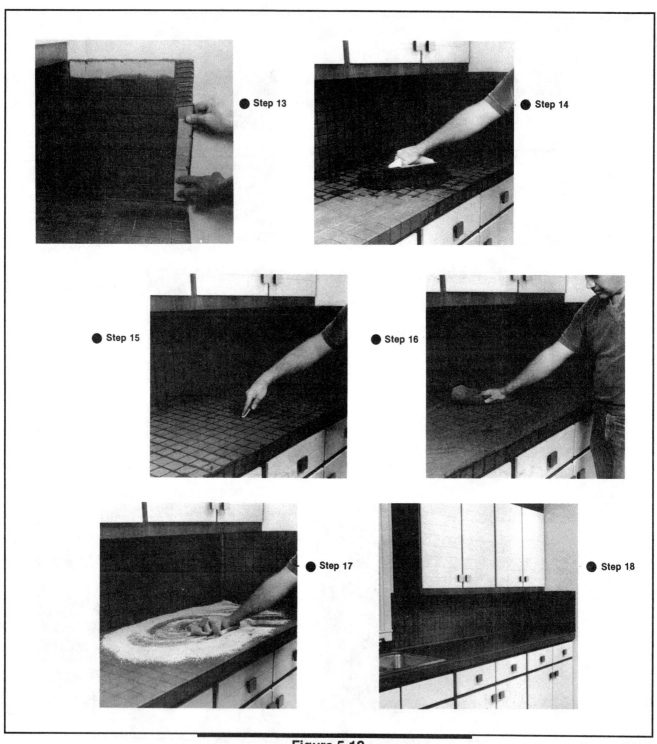

Figure 5-12
Installing tile with dry-set mortar on Wonder-Board over plywood (continued)
Courtesy: American Olean Tile

Step 10: Using a wooden beating block and hammer, compact the tile into the mortar. Use a wet sponge to dampen the paper on the trim strips. Peel the paper off and sponge the excess adhesive from the tile surfaces. Adjust the tiles for straight, uniform joint lines. Sponge off any excess mortar.

Step 11: Apply dry-set to the Wonder-Board backsplash surface using the same 1/4-inch square-notched trowel. Then tile the backsplash. Begin with trim strips of C-833 cove tile, pressing each tile firmly into the mortar ribs.

Step 12: Set the tile sheets on the backsplash, pressing each sheet into place. Adjust the alignment to match the joint lines of the counter tile. Wet the paper on the vertical corner strips and peel it off. Sponge off the excess adhesive.

Step 13: Set the tile on the adjacent side wall the same way as described in Step 12. Be sure the bullnose is straight. Then remove the paper cover from the trim strips and sponge off the adhesive.

Step 14: After the tiles are set and tapped snug, clean off the surface. You can begin grouting immediately, using American Olean sanded grout. Firmly compact it into the joints with a floor trowel, removing the excess grout by moving the trowel diagonally across the joints.

Step 15: To be sure the joints are well compacted, run a wooden spatula or stirrer along each joint line, pressing grout firmly into the joint. This is called *striking*, and it makes the joints stronger, more stain resistant, and easier to clean.

Step 16: Sprinkle dry grout powder over all the tile surfaces. Then use a burlap pad to rub the dry grout powder over the freshly grouted tile, including the backsplash. Rubbing increases the density of the joints, dries the grout out uniformly, and helps loosen surface grout film to make the final cleaning easier.

Step 17: Now sprinkle dry sawdust over the damp grout film on the tile surface. Then rub it vigorously with the burlap pad. Use a brush to remove the sawdust. The tile surface should be completely clean. Remove any remaining smudges or spots of grout haze with a damp sponge.

Step 18: Finish up by installing the drop-in sink. Use silicone rubber caulk under the sink rim. Remove any excess caulk with a cheese cloth pad saturated with denatured alcohol. The job is now completed. You can use dry-set mortar on Wonder-Board with other types of tile surfaces as well.

Figure 5-13 shows cross-sections of each of the tile installations we discussed here. In Figure 5-14 you can see a beautifully finished tile job which used a colorful floral tile. There's a wide range of colors and designs available to suit any theme or color scheme.

Solid-Material Countertops

Du Pont sells a solid, nonporous material under the registered trade name of *Corian*. It could be described as a man-made stone. The color and pattern run through the solid thickness. It comes in cameo white, almond, dawn beige, and satin gray. Because Corian is nonporous, most stains will wipe off with a damp cloth. More stubborn stains (including cigarette burns) can be rubbed off with a common abrasive household cleanser. This makes it an ideal surface material for countertops.

Though the material can withstand higher temperatures and more surface abuse than ordinary countertop materials, it can be damaged if hot cookware is set directly on the surface. Using it as a cutting board will also damage the surface.

Corian Sheets

Corian can be cut, shaped, drilled, routed, and sanded much like hardwood. You can order it from distributors in both sheets and pre-cast form. The sheets are available in three standard thicknesses, 1/4-inch, 1/2-inch, and 3/4-inch.

Adhesive on plywood

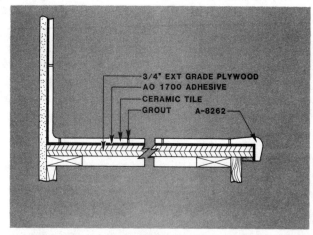

Adhesive on laminate

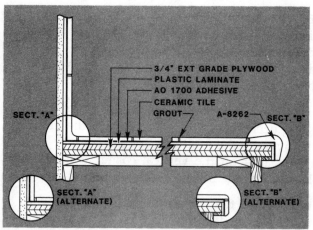

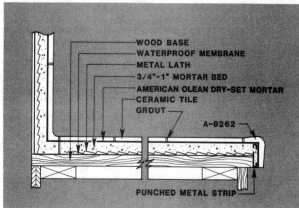

Conventional mortar on wood base

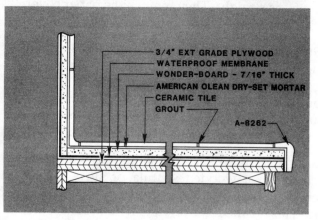

Dry-set mortar on Wonder-Board over plywood

Figure 5-13
Cross sections of tile installation methods
Courtesy: American Olean Tile

Figure 5-14
Ceramic tile countertop
Courtesy: Ceramic Tile Institute

The 1/4-inch sheet is 30 inches wide and comes in lengths of 57 inches, 60 inches, 72 inches, 80 inches, and 98 inches. This thickness is also available in a tub wall kit, with four panels plus a batten strip. The 1/4-inch sheet is too thin for use as a countertop.

The 1/2-inch and 3/4-inch sheets come in widths of 25 and 30 inches, and lengths of 98 inches, 121 inches, and 145 inches.

Corian Integral Countertops and Sinks

You can order solid formed Corian countertops with sinks included. They're available in single or double bowl designs and measure 10 feet long, 25 inches wide, and 3/4 inch thick. All units come with a 4-7/8-inch backsplash and are designed to accept standard faucets and drain hardware.

The large bowl is centered in the 10-foot length in both the single and double bowl units, with the smaller bowl offset to the left in the double bowl unit. See Figure 5-15. You can drill faucet holes using a template and router, or a high speed electric drill with a spade bit, a twist drill, or a hole saw. Don't use auger bits. The dimensions of the double and single bowl units are given in Figure 5-16.

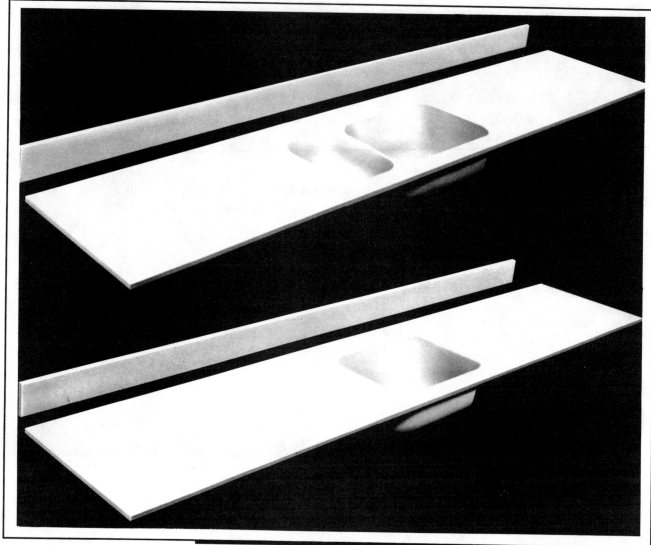

Figure 5-15
Corian integral countertops and sinks
Courtesy: DuPont Co., Inc.

The countertops must be trial-fitted before cutting. Always make sure you allow an 1/8-inch clearance between the countertop and walls for expansion. Never wedge the stone-like tops between two walls.

Tools Required for Working with Corian

You'll need some special tools when working with Corian:

- Safety glasses, safety shoes, a dust mask, and gloves

- A sawhorse and three 2-inch by 4-inch by 8-foot support rails

- A 3-foot and an 8-foot straightedge

- C-clamps

- A circular saw with a 40-tooth carbide blade

- A saber saw with metal-cutting blade (12-14 teeth per inch)

- A router with a sharp 3/8-inch diameter carbide bit, minimum 2 HP

- An electric drill and bits

- An orbital (finishing) sander, minimum 10,000 orbits per minute

- Sandpaper: 120-180 grit and 120-180 grit wet or dry

- 3M Scotch Brite pads (red, general purpose) or similar pads

- A belt sander with 100-120 grit belt

- Regular carpenter tools including square, level, hammer, nails, file, scribe or compass, tape measure, etc.

- Caulking gun

- Caulk remover tool

- Polyethylene, to be used as drop cloth and for dust control

- Masking tape

- Wooden bracing strips and shim material

- Household aluminum foil

- Neoprene panel adhesive, tan colored

- Du Pont silicone sealant, color matched

- Du Pont joint adhesive, color matched

- A block plane

- A 1-inch chisel

- A clean white cloth

- Denatured alcohol (also known as shellac thinner or alcohol stove fuel)

- Aluminum conductive tape (not duct tape)

- Spring clamps

- Hot-melt glue gun and glue sticks

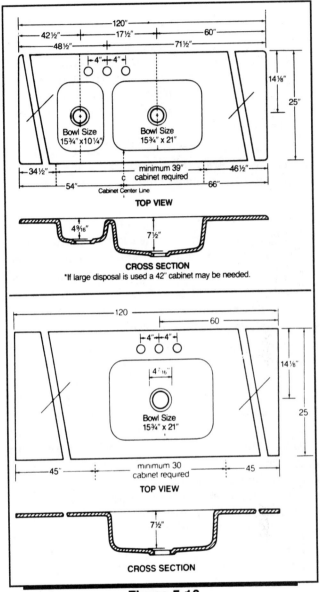

Figure 5-16
Dimensions for Corian integral countertops and sinks
Courtesy: DuPont Co., Inc.

- An abrasive scouring cleanser

- A green (household type) Scotch Brite or similar pad

I'd also take along a toothpaste key for the joint adhesive, a router template, decorative edge router bits, and ear muffs or plugs, for comfort.

Installing a Corian Countertop

When installing Corian, you need a good-sized work area. Set up two sawhorses with three 8-foot long 2 x 4's extended between them to use as support rails for the sheet material. You can do this work outside, weather permitting, to avoid congestion and dust in the kitchen.

If you sand the Corian inside a home, tape drop cloths over interior doors and air ducts to control dust. Also, cover the cabinets to protect them.

Step 1: If you're installing a new countertop on existing cabinets, remove the old countertop, sink, and appliances. Make sure all the cabinets are level. If not, use shims to make corrections. Be sure all the cabinets are secured together. Corian must be installed without underlayment, but it does require cross supports. Install a 1 by 4-inch wood support in the center of the countertop joint locations as shown in Figure 5-17, Step 1.

Step 2: Add extra support to all sink and appliance cutouts within 3 inches of all four edges of the cutout. If there's no cabinet framing along the backwalls, install cross supports to provide complete perimeter support. If you need to build up the edges to raise the countertop, use wooden support strips. Install these supports around the complete perimeter and at cross sections. Check the level on all supports.

Do *not* use a full underlayment or base for the countertop. Corian should be lightly adhered directly to the cabinets or wood supports. Full underlayment can cause the material to warp and crack.

Step 3: Put a layer of paper or duct tape on the cross support under the countertop joint. This keeps the joint adhesive from sticking to the support.

If you're using a *full-height* backsplash, you must install it at this time. It should be positioned *behind* the countertop. The procedure for installing a full-height backsplash is covered in the section on backsplash installation just following this one.

Step 4: Set the countertop sheet into position on the cabinets and examine the fit of all the edges. At the return walls, allow a 1/8-inch clearance for expansion of the sheet.

Step 5: Check the alignment of the surface at the joints. Make sure they're smooth and level. If shimming is needed to match one surface plane to another, have the shims ready. Aluminum tape folded to the necessary thickness makes an excellent shim for leveling joints.

Check to assure that the mating joint edges are parallel. If they're not parallel, remove excess material with a router guided by a straightedge.

Step 6: If the cutouts are fabricated (previously cut out), check their location for proper fit. Add support within 3 inches on each side of the cutout.

If the sink and appliance cutouts aren't fabricated, locate and mark the center line for each cutout on the sheet. Support the piece to be cut out. Put two 1/4 by 1-inch plywood support strips under the area to be cut away to keep it from falling through and damaging the cabinets. Use a router with a sharp, 3/8-inch diameter bit guided by a straightedge or a template clamped to the top to complete the cutout.

Sabre or circular saws are *not* recommended for cutouts. They leave rough edges which could cause the Corian to crack.

Step 7: Provide enough space around appliance and sink cutouts to allow for expansion; a minimum of 1/4 inch on all sides.

Step 8: After you make the cutout with a router, smooth the top and bottom edges with an orbital sander.

Step 9: Tape cooktop cutouts. Apply aluminum conductive tape around the cutout so that it folds over on the top surface. Be sure the tape extends beyond the outermost flange of the cooktop. Cover all the corners with tape. You can trim off the excess tape after the cooktop is installed.

Step 1

Support joint

Step 2

Perimeter support

Step 3

Apply release product on cross support

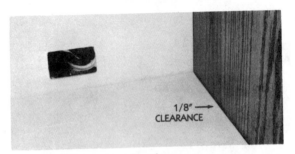

Step 4

Allow clearance for expansion

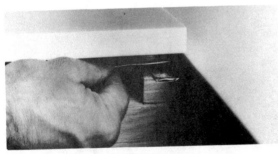

Step 5

Aluminum tape used for shims

Step 6

Support cutouts

Figure 5-17
Installing Corian countertop
Courtesy: DuPont Co., Inc.

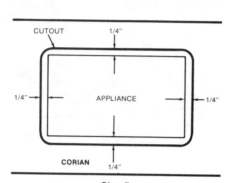

Step 7
Provide space for expansion

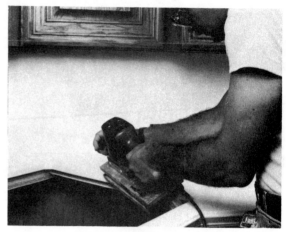

Step 8
Sand top and bottom edges of cutout

Step 9
Conductive tape completely installed

Step 10
Sand edges at joint

Step 11
Clean edges with alcohol

Step 12
Position countertops, leaving gap for joint adhesive

Figure 5-17
Installing Corian countertop (continued)
Courtesy: DuPont Co., Inc.

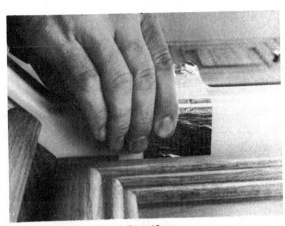

Step 13
Dam underside

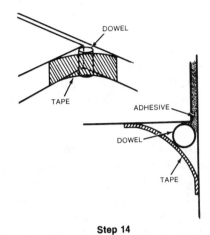

Step 14
Inside corner radius

Step 15
Fill joint with adhesive

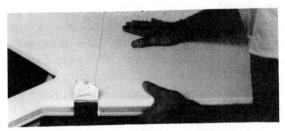

Step 16
Push sheets together to squeeze out excess adhesive

Step 17
Clamp joint together to set

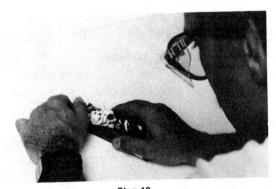

Step 18
Using block plane to remove excess adhesive

Figure 5-17
Installing Corian countertop (continued)
Courtesy: DuPont Co., Inc.

When installing Corian countertops, remember to *support*, *space*, *smooth* and *tape* cooktop cutouts.

Step 10: Prepare the countertop joints by sanding the edges to remove any tool marks or belt sander marks. Use an orbital sander to smooth the edges of each sheet at the joint location.

Step 11: Clean the edges of the sheets with denatured alcohol to remove dirt, dust, pencil marks, and fingerprints. Apply the alcohol with a clean white cloth. Make sure all joint surfaces are clean to assure good adhesion and clean looking joints. It's a good idea not to smoke while using denatured alcohol.

Step 12: Position and secure the Corian countertop to the cabinets. Place one sheet at a time, using one dab of silicone every 12 to 18 inches to secure the sheet to the cabinet or wooden support strips. Clamp the sheet to prevent movement. Position and adhere the second sheet, leaving a gap of 1/16 inch to 1/8 inch between the sheets.

Step 13: You must be ready to complete the joint within 15 to 30 minutes after securing the sheets. The silicone will begin to set up and the sheets will be hard to move together after that time.

Dam the underside of the joint. Place aluminum tape on the underneath surface and the front edge or overhang to be sure that the adhesive completely fills the joint and doesn't leak out.

Step 14: Where two sheets butt to form an angle, you must provide a corner with a radius. One way to do this is to wrap aluminum foil around a piece of 1/2-inch doweling or tubing and tape it to the corner of the joint. When you apply the joint adhesive, pull the dowel away slightly to assure complete filling. Then press the dowel lightly into the corner as shown in Figure 5-17.

Step 15: Prepare the adhesive. Cut open the clear plastic tube (component B). Squeeze any air pockets out of the tube. Then inject the entire contents of the foil tube (component A) into the clear tube. Flatten the foil tube to be sure it's empty.

Squeeze out about half of the air in the plastic tube, then snap the applicator cap onto the tube. Press hard to be sure that the cap locks down tight.

Hold the tube upright and mix the contents together by squeezing and kneading. Mix completely. Poor mixing can result in poor color, poor adhesion, and the formation of pits in the joints.

When completely mixed, trim off the applicator cap square just below the hard white tip. Squeeze out and discard a small amount of the adhesive. It's now ready to apply.

Spread adhesive in the joint. Fill the joint 1/3 to 1/2 full with joint adhesive, working from the rear to the front. Keep the tube vertical, as shown in the Figure 5-17, step 15.

Step 16: Push the sheets together to squeeze out the excess adhesive. Leave the excess adhesive on the sheets undisturbed until it's set. Add joint adhesive to any area that isn't filled to overflowing. Use a clean wooden toothpick to puncture any air bubbles that form in the adhesive.

Step 17: Here's a helpful hint: To clamp the joint together, apply a 3-inch stream of hot melt glue to two wooden strips. Attach the strips to the top of the countertop sheets, one on each side of the joint. Using C-clamps, draw the strips together. Hold the sheets firmly butted until the adhesive sets. Remove the wooden strips and hot melt glue with a sharp putty knife (use one with rounded corners).

Don't use pipe or bar clamps to squeeze the countertop sheets together. They may squeeze too much adhesive out of the joint.

Leave the joint undisturbed until it's set. Depending on the temperature of the countertop sheets, the adhesive should set in 45 to 60 minutes. Cooler temperatures will slow down the setting time. When it's set, your fingernail won't make an indentation in the adhesive.

Figure 5-18
Position the backsplash
Courtesy: DuPont Co., Inc.

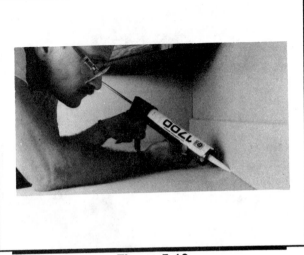

Figure 5-19
Caulk the seam
Courtesy: DuPont Co., Inc.

Step 18: Remove the excess adhesive when the joint is set. Use a block plane or belt sander to level the joints. A block plane with a sharp, low-angle blade and rounded corners is best because it will keep the dust to a minimum.

If you use a belt sander, use 120 grit sandpaper. Hold the sander flat but angled about 45 to 60 degrees from the joint. Be careful not to gouge the adjacent sheet.

At the back wall, you can use a sharp 1-inch chisel to remove the excess adhesive.

Smooth the joint with an orbital sander equipped with 120 to 180 grit sandpaper. To minimize dust, moisten the countertop and use wet or dry sandpaper.

Buff the entire surface using a Scotch Brite pad under the orbital sander to get a smooth surface. Wet the Scotch Brite pad to keep dust to a minimum.

Installing the Backsplash

There are three types of backsplashes: a back-splash up to 5 inches; a full-height backsplash; and a ceramic tile backsplash.

A backsplash up to 5 inches: Use the following steps to install a 5-inch backsplash.

1) Identify and mark the back side of the splash.

2) Check the backsplash for proper fit. Leave 1/8 inch minimum clearance at the return walls. See Figure 5-18.

3) Route the top edges for design appearance if required.

4) Clean all the edges with alcohol.

5) Place a continuous bead of silicone on the bottom center of the edge of the splash.

6) Adhere the splash to the top of the countertop, *not* to the wall.

7) Caulk the seam between the countertop and the splash with silicone. See Figure 5-19. Caulk the seam using a forward motion. Pushing the caulking gun forward along the seam line will make a smoother joint.

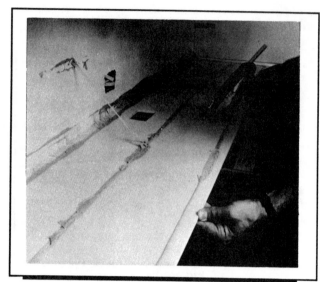

Figure 5-20
Apply adhesive to full height backsplash
Courtesy: DuPont Co., Inc.

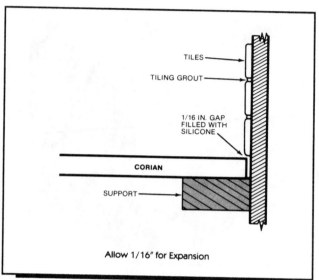

TILES

TILING GROUT

1/16 IN. GAP FILLED WITH SILICONE

CORIAN

SUPPORT

Allow 1/16" for Expansion

Figure 5-21
Ceramic tile backsplash
Courtesy: DuPont Co., Inc.

8) Remove any excess caulking with a caulk remover tool; then smooth the joint with a wet finger. Clean the seam with alcohol.

A full-height backsplash: A full-height backsplash is installed before the countertop, as mentioned earlier in the chapter. If you're installing a long backsplash, you may want to seam the backsplash sheets together before you begin the installation. It makes a nicer overall appearance. Use a color-matched joint adhesive to join the pieces.

The steps for installing a full-height backsplash are:

1) Trial fit the backsplash *behind* the countertop. Check the fit along all the cabinet edges and adjoining walls. Allow a minimum of 1/8 inch for expansion. If the wall is uneven, shim as necessary so you'll have an even caulk line between the splash and the countertop.

2) Mark the location of all the electrical outlets on the backsplash. Make cutouts for them using a router.

3) Use a 3/8-inch diameter drill or router bit to radius all inside corners. Rounded corners will keep the sheet from splitting.

4) Sand all cut edges.

5) If you need to use screws to install cabinets over the backsplash, drill pilot holes in the sheet. The pilot holes should be 1/8 inch larger than the shank of the screw. When you install the cabinets, fasten the screws snugly, but not tight.

6) Apply neoprene panel adhesive to the splash in a continuous 1/4 inch stream around the outer edge and down the middle. See Figure 5-20. Add dabs of hot melt glue to hold the splash on the wall while the adhesive sets. You'll have to install the splash quickly because the hot melt glue sets fast.

7) Install the backsplash and hold it in place a few seconds until the hot melt glue sets.

8) After the countertop has been installed, caulk the seam between the countertop and backsplash with silicone.

9) Remove any excess caulking with a caulk remover tool; then smooth the silicone along the joint with a wet finger. Clean the seam with alcohol.

A ceramic tile backsplash: You can install a ceramic tile backsplash using the same instructions for tile installation given earlier in this chapter. There are only a few additional items to include:

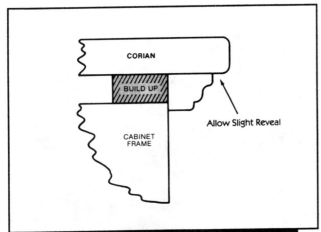

Figure 5-22
Adding a decorative edge
Courtesy: DuPont Co., Inc.

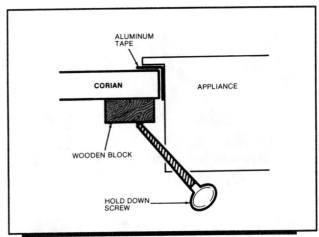

Figure 5-23
Installing appliances with hold-down screws
Courtesy: DuPont Co., Inc.

1) Leave a 1/16 inch gap for expansion between the top of the countertop and the bottom row of tiles. See Figure 5-21.

2) Fill the gap with silicone.

3) Remove any excess caulking with a caulk remover tool, then smooth the silicone seam with a wet finger. Clean the seam with alcohol.

Applying a Decorative Edge to Corian

Your client may request a decorative edging for the countertop. For many jobs, the decorative edge will be installed in the fabricator's shop. If not, then use the following procedure:

1) Cut the edge strips to required length.

2) Sand the edges with an orbital sander.

3) Check the fit.

4) Clean all the surfaces to be glued. Use denatured alcohol to remove dirt, pencil marks, dust, and fingerprints. Cleaning with alcohol will also prevent dirty seam lines and improve adhesion.

5) Apply a stream of silicone on the top of the edge trim so the excess silicone will squeeze out of the seam between the countertop and the strip.

6) Apply dabs of hot melt glue to the strip every 8 to 12 inches to tack the edge in place until the silicone sets.

7) Position the strip directly under the countertop, leaving a slight reveal as shown in Figure 5-22.

8) Secure the strips promptly, using spring clamps.

9) Remove the spring clamps after the hot melt glue sets.

10) Remove any excess silicone using a caulk remover tool. Smooth the seam with a wet finger and clean with alcohol.

Completing the Job

When you complete the installation of the countertop and backsplash, check all the cut edges. Sand any sharp edges with an orbital sander, using 180 grit paper.

Make sure the cooktop cutout is lined with aluminum conductive tape. Install the cooktop. Avoid scratching or chipping the edges of the cutout with the metal frame of the unit. Trim away the excess aluminum tape around the cooktop flange.

Install other drop-in appliances. Make sure each one is properly centered in the cutout. Fin-

Figure 5-24
Corian countertop and work island
Courtesy: DuPont Co., Inc.

ger-tighten the fasteners to keep the appliances in place.

If appliances or sinks are designed to have installation screws going into the countertop, don't use the screws. They can crack Corian. Instead, secure the cooktop with silicone sealant. If you use hold-down screws, insert a wooden block between the end of the screws and the bottom of the countertop as shown in Figure 5-23. Secure the

dishwasher flange to the adjacent cabinets or the wood build-up strip.

Use either silicone sealant or plumber's putty for a watertight seal around all sinks.

Wipe off any marks or smudges on the new countertop with alcohol. The completed job should look like Figure 5-24.

Figure 5-25
A beautifully designed kitchen using Corian countertops
Courtesy: DuPont Co., Inc.

The Care of Corian

Before you leave the home after installing a Corian countertop, show the homeowners how resistant it is to stains. Mark it with a ball point pen, a cigarette burn, and a felt tip pen. Then remove the marks with an abrasive cleanser and a slightly damp cloth. Buff the area with a green Scotch Brite pad using a light circular motion. Leave the pad with the client.

Figure 5-25 shows another kitchen with Corian countertops and work island. A job like this requires a great deal of skill. You may prefer to have a professional do your countertop installations for you. But if you do the work yourself, follow the steps in this chapter carefully. It should give you professional results.

Attractively designed and built cabinets and countertops can sell a kitchen project. The countertop shows off the cabinets. The work you do with cabinets and countertops will help build your reputation as a kitchen and bathroom specialist.

Manhour Estimates

Keep and use *your own* manhour records for installing countertops. Your experience is the best guide when estimating labor for the projects you

Work element	Unit	Manhours per unit
Setting flat tops	10 SF	1.0
Setting molded (factory or shop prefabricated) tops with backsplash	10 SF	2.4
Setting ceramic tile (6" x 6")		
Adhesive on plywood	10 SF	3.5
Adhesive on laminate	10 SF	3.0
Conventional mortar on wood base	10 SF	4.5
Dry-set mortar on Wonder-Board over plywood	10 SF	5.0
Corian sheets	10 SF	3.5

Figure 5-26
Manhour estimates for installing countertops

do. Figure 5-26 shows typical manhour estimates per unit of countertop installation by skilled craftsmen.

The estimated time includes job preparation, installing base top, and clean-up. You must figure in additional time for removing old countertops, leveling and shimming old cabinets, and removing and installing sinks and appliances. Allow 4 hours for installing double stainless steel sinks, and 2 hours for a cooktop or drop-in range.

Kitchen Sinks, Appliances, and Hoods

As a kitchen and bathroom remodeling specialist, you'll be installing a wide variety of kitchen appliances. Most manufacturers include installation instructions with every appliance they sell. Review the instructions before starting work — not after something has gone wrong.

But sometimes you'll be asked to install an appliance or sink that doesn't have instructions. That's why I'm going to provide some general guidelines to follow.

Obviously I can't give installation procedures for every sink, dishwasher, cooktop, oven, and range hood on the market. Instead, I'll concentrate on the basic steps you'll follow on the more common kitchen appliances.

I'll begin with the most important tip: *Never* make cutouts before you have the exact dimensions of the appliance. You can't make the hole smaller once you've cut it.

The Kitchen Sink

Probably the item that you'll be replacing most often will be the kitchen sink. Let's go through the steps involved in installing a new self-rimming sink. We'll choose the Kohler Epicurean K-5904 for our example. Figure 6-1 shows you all the key dimensions for the sink.

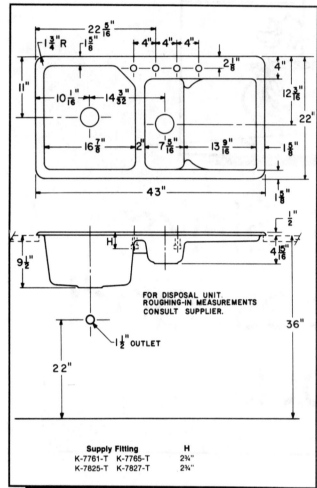

Figure 6-1
Sink dimensions for an "Epicurean" enameled
self-rimming sink
Courtesy: Kohler Company

Installation

Let's assume you'll install the sink on a laminate countertop, since we haven't covered cutouts in laminate before. Refer back to Chapter 5 for planning cutouts in ceramic tile or Corian countertops.

Step 1: Locate and mark the center lines of the sink on the countertop, as shown in Figure 6-2.

Step 2: Now establish the sink outline. The sink dimensions are 43 inches by 22 inches. Measure and mark points 11 inches above and below your horizontal center line. Now measure and mark points

21-1/2 inches to each side of your vertical center line. Draw a rectangle by connecting these points, making sure that your lines are parallel to the center lines. Using the measurements in Figure 6-2, swing a radius at each of the four corners. You could also place the sink upside down on the countertop, draw the outline around it. This is your sink outline, but *not* your cutting line.

Step 3: To establish the *cutting outline,* draw a second line 5/8 inch inside the sink outline. Cut on this line.

Step 4: Assemble the fittings on the sink.

Step 5: Apply two ribbons of polyseam adhesive around the cutout edge within the sink outline you've drawn. Spread it lightly with a blade or putty knife.

Step 6: Place the sink into the counter cutout, using the outline as a positioning guide.

Step 7: Press the sink down firmly into the adhesive.

Step 8: Remove surplus adhesive with a damp cloth or sponge. If there are any gaps in the adhesive, fill them immediately.

Step 9: Using a damp cloth, clean the sink and countertop.

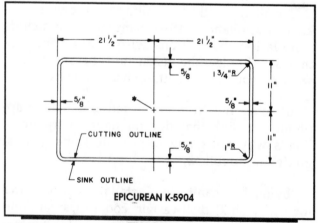

Figure 6-2
Sink cutout measurements
Courtesy: Kohler Company

Figure 6-3
New sink in Formica countertop
Courtesy: Kohler Company

Step 10: If you have to remove the sink for repositioning, heat a thin knife and insert it into the sealant between the sink and countertop. Cut through the sealant, keeping the sink raised to prevent resealing. Heat the knife as often as necessary. Replace the sink in the correct position. Press down firmly into the adhesive once again. Repeat Steps 8 and 9.

Figure 6-3 shows how your sink installation should look when the job is completed.

Built-In Cooktops

Assume your client has selected a 36-inch KitchenAid electric glass surface built-in cooktop, Model KECT 365. You're going to install it in the new ceramic tile countertop which is already completed.

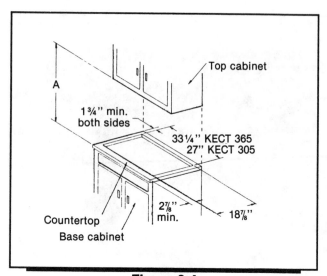

Figure 6-4
Cutout dimensions for countertop installation
Courtesy: KitchenAid, Inc.

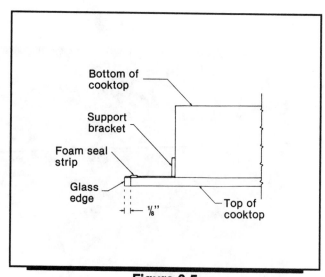

Figure 6-5
Place foam seal strip along underneath edge
Courtesy: KitchenAid, Inc.

Installation

The illustrations that came with the cooktop instructions are shown in Figures 6-4, 6-5, and 6-6. All cooktops are designed for installation in a base cabinet with a countertop depth of 24 inches. The cutout dimensions for this cooktop are given in Figure 6-4.

Following the instructions, you have left a cutout 33-1/4 inches wide by 18-7/8 inches deep in your countertop. You have a remaining front edge of 2-7/8 inches, a back edge of 2-1/4 inches, and more than the necessary 1-3/4 inches required on each side of the cutout.

The vertical clearance required for a cooktop depends on what you plan to install above it. Measurement "A" in Figure 6-4 is the 30-inch minimum clearance required between the top of the cooking surface and the bottom of an unprotected wood or metal wall cabinet.

If the bottom of the wall cabinet is protected, then "A" can be 24 inches. The protection required is 1/4-inch flame retardant millboard (that's the minimum thickness), covered with not less than No. 28 MSG sheet steel, 0.024-inch aluminum, 0.015-inch stainless steel, or 0.020-inch copper.

You can reduce the risk of burns or fire caused by reaching over the heated surface elements of the cooktop by installing a range hood. The hood should project horizontally at least 5 inches out beyond the bottom of the overhead cabinet. You can eliminate these fire risks altogether by not placing storage above the cooktop.

Follow these instructions for installing the new glass cooktop:

Step 1: Remove the mounting hardware and foam seal strip from the packaging.

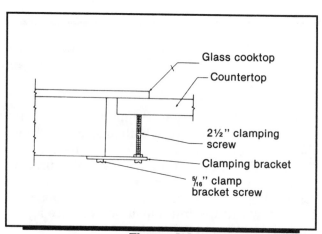

Figure 6-6
Clamp into place
Courtesy: KitchenAid, Inc.

Step 2: Place the cooktop in the countertop cutout. Center and align the cooktop, making sure to maintain the required clearances. Draw an outline of the back edge of the cooktop on the countertop using a pencil or an erasable marker. Remove the cooktop from the opening and place it *upside down* on the inner packaging to avoid damage to the unit.

Step 3: While the cooktop is upside down, remove the backing paper from the foam seal strip and place it along the underneath edge of the cooktop. It should be attached in one continuous piece all around the underside of the cooktop, 1/8 inch from the inside edge. The strip will overlap four support brackets. See Figure 6-5. Cut off any excess material.

Step 4: Using the 5/16-inch screws furnished, loosely screw the plain end of the clamping brackets into the holes provided on the underside of the cooktop. There should be one bracket for each side of the cooktop. Rotate the brackets inward. Return the cooktop to the countertop cutout using the outline as a guide for lowering the unit into place. If the cooktop isn't properly aligned, lift the unit out and lower it again. This should be done carefully to prevent any damage to the form seal strip.

Rotate the clamping brackets out and tighten the 5/16-inch screws. Thread the 2-1/2-inch clamping screws through the inset in the brackets. Tighten the clamping screws with a screwdriver until the screws are tight against the bottom of the countertop. See Figure 6-6.

Step 5: Using the entire length of conduit, connect the power supply leads from the unit to the junction box. Do *not* cut the conduit. NOTE: Improper connection of the wiring may damage the cooktop. If you're joining the wiring to aluminum house wiring, use only the connections designed for joining copper to aluminum.

Figure 6-7 shows the completed installation of the cooktop.

Range Hoods

Let's say your client wants a NuTone decorative range hood in the kitchen addition you're doing. Range hoods can be installed with ducting to the exterior, or non-ducted. This range hood fits under the wall cabinet over the cooktop and requires 7-inch diameter round ducting.

Installation

Range hoods work best when they're mounted so the distance from the lower lip of the hood to the cooking surface isn't more than 30 inches. When venting to the outside, make the duct run as short as possible. Try to avoid using elbows in the duct. In most two-story houses, however, you'll have to use an elbow to duct outside through the exterior wall.

A word of caution: To reduce the risk of fire, always duct to the building exterior, not into a wall cavity, ceiling, attic, crawl space, or garage. Use duct tape at all joints, and never use a duct smaller than the discharge on the hood.

Remember, it's not the size of the hood or range that determines the amount of ventilation you need, it's the size of the kitchen. An average 160-square-foot kitchen with an 8-foot ceiling requires a 320 c.f.m. fan. (Fan capacity is measured in cubic feet per minute.)

The wiring for the range hood must comply with your local codes. With both the fan and the light operating, a hood requires less than 125 watts of power. In most cases the wiring can be connected to one of the 110-120-volt lighting circuits (20-amp) in the breaker or fuse panel. Use at least No. 14 gauge, 2 conductor with ground, copper wire for the connection.

Use the following steps for your range hood installation.

1) Lay the hood upside down on your workbench or floor.

Figure 6-7
Electric glass surface cooktop
Courtesy: KitchenAid, Inc.

2) Unscrew and remove the wiring compartment cover.

3) Slide the lamp cover to the front of the hood and remove it.

4) Remove the filters by pulling the tab on the front of the hood.

5) Punch out the wiring compartment knockout (either top or rear) and install an approved wire connector.

6) Using the illustration for the Model 6300 hood (Figure 6-8), lay out the hood mounting holes, the hole for wiring, and the air duct hole in the wall cabinet.

7) Cut the wiring and cabinet duct hole.

8) With the hood temporarily in place, locate the centerpoint of the duct cutout in the ceiling with a plumb bob. Scribe a 7-1/2-inch diameter hole and cut it out. Remove the hood before you make the cutouts, to keep any debris out. Follow the same procedure for locating the centerpoint of the cutout in the roof. The roof cutout may require a hole larger than 7-1/2 inches because of the roof pitch. Install the duct down through the roof cutout.

Install a collar on the duct at the ceiling to keep air from moving from the attic to the kitchen. Use a roof vent to cap the duct.

9) Put in four mounting screws, leaving about 1/4 inch of thread exposed. No. 8 or No. 10 round head screws will work the best.

10) Install the hood. Feed the wiring through the holes into the wiring compartment. Be sure the duct is positioned over the collar on the hood. Align the hood keyhole slots with the partially installed screws and push the hood against the rear wall. Tighten the four screws.

11) Using a long screwdriver, reach between the fan blades and see that the damper operates freely.

12) Connect the hood wires to the electric supply leads, connecting white to white and black to black. Connect the supply ground to the green screw in the wiring compartment. Make sure your wiring and connections comply with the local code.

13) Replace the wiring compartment cover.

14) Install a 40 to 75 watt bulb in the unit. Replace the filter and lamp covers.

15) Turn on the electrical power and test the hood's operation.

Canopy hoods, island hoods, and flip-out eye-level hoods are installed in much the same way. Except for the ductwork and duct cutouts, you'll also install non-duct hoods this way. A non-duct, or ductless hood, isn't vented to the outside. The fan pushes the air through a charcoal filter and back into the room. Most non-duct hoods also have an aluminum grease filter.

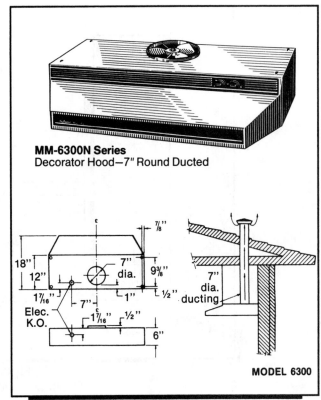

MM-6300N Series
Decorator Hood—7" Round Ducted

MODEL 6300

Figure 6-8
Decorator range hood and mounting diagram
Courtesy: NuTone Inc.

Built-In Ovens

For this example, we'll assume you're installing a KitchenAid electric built-in double oven, model KEBS 277S. One of the most important considerations in the installation of a built-in oven is the selection of an appropriate cabinet.

Look at Figure 6-9. These are the dimensions needed for a built-in double oven. Consider both the cabinet and oven widths when you're selecting the right cabinet for the oven — or the right oven for the cabinet if it's an existing cabinet. The oven selected by your client is 24-1/2 inches wide. This is your *B min* dimension shown in the diagram. It'll fit nicely into a cabinet that's 27 inches wide, which is the *A min* dimension shown in Figure 6-9. Study the oven and other dimensions given.

A solid bottom or runners spaced on 19-1/2 inch centers are required in the bottom of the cabinet opening to support the oven. The front of the cabinet must be at right angles to the supports as well as level. If the oven isn't installed level, foods won't cook properly.

Preparations for Installation

You'll need to provide an electric junction box for the oven. It should be located in the position shown in Figure 6-9. Make sure the wiring meets your local code requirements. The power supply

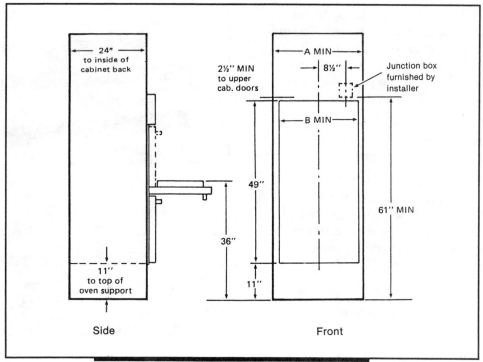

Figure 6-9
Dimensions for built-in oven
Courtesy: KitchenAid, Inc.

to the junction box must be 120/240-volt or 120-208-volt, 60 hertz, AC, single phase, 3-wire. Remember that an oven must have a separate circuit. Never install other electrical equipment or wall receptacles on the oven circuit.

It's a good idea to leave the oven on the carton base until you're ready to install it. Keep the protective pads over the doors. Protect the front and frame of the unit as long as possible.

Installation

Remove all the cords, tape, and wire used to hold the various parts in position during shipment. Carefully examine the unit for damage. (It may have been damaged prior to delivery at the job.) Remove the racks from the inside of the oven and put them aside while you're installing the oven in the cabinet. Take the broiler pan and grill from the packing on top of the oven. Keep them

with the owner's manual and in a safe place until you can give them to the homeowner.

Step 1: Before placing the oven in the cabinet, make your electrical connections. Your first priority is to ground the oven. *Don't work on the oven wiring until it has been properly grounded.* The oven frame is grounded through the bare grounding wire. Connect it to the ground. Connect the white neutral to the service neutral wire at the junction box. Connect conduit from the oven to the junction box, and properly connect it to the power supply leads. Connect the bare wire to the ground, black to L2, red to L1, and white to neutral or according to code.

Step 2: Remove the oven doors to reduce the weight of the unit and provide a better hand-hold while lifting the appliance into the cabinet. Figure 6-10 shows how to disengage the door.

• Open the door completely.

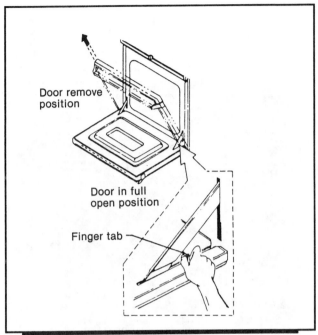

Figure 6-10
Door removal
Courtesy: KitchenAid, Inc.

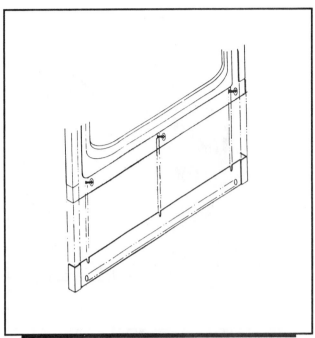

Figure 6-11
The bottom trim strip attachment
Courtesy: KitchenAid, Inc.

- Press down on the finger tab on one side of the oven door hinge area. Push the tab toward the oven. Lift the tab away from door liner and slide it toward the top of the oven door.

- Repeat the step above for the other side of the door.

- Put the oven door in a position approximately 5 inches from fully closed.

- Slide the door off the hinge arm assemblies.

- Repeat this process for the other door.

Step 3: Be sure that the phenolic spacers at each side of the oven are in position to provide proper air flow between the cabinet and the oven. Lift the oven into the cabinet opening.

Step 4: When the oven is properly positioned in the cabinet, install the exterior trim according to the instructions supplied with the trim.

If you're using a bottom trim strip instead, place it on the lower front edge of the frame. Loosen the three screws at the bottom of the front frame.

Slide the trim strip under the screw heads until the strip meets the lower corners of the frame (Figure 6-11). Tighten the screws to hold the trim strip to the front of the frame.

Step 5: Secure the oven to the cabinet with No. 8 screws provided. Don't overtighten the screws. Make sure the edge of the front frame is parallel to the cabinet or to the front edge of the exterior trim.

Step 6: Place the oven racks in the oven.

Step 7: Replace the oven doors.

- Slide the door onto the hinge arms until it's firmly seated.

- Lower the door to the fully opened position.

- Push the finger tabs to the back. Press down on the tabs and slide them forward to lock the door in place.

- Close and reopen the door slowly to make sure it's in place.

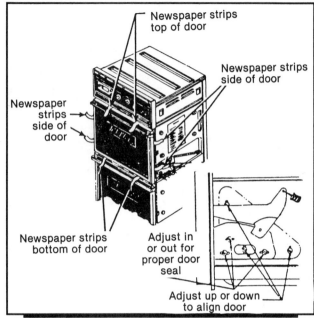

Figure 6-12
Door adjustment procedure
Courtesy: KitchenAid, Inc.

- Repeat these steps for the other door.

Step 8: To adjust the oven doors, look at Figure 6-12. Place two 2-inch by 18-inch strips of newspaper at all four edges of the door, as shown in the illustration. Allow one end of each strip to extend into the oven cavity. With the door closed, tug gently on each strip of newspaper. If the door is properly adjusted, you'll feel firm resistance as you pull each strip. If it's out of adjustment, slide the unit out far enough to expose the hinges on each side. Loosen the screws and move the bottom of the door until the fit is right. Then tighten the screws in both hinges and slide the oven back into place.

Figure 6-13 shows how your completed built-in double oven installation should look.

If you're installing a gas oven, follow the manufacturer's instructions. Figures 4-21 through 4-24 in Chapter 4 show the cabinet cutout dimensions and gas pipe locations.

Figure 6-13
Built-in double oven
Courtesy: KitchenAid, Inc.

Dishwashers

For this example, let's say your clients have chosen KitchenAid's KD-21 Series dishwasher for their kitchen. Of course, you'll install the dishwasher near the sink.

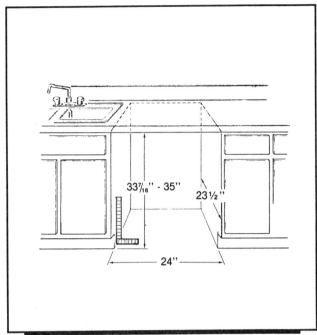

Figure 6-14
Cabinet opening dimensions
Courtesy: KitchenAid, Inc.

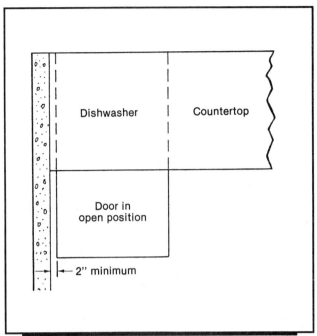

Figure 6-15
Corner installation distance
Courtesy: KitchenAid, Inc.

Built-in dishwashers must be fully enclosed with cabinet on the top, both sides, and the back. If you're installing the dishwasher at the end of a cabinet, the exposed side must be paneled in. The Kitchenaid KD-21 has a right or left side panel kit available to enclose the exposed side.

A standard size dishwasher is 24 inches wide and 23-1/2 inches deep. The heights may vary from 33-11/16 to 35 inches. See Figure 6-14. (If 33-11/16 inches is too high, you can reduce it to 33-7/16 inches by removing the leveling feet.) If you're installing the dishwasher in a corner, you must have a minimum clearance of 2 inches on each side to allow the door to open. See Figure 6-15.

Preparations for Installation

You've left an undercounter cabinet opening in your cabinet layout matching the dimensions of the KD-21 Model dishwasher. Now you need access holes in the cabinets, floor, or rear wall for the hot water supply line, drain line, and electrical supply line. These must be located within the

shaded area shown in Figure 6-16 to avoid interference with the dishwasher's frame or components.

Figure 6-16
Locate pipes and wires within shaded area
Courtesy: KitchenAid, Inc.

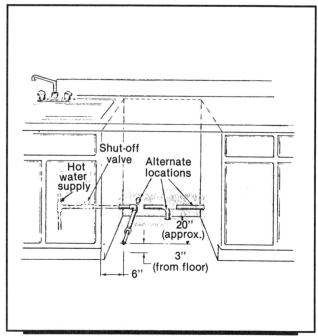

Figure 6-17
Water supply pipe location
Courtesy: KitchenAid, Inc.

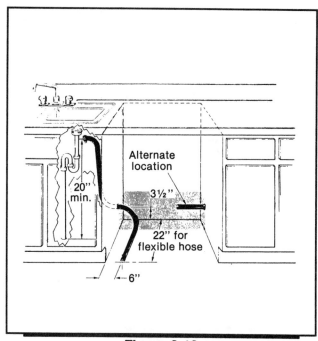

Figure 6-18
Drain pipe location
Courtesy: KitchenAid, Inc.

Hot water supply line: Dishwashers need only hot water connections — 140 degrees Fahrenheit and from 20 to 120 psi. Use 1/2-inch OD copper tubing, or 3/8-inch galvanized or iron pipe for the water supply. The dishwasher fill valve has a 3/8-inch NPT female connection.

After you determine where the water supply line will enter the dishwasher opening, drill a 1-inch access hole. Run the line to the appropriate fill valve location as shown in Figure 6-17.

To make servicing more convenient, install a shut-off valve in the supply line. Make sure it's easily accessible, usually under the sink. Install a union in the supply line near the dishwasher fill valve. (To prevent head damage to the fill valve, make all your solder connections *before* the water line is connected to the dishwasher).

Drain line: The drain line should be a 9/16-inch ID (minimum) flexible hose or 5/8-inch OD copper tubing. The flexible hose you use must be resistant to both heat and detergent. Most plumbing, hardware, and automotive supply stores sell hose like this. Do *not* use any fittings anywhere in

the drain line that are less than 1/2-inch ID. The access hole for the drain line should be 1 inch.

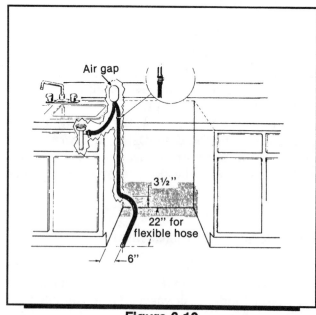

Figure 6-19
Drain connection to an air gap
Courtesy: KitchenAid, Inc.

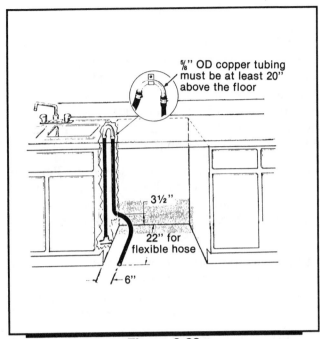

Figure 6-20
High loop installation
Courtesy: KitchenAid, Inc.

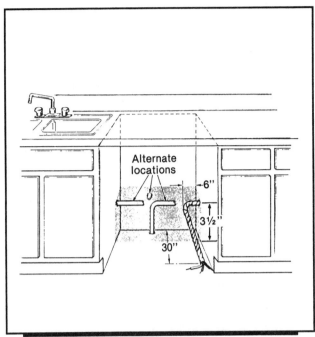

Figure 6-21
Electrical supply cable location
Courtesy: KitchenAid, Inc.

When using copper drain line, clamp a 12-inch length of 9/16-inch ID flexible hose (heat and detergent resistant) to the end of 12 inches of copper tubing. This makes the connection of the drain line to the dishwasher check valve easier.

If you're connecting the drain line to a waste disposal, be sure to remove the knockout or plug from the fitting on the disposal before you connect it to the drain line. Figure 6-18 shows how the placement of the drain line to the sink plumbing connections should look. If your local codes require an air gap, the drain to air gap connections are shown in Figure 6-19.

The drain line connection should be at least 20 inches above the floor to insure proper draining of the dishwasher. If it isn't, you'll have to make a 20-inch high loop in the tubing to bring it up to that height. See Figure 6-20.

To form a high loop in the tube, cut the flexible drain hose and clamp the two cut ends to a semi-circle (3-inch minimum radius) of 5/8-inch OD copper tubing. Support the copper tubing a min-

imum of 20 inches above the floor, making sure that no kinks develop in the hose or copper tubing.

Electrical supply: For the electrical supply, use a properly grounded 115-volt, 15-amp branch circuit. Figure 6-21 shows several possible locations. Don't put any other appliance or outlets on the same circuit. As with everything else you do, all your electrical work must comply with local codes.

Installing the Dishwasher

Remove the kickboard and lower panel to get access to the dishwasher connections (Figure 6-22). Take off the kickboard by removing the two screws that secure it. Pull out the bottom panel to unhook the tabs from the frame. Pull the panel downward to slide the panel flanges from behind the support channel.

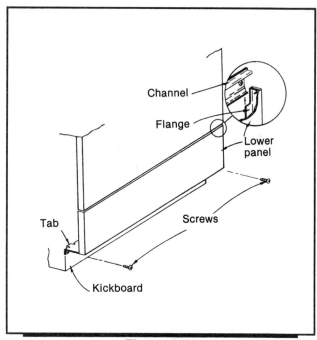

Figure 6-22
Lower panel and kickboard removal
Courtesy: KitchenAid, Inc.

Set the dishwasher in front of the cabinet opening and adjust the four leveling feet to the desired height. (If you've removed the feet to make the unit fit a lower opening, level it with shims.)

Slide the dishwasher into the cabinet opening. Be careful to avoid damaging the floor covering or interfering with the water, drain, and electrical lines. If the rear cross channel on the frame interferes with the plumbing or electrical connections, you can reposition it as shown in Figure 6-23. Angling the cross channel will provide more clearance space for the connecting lines. But don't remove the rear cross channel.

Unlatch and open the dishwasher door. Remove the foam shipping cushions and make sure there's equal cabinet clearance on both sides of the dishwasher. Don't let the cabinet interfere with or distort the dishwasher tank.

With the door still open, place a spirit level against the front tank flange (Figure 6-24) and level the dishwasher. Adjust the feet to level front-to-back and side-to-side as necessary.

If the dishwasher isn't properly leveled or if it's distorted by cabinet interference, the door may not seal properly and the unit may leak. If necessary, adjust the leveling feet to correct any distortion and to balance the alignment of the tank in the cabinet space.

To maintain the dishwasher's position and alignment, secure the adjustable brackets on the

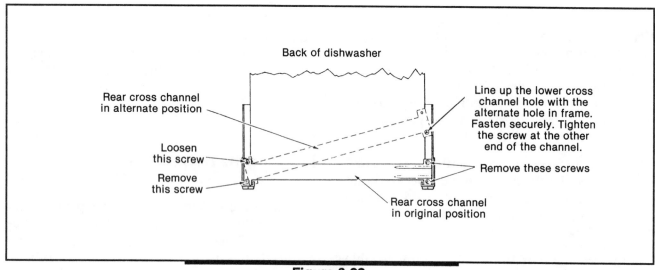

Figure 6-23
Rear cross channel positions
Courtesy: KitchenAid, Inc.

upper tank corners to the countertop. Use No. 10 flat head screws and fasten the brackets as shown in Figure 6-25. Make sure the screw heads don't interfere with the top of the door. If the brackets aren't compatible with the countertop, you can anchor the dishwasher to the floor. Use 1/4-inch lag bolts and fasten them through the holes on each side of the dishwasher frame as shown in Figure 6-26.

Connecting the water supply line: Before you connect the water supply line to the dishwasher, flush it to clear the line of any foreign material. Make sure there aren't any sharp bends or kinks that would reduce water pressure.

To make connecting the water line to the dishwasher easier, connect a 3/8-inch NPT street elbow to the fill valve and a 90-degree compression elbow (3/8-inch NPT one end) to the street elbow. (See Figure 6-27). Connect the supply line to the compression elbow. If you're using galvanized or iron pipe, substitute a second 3/8-inch street elbow for the compression elbow.

Use pipe joint compound or Teflon thread seal tape at all the pipe threads when making the connections. Turn on the water supply and check for leaks in the joints. After you make your checks, turn the water off again and continue with your other connections.

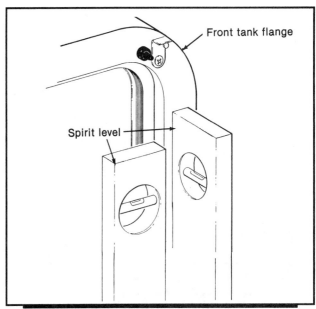

Figure 6-24
Leveling the dishwasher
Courtesy: KitchenAid, Inc.

Connecting the drain line: Using a hose clamp, connect the prepared drain line directly to the dishwasher check valve as shown in Figure 6-28. Make sure there are no sharp bends or kinks in the drain line to restrict the water flow.

Connecting the electrical supply: Begin by turning off the power at the circuit breaker or fuse box.

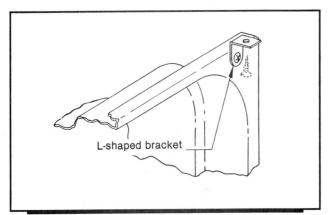

Figure 6-25
Bracket upper tank corners to countertop
Courtesy: KitchenAid, Inc.

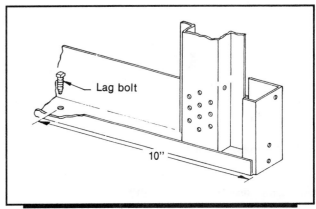

Figure 6-26
Anchor dishwasher frame to floor
Courtesy: KitchenAid, Inc.

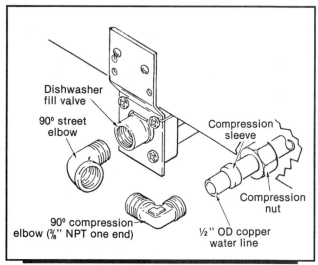

Figure 6-27
Connect the water supply line
Courtesy: KitchenAid, Inc.

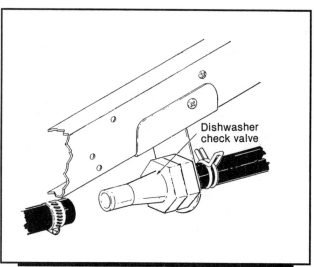

Figure 6-28
Connect the drain line
Courtesy: KitchenAid, Inc.

Connect the dishwasher to a grounded metal permanent wiring system, or run an equipment-grounding conductor with the circuit conductors and connect it to the equipment-grounding terminal or lead on the appliance. To ground the dishwasher:

1) Remove the junction box from the dishwasher.

2) Install a UL listed conduit connector (if you're using conduit), or a UL listed strain relief bushing (if you're using a non-metallic cable).

3) Connect the branch circuit white lead to the unit's white lead, and the branch circuit black lead to the unit's black lead using wire nuts. Secure the ground wire under the green ground screw on the dishwasher.

4) Reinstall the junction box.

Use UL listed aluminum to copper connectors if the house wiring is aluminum.

Make sure that the water supply, drain line, and branch circuit wiring don't touch any exposed terminals of dishwasher wiring.

The Final Checklist

Open the dishwasher and remove all the cardboard packing materials and anything else the manufacturer stored packed in the unit. Review the operating instructions supplied with the dishwasher. Turn on the water supply and check for leaks. Turn on the electrical supply. Test the dishwasher operation.

Turn off the electrical supply and test for leaks under the dishwasher. Make sure no kinks have developed in the fill or drain lines.

Replace the lower panel and kickboard. Look again at Figure 6-22. Line up the panel flanges to fit under the lip of the channel. Slide the panel up until it stops, and then push the tabs up to hook over the frame. Secure the lower panel and replace the kickboard using two screws. Check to make sure that the opening at the bottom of the kickboard isn't blocked by molding, carpeting or anything else that would keep air from circulating around the motor.

Figure 6-29 shows the KitchenAid Model KD-21 installed in a newly remodeled kitchen.

Figure 6-29
Properly installed KitchenAid dishwasher
Courtesy: KitchenAid, Inc.

The Ironing Center

Unfortunately, the invention of permanent press materials didn't make the ironing board obsolete. Most homes have at least one iron and ironing board. For those who regularly struggle to get the ironing board out of a closet and set it up, the ironing board is one of the most aggravating "conveniences" ever made. It's awkward and cumbersome whether it's in use or stored away.

If you have a client whose kitchen has adequate floor and wall space, a built-in ironing center might be a welcome addition. Let's look at the NuTone Ironing Center, Model Avc-40, which is similar to the illustration in Figure 6-30.

The unit fits easily into the wall space between 16-inch OC studs. It requires a recessed opening 14-1/4 inches wide by 60-1/4 inches high by 3-3/4 inches deep. The cabinet is 16 inches wide by 62 inches high by 5-1/2 inches deep, and projects 2-5/8 inches from the finished wall.

The cabinet door is hinged on the right, so be sure you locate it in an area that would allow space for the door to open completely. If you install the unit at the manufacturer's suggested height of 22 inches up from the floor, it provides adjustable heights of 32, 35, and 38 inches for the ironing board.

Installation

Before installing the unit, check to see if your client has a work height preference. The following chart gives ironing board height positions available for each installation height (measured from the floor to the bottom of the unit) from 16 to 28 inches.

Figure 6-30
Built-in ironing center
Courtesy: NuTone Inc.

For work height range:	Make rough opening this height from floor:
26" - 29" - 32"	16"
28" - 31" - 34"	18"
30" - 33" - 36"	20"
32" - 35" - 38"	22"
34" - 37" - 40"	24"
36" - 39" - 42"	26"
38" - 41" - 44"	28"

Figure 6-31
Top wiring compartment
Courtesy: NuTone Inc.

When you've decided on the location and proper height, you can begin the installation.

1) Start by removing the top wiring compartment cover. Press in on both sides, and use a small, thin-blade screwdriver to detach the cover edges from tabs in the cabinet. See Figure 6-31.

2) Mark the cutout location on the wall as shown in Figure 6-32.

3) Make the cutout in the wall.

4) Place the ironing cabinet in the cutout.

5) Make sure the cabinet is flush to the wall. Mark two bottom mounting holes with the board in the "up" position (Figure 6-33, section A). Release the board and let it drop down into the working position (section B). Mark two top mounting holes with the board in its "down" position.

6) Remove the unit from the wall cutout.

7) Drill pilot holes in the wall studs where you marked the top and bottom mounting screw locations.

8) Run electric cable to the top of the cutout location. You'll need a separate 120-volt, 15-amp circuit for the electrical connections.

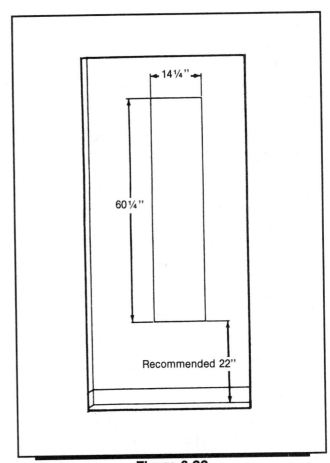

Figure 6-32
Mark the ironing center location on the wall
Courtesy: NuTone Inc.

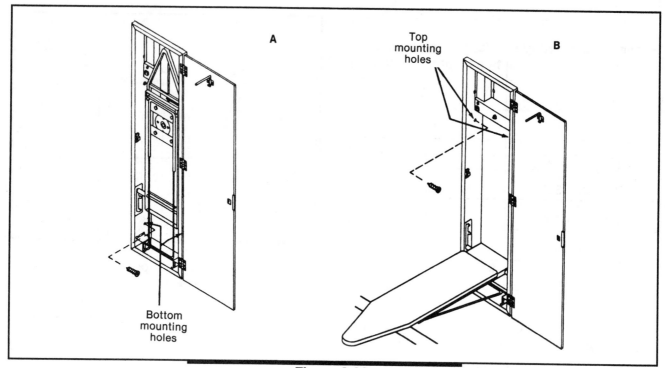

Figure 6-33
Mark the mounting holes
Courtesy: NuTone Inc.

Use code approved connectors, leaving about 20 inches of cable for the connections.

9) Angle the top of the unit into the cutout and run electric cable through the top wiring access hole. See Figure 6-34.

10) Place the unit fully into the cutout and align the mounting holes with the predrilled pilot holes in the wall studs.

11) Use four No. 14 by 1-1/14 inch mounting screws to secure the unit to the wall studs. Refer back to Figure 6-33.

Wiring connections:

1) Remove the two screws holding the bottom wiring compartment cover in place.

2) Install an approved connector into the bottom access hole in the top shelf of the wiring compartment shown in Figure 6-34.

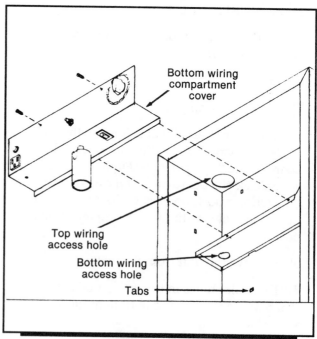

Figure 6-34
Wiring access holes
Courtesy: NuTone Inc.

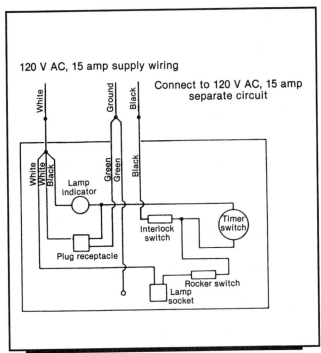

Figure 6-35
Wiring diagram
Courtesy: NuTone Inc.

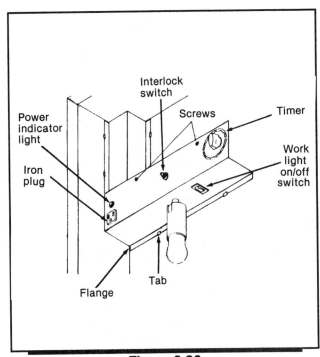

Figure 6-36
Replace bottom wiring compartment cover
Courtesy: NuTone Inc.

3) Run the electrical cable through the connector and tighten (but don't overtighten) the connector.

4) Use the diagram in Figure 6-35 to make the wiring connections. All the wiring must comply with your local codes, and the unit must be properly grounded.

5) Replace the top wiring compartment cover. Place one edge behind the cabinet's tabs and then squeeze the cover and slide the second edge behind the tabs.

6) Replace the bottom wiring compartment cover. Hang the cover's bottom flange behind the cabinet's tabs. Secure the top of the cover with the two screws. See Figure 6-36.

7) Install an R-20, 50-watt (maximum) reflector type lamp into the lamp socket.

8) Adjust the ironing board according to the instructions on the label inside the cabinet. It's now ready to use — and it tucks away easily and unobtrusively when not in use.

Estimating Appliance Installation Manhours

If you don't have your own records, use my manhours (Figure 6-37) for installing appliances. But compile your own labor records to make your estimates more accurate.

These labor estimates include costs for moving on and off the job, preparation, and clean-up. You'll need to add extra manhours for running separate electric branch circuits, water lines, and gas pipe.

Work element	Unit	Manhours per unit
Sink		
Double stainless steel	each	4
Double iron enamel	each	5
Cooktop		
In existing cutout	each	3
Installer makes cutout	each	4.5
Oven, built-in		
Single	each	3.5
Double	each	4.5
Drop-in range		
In existing cutout	each	3
Installer makes cutout	each	4.5
Range hood	each	2.3
Dishwasher	each	7.5
Ironing center	each	6.5

Figure 6-37
Manhours for installing appliances

Bathroom Design and Layout

Custom bathrooms, like custom kitchens, can be a personal design statement made by the owner. There's no limit to the combination of colors, styles, and materials for floor and wall coverings, vanities, lavatories and fixtures.

Can you make an old bathroom into a showplace? Of course! Look at Figure 7-1. Here you have a unique mix of modern materials accented by classic fixtures. Adding new fixtures, lavatory, storage cabinets and separate built-in vanity table provide modern convenience and function. But the traditional look is preserved with oak and brass accents and antique lighting fixtures. The four-legged cast iron tub and pull-chain toilet remind us of a more leisurely time. Notice that this bathroom is much larger than the 4 by 5 foot

bathroom in most homes built today. But many older homes have bathrooms this large.

Figure 7-2 is a more modern bathroom remodeled to make use of a similar old-fashioned style. Notice the detail in the cabinetry work. The decorative wallpaper, lighting, sink fixtures and carpeting add a plushness to the decor. The vanity, with two separate lavatories, is designed to accommodate the modern busy couple who must share the bathroom.

As a kitchen and bathroom specialist, you'll be called on to remodel all kinds and sizes of bathrooms. Usually your creativity will be cramped by space limitations. However, even where there's a minimum of space, you can use colors, fixtures and accessories to make the bathroom attractive as well as efficient.

Figure 7-1
Design an "old-fashioned" bathroom
Courtesy: Merillat Industries, Inc.

Bathroom Design

Bathroom remodeling isn't complicated, but it does take know-how. Keep up with trends in bathroom design and fixtures. Subscribe to one or more of the home decorating magazines. Study the articles with pictures of new or remodeled bathrooms. Look over the brochures put out by the companies that manufacture bathroom fixtures.

You don't have to be as creative as the designers who get their names in the magazines. All you have to do is adapt their ideas to your jobs. Let the experts guide your recommendations on style, wall finishes, color combinations, floor coverings, lighting, and layout. Your customers are going to

Figure 7-2
Design an atmosphere
Courtesy: Merillat Industries, Inc.

be looking for designs featuring the latest trends. It's up to you to stay one step ahead of them.

Subscribe to *Builder* magazine and use the information services to request free information on building materials. The address is given in Chapter 2. Use the brochures and photographs you get in your sales presentations. Have a notebook filled with attractive bathroom pictures collected from magazines and sales literature. Make up another notebook with color charts, fixtures, lighting arrangements, floor plans showing fixture placement for different sized bathrooms, and wall and floor coverings. Have your notebooks ready to show your potential clients. Let them know what's available, and what you can do for them.

The modern bathroom trend is glamor and glitz. An up-to-date bathroom can accommodate just about any design. You can include dressing rooms, workout rooms, jacuzzis and saunas. Of course, not every bathroom you remodel needs a sauna. But be aware of the possibilities and be ready to offer these ideas when they meet the homeowner's needs.

Every custom bathroom should reflect the owners' personal tastes. Find out what they like. Use your imagination. There are very few limitations in bathroom design and layout. Consider barn planks, tile, stone, brick, glass block, carpeting, wallpaper, mirrors, paint, or any combination of these to create an interesting and functional decor. Suggest a sliding glass door that opens out to a tropical rock garden or a waterfall. Use flowers, plants, murals, skylights or even piped-in music to create an appealing atmosphere for your clients.

Each year thousands of bathrooms are remodeled. It's big business, and a very profitable one for the alert and imaginative remodeler. Unlike kitchen appliances, you can safely supply bathroom fixtures for your remodeling jobs. Credit the markup on the fixtures to your profit ledger.

Try to make every bathroom you remodel the most beautiful room in the house. Homeowners who love their new bathroom are good prospects for a kitchen remodel next.

Remodeling the Modern Bathroom

Today, you don't need to limit your planning to accommodate the existing plumbing. Placement of bathroom fixtures isn't dictated by the shortest possible pipe run. At one time, bathrooms shared a common wall with the kitchen, and all the water lines and drain pipes were located in that common wall. It's true that less pipe was used, but don't let the tail wag the dog. Design an attractive, functional bathroom that uses a few feet of extra pipe, if necessary. Low-cost plastic pipe lets you locate fixtures anywhere design dictates.

The exception to this would be homes built on slab floors where the plumbing lines are in the floor instead of the wall. In this case, leave the fixtures in their original positions unless you can relocate them without tearing up the slab.

Plan Carefully

It's essential that you think through every part of the job before proposing any changes. Work out all the plumbing and electrical problems during the design and layout stages — not after construction begins. You may want to get the help of your plumbing and electrical subs, not only for design advice, but to be sure your estimate is accurate. The following points could affect your profit if you aren't careful. Be sure you get good advice on such items as:

- Adding a new soil stack.

- Connecting to lead pipe or removing old pipe.

- Relocating old plumbing or extending drain and water lines.

- Bringing old plumbing up to code requirements, such as installing fixture cut-off valves.

- Mating new pipe to old.

- Adding electrical circuits, switches, and outlets.

- Relocation of ductwork and electrical lines.

Bathroom remodeling can be very expensive. Many times you'll find that the floors have to be torn out because of water damage. You could even have to replace damaged studs.

Removing old steel or iron tubs can mean removing the door casings as well, at least temporarily.

You have to cut old fiberglass tub or shower units into small sections before you can take them out of most bathrooms. Keep that in mind before agreeing to install a one piece tub/shower unit. You may have to remove a section of wall to get the unit into the bathroom (or even into the house). That can add plenty to the cost of the job.

Room Size

When designing a bathroom layout, your first consideration will be the amount of space you have to work with. A 5 by 7 foot bathroom limits your alternatives unless you can get extra space from a closet, porch, or adjoining room. It's often possible to steal space from other rooms, especially in a home where the children are grown and gone. Your clients may not mind cutting down an adjoining closet or even eliminating a closet or spare bedroom entirely. In that case, you can let your imagination soar. You have the space to show your designing ability.

Bathroom Fixtures

Your next consideration will be the type and style of fixtures to use.

Standard tubs: A 5-foot tub is often considered the standard. It's the size most widely used. Rectangular tubs are available in 4 to 6 foot lengths, and widths of 30 inches or more. Tubs can be cast iron, steel, acrylic, fiberglass, or even teak wood.

When you're planning a remodeling job, remember that your clients don't have to select a standard 5-foot tub. There are many styles to choose from. Tubs come in a variety of shapes and sizes, including squares, ovals, and triangles that fit into a corner. A plain tub doesn't add much elegance to a bathroom. When possible, select tubs designed to create a mood or particular style for the bath. They should be accent pieces as much as fixtures.

Cast-iron tubs hold heat the longest and are the most durable. The porcelain finish on a quality tub is approximately 1/16-inch thick. With proper care, a cast-iron tub can last a lifetime. But they're expensive, and can weigh as much as 500 pounds. Steel tubs aren't as expensive as cast iron and weigh only about 100 pounds. Although they aren't as rugged as cast iron, steel tubs offer excellent service.

Modular fiberglass tub/shower combinations come in large one-piece units, or a somewhat easier-to-handle two-piece unit. Tub and shower modules eliminate the need for waterproof finishes in the tub compartment. ABS plastic wall surround also provides the same advantage. Their disadvantage is that they scratch easily, and need frequent cleaning. Remember also that the combination units are large, and may not fit through the doorway. If you have to remove a partition or enlarge a doorway, you've got a big disadvantage, especially if you didn't include that in your price.

Teak wood tubs are available with matching toilets and lavatory.

Most American homes are equipped with rectangular metal tubs recessed into a tub compartment or niche. The surrounding walls are commonly finished with some type of waterproof material. Ceramic tile is the most popular choice. There's also a metal tub with one finished end available. It can be used in a corner with the finished end completing a three-sided enclosure.

When choosing fixtures, consider safety as well as design. Tub bottoms should have a non-skid surface for safety. Today, most metal tubs are built with non-skid bottom surfaces. Tub enclosures should include grab bars and hand grips that are properly positioned and firmly secured. Glass enclosures should always be made of safety glass.

Shower heads are usually placed 60 inches or more above the shower floor. If the bathroom doesn't have a window, you'll need to install an exhaust fan. The fan pulls out excess moisture and odors, protecting the walls and ceilings.

Whirlpool tubs: Whirlpool tubs can be installed like a regular tub. But for an elegant effect, provide steps up to the tub rim. Steps are usually covered in ceramic tile, as shown in Figures 7-3 and 7-4. Figure 7-5 shows steps covered in carpet, a plush and lower cost alternative to tile.

Another alternative is to have the whirlpool tub sunken, with the top rim level with the floor. You can create a striking bathroom design in a multi-level home with a step-down bath, as shown in Figure 7-6.

Shower coves and modules: Shower units made of polypropylene or fiberglass offer excel-

Figure 7-3
Elegant bathroom with whirlpool tub
Courtesy: Merillat Industries, Inc.

lent service and are fairly easy to clean. The modules require special framing, which we'll cover in Chapter 8.

Shower coves, separate from the tub, offer a useful alternative to the usual tub/shower combination if there's space available. Molded units come in various sizes, the most popular units ranging in size from 32 by 36 by 72-1/2 inches to 48 by 36 by 72-1/2 inches. Most sizes will accom-

modate a glass shower door. Figure 7-7 is a 36-inch shower cove which fits nicely into the design of this remodeled dressing room/bathroom combination.

An elegant bathroom is the result of good design and your choice of appropriate materials. If you rob space from a closet to enlarge a bathroom, the shower cove shown in Figure 7-7 or the tub and shower combination in Figure 7-8 would be

Figure 7-4
Whirlpool tub with ceramic tile step-up
Courtesy: Kohler Company

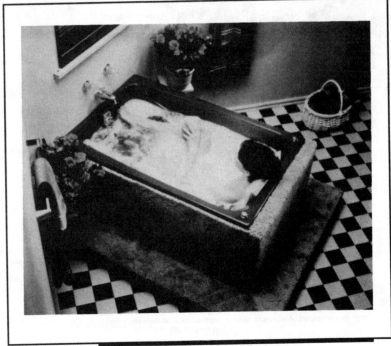

Figure 7-5
Whirlpool tub installation with carpeted step-up
Courtesy: Kohler Company

Figure 7-6
Step-down tub design
Courtesy: Kohler Company

Figure 7-7
Shower cove offers smart use of space
Courtesy: Kohler Company

Figure 7-8
New tub in old closet
Courtesy: Merillat Industries, Inc.

good ways to use that space. Notice that using a curtain instead of a glass enclosure adds to the soft tone and atmosphere of the rooms, merging with the cabinetry and wallpaper. These bathrooms didn't just happen. They were *designed* with careful attention to detail. When you're designing any bathroom, give full attention to all the details.

Lavatories: Lavatories come in all shapes and colors. They're made from cast iron, steel, vitreous china, or they may be formed as part of the vanity top in Corian, cultured marble or other materials. The pedestal lavatory shown in Figure 7-9 is a popular modern fixture available in many styles and materials, including teak wood. If you design a bathroom using a pedestal lavatory, you

Figure 7-9
Pedestal lavatory
Courtesy: Kohler Company.

Figure 7-10
Corner lavatory installation
Courtesy: Kohler Company

lose the storage space that a vanity cabinet below the lavatory usually offers. Be sure you compensate by creating alternative storage close to the lavatory stand.

Lavatories may be self-rimming, rimless, or under-counter models, and molded in rectangular, oval, round, or square shapes. Sizes are also available for narrow or odd-shaped countertop installations. Figure 7-10 shows a self-rimming lavatory installed in a corner vanity. Whatever bathroom design your clients choose, there's sure to be an elegant lavatory available to suit their taste.

Toilets: A good toilet is expensive but is usually worth the extra cost. A poor quality toilet is likely to overflow, leak or drip. If you're going to supply new bathroom fixtures for your client, be sure to look for toilets that have non-overflow features and vacuum breaker safeguards against back siphonage. If your clients are interested in water conservation, you can install toilets with siphon vortex flushing action which will flush with only 3.5 gallons of water.

Several types of toilets are available. The close-coupled (two-piece) type is standard. The modern one-piece, low-silhouette design in Figure 7-8 is the most popular alternative. Special designer or fashion toilets like the pull-chain, high-tank model in Figure 7-1 are also available. For the more practical homeowners, there's a wall-mounted toilet available that's designed to make floor cleaning easier.

If you're remodeling a bathroom with concrete slab floors, there's a rear outlet close-coupled toilet designed especially for installation on concrete slab. The rear outlet permits the drain pipe to be installed in the wall instead of the floor.

A good quality toilet should have a sturdy seat and strong hinges. Plastic toilet seats, though not as sturdy as the heavier wood, often last longer because the paint on wood seats chips off and becomes unsightly.

Bidets: The bidet (pronounced *be-day*) has been a standard in European bathrooms for many years. They're becoming more popular as an addition to the modern American bathroom. The bidet is usually installed next to the toilet, as shown in Figure 7-6.

Faucets and accessories: Your design isn't complete until you and your client have decided on the style and type of faucets and accessories best suited for the bathroom. Selection here is almost unlimited. There are modern European designs, traditional styles, antique fashions, and many more. Finishes are available in stainless steel, brushed nickel, polished brass, gold-plating or a variety of colors, with accents of cut crystal, ceramic, or wood.

The hardware should complement your design. If the design is elegantly modern, the hardware should be the same. If your clients prefer old-fashioned charm, use faucets and accessories to highlight the period they've chosen to accentuate. Consult manufacturer's catalogs and brochures to find what's available. The faucets and accessories you choose will play a key role in your bathroom design.

Lighting and electrical outlets: A bathroom without enough light and electrical outlets is as bad as one without adequate storage. Too many baths have too little of both. As a bathroom remodeler, keep in mind that this room needs special lighting in specific areas as well as general or decorative lighting for the entire room.

Special fixtures are available to meet almost any need in a remodeled bathroom. There are waterproof lights for over showers and tubs; heat lamps and sun lamps for a quick warm-up while drying off after a bath or shower; luminous ceiling lights which brighten the entire room; indirect lighting from bulkheads for a softer look; and special theatrical lights for the vanity area. Your choice of lighting should be practical and functional as well as decorative.

Figure 7-11 shows some of the fixtures that are available for lighting wall cabinets. Windows and skylights can also provide natural light during the day. Figure 7-12 is a nicely designed, well-lighted bathroom using glass block for additional daytime light.

Be sure to provide enough receptacles for all the small appliances used in today's bathrooms. Keep outlets above the vanity or lavatory level for easy access. Always consider safety. Don't install switches or receptacles within reach of the shower or tub.

Vanities, Cabinets and Bathroom Storage

Cabinetry plays a key role in bathroom design. Bathroom vanities come in as many styles as kitchen cabinets: early American, modern, Mediterranean, and many others. The vanity treatment — that is, color, trim, doors, and hardware — is virtually unlimited. You can use wood stains, veneers, or paint to create cabinets in any color scheme or style.

The kitchen isn't the only room where you can make use of wall cabinets. Figure 7-13 shows how you can work wall cabinets into your bathroom design as well. The designer who planned this bathroom wasted no space. Every available foot is used to good advantage. There's a spacious vanity with a dressing table at one end; the seat for the dressing table doubles as a hamper for dirty clothes. Wall storage cabinets, drawers and shelves occupy one wall while an over-toilet storage cabinet gives the cabinetry balance.

A good bathroom design includes adequate closet and drawer space to store all the items needed in the bathroom. You can't provide too much storage space. All sorts of gadgets are made for use in the bath area: hair dryers, curling irons, electric toothbrushes, shavers, water pics, hot water bottles, and heating pads to name the more obvious. There are also the linens, tissues, soaps, shampoos, toothpaste, mouthwash, medicines, first aid supplies, cleaning supplies and storage for dirty clothes. Think *storage* when you design a bathroom. In Figure 7-14 you'll find data and dimensions for vanities, vanity components, and bathroom cabinets that will be useful for your designs.

Figure 7-11
Lighting must be functional as well as decorative
Courtesy: NuTone Inc.

Figure 7-12
Glass block adds daytime light
Courtesy: Merillat Industries, Inc.

Wall and Floor Coverings

Ceramic tile is the most common choice for bathroom walls and floors. But many other materials are available to the creative designer. Combinations of wood, stone, brick, paneling, wallpaper, and mirrors will give your designs a distinct look. A good designer makes use of a variety of materials for function and aesthetic value.

Your client's taste and pocketbook will usually be the determining factor in choosing wall and floor coverings, but your ideas can influence those choices. It's important that you show your clients what materials are available in their price range. Sometimes people simply don't know what's available. Your job is to show them. A

Figure 7-13
Plan bathroom storage carefully
Courtesy: Merillat Industries, Inc.

good designer gives the clients what they want. But it's the way the materials are put together that makes the difference between an ordinary remodeling job and a showplace.

If your clients decide on ceramic tile, you can help them choose from a wide assortment of colors and sizes. When color-blended or contrasted with other materials or bathroom fixtures, ce-

ramic tile presents a striking room. It's a hard material to beat for bathroom use. Don't hesitate to use tile for design and beauty as much as serviceability.

When you install ceramic tile, be sure to use floor tile on the floor and wall tile on the walls. Mottled or crystalline glazed tile is better for floors than highly glazed wall tiles. Glazed wall

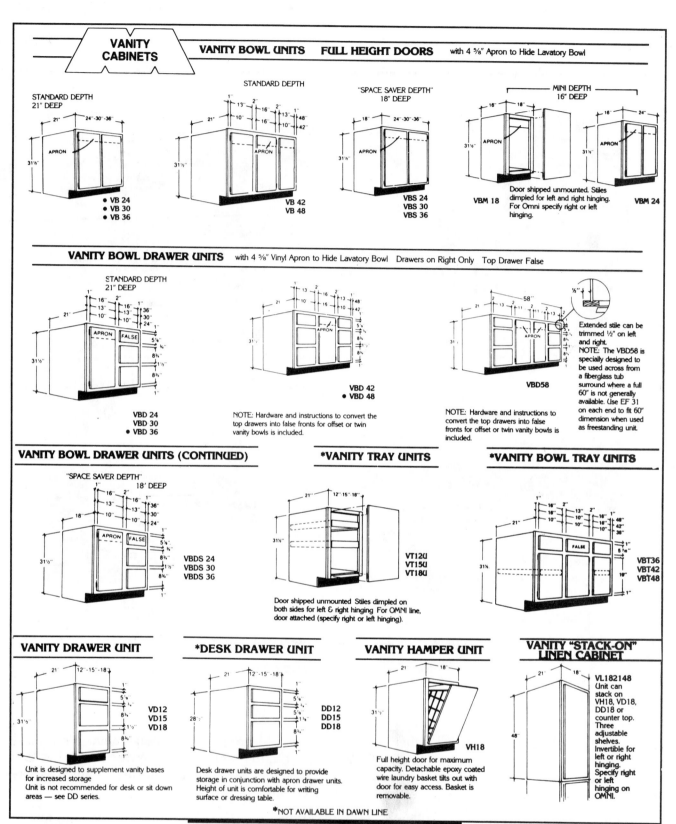

Figure 7-14
Vanity cabinetry
Courtesy: Merillat Industries, Inc.

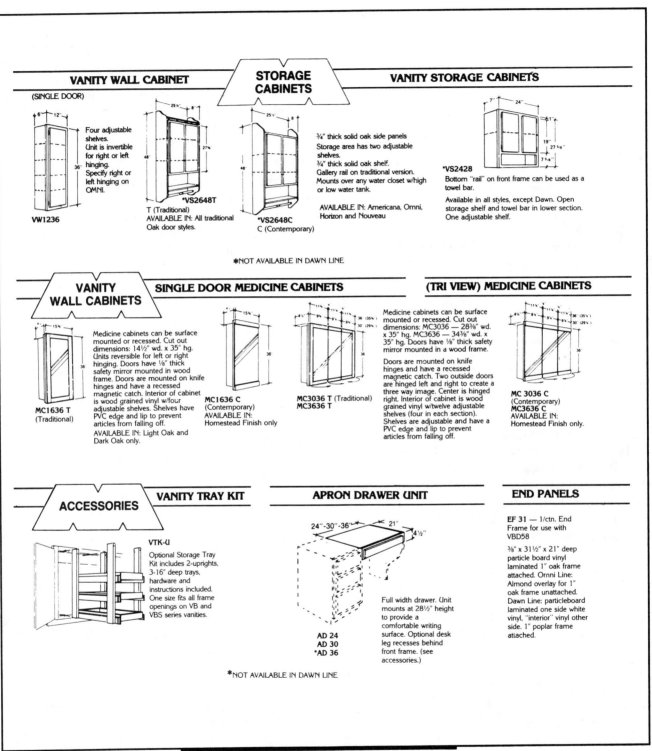

Figure 7-14
Vanity cabinetry (continued)
Courtesy: Merillat Industries, Inc.

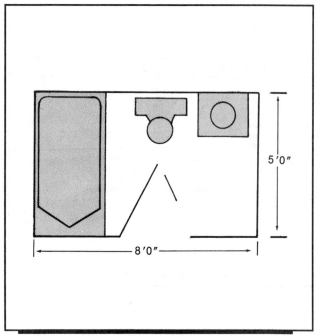

Figure 7-15
Bath with common wall plumbing

You can create a plush atmosphere in the bath using carpeting or a combination of carpeting and tile or marble. Of course, carpeting isn't always the most practical choice. It can easily get saturated, especially if small children use the bathroom. Suggest a loose-laid carpet (matching the carpeting in the adjoining room) which can easily be taken up, dried, and replaced by the homeowner.

Marble, either synthetic or natural, is another good material to use in the bathroom. Or, if cost is a limiting factor, suggest plastic laminates and plastic-finished hardboard. Whatever you use, blend the various bathroom components into a unified whole.

Bathroom Layout

There are large bathrooms and very small bathrooms, and you need to be prepared to handle both. For a kitchen and bath remodeler, *where there is space, there is elegance.* Look again at Figures 7-12 and 7-13. A good bathroom layout is attractive and functional. That's not a difficult combination if you have plenty of space to work with. But a compact bathroom needs to be functional and comfortable as well.

Where floor space is limited, you'll have to plan the arrangement of the bathroom fixtures carefully. Figures 7-15 and 7-16 show how you might place fixtures in a small bathroom where the plumbing is limited to a common wall or two adjacent walls. Don't crowd the placement of fixtures. They'll be awkward to use. Figures 7-17 and 7-18 show minimum and recommended spacing for the comfortable use of fixtures.

If there's plenty of space available, spread the fixtures out to suit your design. Figure 7-19 shows a layout for a luxurious bathroom and dressing room which includes a step-up whirlpool tub. You'll seldom have that much space to work with, except in a large older home.

tiles can be dangerously slick on the floor, especially in an area where people will be walking in stocking feet. Floor tile comes in a variety of shapes, including large and small squares, rectangles, hexagons, and octagons. Wall tiles are also available in various sizes. The 4-1/4-inch and 6-inch square wall tiles are the most popular.

Quarry floor tiles are a good alternative to ceramic tile. They make a durable and attractive floor. You can find quarry tile in different shades of red, brown and tan. The 6 x 6 x 1/2 inch and 3-7/8 x 8 x 1/2 inch tile are most popular.

A patterned wall tile in a similar or contrasting shade makes a striking combination with quarry tile floors.

Sheet vinyl is another popular choice for floor covering. It comes in 6 foot and 12 foot widths. You can use the narrower width for small bathrooms and the 12 foot width for larger rooms. Try to avoid seams when you install sheet vinyl.

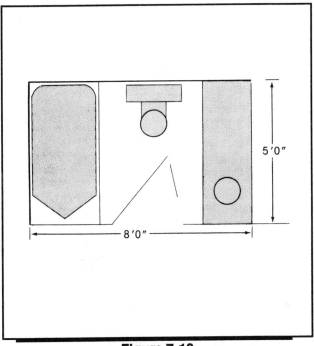

Figure 7-16
Fixtures on two walls—lavatory pipe runs under vanity

Some homes built in the early 1900's had very large bathrooms, 10 by 12 feet or even larger. If you have a job like that, suggest a layout that lets two people share the bathroom with some degree of privacy. Figure 7-20 is an example of how you can remodel an old bath to comfortably accommodate two or even three in privacy.

Figure 7-21 shows the floor plan of an older home with a bedroom that measured 14 by 16 feet. Figure 7-22 shows how a bathroom was added without eliminating the bedroom. Figure 7-23 shows how a porch was enclosed and made into a bathroom adjacent to the bedroom.

While it's very good for your business to be able to offer these ideas to your clients, don't go overboard in looking for bathroom space in old homes. While bathrooms can be added in unused areas such as a large closet, pantry or small back bedroom, not every unused space is a candidate for an additional bathroom. For example, converting a pantry off the kitchen into a bathroom

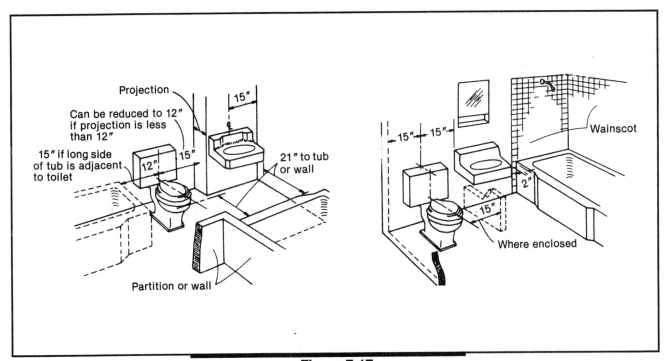

Figure 7-17
Minimum dimensions for bathroom fixture spacing

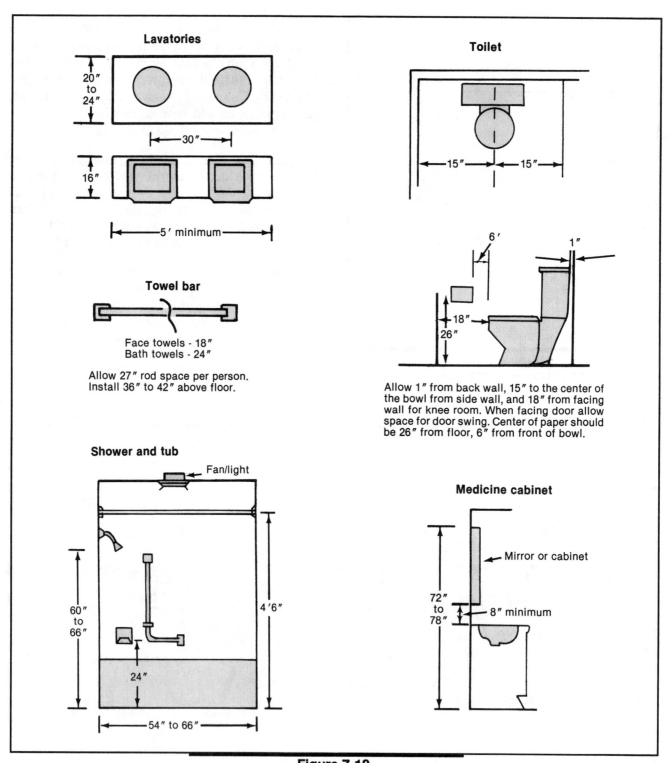

Figure 7-18
Recommended space requirements for bathroom fixtures

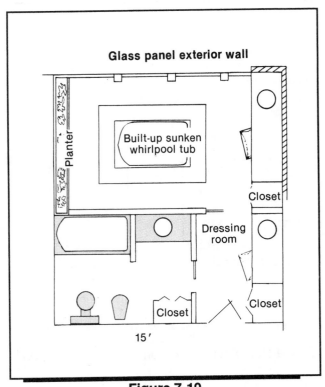

Figure 7-19
Modern luxury bath with whirlpool bath, bidet and dressing room

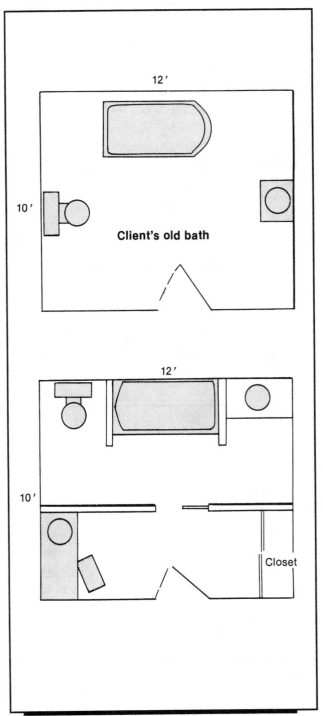

Figure 7-20
Bathroom divided to provide privacy

isn't a good arrangement if it adds traffic through the kitchen work area. However, a half-bath adjacent to the kitchen and off the living area can be a very convenient alteration.

The minimum space needed for a full bathroom with a tub is 5 by 7 feet. You can frequently find exterior space to add on a small bath. In a 1-1/2 story house, add on in the area under the shed dormer, running the plumbing through the wall on the first floor.

If you can't find room for a full bath, there's probably space for a half bath. Locate it near the work and living areas to save steps and relieve the traffic in the main bath. You can put a half bath in a space that's just 3 by 5-1/2 feet, as

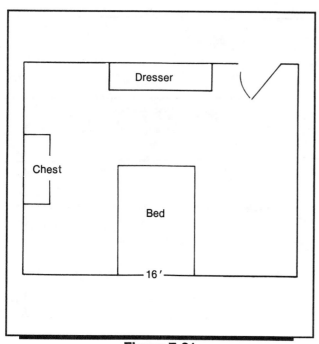

Figure 7-21
Large bedroom permitting bath addition

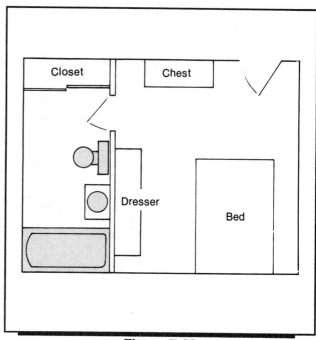

Figure 7-22
Conversion of large bedroom into bedroom & bath

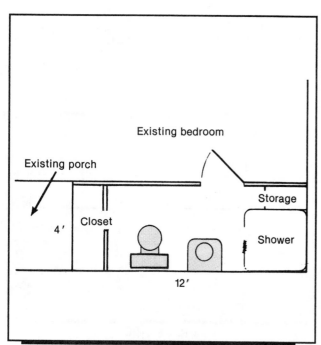

Figure 7-23
Converting part of back porch into a bathroom

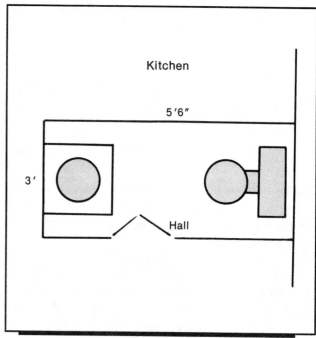

Figure 7-24
Utilizing small area for half-bath

shown in Figure 7-24. The space can be taken from a back porch or closet, or found under a stairway.

Keep in mind our earlier discussion on the use of color. Light colors make a small room larger, and dark colors close it in. Today you can make the bathroom a color event. Anyone can paint walls and change wallpaper at will. But colored fixtures, ceramic tile and marble are more permanent. Be sure your clients are completely happy with the colors you're going to install. For fixtures and countertops, use colors that will blend with several styles and color schemes. That way the homeowners can keep the bath looking modern without another major remodeling.

Bathroom Checklist

When you plan a bathroom remodeling job, use a checklist to get off to a good start. Remember, your design should reflect both an up-to-date approach and what your client wants and needs. You know what can be done in basic bath design and what's appropriate for larger and more elaborate baths. Your kit should include plans and information on various types of basic baths, half baths, and fancy bathrooms. Your checklist should include all the items you'll need to complete the design for these baths.

Figure 7-25 is a bathroom checklist that will help you and your clients get down to specifics. Make copies of it and use them when you meet with potential clients.

The cost of a basic bathroom remodeling job will range from $4,500 to $6,500. Fancy jobs, where elegant design is the most important factor, can easily exceed $10,000, depending on the

fixtures and treatment. When the homeowners want a ballpark figure, give them a price range close to what you know it might be. Don't be specific in your quotes until you've made a careful on-site inspection and calculated *all* the costs. Guesses about costs have no place in the remodeling business except to eliminate your company from the competition.

Bathroom Plans and Specifications

The bathroom specifications and estimate sheet, shown in Figure 2-10 in Chapter 2, lists the labor and material costs included in a job. The cost is the amount charged to the contract, not your actual cost.

You're going to need current costs for your estimate. Several trades are usually involved in bathroom construction, depending on the amount of work you can do yourself. Be sure and get the latest prices for materials and subcontract work before figuring the job. It's the only way to guard against a loss.

Also, keep in mind that this week's prices won't always apply to next month's work. If you're estimating a job to be done two or three months in the future, put a price escalation clause in the contract to protect yourself. Three months from now the tile sub might inform you that his price is $200 above what he previously quoted you. If you're not protected, the loss is yours.

You might want to make copies of the specification sheets for your own use. Make them part of your contract with your clients. Whether you use these specification sheets or make up your own, be sure your documents are clear and detailed enough to eliminate any misunderstanding.

Bathroom Checklist

Owner's Name _____

Address _____

Phone_____

Construction Requirements

- ☐ Replace floor joists
- ☐ Replace subfloor
- ☐ Replace underlayment
- ☐ Remove partition
- ☐ Add partition
- ☐ Relocate door
- ☐ Add closet
- ☐ Raise floor level
- ☐ New window
- ☐ Add shutters
- ☐ Install sliding door
- ☐ Install folding door
- ☐ Bulkheads (locations _____)

Floor

- ☐ New
- ☐ No change
- ☐ Remove (manhours _____)
- ☐ Repair (manhours _____)
- ☐ Tile
- ☐ Carpet
- ☐ Vinyl
- ☐ Other
- ☐ Style
- ☐ Color
- ☐ Floor size (_____)

Plumbing Requirements

- ☐ Remove fixtures
- ☐ Remove radiator
- ☐ Rough-in:
  - Supply _____ feet
  - Waste _____ feet
  - Vent _____ feet
  - Gas _____ feet
  - Steam _____ feet
- ☐ Install fixtures
- ☐ Install spa
- ☐ Install bidet
- ☐ Other (_____)

Walls

- ☐ New
- ☐ No change
- ☐ Remove (manhours _____)
- ☐ Repair (manhours _____)
- ☐ At tub area (sq ft _____)
- ☐ Color (_____)
- ☐ Paint (_____)
- ☐ Paper (_____)
- ☐ Tile (_____)

Ceilings

- ☐ New
- ☐ No change
- ☐ Remove (manhours _____)
- ☐ Repair (manhours _____)
- ☐ Sheetrock
- ☐ Luminous
- ☐ Skylight
- ☐ Beam
- ☐ Other
- ☐ Paint
- ☐ Color

Storage

- ☐ New
- ☐ No change
- ☐ Remove (manhours _____)
- ☐ Closets (type_____)
- ☐ Linen
- ☐ Laundry
- ☐ Washer/dryer
- ☐ Expand shelving
- ☐ Electrical appliances
- ☐ Cleaning supplies
- ☐ Scales
- ☐ Panel (_____ sq ft)
- ☐ Glass (_____ sq ft)
- ☐ Mirrors (_____ sq ft)
- ☐ Other (_____ sq ft)

Enclosures

- ☐ New
- ☐ No change
- ☐ Remove (manhours _____)
- ☐ Repair (manhours _____)
- ☐ Shower stall

Figure 7-25
Bathroom checklist

☐ Shower/tub modular (size _____)
☐ Tub doors (size _____)
☐ Shower doors (size _____)
☐ Style of doors _____
☐ Shower rod

Heating/Cooling

☐ New
☐ No change
☐ Relocate unit/registers
☐ New duct
☐ Close duct
☐ Baseboard
☐ Radiant
☐ Gas/space
☐ Electric/space

Electrical

☐ New
☐ No change
☐ Type wiring
☐ Wiring (_____)
☐ Heater switch
☐ Infrared heat lamp switch
☐ Fan switch
☐ Wall outlets
☐ Other

Ventilating

☐ New
☐ No change
☐ Ceiling fan
☐ Wall fan
☐ Vent
☐ Fan, lamp, heater unit

Lighting

☐ New
☐ No change
☐ Ceiling (type_____)
☐ Wall
☐ Bulkhead
☐ Indirect
☐ Waterproof
☐ Medicine cabinet
☐ Drop
☐ Other

Accessories

☐ New
☐ Remove (manhours _____)
☐ Towel ring
☐ Towel bars
☐ Paper holder
☐ Mirror (size _____)
☐ Soap dish
☐ Tumbler/toothbrush holder
☐ Match tile type
☐ Other finish type
☐ Other

Medicine Cabinet

☐ New
☐ No change
☐ Recessed
☐ Surface
☐ Type
☐ Shape
☐ Size
☐ Mirror

Shower Cabinet or Cove

☐ New
☐ No change
☐ None
☐ Fiberglass
☐ Polypropylene
☐ Size
☐ Color
☐ Door

Lavatory

☐ New
☐ No change
☐ Self-rim
☐ One-piece
☐ Wall hung
☐ Flush mount
☐ Undermount
☐ Rectangular
☐ Oval
☐ Size
☐ Color
☐ Other

Figure 7-25
Bathroom checklist (continued)

Tub

- ☐ New
- ☐ No change
- ☐ None
- ☐ Fiberglass tub/shower modular
- ☐ Steel
- ☐ Cast iron
- ☐ Sunken
- ☐ Whirlpool
- ☐ Size
- ☐ Style
- ☐ Color

Toilet

- ☐ New
- ☐ No change
- ☐ Reset
- ☐ Floor mount
- ☐ Wall mount
- ☐ Style
- ☐ Color

Vanity

- ☐ New
- ☐ Existing
- ☐ None
- ☐ Replace
- ☐ Remove
- ☐ Finish (_____)
- ☐ Style
- ☐ Color
- ☐ Size
- ☐ Doors
- ☐ Pulls (style _____)
- ☐ Drawers
- ☐ Height
- ☐ Knee space
- ☐ Hamper space

Bidet

- ☐ New
- ☐ None
- ☐ Style
- ☐ Color

Vanity Top

- ☐ New
- ☐ No change
- ☐ Material
- ☐ Color
- ☐ Splash height
- ☐ Edging
- ☐ Molded splash
- ☐ Separate splash
- ☐ Number of cutouts
- ☐ Other

Fittings

- ☐ New
- ☐ No change
- ☐ Type valve (_____)
- ☐ Diverter type (_____)
- ☐ Massage
- ☐ Style
- ☐ Color
- ☐ Quality (_____)
- ☐ Other

Salvage Value

- ☐ Tub
- ☐ Shower
- ☐ Lavatory
- ☐ Toilet
- ☐ Fiittings
- ☐ Pipe
- ☐ Lumber
- ☐ Mirrors/glass
- ☐ Accessories
- ☐ Radiator
- ☐ Heating/cooling unit

Figure 7-25
Bathroom checklist (continued)

The Finished Job

The more subcontractors you use, the more chances there will be of foul-ups, delays, and questionable quality. Make certain that your subcontractors perform professionally.

The subcontractor's reputation isn't on the line like yours. Do yourself a favor; use only qualified, professional subs for bathroom work. You don't want the tilesetter standing in an expensive new tub, grinding sand into the finish. Some subs are careless and less reliable than others. You're responsible for their carelessness, just as you are for their delays. A prolonged delay by an otherwise very competent sub can cause both you and your client considerable irritation. You want the trades you hire to come in, do the work, and be out as scheduled. That's essential when you're working in an occupied home!

Protect the tile and fixtures while there's work in progress, even if they aren't new. Scratched porcelain or chipped tile aren't design problems, but they'll affect the finished product. You're going to spend a lot of time working up a design for your client — don't let someone else spoil it for you. Pay attention to detail, from the design stage right through to completion.

A bathroom specialist who's good at design, is careful with every client's property, and gets the job done on time, is likely to have all the bathroom work anyone can handle.

Installing Bathroom Fixtures

Every installation begins with the floor. Before estimating the job, you should have made a thorough inspection of the bathroom floor from above *and* below. If any repairs are needed, you'll have to do them before you can install the fixtures. You may have to restore the sills, floor joists, subfloor and underlayment.

If you found damaged floor joists but the subfloor was solid, you may be able to replace the joists from underneath. Where there's damage to only one or two joists, it's better to make your repairs from below. It saves you from having to take out a section, or possibly the entire floor, and replace it with all new materials. Of course, you can't replace the joists from underneath unless you have adequate working space. Working in a crawl space can be a very difficult and time-consuming job.

If you found extensive water damage to the subfloor, under the toilet for example, you'll have to replace the damaged area. You'll need to cut

out the section and replace it, or redo the entire floor. Another common area for water damage is under the tub. Figure 8-1 shows how the joists and subfloor should be placed under the tub. Notice the double joists under the edges of the tub. A cast iron tub filled with water weighs about a thousand pounds. And the person getting into it will add another hundred or two. It's a good idea to reinforce the tub area when you're putting in new floors.

If you're going to change the walls or wall finishes, you'll first have to run electrical circuits for outlets, heaters and lights, and install new water pipes and drains. If the wall studs are water damaged or infested with termites, replace them. Don't waste your time, and your client's money, applying a new finish over deteriorated floors, walls, or ceilings. That's why a *thorough inspection for structural damage or weakness* is so important. Many kitchen and bath remodelers have lost money on jobs that started with a careless inspec-

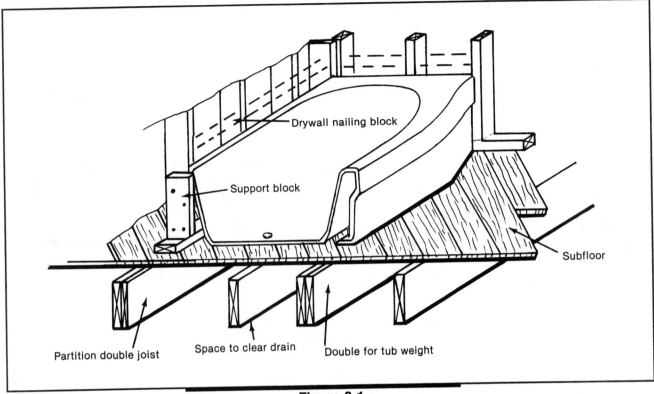

Drywall nailing block

Support block

Subfloor

Partition double joist   Space to clear drain   Double for tub weight

Figure 8-1
Framing for bathtub (block support)

tion and a consequent low estimate. My tuition for this little lesson was about twenty times what you paid for it, and for all the other lessons in this book.

Installing the Tub

Once you complete any needed repairs, begin installing the bathroom fixtures. Let's say your clients select a regular cast iron tub for the main bathroom (Kohler's K-790-S), and a cast iron whirlpool tub for their master bath. The whirlpool tub is Kohler's K-792, steeping bath.

The regular tub's specifications are shown in Figure 8-2. Figure 8-3 shows the specifications for the K-792 whirlpool tub. We'll discuss the installation of both tubs.

Keep in mind there are a variety of installations possible for these tubs. No two bathroom remod-

eling projects are exactly alike and few remodelers do things the same way. One job may be just like the one we'll be discussing, and another may require a little different framing procedure.

Tools and Materials Required

In addition to the conventional woodworking tools, you'll need:

- Arc pliers or a 14-inch pipe wrench
- Ruler
- Level
- Square
- Screwdriver
- Pliers

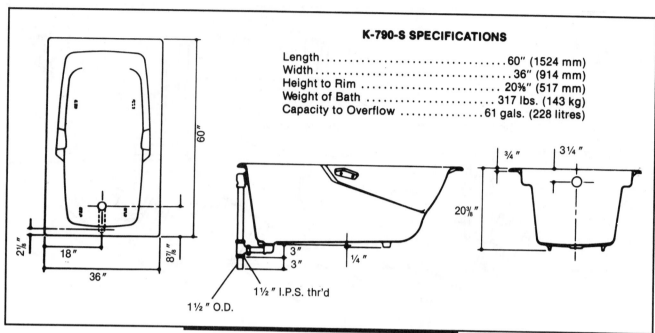

Figure 8-2
Tub specifications
Courtesy: Kohler Company

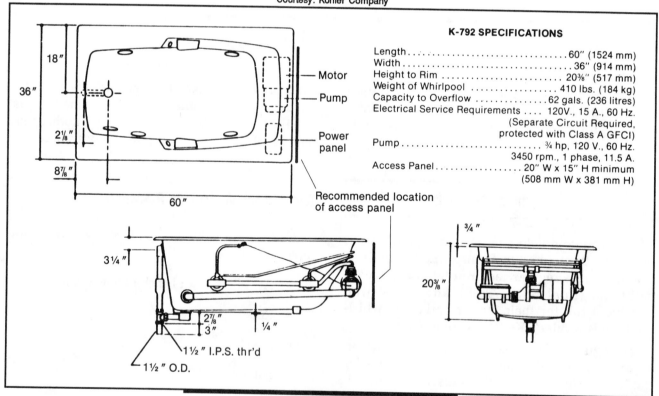

Figure 8-3
Whirlpool specifications
Courtesy: Kohler Company

- Plumber's putty

- Water-resistant sealer

- Safety shoes

Framing a Standard Tub

The tub we're installing is designed for installation in either a new or an existing bathroom. Measure the area where you're going to install it to be sure it fits. Check the existing plumbing to make sure it corresponds to the new tub. Remember, cast iron tubs are heavy. Protect the floor by slipping boards under the tub while you move it in or out of place. See Figure 8-4.

Construct a frame to fit your particular tub installation. The type of frame depends on the method of installation. You can install the tub in a variety of ways: in a recess, corner, peninsular, or sunken position. Figure 8-5 shows types of tub framing you can use. Be sure you provide adequate support for these tubs under the legs — not just the rim.

Installing the Tub Drain

There are several types of tub drains. Each installs a different way. In any case, read and follow any instructions packed with the drain. In this installation, you're going to use Kohler's Clearflo drain.

1) Look at Figure 8-6, Diagram A. Apply a bead of plumber's putty about 1/4 inch thick under the lip of the strainer flange. Insert the strainer through the drain hole of the tub. Place the black, flat gasket over the strainer from the underside of the tub.

2) Attach the strainer firmly to the drain ell. The drain ell tube should face the overflow hole. Tighten the strainer into the drain ell with the handle of your pliers, as shown in Diagram B. Be sure there's a complete putty seal around the strainer body. Remove any excess putty. *Do not* reposition the drain after you tighten the strainer or you'll break the putty seal.

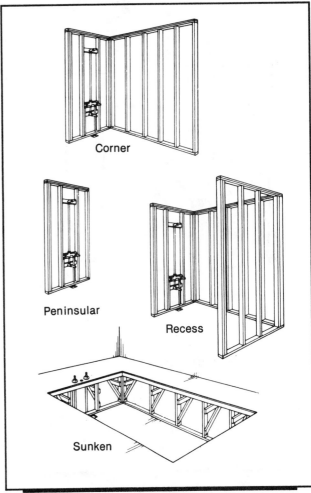

Figure 8-5
Framing for various tub installations

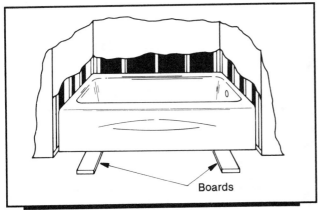

Figure 8-4
Use board skids to remove or install tub

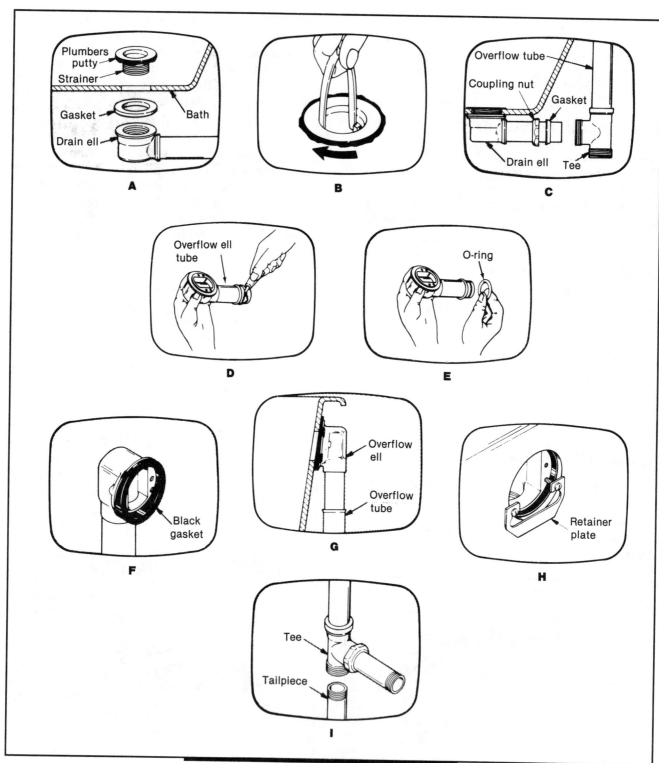

Figure 8-6
Installing a Clearflo tub drain
Courtesy: Kohler Company

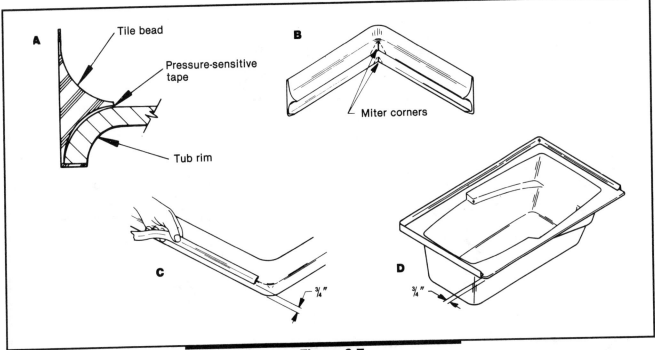

A — Tile bead
Pressure-sensitive tape
Tub rim

B — Miter corners

C — ¾"

D — ¾"

Figure 8-7
Vinyl tiling-in bead installation
Courtesy: Kohler Company

3) Assemble the coupling nuts and tapered gaskets on the overflow and drain ell tubes (Diagram C). Notice the position of the tapered gasket on the tube. Align the parts with the tee as shown in the illustration. Insert each tube completely into the tee. Align and hand tighten the coupling nuts.

4) Thoroughly lubricate (with grease) the two O-rings provided with the overflow ell. Slide them into the grooves on the overflow ell tube. See Diagrams D and E.

5) Apply a bead of RTV sealant to the overflow ell. Attach the black gasket to the overflow ell as shown in Diagram F. The gasket is tapered. Make sure you place the thickest part of the gasket at the bottom.

6) Insert the overflow ell into the overflow tube. Align the overflow ell with the overflow hole in the tub. Apply a bead of RTV sealant between the gasket and the tub. The tapered gasket will fit snugly into the tub's contour. See Diagram G.

7) From inside the tub, attach the retainer plate to the overflow ell with the two screws provided. Tighten the screws securely (Diagram H).

8) Tighten all the coupling nuts on the tee to secure the assembly. Attach the tailpiece to the tee (as shown in Diagram I) and tighten it securely. You may need to cut the tailpiece so it'll fit properly. There should only be 1 to 2 inches of tailpiece inside the trap.

Vinyl Tiling-in Bead Installation

Before you position the tub in place, apply vinyl tiling-in bead to the sides of the tub which contact the wall. The vinyl bead keeps water from seeping between the tub and the wall. Use it for a water-tight installation. The vinyl bead comes in a kit (K-1179) and contains 14 feet of bead, enough for three sides of the tub. The kit also has 14 feet of pressure-sensitive tape, which you need to seal the vinyl bead to the tub. See Figure 8-7 A.

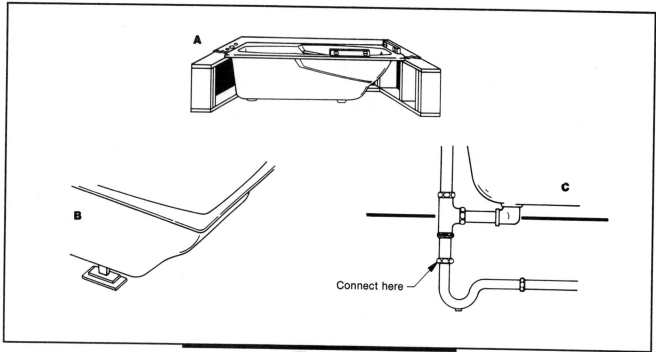

Figure 8-8
Leveling and setting the tub
Courtesy: Kohler Company

1) Before you install the vinyl bead, clean all the dust, grease and foreign material off the tub. Don't install vinyl bead or pressure sensitive tape in cold weather — temperatures below 40 degrees Fahrenheit.

2) Temporarily position the bead around the edge of the tub, measuring for correct installation. (Don't use the sealing tape until you're ready to put it permanently in place.) Bend the bead and clip the excess material from the corners to form a miter joint. See Figure 8-7 B. Be careful not to cut through the bead when you miter the corners.

3) When you have a good fit with the bead, apply the pressure-sensitive tape to the tub rim. Using the bottom edge of the rim as a guide, place the tape 3/4 inch in from the edge of the tub rim. See Figure 8-7 C. Leave the paper backing on. Cut the excess material from the corners to form a miter joint.

4) Now remove the paper backing from the tape. Start the vinyl bead 3/4 inch in from the edge of the rim as you did with the tape. Position the bead around the tub as shown in Figure 8-7 D. (The figure shows bead installation for a recessed tub enclosed by three walls.) Press the bead firmly in place with heel of your hand to seal it properly. Continue to work the bead firmly in place until you reach the opposite end. After you've secured the bead in place, you can install the tub.

Leveling and Setting the Tub

The tub must be level and resting on all four feet when you complete your installation.

1) To position the tub, slide it into place and insert the tailpiece into the trap. Check for level along the sides and across the drain end as shown in Figure 8-8 A.

2) You may need to shim under the tub feet with solid shims (Figure 8-8 B). If the feet aren't accessible from the back or side, you'll have to move the tub in and out of the recess area until it's shimmed properly.

3) When the tub is level and secure, connect the drain into the trap as shown in Figure 8-8 C. You may have to remove the tailpiece and cut it to fit the trap.

4) Construct an access panel on the drain-end wall to simplify future maintenance. An access panel may be required by code. Few things are more irritating to homeowners or plumbers than a sealed up fixture drain and water pipes.

Installing Finish Wall Material

When you install a tub in a corner, peninsular, or recessed position, you'll need a finish material to protect the wall from moisture. Figure 8-9

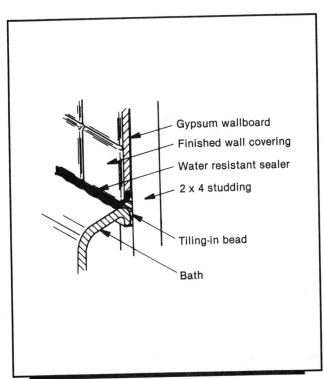

Gypsum wallboard
Finished wall covering
Water resistant sealer
2 x 4 studding
Tiling-in bead
Bath

Figure 8-9
Finish wall installation

shows how to protect the tub area from water damage.

Cover the framing and walls with gypsum wallboard or other material appropriate for the wall finish you're using. Install the wall finish on the subwall. Seal the joints under the tub rim between the tub and finish wall with a water-resistant sealer.

During construction of the framing and while you're installing finish wall materials, be sure to protect the tub from damage.

Whirlpool Tub Installation

You probably won't get asked to do a lot of whirlpool tub installation jobs unless you're working in a high-income area, but customers who are getting a good-sized bathroom remodeled may be open to your suggestion. If you can do it efficiently, installing a whirlpool tub can make a nice increase in the profits of a job, and provide a showplace that should bring in a good many referrals. When people have something their friends and neighbors don't have, they're usually very eager to let them see it.

If one of these jobs comes your way, read very carefully the installation instructions provided with the tub.

You'll need good access to make the final connections. The whirlpool requires an access panel 20 inches wide by 15 inches high so there's clearance to service the pump and controls. Access has to be at the pump end of the whirlpool. Refer back to Figure 8-3. Securely tighten the pump connections before you begin.

The Electrical Connections

The whirlpool controls are usually prewired at the factory. You must have a separate 120-volt, 15-amp, 60 hz, circuit with a ground fault circuit interrupter (GFCI) for installation. The GFCI provides additional protection against line-to-ground shock hazard.

Connect the supply leads to a 3-foot length of 3/8-inch watertight conduit. The conduit will usually have black and white leads and a green ground wire. See Figure 8-10. Provide a separate equipment grounding conductor for the green ground wire. *Do not* connect the ground to any current-carrying conductor except at the main fuse or service breaker panel.

Framing Under the Whirlpool Tub

Figure 8-11 shows (A) corner, (B) peninsular, (C) recessed, and (D) sunken installation of a whirlpool tub.

Build a strong frame out of 2 x 4s. Be sure there's good access to the pump or power panel. Notch the framing as necessary for the control body. Also consider the thickness of the subwall and finish materials. If you want an apron wall with-

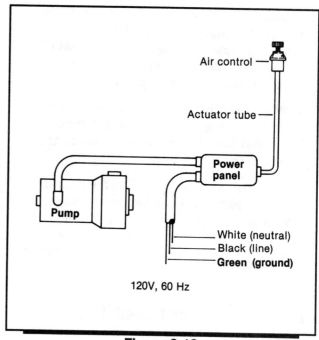

Figure 8-10
Whirlpool electrical connection
Courtesy: Kohler Company

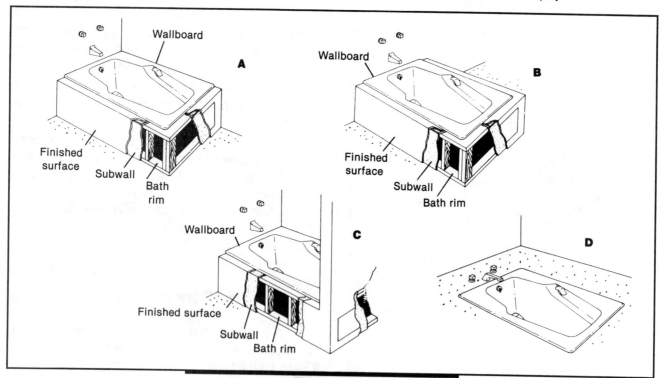

Figure 8-11
Framing under the tub
Courtesy: Kohler Company

out a ledge, the finish apron wall must be 1/32 inch under the tub rim.

You need good support for the tub and the tub must be level. Don't support the weight of the tub by the rim, and never use the piping or the pump for structural support or positioning. In a sunken installation, support the bottom of the tub with four supporting blocks.

Before you cover the framing in the apron area, open the hot and cold valves and check all supply connections for leaks. Fill the tub to the overflow and drain connections to check for leaks. Operate the whirlpool for at least 5 minutes and check again for leaks.

Whirlpool Trim and Other Assemblies

Setting the whirlpool tub into position and putting up the finish wall is the same as for a standard tub. When the whirlpool tub is in place, begin installing the trim kit, ball and retainer assemblies, and suction assembly.

The on/off button assembly: The trim kit will probably include two plated air caps and two tapered trim caps. These adjust the on/off and whirlpool jet settings on the tub. To assemble:

1) Place a ring of RTV sealant around the base of the air control body as shown in Figure 8-12 A. Slip the tapered trim cap over the body until it fits onto the tub surface. Repeat this procedure for the other control.

2) Align the two holes on the bottom side of the dual-control air cap (whirlpool jets, on/off and high/low) with the two tabs on the actuator that can be depressed (Figure 8-12 B). Snap the dual-control air cap into place. You may need a small amount of force to attach the cap. See Figure 8-12 C.

3) Place the air cap (whirlpool jets, high/low) on the control that rotates but can't be depressed. Attach it the same way as you did the first control.

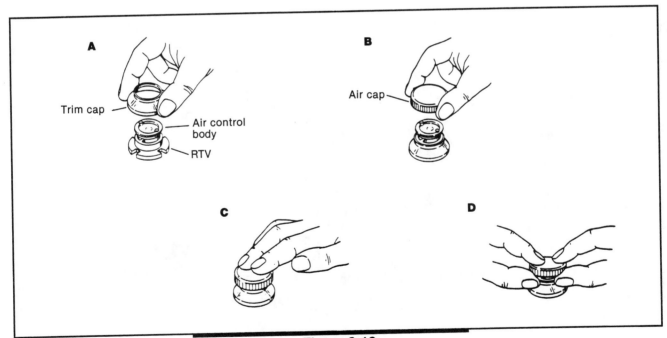

Figure 8-12
Installing the whirlpool trim kit
Courtesy: Kohler Company

4) If you need to remove the air caps for any reason, grip the cap gently but firmly with the ends of your fingers. Then pull up. See Figure 8-12 D.

The ball and retainer assemblies: Install these in the whirlpool jet housing one at a time:

1) Remove all dirt, grease, dust and moisture from the tub flanges. Disassemble the ball and retainer assembly. Carefully press the ball, retainer, and plastic bearing out of the trim ring. See Figure 8-13.

2) Apply a bead of RTV sealant to the edge of the trim ring as shown in Figure 8-13.

3) Carefully snap the trim ring into the flange on the tub. Make sure the dimples in the trim ring align with the notches in the flange. Fill any gaps between the bathtub wall and trim ring with RTV. Carefully remove any excess sealant from around the trim ring.

4) Remove the plastic bearing, ball, and O-ring from the inside of the retainer. Apply a light film of lubricant to the O-rings. Lubricant is usually shipped with the tub. Place the O-rings back in the retainer. Place the ball back into the retainer as well.

5) Apply a light film of lubricant to all surfaces of the plastic bearing. Reassemble the bearing into the ball and retainer assembly.

6) Apply a light film of lubricant to the O-ring on the outside of the retainer.

7) Insert the ball and retainer assembly into the jet housing on the tub. Be careful not to drop the plastic bearing into the housing.

8) Align the screw holes and fasten the retainer assembly with two of the phillips head screws provided. Tighten the screws until the ball moves freely from side to side with slight pressure.

9) Repeat the above steps for each of the remaining jets on the whirlpool tub.

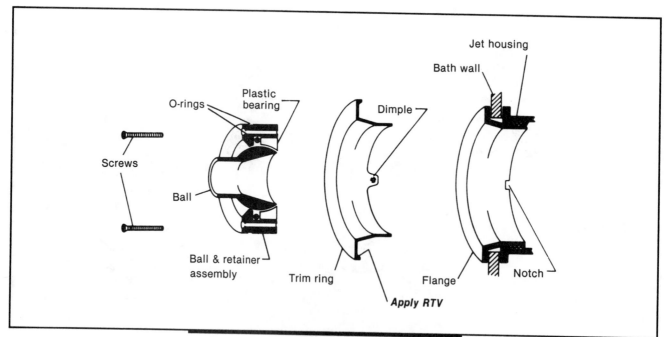

Figure 8-13
Ball and retainer assembly
Courtesy: Kohler Company

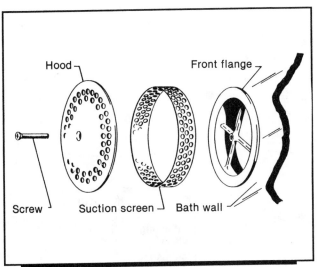

Figure 8-14
Suction assembly
Courtesy: Kohler Company

The suction assembly: To install the suction assembly (Figure 8-14), fit the suction screen into the groove on the back of the hood. Attach the screen and hood squarely to the front flange of the tub so the riveted portion of the suction screen faces downward. Secure the hood with a screw.

Installing the Drain Linkage

Assume you're using Clearflo drain linkage with the whirlpool tub. You may need to loosen the set screw on the linkage and adjust the linkage to the proper tub size. Begin by adjusting the block to 16 (Figure 8-15, Diagram A). Tighten the screw after you make the adjustment. Install the drain linkage as follows:

1) Insert the lift assembly (Figure 8-15, Diagram B) into the overflow. Tighten the overflow hood to the overflow ell with two screws. See the inset in the diagram.

2) Attach the dial assembly to the overflow hood with screws (Diagram C).

3) Insert the lift assembly into the drain hole in the tub (Diagram D). You may need to adjust the dial to the desired position.

4) The drain stopper should sit about 3/8 inch above the drain hole. If you need to make an adjustment, remove the stopper and loosen the nut below the stopper (Diagram E). Raise the stopper by turning it clockwise.

5) If you can't adjust the stopper for enough drain clearance, you'll have to remove the lift assembly. Loosen the adjusting screw on the linkage (Diagram F). Slide the adjusting block up to increase clearance, or down to decrease clearance. Tighten the adjusting screw and then reassemble the lift assembly.

6) Install the finish faucet trim according to the manufacturer's instructions, then clean up the tub area.

Never use an abrasive cleaner on the tub. It may scratch and dull the surface. Use warm water and a liquid detergent to clean the tub's surface after you complete the installation.

Installing a Fiberglass Shower Cove

You can make a bathroom more convenient by adding an attractive fiberglass shower cove. They're easier to install and take up less space than the larger tub/shower modules. The units fit through most standard door openings. However, take very careful measurements to make sure the unit you're installing fits into the area you're working. You may need to have it within the installation area before you complete the framing.

Preparation Tips

Protect fiberglass units before and after installation. Keep them wrapped in protective packaging until you're ready for installation. During installation, the shower floor protector will prevent abrasions and scratches on the finish. If you must store a unit outdoors, place it upside down to protect it from the elements. When you move the shower cove, avoid flexing the sidewalls to keep the radius from cracking.

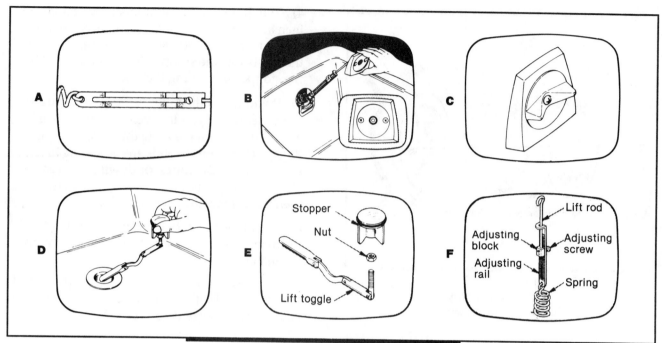

Figure 8-15
Drain linkage installation
Courtesy: Kohler Company

Provide access to plumbing connections: Before installation, plan your plumbing access. Consider these suggestions:

In locations where the plumbing is adjacent to a masonry wall, build a separate wall at least six inches in from the masonry wall. You can access connections through this space. See Figure 8-16. Install furring if the back of the unit is against the masonry wall.

If you're installing a unit on a slab at the corner of two outside walls, make your plumbing connections at the accessible end.

When units are installed back-to-back on a slab and against outside walls, access depends on the type of partition the units sit against. For wood partition construction, at least one unit should have an access. You can then reach the others through the accessible unit. In masonry or fire-rated partitions, each unit will need its own access.

When you're installing units on a slab in a cluster of four, back-to-back and end-to-end, build a

plumbing wall that gives access to all four units. Otherwise you have to make plumbing connections from an accessible end.

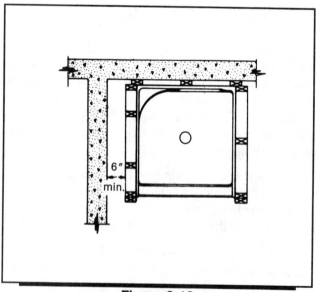

Figure 8-16
Construct a separate wall to access plumbing
Courtesy: Kohler Company

If you install a unit above a basement or anywhere drain connections are accessible from below, make your connection from beneath.

The base: Since the fiberglass shower cove is a single unit, you don't need to do hot mopping or provide a shower pan. There is no additional support needed under the basin area as long as you nail the unit securely into the recess.

The walls: If you're installing a shower cove adjacent to a vertical duct or chase, install fire-rated gypsum drywall around the unit. Whenever a fire-rated wall is specified, you must have it in place before installing the unit.

Also be sure to insulate exterior walls before installing the shower cove.

Framing

The fiberglass shower cove requires special framing. Follow the instructions here and the illustrations in Figure 8-17 for proper framing procedures.

Step 1: Construct the framing as shown in the illustration. The frame must be square and plumb. If you're installing grab bars, provide 2 by 6 bridging for their attachment. (See Step 10 for grab bars.)

Step 2: The illustration shows drain installations for both wood and concrete flooring. Locate the rough plumbing for the shower cove drain according to the dimensions specified in the manufacturer's instructions. Notice the opening required in the subfloor for the drain fittings. The 2-inch waste pipe extends 7/8 inch above the subfloor or slab. In slab construction, you must have a pocket to accommodate the drain fitting.

Step 3: Position the rough plumbing for the supply, but don't strap it. Where you have limited access to supply fitting connections, consider using soft copper tubing as a riser between the valve and supply line. Connect the supply fitting and riser before positioning the unit. The soft tubing can be bent into position for the supply fitting and shower arm after the unit's in place.

Install the shower drain fitting in the unit's drain outlet using a non-hardening mastic sealant. Use a sealant that meets code requirements.

Step 4: On the outside of the unit, lay out the location of all fitting holes. Using a quarter-inch drill, make the pilot holes from the outside of the unit.

For multiple installations where you've located supply fittings accurately during rough plumbing, use a template to mark pilot holes in each unit. Make the template out of 3/8" plywood.

Step 5: Working from the finished face of the unit, enlarge the pilot holes with a keyhole saw.

Step 6: Clean the framed recess thoroughly and set the unit squarely into the pocket of the subfloor or slab. Make sure it fits evenly over the drain pipe extension. Plumb the front and side nailing-in flanges and level the rim of the unit. You may need to shim the unit to level it. Shower cove units are plumb and level when you install them properly. You may need to make some framing adjustments due to variations in the cove widths or framing.

Before nailing, always check to see that the nailing-in flanges are pressed firmly against the wall studs. This will help prevent the unit from moving while you nail it into place. Using No. 6 large-head galvanized nails, fasten the back wall nailing flange to the wall studs. Attach the side wall nailing flanges the same way. Then nail the front vertical nailing flanges to the studs on 8-inch centers. Be careful to avoid damaging the unit. I suggest that you pre-drill the holes in the flange before nailing it. This will prevent buckling. (In metal stud construction, drill the holes through the nailing-in flanges and metal studs, then secure them with sheet metal screws.)

Step 7: Caulk and lead the drain. Plug it and test for leaks.

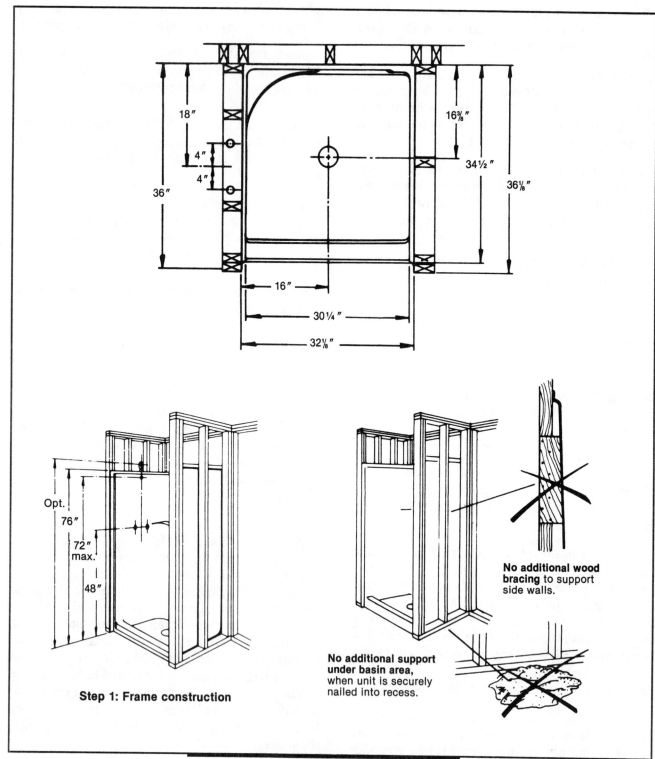

Figure 8-17
Installing a shower cove unit
Courtesy: Kohler Company

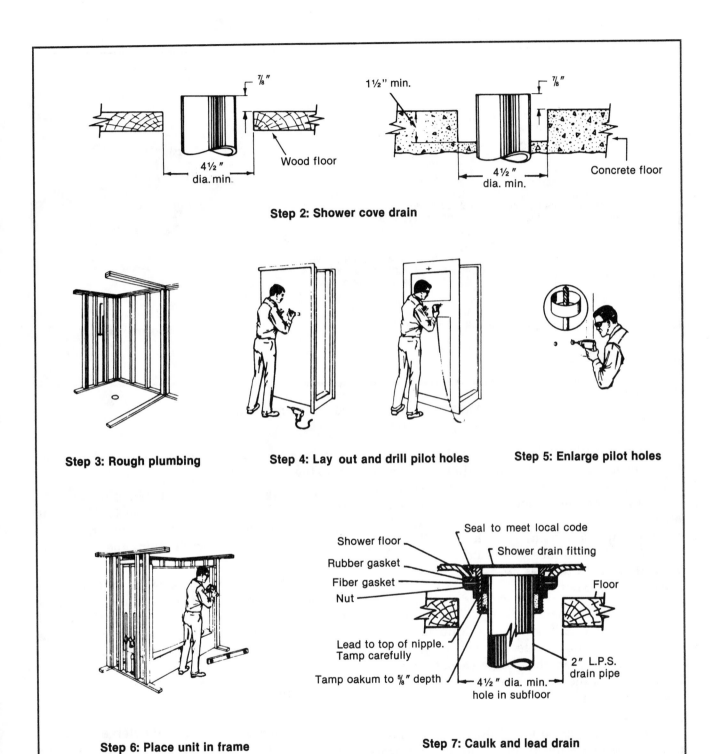

Figure 8-17
Installing a shower cove unit (continued)
Courtesy: Kohler Company

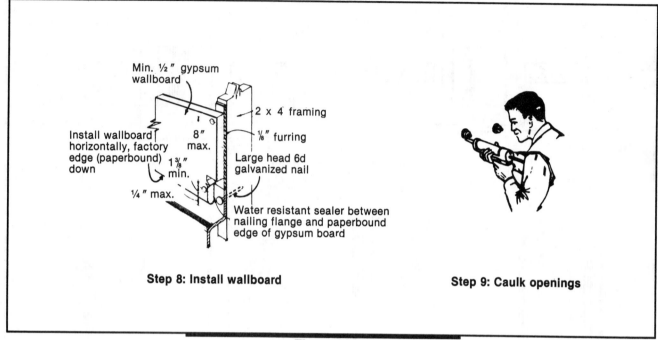

Figure 8-17
Installing a shower cove unit (continued)
Courtesy: Kohler Company

Step 8: Apply 1/8-inch-thick furring strips to the studs to insure your wallboard installation is true and level. Next, apply a water-resistant sealer to the nailing flange. Install the wallboard horizontally. The factory (paperbound) edge should be no more than 1/4 inch above the horizontal finished surface of the unit. Extend the wallboard out at least as far as the next stud on each side of the unit.

Fur the vertical nailing flanges. Then seal the wallboard to the nailing-in flange. Mud, tape, and finish the wallboard true and level. After you apply the finish, seal the area between the paperbound edge of the wallboard and the unit with a water-resistant sealer.

Step 9: Strap the supply fittings. Caulk all the openings around the fittings and shower arm with a water-resistant sealer.

Step 10: Install the finish trim. You can install the grab bars or towel bars through the cove walls and fasten them directly to the bridging. Secure the grab bars with the proper screws, bolts, and backing.

You can also attach the grab bars directly to the shower cove. But be sure to use the fastening device suggested by the manufacturer. Always follow the manufacturer's guidelines when installing grab bars.

Install the shower rod above the unit and position it so the shower curtain will hang inside the dam. Follow the manufacturer's installation instructions if you're putting in a shower enclosure.

Clean-Up

Use warm water and a liquid detergent to clean the surface of the shower cove. Again, don't use abrasive cleaners.

You can remove stubborn stains, paint or tar with turpentine or paint thinner. Remove plaster by scraping with a wood edge. Don't use metal scrapers, wire brushes or other metal tools. A powdered detergent and a damp cloth provide enough mild abrasive action to take off residual plaster.

Restore the finish to dulled areas by rubbing them with a liquid cleaning compound. Use the same kind you would use on automobile bodies. Follow with a light application of liquid wax. Figure 8-18 shows a finished shower cove installation.

Fiberglass Tub and Shower Units

The procedure is the same when installing a fiberglass tub and shower module. Figure 8-19 shows the details you need for framing and installing the module. Provide an access panel to the drain connections and water supply pipes for servicing.

Figure 8-18
Completed shower cove installation
Courtesy: Kohler Company

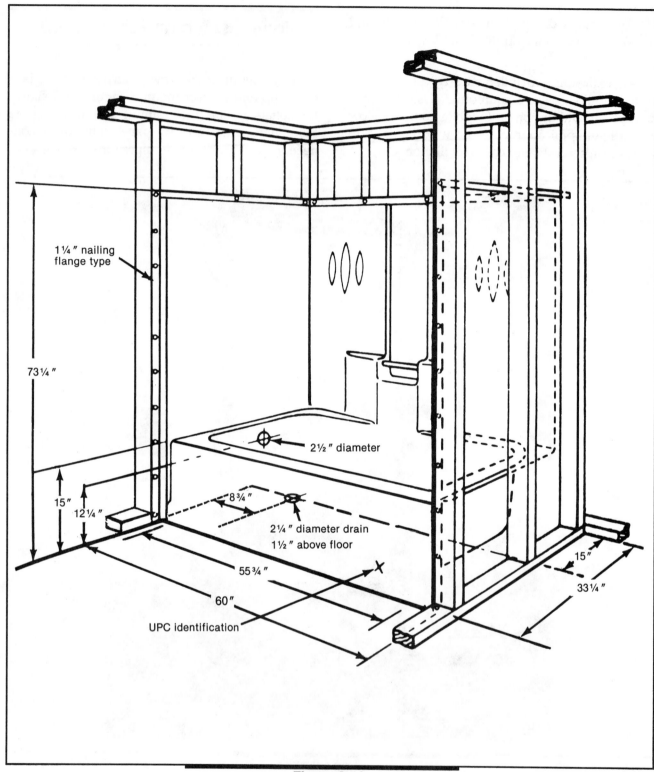

1¼″ nailing
flange type

73¼″

2½″ diameter

15″

12¼″

8¾″

2¼″ diameter drain
1½″ above floor

55¾″

X

60″

15″

33¼″

UPC identification

Figure 8-19
Framing and installation of a tub/shower unit

Installing the Toilet

Let's say you're going to install a Kohler low-profile, one-piece toilet (Model K-3397-EB) for your client. You're probably experienced enough to know that you must be very careful when you work with vitreous china products. If not, let this be a warning — vitreous china breaks and chips easily if you overtighten the bolts or handle it carelessly.

Tools and Materials

You'll need the following tools for installing a toilet:

- A 10-inch adjustable wrench
- A 12-inch pipe wrench
- A metal file (fine cut)
- Tape measure
- Level
- Tubing cutter
- Hacksaw
- Putty knife
- Screwdriver

You'll need the following materials for your toilet installation:

- Toilet setting compound
- Toilet gasket
- Toilet seat
- Toilet T-bolts (2)
- Toilet supply shut-off valve

The Installation

This Kohler toilet needs a full 1/2 inch ID water supply. The water supply tubing should be 2-5/8 inches above the floor and 6-1/2 inches to the left of the centerline. The toilet needs 25 psi of running pressure at the shut-off valve. See Figure 8-20, Diagram A for installation dimensions. Use the following steps to install the toilet, but always follow local codes if their requirements are different from these instructions.

1) To remove the old toilet, turn the water off at the shut-off valve or at the water meter. Flush the toilet and sponge out the remaining water from the tank and bowl.

2) Disconnect the coupling nut from the water supply that comes from the wall or through the floor. Remove the tank from toilet bowl, as in Diagram B.

3) Pry off the bolt caps at the base of the toilet (see the inset in Diagram C). Unscrew the nuts from the bolts that secure the bowl to the floor. Lift the bowl by the sides to remove it from the floor. A rocking motion, as shown in Diagram C, will help dislodge the toilet from the floor flange.

4) Remove the old gasket from the floor and closet flange with a putty knife (Diagram D) and discard it. If you won't be installing the new toilet immediately, stuff a rag in the closet flange to keep sewer gas out of the room.

If the floor needs repairing, make the repairs and install any new flooring before you set the new toilet. If you raise the level of the floor, add a collar to the soil stack. Now is the time to make any changes or add on plumbing that you'll need to mate the soil stack with the new toilet.

5) Install new T-bolts as shown in Diagram E. Temporarily set the new toilet over the closet flange. Align the T-bolts with the holes at the base of the toilet.

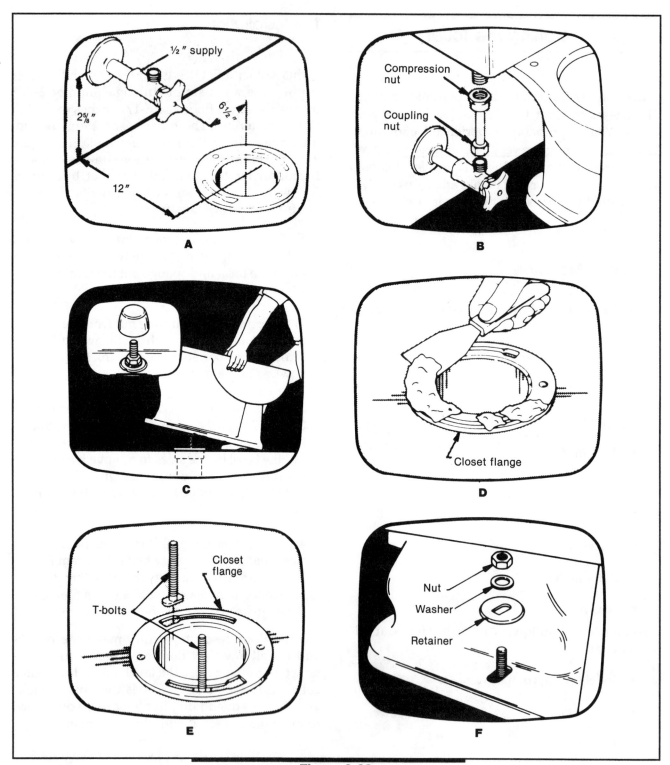

Figure 8-20
Toilet installation
Courtesy: Kohler Company

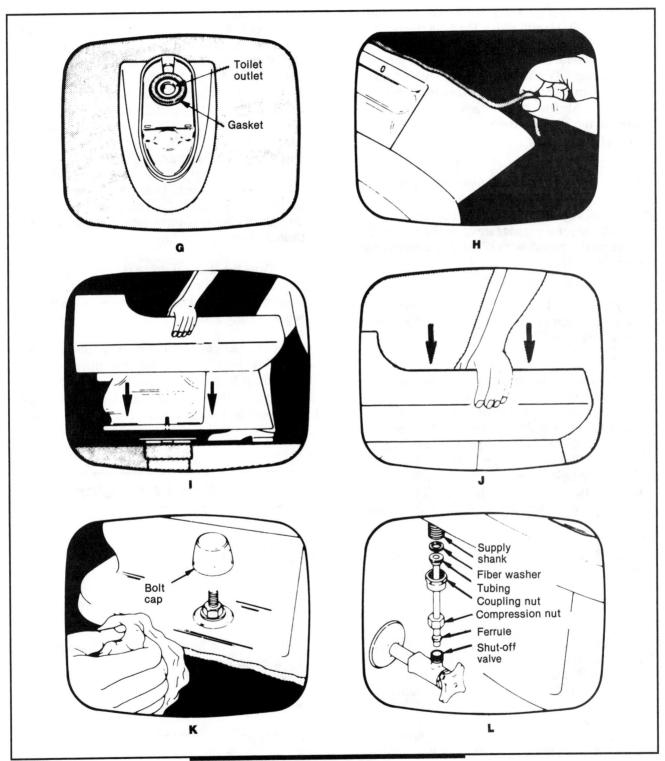

Figure 8-20
Toilet installation (continued)
Courtesy: Kohler Company

6) Place a retainer and washer over each bolt (Diagram F). Hand tighten the nuts. Mark the bolts 1/4 inch from top of the nut. Remove the nuts, washers, retainer, and toilet from the closet flange. Remove the T-bolts and thread the nuts onto them. Cut the bolts off at the mark and file the rough edges. Once again, remove the nuts. Replace the T-bolts in the closet flange.

7) Place the toilet upside down on a pad or throw rug. Firmly place a gasket on the toilet outlet, as in Diagram G. If you use a gasket with an integral plastic sleeve, make sure you position the gasket with the sleeve facing *away* from the toilet.

8) Place a bead of toilet setting compound, about 1/8 inch thick, evenly around the base of the toilet. See Diagram H.

9) Remove the rag or any other obstruction from the closet flange before setting the toilet in place. Carefully lower the toilet onto the closet flange, aligning the holes in the base with the T-bolts, as shown in Diagram I. Be sure the toilet sits squarely over the closet flange and bolt holes. If you have to lift the toilet off the floor to realign it, you'll have to apply a new gasket to ensure an adequate seal.

10) Apply your full body weight to the rim of the toilet to set the seal (Diagram J). But *don't rock the toilet* — that would break the watertight seal.

11) Assemble the retainers, washers, and nuts over the exposed T-bolts (Look back to Diagram F). Hand tighten the nuts, then tighten them 1/2 turn more with a wrench.

12) Remove the excess setting compound from around the base. Wipe off any wax, setting compound, or dirt from the area around the bolts. Then snap on the caps (See Diagram K).

13) To connect the water supply, remove the coupling nut from the supply shank. Carefully bend the tubing to fit between the supply shank and the shut-off valve. Using a tubing cutter, cut the tube 1/4 inch longer than the connecting distance. Remove any burrs from inside the tubing. Slip the coupling nut, compression nut, and ferrule onto the tubing. Insert the cut end of the tubing into the shut-off valve and the other end into the supply shank. Tighten the coupling nut first, but don't overtighten. Don't use pipe sealant on the supply shank. Complete the assembly by tightening the compression nut. (Diagram L illustrates this procedure.)

14) Turn the shut-off valve on and check for leaks. If the pipe connections are squarely assembled, a slight retightening of the nuts will stop any leaks.

You can also get flexible hose with factory-assembled fittings for easy water supply hook ups. It's good for both hot and cold lines, and requires no cutting or flaring. It comes in various lengths for commode, lavatory, and sink installations.

Installing the Lavatory

Let's say your clients want a Kohler self-rimming lavatory in their main bathroom.

Tools and Materials

You'll need the following tools for installing a self-rimming lavatory:

- Putty knife
- A 10-inch adjustable wrench
- Saber or keyhole saw
- A 12-inch pipe wrench
- Tubing cutter
- Screwdriver

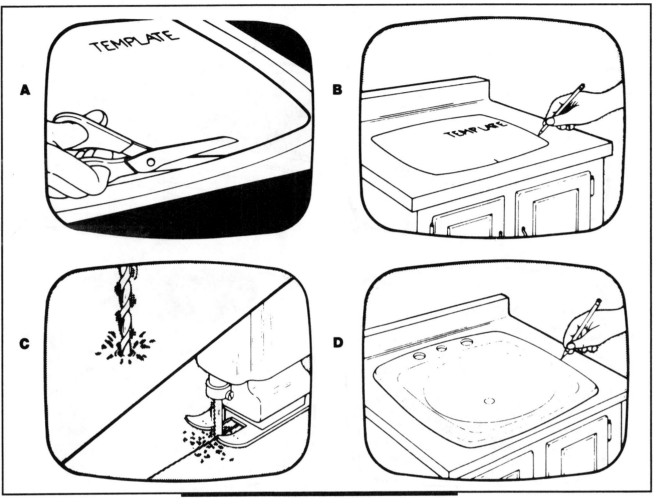

Figure 8-21
Lavatory installation
Courtesy: Kohler Company

- Hacksaw
- Ruler
- Drill
- A 1/2-inch drill bit
- Scissors

You'll also need the following materials for installation:

- Polyseam seal
- Plumber's putty
- Faucet unit
- Shut-off valves

The Installation

Before you begin installing the lavatory, make sure it fits correctly into the vanity cabinet. It shouldn't keep drawers and cabinet doors from opening and closing properly. If it doesn't fit, you'll need a smaller lavatory — one designed especially for narrow countertops.

1) You'll need a template as an aid in making the cutout for the lavatory. Cut the template to the size you need for the opening, as shown in Figure 8-21, Diagram A.

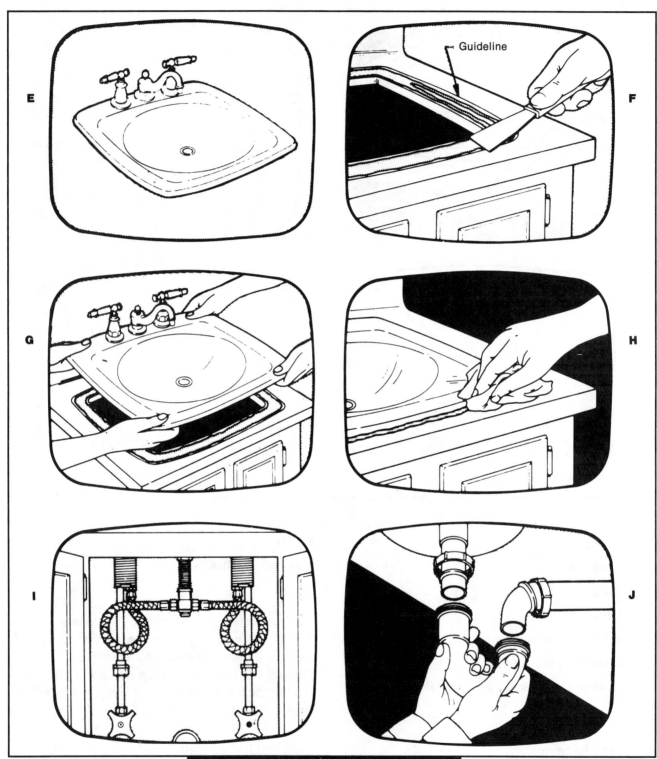

Figure 8-21
Lavatory installation (continued)
Courtesy: Kohler Company

2) Trace the template onto the countertop using a soft lead pencil. See Diagram B. Templates have the centerlines marked to help you align the opening.

3) Before you make a cutout in a new countertop, use a 1/2-inch drill to make a pilot hole. Then use a saber or keyhole saw to cut out the opening. Carefully follow the pencil line traced from the template, as shown in Diagram C. If you're installing the lavatory in a ceramic tile countertop, make the opening during the tile installation.

4) Temporarily place the lavatory in the opening and adjust it for exact positioning. Lightly trace a pencil line around the outside edge of the lavatory (Diagram D). This line will be your guide when you apply the polyseam seal. Then remove the lavatory from the countertop.

5) Assemble the faucet and drain to the lavatory, following the manufacturer's instructions. See Diagram E.

6) Apply two ribbons of polyseam seal on the countertop, between the edge of the opening and the guideline you just traced. Spread the seal evenly with a putty knife as shown in Diagram F. Polyseam sets up in a few minutes, so spread it quickly.

7) Carefully place the lavatory in the countertop opening. Use the guide line to position it properly, as in Diagram G. Press it firmly into the polyseam seal.

8) Immediately remove the excess polyseam seal with a damp cloth (Diagram H). Fill any voids in the joint if necessary.

9) Allow the polyseam seal to set 30 minutes before connecting the supply lines and drain. When you connect the lines and drain, be careful not to move the lavatory out of position. Connect the water supply lines the same way as described in step 13 for the toilet installation. Your completed connections should look like Diagram I.

10) Connect the drain pipe and trap to the fixture and the wall outlet, as shown in Diagram J. Turn the tailpiece into the drain body. Align the trap inlet with the tailpiece and insert the tailpiece into the trap. You may have to cut the tailpiece to fit; it should extend only 1 to 2 inches into the trap.

11) Turn on the water and check for leaks at the supply and drain connections. Tighten the nuts to stop any leaks.

12) Clean up after you finish installation, but don't use abrasive cleaners on new fixtures. Use only warm water and a non-abrasive liquid detergent to clean a new lavatory.

The Pedestal Lavatory

The following instructions are for installing a pedestal lavatory in a bathroom with frame-type construction. If you don't have frame-type construction, you'll have to supply suitable bracing and fastening devices to support the unit. Make sure they're strong enough for the weight of the lavatory.

Installation Instructions

We'll assume that the wall and floor where you're working are both square and plumb. Figure 8-22 shows the top and front view of a standard pedestal lavatory. Follow along in this figure as I describe the work.

1) Rough in the supplies and drain pipe according to the manufacturer's dimensions. Be sure to follow the plumbing code that applies.

2) Install enough backing behind the finished wall to support hangers and anchoring devices.

3) Install hangers according to roughing-in dimensions. The hangers may have to be repositioned later to compensate for slight variations in china.

4) Before installing the lavatory, attach the supply and drain fittings.

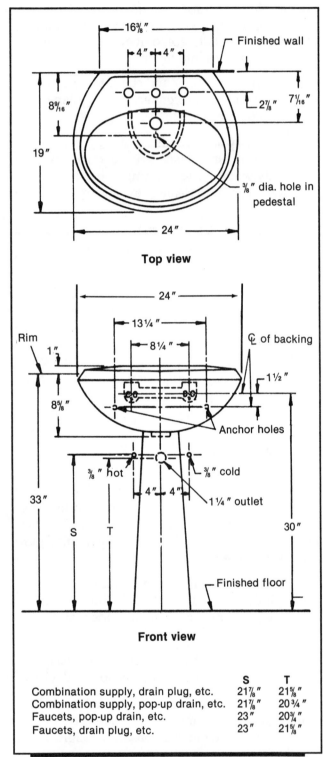

Top view

Front view

	S	T
Combination supply, drain plug, etc.	21⅞"	21⅝"
Combination supply, pop-up drain, etc.	21⅞"	20¾"
Faucets, pop-up drain, etc.	23"	20¾"
Faucets, drain plug, etc.	23"	21⅝"

Figure 8-22
Installation instructions for pedestal lavatory
Courtesy: Kohler Company

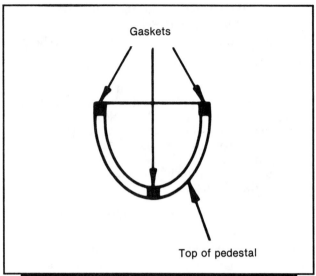

Figure 8-23
Installation of pedestal lavatory
Courtesy: Kohler Company

5) Install the trap so the inlet is 7-1/8 inches from the finished wall. Slip the 1-1/4inch O.D. drain tailpiece into the trap.

6) Place the pedestal so the mounting hole is about 8-9/16 inches from the finished wall.

7) Apply the self-adhesive gaskets provided with the unit to the top edge of the pedestal, as shown in Figure 8-23.

8) Carefully position the lavatory over the hanger and the pedestal. Move the pedestal slightly, if necessary, to be sure that it sets properly in place. If the bottom of the lavatory makes direct contact with the china on the top edge of the pedestal, use more gaskets to shim and protect the base. The lavatory must be supported by both the hanger and the pedestal. Check and make sure you have proper drain alignment and the lavatory is level. *Note*: Because of variations in china, you may have to raise or lower the hanger slightly. The lavatory must contact the wall evenly and rest firmly on the pedestal.

9) Mark the centers of the anchoring holes for the lavatory and the pedestal.

10) Remove the lavatory and pedestal. Drill holes for the 1/4-inch lag bolts and washers you need to secure the lavatory to the backing. (You may need to use other fastening devices for installation in a home that doesn't have frame construction. Make sure they're long enough and strong enough for the unit.) Drill the hole for attaching the pedestal to the floor.

11) Place the pedestal and lavatory back into their mounting position. Install the 1/4-inch lag bolts and washers, and secure the lavatory to the wall. Attach the pedestal to the floor in the same way. Tighten the bolts carefully, leaving them about a half turn loose.

12) Connect the hot and cold supplies to the fitting. Then connect the 1-1/4 inch O.D. tailpiece to the drain body. Secure the trap connections, and your installation is complete.

Figure 8-24 shows how your finished pedestal lavatory installation should look.

Integral Vanity Tops and Bowls (ITB)

I've found that many clients prefer molded one-piece vanity tops. See Figure 8-25. They're available in several popular lengths, with single or double bowls. The bowls come in several sizes and can be located in several positions in the countertop. You can even order them with standard pre-drilled faucet holes. All the tops include hole-drill templates, installation instructions, and a separate 2-7/8-inch backsplash. You can also order side splashes and front aprons if you need them with your installation.

Dimensions

Figure 8-26 gives you the width dimensions and bowl sizes for countertops. Typical mounting installations are shown in Figure 8-27.

Figure 8-24
Finished pedestal lavatory installation
Courtesy: Kohler Company

One-piece countertops are usually made to a tolerance of plus or minus 1/8 inch. Check any close fits between the front edge and overflow tubes, and the back edge and faucet holes before installing support frames or cabinetry.

Installation

Installation of one-piece bathroom vanity tops is the same as for kitchen countertops. Check Chapter 5 for details. Remember, the maximum allowable unsupported distance between support

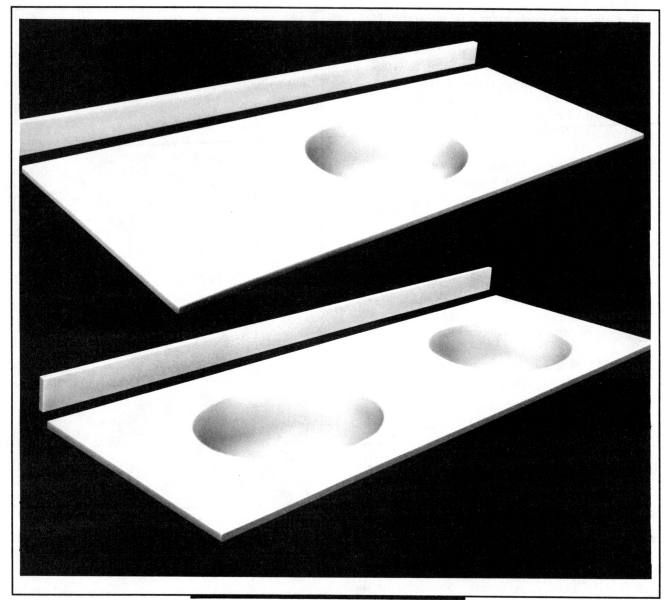

Figure 8-25
Corian integral vanity tops and bowls
Courtesy: DuPont Co., Inc.

members is 24 inches. Be sure to stud mount all brackets.

For bathrooms, set the backsplash and sidesplash using mildew-resistant, color-compatible silicone sealant. It should be available from the distributor who supplies the tops you use. Remove excess silicone with a putty knife or caulk-remover tool. Wipe the seam clean with denatured alcohol.

If the top doesn't have pre-drilled faucet holes, use the template provided to mark their locations. Drill the holes using a router or a high-speed electric drill. Attach either a spade bit, twist drill or hole saw to the drill. Don't use auger bits.

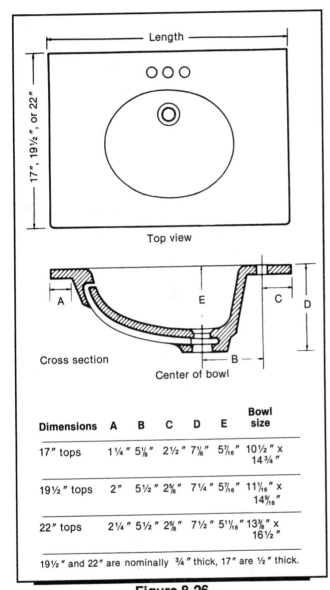

Figure 8-26
Bowl specifications for Corian integral vanity tops
Courtesy: DuPont Co., Inc

Dimensions	A	B	C	D	E	Bowl size
17″ tops	1 1/4 ″	5 5/8 ″	2 1/2 ″	7 1/8 ″	5 7/16 ″	10 1/2 ″ x 14 3/4 ″
19 1/2 ″ tops	2 ″	5 1/2 ″	2 5/8 ″	7 1/4 ″	5 7/16 ″	11 1/16 ″ x 14 9/16 ″
22 ″ tops	2 1/4 ″	5 1/2 ″	2 5/8 ″	7 1/2 ″	5 11/16 ″	13 3/8 ″ x 16 1/2 ″

19 1/2 ″ and 22″ are nominally ³⁄₄ ″ thick, 17″ are ½ ″ thick.

Install the faucets and drain fittings according to the manufacturer's instructions. Don't overtighten the fittings.

Cultured marble integral vanity tops and bowls are also available in most areas. They come with a molded backsplash and pre-drilled faucet and drain holes. Install them the same way as any one-piece top.

Electric Wall Heaters

Electric wall heaters provide extra heat in a bathroom. If your clients want or need more heat in a new or existing bathroom, an electric wall heater is usually the best choice. They range from 1,000 watts to 4,000 watts. The size you recommend depends on the size of the bathroom, climate and insulation values built into the home.

I'll assume you're installing a NuTone wall heater, model 9819. It's a 120-240 volt heater with 1,920 total watts. Dimensions are:

Housing: 12-1/2 inches high by 10-1/2 inches wide by 3-3/8 inches deep.

Grille: 14-3/4 inches high by 11-9/16 inches wide by 1 inch deep.

Wall cutout: 12-5/8 inches high by 10-5/8 inches wide.

Mounting the Housing

Mount the wall heater vertically at least 6 inches above the finish floor. To reduce the fire hazard, don't locate the heater closer than 12 inches to an adjacent wall or behind a door. And, no matter how limited the bathroom wall space is, don't place towel racks above a wall heater. And never mount a bathroom heater over a bathtub or in a shower stall enclosure.

1) Choose the heater location.

2) If you have access from both sides of the stud wall, mount one side of the housing to a stud, as shown in Figure 8-28 A. Position the flange flush to the stud.

3) In existing construction, make a wall cutout next to a stud. It should be 12-5/8 inches high by 10-5/8 inches wide. See Figure 8-28 B.

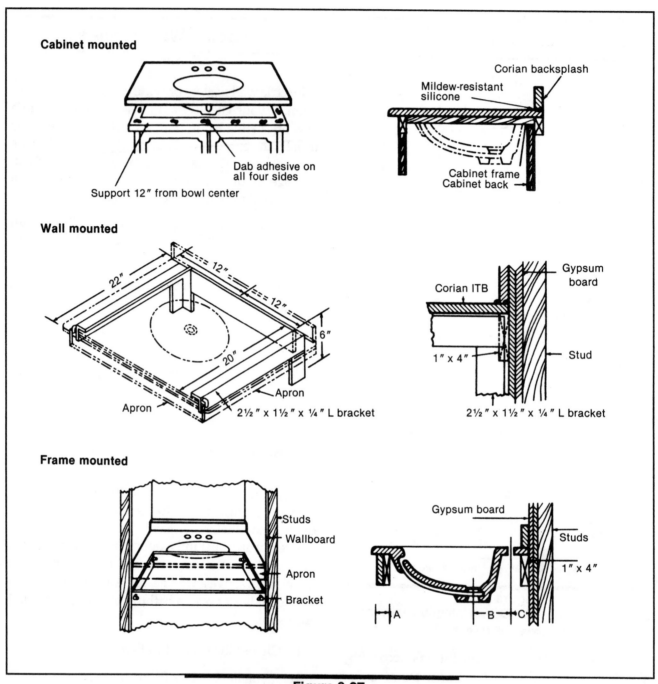

Figure 8-27
Corian integral vanity top installation alternatives
Courtesy: DuPont Co., Inc

4) Run wiring from the circuit breaker or fuse box to the heater location. Make sure the wire size meets code requirements.

5) Install a box connector into the wiring entrance hole in the housing junction box.

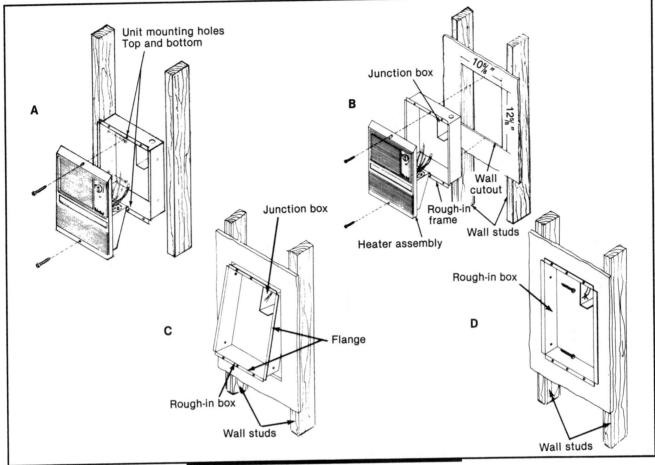

Figure 8-28
Installing electric wall heater housing
Courtesy: NuTone, Inc.

6) Pull the wiring through the cutout and secure the cable to the box connector. Allow 6 inches of wiring to make the connections.

7) Insert the top of the housing into the cutout first, so the box connectors clear the wall. See Figure 8-28 C. Then insert the bottom of the housing into the cutout. The housing frame should be flush with the wall.

8) Use screws to fasten the housing to the wall stud as shown in Figure 8-28 D.

Wiring Connection

You can wire the heater for either 20 amps/120 volts or 15 amps/240 volts. You need a separate circuit for either wiring method. All wiring must follow local code, and the unit must be properly grounded.

1) Support the heater assembly on the bottom of the rough-in frame while you make the wiring connections.

2) For 120-volt wiring, make the connections as shown in Figure 8-29 A.

3) For 240-volt wiring, make the connections as shown in Figure 8-29 B.

4) Use wire nuts to make all the connections, and insulate them with electrical tape.

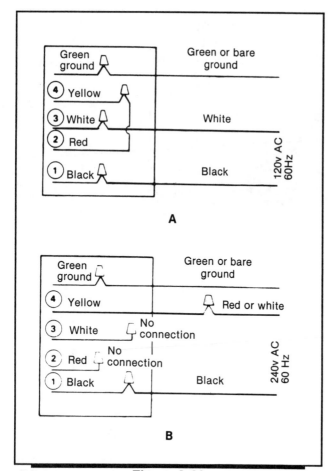

Figure 8-29
Wiring connections for electric wall heater
Courtesy: NuTone, Inc.

Securing the Heater

1) Thread all wiring back into the junction box.

2) Locate the center holes in the housing flange and line them up with the mounting holes in the grille.

3) Use two screws to attach the grille to the housing, as shown in Figure 8-30.

Operation

Turn the thermostat control clockwise to the high position. Allow the heater to run until the room is at the temperature you wish. Adjust the

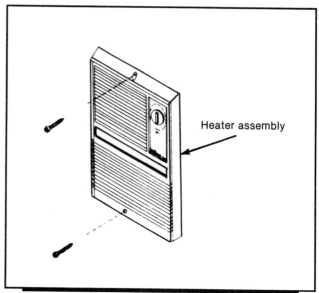

Figure 8-30
Securing wall heater
Courtesy: NuTone, Inc.

thermostat as needed to maintain the temperature. Turn the heat off by turning the thermostat control fully counter-clockwise.

Installing the Exhaust Fan

I recommend installing an exhaust fan in every bathroom you remodel, even if the bathroom has a window. People prefer to keep windows closed in cold weather, so the exhaust fan is needed.

Let's say your customer wants you to install a NuTone bathroom exhaust fan/light combination unit. The model number is 8663. The unit consists of the housing, power unit/blower assembly (motor, wheel, mounting plate), grille, reflector/lamp socket assembly, and duct collar. See Figure 8-31.

The units dimensions are:

Housing: 9 inches long by 9 inches wide by 5-1/2 inches deep.

Housing bottom rim: 13-1/8 inches in diameter.

Grille: 14-1/2 inches in diameter.

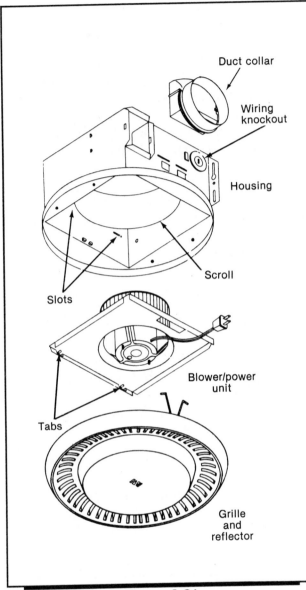

Figure 8-31
Assembly for ceiling exhaust fan with light
Courtesy: NuTone, Inc.

Installation in a New Ceiling

If you're remodeling a bathroom, install the unit housing before installing the finish ceiling. You can install the blower unit and grille after the finish ceiling is in place. If you aren't making changes involving the ceiling, we'll also discuss installation in an existing ceiling.

Plan the ductwork: Ducting will run from the discharge opening of the fan to the exterior. For the most efficient fan performance, make the duct run as short as possible and use a minimum number of elbows. Use 4-inch round duct for your installation. You can use flexible pipe with optional accessories such as caps, roof caps, and elbows.

Plan the wiring: Use a 120 volt circuit with a ground from your power source. Run it through the wall switch and into the junction box in the fan housing. If you want separate controls for the light and fan, use the optional NuTone model VS-86 switch.

Disassemble the unit: Follow Figure 8-31 as I describe how to disassemble the unit.

1) Remove the blower/power unit assembly from the housing.

2) Unplug the blower/power unit.

3) Remove the screw (located next to the plug-in receptacle) holding the blower/power unit mounting in place. Save the screw.

4) Lift the mounting plate at the end, near the plug-in receptacle, until the blower wheel clears the scroll.

5) Remove the plate by pulling its tabs out of the slots in the housing. Set the blower/power unit aside until it's needed.

6) Remove one of the wiring knockouts from the housing.

Mount the housing: You can mount the housing with tabs or on hanger bars.

Mounting with tabs—

1) Locate the fan housing next to the ceiling joist.

2) Loosely attach the housing to the ceiling joist. Use a wood screw to make the attachment through the keyhole slots in the mounting tabs. See Figure 8-32 A.

3) Adjust the housing so it'll be flush with finish ceiling. For the grille to fit properly, the housing rim shouldn't extend beyond the ceiling surface.

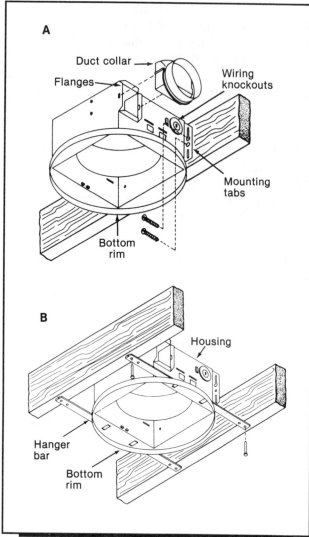

Figure 8-32
Mounting the housing
Courtesy: NuTone, Inc.

2) Insert the hanger bars through the mounting tabs located on the bottom rim of the housing. Nail one bar to the joists. See Figure 8-32 B.

3) Slide the housing to the desired location between the joists, then nail the second hanger bar to the joists. Note that the housing will have no vertical adjustment. The rim extends 1/2 inch below the hanger bars.

Install the ductwork: You've already planned the run. Now make the installation.

1) Place the duct collar over the flanges at the discharge opening of the fan. Secure the collar by snapping the tabs into the slots in the flanges. See Figure 8-32 A.

2) Run 4-inch round duct from the fan discharge opening to the outside and terminate it as shown in Figure 8-33.

3) Connect the duct to the fan duct collar.

Wiring: Be sure all wiring complies with local code, and that the unit is grounded.

1) Run a 120 volt circuit with a ground from the wall switch to the fan.

2) Install a box connector into the wiring entrance hole.

3) Pull the wires through the box connector and into the junction box. Tighten the box connector, but don't overtighten on the wiring.

4) When you've adjusted the housing for the ceiling finish thickness, tighten the screws in the slots.

5) Permanently secure the fan housing to the joist with screws through the center holes in the mounting tabs.

Mounting with hanger bars—

1) If the joists are spaced 24 inches apart, use the hanger extension sleeve. For 16-inch spaced joists, you can discard the extension sleeve.

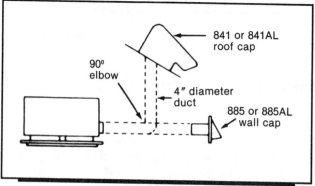

Figure 8-33
Duct installation
Courtesy: NuTone, Inc.

4) If you're installing a single switch for both the fan and the light, make the wiring connections as shown in Figure 8-34 A. If you're using a double switch for separate control of the fan and the light, make your connections as shown in Figure 8-34 B.

5) Connect the green (or bare) ground wire to the green ground screw.

Install the power/blower unit: See Figure 8-35.

1) Place the power/blower unit into the housing so the mounting plate tabs insert into the slots in the housing.

2) Press the other end of the mounting plate until it's firmly seated over the scroll and plug-in receptacles.

3) Secure the mounting plate to the housing with a screw.

4) Insert the motor plug into the junction box receptacle (Figure 8-35).

Install the lamp: Figure 8-36 shows lamp installation.

1) Loosen the retaining screw securing the lamp socket bracket to the reflector.

2) Remove the lamp socket through the hole in the reflector.

3) Install a lamp (100 watt maximum) in the socket.

4) Replace the lamp socket bracket in the slot. Tighten the screw.

5) Insert the light plug into the junction box receptacle.

Install the grille: Squeezing the grille mounting springs together, insert the springs into the tabs on both sides of the housing. See Figure 8-37. Press the grille firmly into place against the ceiling.

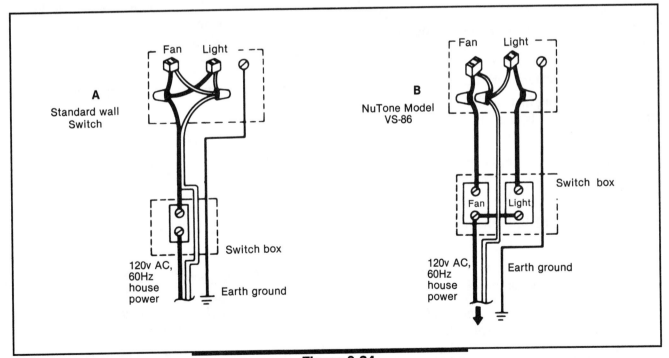

Figure 8-34
Wall switch connections for exhaust fan and light
Courtesy: NuTone, Inc.

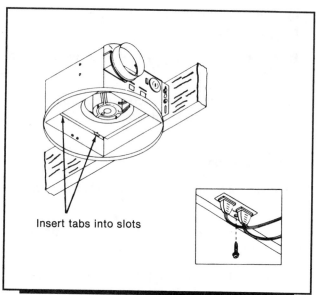

Figure 8-35
Install power/blower unit
Courtesy: NuTone, Inc.

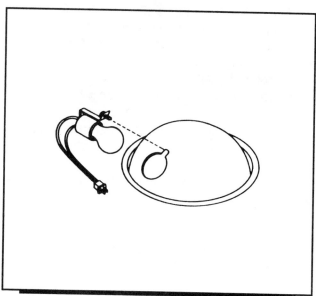

Figure 8-36
Install light
Courtesy: NuTone, Inc.

Hanging the Fan in an Existing Ceiling

Inspect the area where you're planning the installation. Make sure there's either space for proper venting above, or at least enough area to install ducting. Also be sure you can run wiring to the location, and that no other wiring or obstruction will interfere with the unit.

Use the following instructions as a guide. Much of the installation is the same as we have just discussed.

1) You must mount the fan between ceiling joists. Decide where you want to locate the fan, then find the nearest joist.

2) Drill a starter hole in the ceiling between the joists.

3) Saw a line from the hole to the joist to locate the exact edge of the joist.

4) Remove the power/blower unit from the housing, as previously described.

5) Use the housing pan as a template to mark the cutout. Center the pan between the joists and trace around the pan.

6) Make your cutout along the outside of the line.

7) Install 2 x 4 cleats to both ceiling joists. In some cases you may need more than a single cleat on one side. There must be no more than 9-1/2 to 10 inches between cleats. See Figure 8-38.

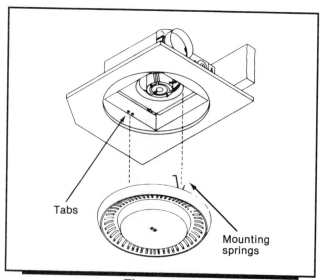

Tabs

Mounting springs

Figure 8-37
Install grille
Courtesy: NuTone, Inc.

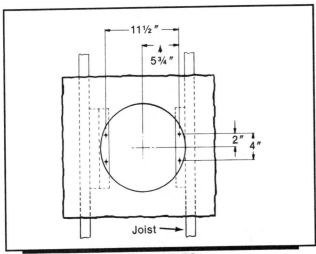

Figure 8-38
Install cleats to ceiling joists
Courtesy: NuTone, Inc.

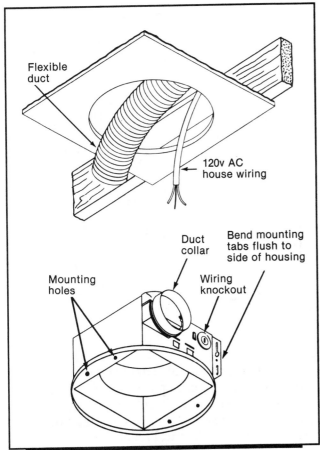

Figure 8-39
Installation in an existing ceiling
Courtesy: NuTone, Inc.

8) Remove the side wiring knockout and insert and secure the box connector into the wiring entrance hole.

9) Using pliers, bend both mounting tabs to the side of the housing. Make sure they're flush with the housing.

10) Install the duct collar.

11) Pull the wire through the box connector and connect the 4-inch flexible duct to the duct collar.

12) Carefully push the ductwork and the wiring back into the cutout. Slide the housing into the cutout. See Figure 8-39.

13) Use wood screws to secure the housing to the cleats through the four holes in the housing pan. Make sure the pan is flush to the finish ceiling.

14) Install the power/blower unit. Complete the installation as previously described.

Wall Mounted Hair Dryer

Hair dryers have become a popular bathroom remodeling appliance. Installing a unit on the wall keeps the hair dryer available, yet out of the way. It's an ideal accessory for people who don't like clutter or those who have a shortage of storage space. I'll describe installing a NuTone, Model HD-100 in your client's bathroom.

The Installation

Mount the unit so the base is approximately 5-1/2 feet above the floor. Installing the hair dryer at this level will reduce the wear on the hose. Your client will be pulling straight out or down on the handle of the hose instead of up. This minimizes stress on the connection and keeps the hose from kinking. See Figure 8-40 A.

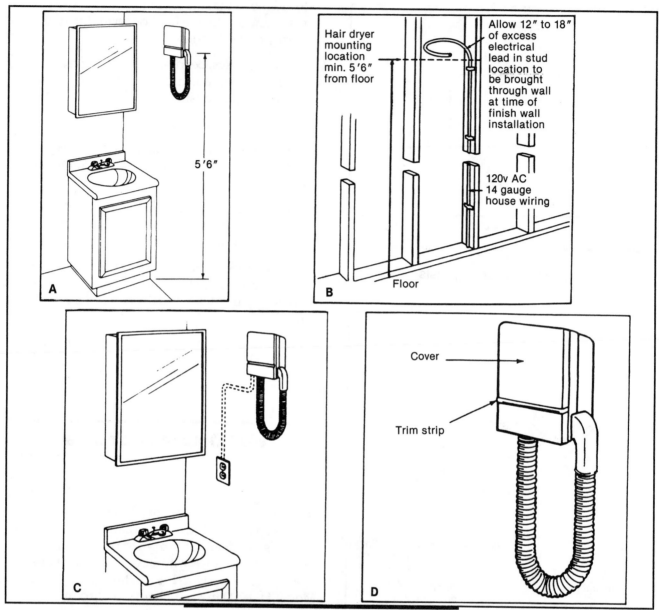

Figure 8-40
Installing a wall mounted hair dryer
Courtesy: NuTone, Inc.

Of course, if you have a client who is very short or very tall, adjust the height accordingly. Once you've settled on height and location, begin installation.

1) If you have access to an open stud wall, run the wiring as shown in Figure 8-40 B. If you don't have access to open studs, run a minimum 14 gauge cable to the mounting location. The power requirements for the NuTone HD-100 are 120 volt, 6.5 amps, and 850 watts. If possible, install the unit on the same wall as an electrical razor outlet. Snake the cable behind the finish wall. See Figure 8-40 C. Be sure all the wiring is done according to code.

Work element	Unit	Manhours per hour
Bathtub		
Cast iron, standard	each	7.8
Cast iron, whirlpool	each	10.5
Toilet		
One-piece	each	4.0
Two-piece	each	4.5
Lavatory		
Self-rimming in cutout	each	4.5
Pedestal	each	3.8
Integral vanity top and bowl	each	5.0
Electrical wall heater	each	4.5
Exhaust fan	each	3.5
Hair dryer	each	2.0
Running electrical circuit (non-metallic sheathed cable) in existing structure	50 LF	2.5
Extending/modifying water supply pipe to mate with relocated fixture	each	2.0
Extending/modifying soil pipe to mate with new toilet	each	3.0

Figure 8-41
Manhours for installing bathroom fixtures

2) Drill mounting holes, using the template provided by the manufacturer. Drill the proper size holes for the type of fastener you're using: screws, toggle bolts, molly bolts, etc.

3) Run the wiring through the access hole in the back of the unit. Using wire nuts, connect the white supply lead to the unit's white wire and the black supply lead to the unit's two black wires.

4) Attach the unit to the wall through the three mounting holes using screws or other fasteners.

5) Install the cover using two screws. Place the trim strip over the screw area as shown in Figure 8-40 D.

Installation Tips

The modern bathroom is only as efficient as the installation of the fixtures and equipment. A good design and layout means very little if nothing works as it should. Proper installation is also essential for safety. The installation procedures we covered in this chapter were prepared by the manufacturers of the equipment. There's no better installation

Work element	Unit	Manhours per unit
Bathtub		
Cast iron, standard	each	4.8
Cast iron, whirlpool	each	5.5
Toilet		
One-piece	each	1.5
Two-piece	each	1.8
Lavatory	each	1.5
Vanity	each	1.5
Fiberglass tub/shower module	each	4.5

Figure 8-42
Manhours for removing bathroom fixtures

method than the instructions prepared by those who made the fixture or equipment.

Take the time to study the installation instructions furnished with the units you're installing. You make no profit in callbacks. If you're called back to fix something, it will cost you triple in lost profits. First, you have to undo. Then you redo. In that same time you could be earning money somewhere else. Callbacks due to poor workmanship can only hurt your reputation.

As one oldtimer instructed his crew, "Don't install nothing without a map and pictures, and don't pull no wires before you pull the switch!"

Manhour Estimates

Figure 8-41 shows my manhour figures for installing bathroom fixtures, including tubs, fiberglass tub and shower modules, toilets, lavatories and vanities. The time includes moving on and off site, unloading, uncrating, clean-up and repairs as needed. It doesn't include time for framing the bathtub installation.

Figure 8-42 shows manhours for removing bathroom fixtures. The time includes removal, hauling from the site and clean-up.

Installing Tub and Shower Surrounds

Kitchen and bathroom remodeling usually includes many trades: carpentry, plumbing, electrical, painting, flooring, tile and more. But don't get the impression that simple jobs requiring only one or two trades aren't profitable. Even small jobs can be good money-makers. To the craftsman with limited capital, small jobs can be ideal. They're steady work and a reliable source of income. You get in, get the work done, get paid and get on to the next job — often in the same week. Remodelers and craftsmen who build a reputation for professionalism and honesty handling smaller jobs usually have all the work they can handle. Most communities I'm familiar with have several remodeling companies anxious to quote on major kitchen or bathroom jobs. That's prestige work — and usually very competitive. But in some communities, finding a contractor willing to tackle small one or two trade jobs is much harder.

Installing tub and shower surrounds is one of those small jobs that many remodelers prefer to ignore. For some, it doesn't offer enough profit unless it's part of a larger job. You'll have to decide for yourself if this kind of job is worth the effort. For my company, it is. But even if you won't do tub and shower enclosures except as part of a larger job, you'll have to handle this work occasionally. Read on.

In this chapter I'll explain how to install three types of tub and shower surrounds. My examples will assume you're using Corian tub enclosures. Of course, that's just one popular brand name. There are others. All require about the same installation procedures.

The first type I'll describe uses a simple bathtub wall kit with an accessory trim kit. The second installation is a little more complex. It's a custom shower wall surround using a 1/2-inch Corian sheet. The third installation is Corian over an existing tile surround, a frequent request in renovation jobs.

Installing a Bathtub Wall Kit with Accessory Trim Kit

Let's say you're installing a standard 5-foot recessed tub with a Corian surround. You've completed the rough-in plumbing and the tub is in place. Before you install the tub surround, attach moisture-resistant wallboard to the 2 x 4 studding in the surround area. This will ensure a sound, long-lasting installation.

There are a couple of precautions you should take when you're working with Corian. Check and make sure your installation meets the following conditions:

Above grade: Never install Corian directly to cinder block, concrete or masonry walls. Always stud out these walls with 2 x 4s and install water-resistant gypsum board. This guarantees the smooth surface you need for a watertight seal using Corian sheets.

Below grade or on-grade: Never use Corian on exterior masonry walls or on any other wall construction that may become damp. Even using water-resistant gypsum board over studs won't provide an effective moisture barrier when the base wall is damp.

Preparation

The Corian bathtub wall kit consists of four precut 1/4-inch sheets, 29-5/16 by 57 inches and a 1/4-inch batten strip, 6 by 57 inches long. The optional trim kit gives your installation a deluxe finished appearance. It contains four pieces of 1/2 by 2 by 74-inch trim. You need to do very little fabrication if you order both the bathtub wall kit and trim kit.

Use a commercial adhesive and caulk kit for the installation. The kit will probably have three tubes of neoprene panel adhesive for bonding the sheets to the wall. The adhesive is a light tan color and doesn't show through the sheets. Use silicone sealant for caulking sheet joints, battens, and trim pieces. There's a silicone sealant made especially for Corian installations.

If your installation is non-standard and requires custom work, you can order Corian sheets that are 1/4 by 30 inches wide and 57, 72 and 98 inches long.

Tools required: You'll need the following tools and supplies for your installation.

- Electric drill and drill bits

- Saber saw with plastic cutting-blade (10 to 14 teeth per inch)

- Belt sander with 50 to 80 grit paper

- Caulking gun

- Sawhorses and three 8-foot long 2 x 4s for support rails

- Ordinary carpenter tools

- Clean-up tools and supplies, including masking tape, putty knife or caulk remover tool, cheesecloth and alcohol

- Blanket or padding to protect the tub from scratches

The additional tools and supplies listed below can make the job easier and reduce your installation time:

- Hole saw for electric drill

- Orbital (vibrating) finish sander

- 1-inch by 1-inch, or 1-inch by 2-inch wood bracing strips

Wear gloves when carrying sheets of fiberglass or Corian to protect your hands against the sharp edges.

Setting up the work site: On the job, set your sawhorses in place with two 2 by 4 rails on top to

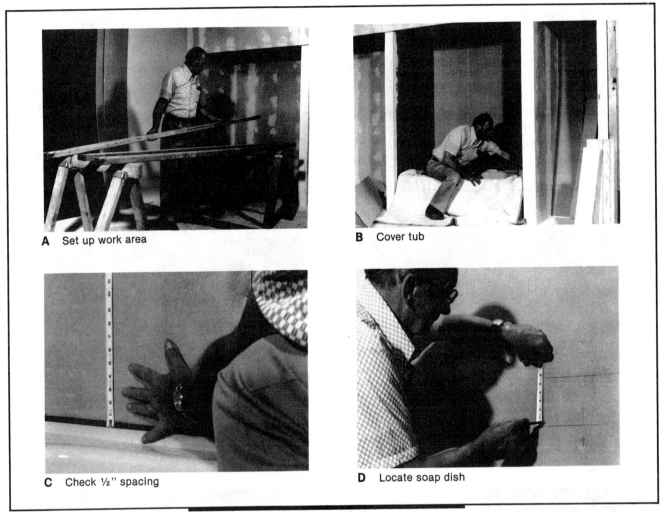

A Set up work area

B Cover tub

C Check ½" spacing

D Locate soap dish

Figure 9-1
Preparation for installing bathtub wall kit
Courtesy: DuPont Co., Inc.

support the sheet material. You need the third 2 by 4 rail to support the underside of the sheet in the area that you're cutting or drilling. See Figure 9-1 A.

Cover the tub with padding to protect it against damage or scratches. See Figure 9-1 B.

Make sure you have a 1/2-inch space between the bottom edge of the wallboard and the tub flange, as shown in Figure 9-1 C. If not, make the 1/2-inch gap with a utility knife. If a leak ever develops, this gap prevents water from wicking up the gypsum board behind the Corian sheets.

If you're installing a recessed soap dish, locate the desired position on the wall. Cut an opening in the gypsum board. Make sure you avoid stud locations (Figure 9-1 D). If you're installing grab bars as well, check the design to make sure you can anchor the bars to the studding.

Wipe the wallboard clean with a cloth moistened in alcohol. Avoid wetting the wall with water. The alcohol evaporates quickly, leaving the clean, dry surface you need for a good bond between the wallboard and sheet material.

Panel Installation

Begin your installation with a trial fit of the first panel.

Step 1. Trial fit the first panel: Using your level, locate the lowest point of the tub ledge (Figure 9-2 A). Place the first panel here. Double check the color match and length of all the panels. If they aren't all the same length, start your installation with the shortest panel.

Put 1/16-inch shims on the tub ledge. You can use small nails like the ones in Figure 9-2 B for shims. Place the first panel in position on the wall. Plumb the panel with a level.

Hold the sheet up in position. The sheets are always square, but the walls and tub may not be.

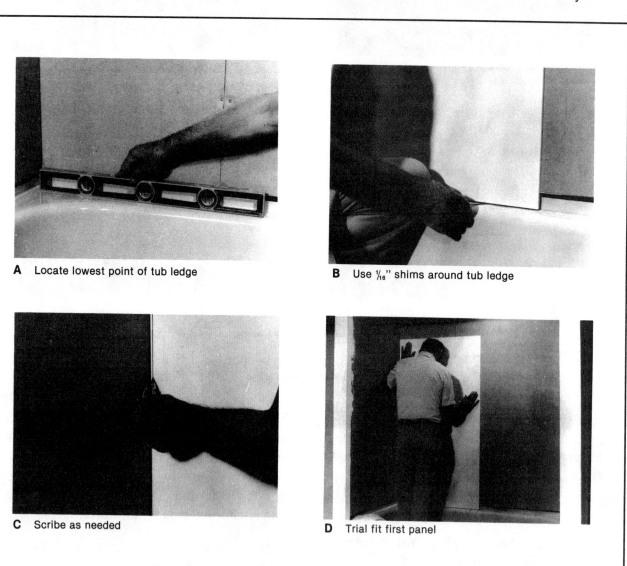

A   Locate lowest point of tub ledge

B   Use ¹⁄₁₆" shims around tub ledge

C   Scribe as needed

D   Trial fit first panel

Figure 9-2
Installing Corian bathtub wall kit
Courtesy: DuPont Co., Inc.

E   Mark level line around walls

F   Apply adhesive to wall

G   "String" adhesive and press in place

H   Bracing for tight adhesive bond

I   Installing second panel

J   Locate soap dish cutout on Corian panel

Figure 9-2
Installing Corian bathtub wall kit (continued)
Courtesy: DuPont Co., Inc.

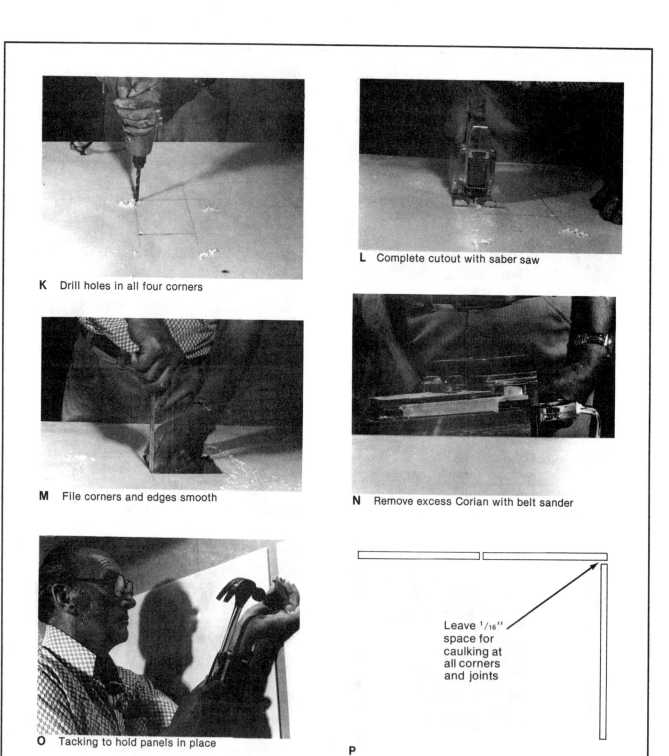

K Drill holes in all four corners

L Complete cutout with saber saw

M File corners and edges smooth

N Remove excess Corian with belt sander

O Tacking to hold panels in place

P

Leave $^1/_{16}''$ space for caulking at all corners and joints

Figure 9-2
Installing Corian bathtub wall kit (continued)
Courtesy: DuPont Co., Inc.

If the vertical gap between the sheet and the wall is 1/8 inch or more, you'll have to trim the sheet so it fits plumb. Use a pencil compass to scribe the sheet edge to the corner wall (Figure 9-2 C). If the tub isn't level, you'll need to scribe the tub ledge also. Use a belt sander to trim the excess from the panel.

After trimming, set the fitted panel in position on the shims (Figure 9-2 D). Use a pencil to out-

line the top and side panel edges on the wall-board.

Set the panel aside. Extend the top edge line around all three walls using a level. See Figure 9-2 E. Use this line to match up the heights of the other three panels. The line along the panel edges shows you where to apply the panel adhesive.

Step 2. Install the first panel: Clean the back of the panel with an alcohol-dampened cloth. Apply

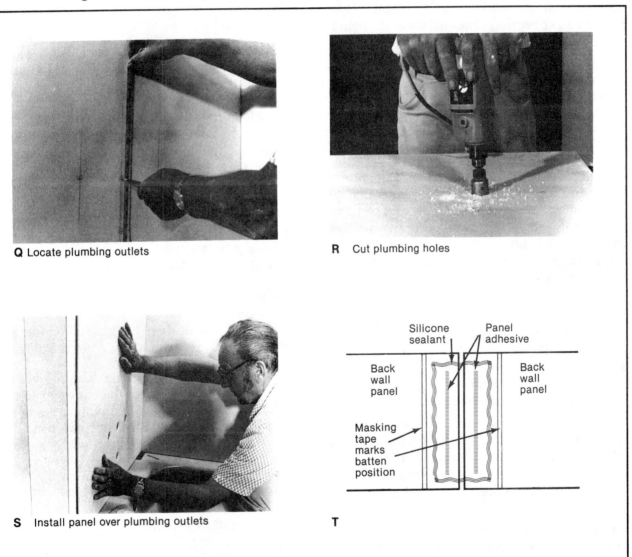

Q Locate plumbing outlets

R Cut plumbing holes

S Install panel over plumbing outlets

T

Figure 9-2
Installing Corian bathtub wall kit (continued)
Courtesy: DuPont Co., Inc.

neoprene adhesive to the wall with a caulking gun. See Figure 9-2 F. Place a 1/4-inch bead of adhesive about an inch in from all the edges of the panel. Apply additional vertical beads 8 to 10 inches apart in the center area of the panel. Within two minutes, press the panel firmly against the wall.

Pull the panel away from the wall to string the adhesive and allow it to vent (Figure 9-2 G). This usually takes about two minutes. Press the panel back against the wall. Press the palm of your hand firmly over the entire surface of the panel to make sure you have a good bond.

You may need to brace the panel while the adhesive sets up completely. This may not be necessary if the wall is smooth and even. If you do need to brace, use 1 x 1 or 1 x 2 wood braces. Cut the braces slightly longer than the distance you need to span to ensure a snug fit. See Figure 9-2 H.

Step 3. Install the second panel: Put shims in place and repeat the same procedures that you used to install the first panel. If the first panel was on the rear wall, install the second panel as shown in Figure 9-2 I. If the first panel was an end panel, install the other end panel next. You want both end panels to extend the same distance from each corner.

If the second panel is the one with the recessed soap dish, carefully measure the location of the opening in the wallboard. Transfer the dimensions to the front of the panel. See Figure 9-2 J. Drill holes in all four corners of the cutout using an electric drill (Figure 9-2 K).

Complete the cutout using a saber saw. Be careful not to cut into the corners with the saw blade (Figure 9-2 L). File or sand smooth all the corners and edges of the cutout, and round the corners. This is necessary to prevent the sheet from cracking. See Figure 9-2 M.

Trial fit the panel. Scribe the bottom and corner edges, and remove any excess material with a belt sander. See Figure 9-2 N. Make a repeat trial fit. Match the level line to the top edge and scribe. Continue to install the panel using the same installation procedures you used for panel one.

Tack a nail into the wallboard, against the edge of the panel (not through it). This will hold the sheet in place until the adhesive sets (Figure 9-2 O).

Step 4. Install the third panel: The third panel we'll assume to be the end panel of the wall without plumbing outlets. Repeat the procedures for the other two panels, leaving a 1/16-inch gap for caulking the corners where the sheets abut. Scribe the sheet to get a uniform corner fit, as in Figure 9-2 P.

Step 5. Install the fourth panel: With shims in place, measure the location of the plumbing outlets on the back of the panel. Transfer these dimensions to the front side of the panel (Figure 9-2 Q). Make the cutouts about 1/4 inch larger than necessary for the plumbing. Before cutting, be sure that the escutcheon plates will completely cover the cutouts.

Make starter holes with the drill and complete the cutouts with a saber saw, or a hole saw, Figure 9-2 R. Be sure to support the sheet underneath with a 2 by 4 rail when you make your cutouts. File all cutout edges and corners smooth.

Place the panel in position for a trial fit. Scribe as necessary so that the panel fits both the tub ledge and the inside of the tub surround. (Figure 9-2 S). Install the panel as you did the others.

Step 6. Install batten strip: Use a level and a measuring tape to center the batten strip on the rear wall. Mark the position with strips of masking tape (Figure 9-2 T). Don't use pencil lines. They may show through when you complete the final caulking.

Trial fit the batten. Scribe as needed to match the height of the two rear panels. Round off any sharp edges by sanding or filing.

Clean the batten with an alcohol-dampened cloth. Apply both panel adhesive and silicone sealant as shown in Figure 9-2 T. Install the batten by pressing it firmly into position. Remove the masking tape. Also, quickly remove any excess sealant with an alcohol-saturated cloth before the sealant sets or cures.

If the walls are uneven, you may need to brace them as shown earlier in Figure 9-2 H.

Trim Strip Installation

The trim strip kit gives your job a clean, finished look that will please your client.

Step 1. Back wall trim strip: Measure the back wall above the panels and cut the trim strip 1/8 inch shorter than the length of the wall. This will leave you a 1/16-inch gap in the corner for caulking. Sand the exposed edges. Clean the back surface of the trim strip. Apply a bead of panel adhesive to the back of the trim strip and press it to the wall.

Step 2. End wall trim strip: Cut the top end strip 1/16 inch shorter than the length of the wall to

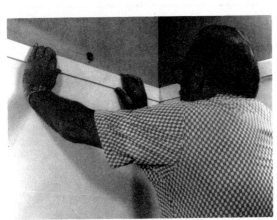

A   Install top trim

B   Scribe vertical trim to fit tub

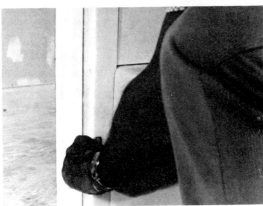

C   Install front vertical trim strips

Figure 9-3
Trim strip installation
Courtesy: DuPont Co., Inc.

leave a corner for caulking. Make sure the front end of the trim strip is flush with the front edge of the end wall panel. Install this strip the same way that you did the back wall trim strip. See Figure 9-3 A.

Step 3. Front vertical trim strips: Measure the front edge trim from the floor to the top trim height. Cut the strip to length and make a trial fit. Often you'll have to scribe and trim the strips to fit snugly against the tub all the way to the floor. See Figure 9-3 B.

Cut away the scribed material using a saber saw. Sand all the edges, clean the strip, and install it as shown in Figure 9-3 C.

Final Clean-up and Caulking

The final steps are installing the fixtures, cleaning off and smoothing the surface, and caulking all the joints.

A Round exposed edges

B Clean before caulking

C Caulk all joints, corners, and edges

Figure 9-4
Clean-up and caulking
Courtesy: DuPont Co., Inc.

Figure 9-5
Your completed installation
Courtesy: DuPont Co., Inc.

Step 1. The fixtures and accessories: Install the soap dish, grab bars, shower door, and any other fixtures your client requested. If you need to drill screws into the panels, drill the holes oversize and fill with caulk.

Step 2. The clean-up: Check to be sure that you've sanded and rounded off all the exposed edges (Figure 9-4 A). Clean all the Corian panels and trim before you caulk the joints. This prevents dust and dirt from getting into the sealant. See Figure 9-4 B.

Clean all the joints with an alcohol-moistened cloth to get a good caulk seal. Use an orbital sander with a Scotch-Brite pad to remove pencil marks, surface dirt, and scratches. This will also restore the original sheen to the finish.

Step 3. Caulking: Carefully caulk all the joints, corners and edges with a mildew-resistant silicone sealant. The sealant guarantees an attractive, long-term, watertight installation.

Remove all the shims and nails. Caulk the interior corners, batten edges, trim joints, and the 1/16-inch space you left between the panels and tub (Figure 9-4 C). Fill the joints completely. Remove any excess sealant with a putty knife or caulk remover tool. Smooth the silicone with your finger or an alcohol-moistened cloth.

Figure 9-5 shows the completed job.

Installing a Shower Wall

Many of the steps and procedures are the same for installing a shower wall. The precautions are the same also. Review the procedures I've described for a tub kit installation before beginning to install a shower kit. I won't waste space duplicating the instructions.

Planning your shower wall installation is important. Shower pans come in many sizes and shapes. Figures 9-6, 9-7 and 9-8 show three of the more popular pan types and shower layouts.

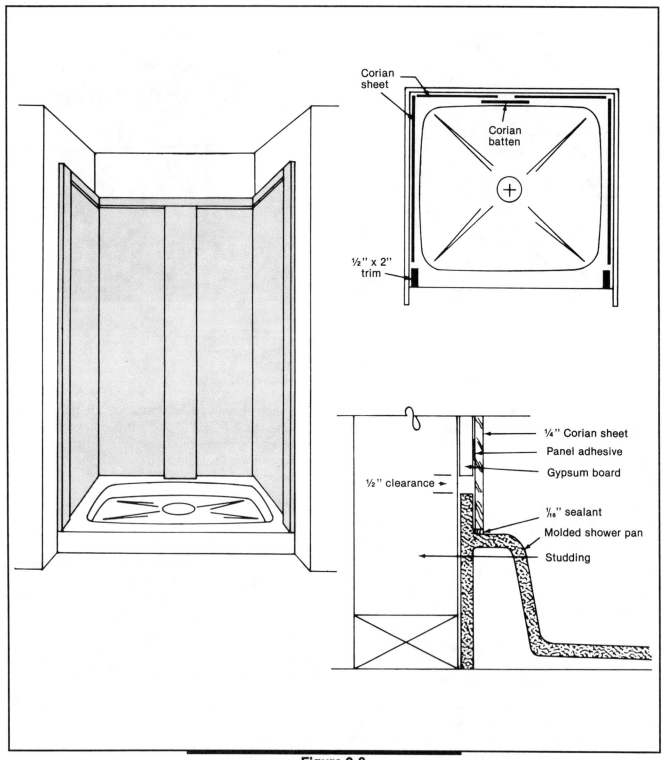

Figure 9-6
Batten style Corian shower surround with molded shower pan
Courtesy: DuPont Co., Inc.

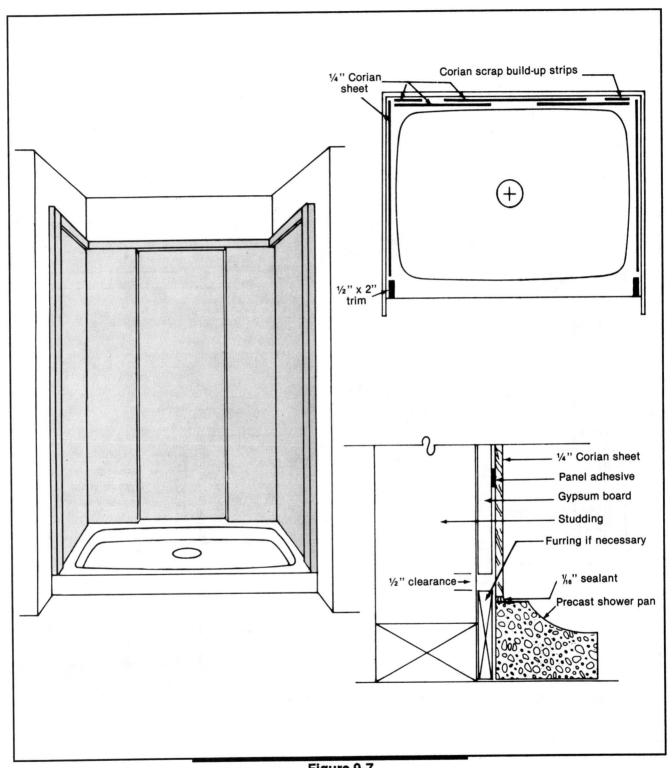

Figure 9-7
Lap style Corian shower surround with precast terrazzo shower pan
Courtesy: DuPont Co., Inc.

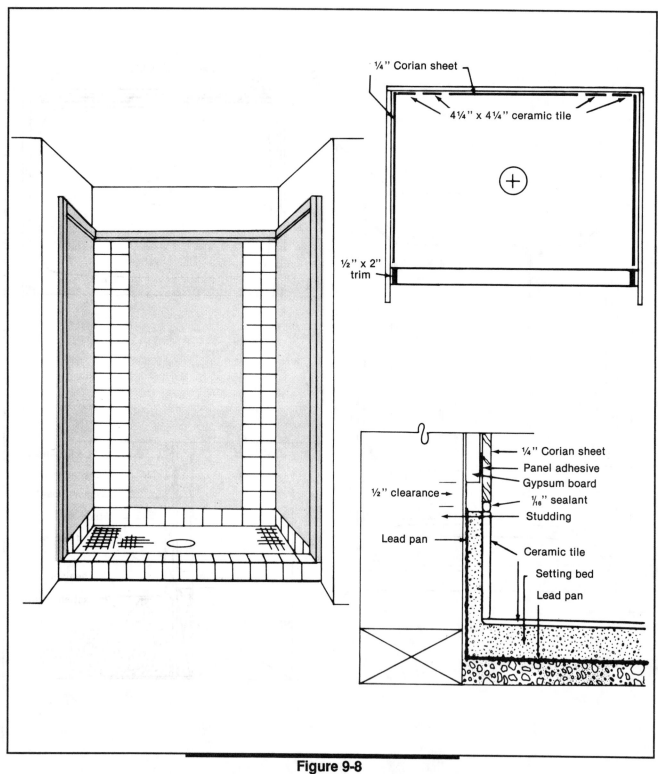

Figure 9-8
Corian shower surround with ceramic tile floor and accents
Courtesy: DuPont Co., Inc.

Since most showers are wider than the standard plastic wall sheet, there are three ways to span the wall. You can join panels with batten strips or lap joints, or use panels in combination with ceramic tile. But in any event, don't extend panels all the way to the floor or below the level of a ceramic tile shower floor. Use a shower pan or a base course of ceramic tile as shown in Figure 9-8.

Planning and Preparation

Have your clients select the type of shower layout and shower pan they prefer.

Step 1. Specifications and layout: Assume you're going to install a molded shower pan (any one of the pan types shown in Figures 9-6, 9-7, or 9-8 will do) and floor-to-ceiling shower walls that meet the following specifications:

- Color — Dawn Beige

- Dimensions — 32 by 48-inch shower pan

- Wall height — full height (89 inches from shower pan edge)

- Rear wall design — 6-inch batten over 23-inch wide sheets

- Side wall design — 30-inch sheets with 4-inch lap strips

- Ceiling design — Corian sheets with a front-to-rear center batten strip

- Ceiling trim — 1/4 by 2-inch trim

- Fascia trim — 1/4 by 4-inch, floor to ceiling

- Soap dish — recessed, left rear panel, 48 inches high

- Grab bar — none

- Plumbing fixtures — on hand

Prepare a drawing like the one in Figure 9-9 to help you lay out the installation. Use the drawing when ordering and cutting the materials.

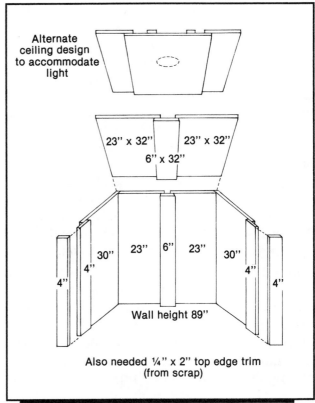

Figure 9-9
Prepare a reference drawing
Courtesy: DuPont Co., Inc

Step 2. Ordering materials: Corian sheets come in 1/4 by 30-inch stock for showers. The sheets are available in 72- and 98-inch lengths. Try to use sheets from the same package to minimize variations in color or pattern.

You'll need the following materials for this job:

- 6 sheets of 1/4 by 30 by 98-inch Corian (Dawn Beige)

- 2 commercial adhesive and caulk kits

- Scotch-Brite wiping pads for cleaning the sheet surface

Step 3. Installation tools and supplies: Use the same tools and supplies for the custom shower surround installation that you use for the tub kit installation. Add to that list a power circular saw equipped with a 40-tooth, 6- or 7-1/4-inch carbide blade.

Step 4. Handling and delivery of the sheets: Any time you take delivery of Corian sheets, peel back the film and make sure the sheets are in good condition. Check also to make sure they match. If you're picking them up in your truck, make sure you cushion the truck bed with a soft material such as carpeting or a blanket. Protect the sheets from damage, especially the edges. Sandwich them between paper or cardboard to protect the surfaces.

Step 5. Wall preparation: Install the rough-in plumbing and wall studs. Set in the shower pan according to the manufacturer's instructions. Protect the pan from scratches or other damage by covering it with padding or a blanket.

Install water-resistant gypsum wallboard against the studs. Leave a 1/2-inch space between the bottom edge of the wallboard and the shower pan flange. See Figure 9-10 A.

Locate the recessed soap dish position on the wall and cut an opening in the wallboard. Avoid placing the soap dish at a stud location. See Figure 9-10 B.

Now wipe down the wallboard with an alcohol-moistened cloth.

Sheet Installation

Begin your shower wall installation with the ceiling.

Step 1. Installing the ceiling: First, measure the ceiling. You'll need two 23 by 32-inch ceiling panels with a 6-inch batten strip.

Place a 30 by 98-inch sheet face up on your workbench. Support it with three 2 by 4 rails. Before cutting the sheet, remove the protective film and inspect the face of the sheet. Mark the dimensions you need and clamp a straightedge to the sheet as a cutting guide. See Figure 9-11 A.

Cut a 6-inch batten strip using a circular saw. Set the batten strip aside for use on the rear wall. Now cut the two ceiling panels and the ceiling batten. Always use the third 2 by 4 rail to support the area being cut. The circular blade should be

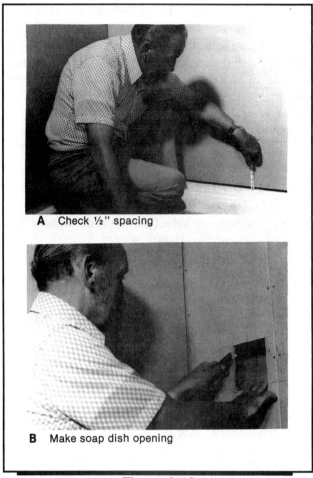

A   Check ½" spacing

B   Make soap dish opening

Figure 9-10
Preparation for installing Corian sheets
Courtesy: DuPont Co., Inc.

set to penetrate about 1/4 inch through the sheet (Figure 9-11 B).

Install the ceiling panels using the installation procedures for the tub surround. However, with a ceiling installation, it's easier to apply the adhesive to the back of the panel rather than to the ceiling (Figure 9-11 C). Set the ceiling batten aside. You'll install that later.

The manufacturer probably recommends holding the ceiling panels in place by tacking a few nails into the wallboard immediately below and alongside the panels (Figure 9-11 D). It takes a short time for the adhesive get a good bond.

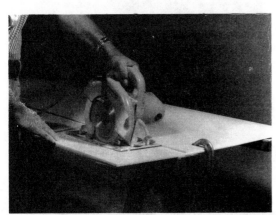

A   Support Corian with 2" x 4" rail

B   Saw blade should barely penetrate the Corian

Figure 9-11
Installing Corian shower walls
Courtesy: DuPont Co., Inc.

Instead of nails, I like to use hot melt glue to hold the ceiling panels in place temporarily. After you apply the adhesive, spot glue at the corners with a hot melt glue gun. Place the sheet in position. Hot melt glue hardens quickly, so you'll have to work fast. Hold the panel up for about 20 seconds. Hot melt glue will hold the panel in place until the adhesive forms a firm bond. Remember, hot melt glue is just for tacking. It's not a substitute for adhesive.

Step 2. Installing the first panel: The design calls for a full 30-inch wide side wall extended by a 1/4 by 4-inch lap strip. The total front to back dimension is 32-1/2 inches. Start with the 30-inch side panel that will have the plumbing outlets. Measure the floor to ceiling height and cut a 30 by 98-inch sheet to the correct length. (In a different design layout, if the sheets weren't full ceiling height, you would locate the lowest point on the pan ledge for your first sheet installation.)

With the shims in place (Figure 9-11 E), measure and mark the location of the plumbing outlets on the face of the panel. Make the cutout holes 1/4 inch larger than you need for the plumbing.

Before cutting, make sure the escutcheon plates will completely cover the cutout holes. See Figure 9-11 F. File the cutouts smooth.

Install the panel following the procedures I've described. (Figure 9-11 G).

Step 3. Installing the second side panel: Install the second 30-inch panel on the opposite wall.

You'll cut and install the narrow lap strips later, using strips cut from the rear wall panel sheets.

Step 4. Installing the left rear panel: Cut a 4-inch lap strip from a 30 by 98-inch sheet and set it aside. Now cut the sheet to the correct width and length for the left back wall panel. Measure the position for the soap dish and make the cutout as described earlier. (Refer to Figures 9-2 I through 9-2 L.)

C   Apply adhesive to ceiling panels

D   Cut and install ceiling panels

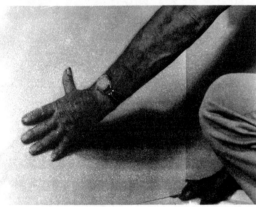

E   Use ¹⁄₁₆" shims between Corian sheet and pan

F   Check plate size before cutting plumbing holes

G   Install side panel

H   Leave ¹⁄₁₆" gap in corners for caulking

Figure 9-11
Installing Corian shower walls (continued)
Courtesy: DuPont Co., Inc.

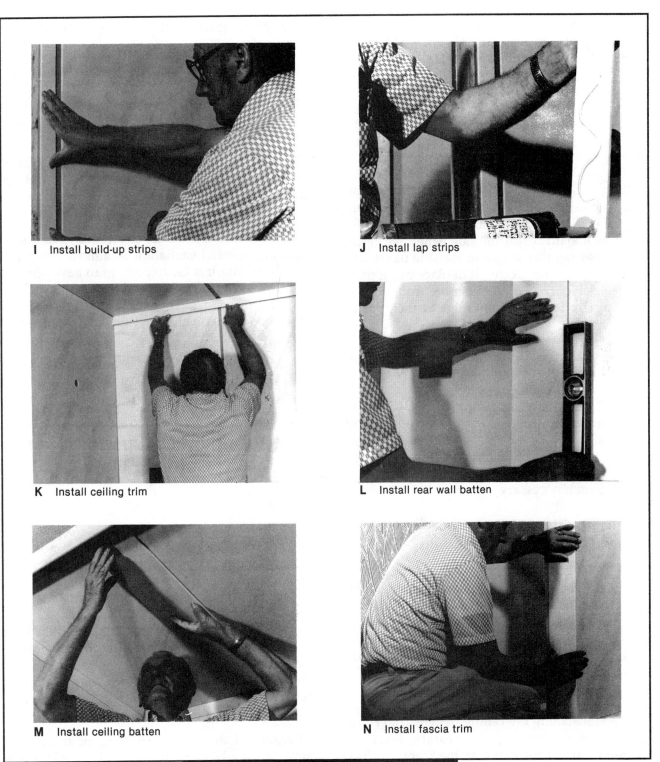

I   Install build-up strips

J   Install lap strips

K   Install ceiling trim

L   Install rear wall batten

M   Install ceiling batten

N   Install fascia trim

Figure 9-11
Installing Corian shower wall (continued)
Courtesy: DuPont Co., Inc.

Install the panel, scribing and trimming as necessary. Be sure to leave a 1/16-inch gap in the corner for caulking (Figure 9-11 H).

Step 5. Installing the right rear panel: Cut the second 4-inch lap strip from another 30 by 98-inch sheet and set it aside. Cut the sheet to the width and length needed for the right rear panel. Install this panel the same way as the previous panel.

Step 6. Installing the side wall lap strips: From scrap pieces, cut a 1/4-inch wide by 30-inch long strip. Use panel adhesive to bond the scrap piece to the wallboard beside the side panel. See Figure 9-11 I. Overlap this strip and the side panel with the 4-inch lap strip. Secure it in place using panel adhesive (Figure 9-11 J). Flush the front edge of the lap strip with the front edge of the gypsum wallboard.

Repeat this procedure for the other side wall lap strip.

Step 7. Installing the ceiling trim: Cut 1/4 by 2-inch trim strips to go along the top edges of all four walls. The trim strips should be 1/16 inch shorter than the wall length so you have a space in the corners for caulking. Trial fit the pieces and scribe them if necessary.

Clean the strips. Apply a bead of adhesive to the back of each strip and press it into place. See Figure 9-11 K.

Step 8. Installing the rear wall center batten: Take the 6-inch batten strip you cut earlier and trial fit it. Then cut it to the necessary length. Install the batten on the rear wall, the same way as the tub batten. The batten should overlap the sheets at least 2 inches on either side. See Figure 9-11 L.

Step 9. Installing the ceiling batten: Trial fit the ceiling batten. Trim it, if necessary, leaving a 1/16-inch space for caulk at the front and rear edges. Round off the edges by sanding. Install the ceiling batten using the same procedures you used for the rear wall batten (Figure 9-11 M).

Brace or hot glue if necessary until the adhesive sets.

Step 10. Installing the fascia trim: In this design, you're using a 4-inch vertical fascia trim to dress up the shower. From the sixth sheet of Corian, rip two fascia trim strips. They should each be 4 inches wide, and cut to length.

Trial fit and scribe the fascia trim to exactly match the vertical lap strips. Install the trim strips using both silicone sealant and panel adhesive. See Figure 9-11 N.

Step 11. Install fixtures, clean and caulk: Your custom shower installation is almost complete. Install the fixtures (soap dish, grab bars, shower door, etc). Carefully clean and caulk all the joints, corners, and edges. Follow the same procedures described in the section on tub wall installation.

Installing a Tub Surround Over Ceramic Tile

Corian offers a major benefit in tub renovation jobs. You can install it directly over watertight ceramic tile, reducing your installation and labor costs. You also eliminate the messy job of removing old tile. Be careful however, not to install Corian over loose or leaking tile, any plastic or metal tile, moist walls, coated hardboard, or plastic laminates. If you have to remove old tile, also check the condition of the drywall or plaster base. If it's not sound and dry, replace it with new water-resistant gypsum wallboard.

Because of the many variations in shower design, it may be hard to know if the old tile is watertight. If you have any doubts, it's best to remove the old tile and tiled receptors before installing Corian.

The Installation

The instructions for installing Corian or sheet plastic tub surrounds over ceramic tile are the same as for installing the same materials against a wallboard base. There are just a few modifications. Review the section on installation against wallboard, because not all of that information is repeated here.

Step 1. Wall preparation: Remove the bottom course of tile and base around the tub ledge with a rubber mallet and chisel. Install a new strip of water-resistant gypsum board in this space. Leave a 1/2-inch air gap between the gypsum board and the tub flange. Shim as necessary to make the strip flush with tile surface.

With a mallet and chisel, remove any protruding fixtures, such as the soap dish shown in Figure 9-12 A. Also remove any loose tile or extra-thick edge tile trim.

Fill void spaces larger than 4 inches square with scrap pieces of Corian or old tile. Use panel adhesive to attach the pieces. See Figure 9-12 B.

Step 2. Plumbing fixtures: Inspect the plumbing fixtures to make certain you can attach them over the additional thickness of the new finish. Extend the plumbing if necessary by substituting longer nipples.

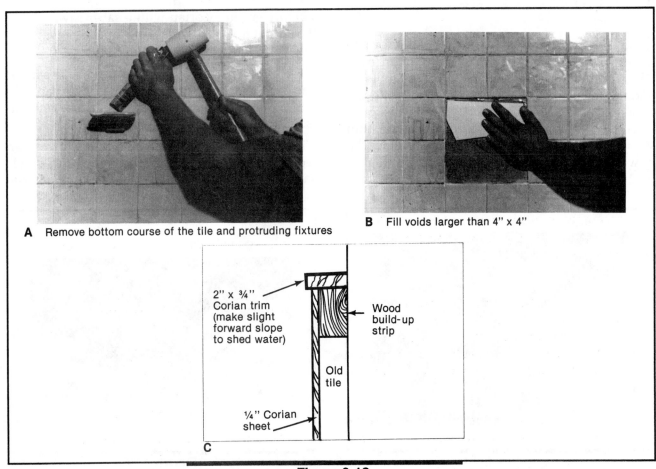

A Remove bottom course of the tile and protruding fixtures

B Fill voids larger than 4" x 4"

2" x ¾" Corian trim (make slight forward slope to shed water)

Wood build-up strip

Old tile

¼" Corian sheet

C

Figure 9-12
Installing Corian tub surround over ceramic tile
Courtesy: DuPont Co., Inc.

Step 3. Clean the tile surface: You need a thoroughly clean and dry tile surface to get a good bond between the old tile and the Corian sheet. Clean the ceramic tile and grout with one of the tile cleaners available at hardware stores. They do a good job of removing dirt, soap scum, and mildew.

Follow the manufacturer's instructions for cleaning. Let the surface dry for 24 hours before doing the installation.

Step 4. Install the tub surround: You could install either a bathtub wall kit or custom cut sheets. Follow the directions given earlier for whichever installation your client prefers.

You'll need to order a 3/4-inch trim kit for finishing the edges when you install Corian over tile. Occasionally, 3/4-inch edge trim isn't enough to cover the thickness of both the old tile trim and the new material. If this is the case, remove the old tile trim piece. Then use thin wood build-up strips to fill in the space. Place the new finish trim over the wood strips. See Figure 9-12 C.

Scalloped Corian Trim

Because you can work this material like wood, you can create different treatments to enhance the beauty of your client's bathrooms. The scalloped edge you see in Figure 9-13 is a good example of a customized trim. Draw your design on a 1/4 by 4-inch strip. The bottom of a round can makes a good template. Cut the strips with a saber saw, then smooth with a sander. Use panel adhesive to attach the custom trim, placing it just beneath the 3/4-inch top trim strip.

Hints for Working with Corian

Before cutting Corian with a saber saw, outline the cutout holes with masking tape to prevent the saw from scratching the surface.

Use a Scotch-Brite pad with your orbital sander and let the sander do the buffing. The pad will remove scratches and restore the factory-new finish. See Figure 9-14.

Tape 1/16-inch shims to the tub or shower pan ledge when you start the job (Figure 9-15). This saves you time and makes sure that all your trial

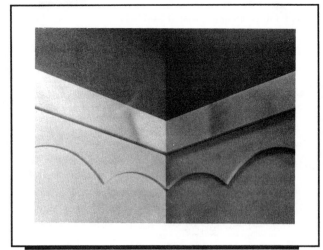

Figure 9-13
Scalloped Corian trim
Courtesy: DuPont Co., Inc.

Figure 9-14
Buff with Scotch-Brite pad
Courtesy: DuPont Co., Inc.

fittings and panel installations have the necessary caulking space.

Brace with wood strips as described earlier, or tack with hot melt glue to hold the panels in place for a good solid bond. See Figure 9-16.

Other Bathtub Surround Kits

Of course, Corian isn't the only bathtub surround kit that's available. Your local lumber dealer probably sells several brands. Plastic kits come in plain to fancy styles and offer an economical and practical remodeling alternative. You can install these kits over ceramic tile, wood, masonry, plaster, or wallboard. Follow the manufacturer's installation instructions.

With all the products available, a versatile remodeler can offer homeowners a bathroom package in almost any price range. While many homeowners prefer ceramic tile tub and shower surrounds, others may want to select a different material. You'll have the advantage over your competition if you can offer your clients several alternatives. Attractive and long-lasting surrounds can be made from several types of material.

Estimating Tub/Shower Surround Installation

If you don't have your own labor records, use the manhour estimating data in this book as a guide in estimating the job. My figures for this part of the job are in Figure 9-17. But if you've developed labor records based on your own experience, use those. No two kitchen and bath remodelers will have the same production rates, and my data is no substitute for your own experience.

Keep a detailed record of manhours devoted to each task on your jobs. Refer to these records when estimating future jobs. Eventually, all your estimating will be based on personal experience and the variables peculiar to your remodeling work.

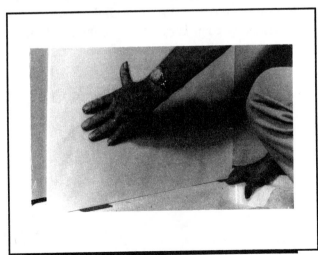

Figure 9-15
Tape shims to tub or shower ledge
Courtesy: DuPont Co., Inc.

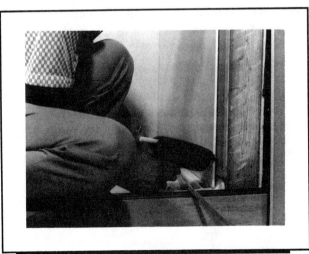

Figure 9-16
Tack with hot melt glue to hold in place
Courtesy: DuPont Co., Inc.

Work element	Unit	Manhour per unit
Corian bathtub wall kit		
Recessed standard tub	each	8.0
Accessory trim	10 LF	2.0
Corian shower stall, 32" x 48"	each	9.5
Ceiling	each	2.0
Trim	10 LF	1.5
Shower receptor, 32" x 48"	each	3.0
Shower door	each	1.5
Plastic tub surround kit	each	6.5
Time includes water supply hook-up and clean-up		

Figure 9-17
Estimating tub/shower surround installation

If you aren't sure how to keep production records, I'll recommend Volume 2 of *Handbook of Construction Contracting*. It shows you how to set up a Construction Estimate File (CEF) for all the construction work you handle. This book is listed on an order form at the back of this manual.

While the CEF was designed for new construction, it works just as well for remodeling. Of course, you have to remember that most remodeling work includes demolition as well. A good rule of thumb to follow is that remodeling work generally takes twice as long as new construction.

Ceramic Tile Tub and Shower Wall Installations

Ceramic tile has been used in building and decorating for centuries. You can find it in the Egyptian pyramids, the great mosques of the middle east, and ancient castles in the old world. Skillfully installed ceramic tile has a timeless beauty. But there's no way to hide a poor ceramic tile job. Even a child can point out the flaws in substandard work.

If you're not a skilled tilesetter, hire someone who is to do your jobs. Tile is tough enough to last longer than a lifetime when properly installed. Its hard surface resists cuts, bumps, and gouges. Don't create sloppy tile work that can blemish your professional reputation well into the next century.

Figure 10-1 shows the beautiful clean lines of a professional tile job. If you demand expert work from your tilesetters, you'll soon have a reputation as a quality kitchen and bathroom remodeler.

Types of Ceramic Tile

Ceramic tile is a mixture of clays hardened at high temperatures. If the color is sprayed on before firing, the tile is glazed. Glazed surfaces vary from bright and shiny tiles, to those with a softer satin-like or matte finish, to those made with a pebbly lustre. The colors run from light pastels to brilliant accent colors, with surfaces that are rough-hewn, textured, or smooth.

Figure 10-1
A professional tile installation
Courtesy: Ceramic Tile Institute

There are two types of tiles that are a solid color throughout, rather than surface colored. One is *quarry tile*, which comes in natural clay colors. The other is *ceramic mosaic* tile made of clays mixed with colored pigments.

The sizes vary from 1-inch by 1-inch ceramic mosaics to 12-inch by 12-inch glazed tiles. Most tiles are simple squares, but you can also get tiles made in hexagon, Valencia, or octagon shapes.

Grout

Grout is the filler material you put between the tiles. It gives your installation a finished look. You can use drywall, sanded, or epoxy grouts to meet the specific tile requirements of your job. Blend colored grouts to harmonize with the tile colors. They can be a subtle design element of the ceramic tile installation.

The American National Standard Institute (ANSI) A118.6 gives specifications for ceramic tile grouts.

Redi-Set, Sheets of Pregrouted Tile

American Olean Tile Company manufactures *Redi-Set*, sheets of tile that are pregrouted with a special water-repellent silicone rubber. The grout won't crumble, and wipes as clean as the tile itself. Instead of installing tiles one at a time, you can put up as many as 64 tiles at once. Because it's flexible, it "gives" if the structure settles.

Installation Details

Even if you subcontract ceramic tile work, you need to know what's involved in creating a professionally finished job. While most tilesetters are competent and reliable, there are a few less than professional types who pass themselves off as experts. If you can't tell the difference until the job is completed, you can lose a lot of money and do more than a little damage to your reputation.

The illustrations in Figure 10-2 show everything you need for quality installation of wall tile. The components are divided into those installed by the tile contractor and those installed by other trades. On many remodeling jobs, however, the tile contractor will install the waterproof paper, metal lath and scratch coat, as part of the tile installation. They usually have a crew or a craftsman who prepares the job for the tilesetter. In some areas the tilesetter may do all the preparation work as well, depending on rules or local custom. Study the details in the figures so you'll know what to look for in each type of installation.

Bathtub Walls

You can install tile over several different types of base walls. There are also a number of treatments you can use as the bed for the tile. Some work better with different types of wall bases than others. Recognize the difference so you can produce a long-lasting, waterproof bath wall.

Using Cement Mortar

Figure 10-3 shows the construction details for installing ceramic tile using cement mortar over wood or metal studs. Wood studs should be solid, dry, well-braced, and spaced 16 inches on center. Wood studs work best in this type of installation. Apply 15-pound felt (roofing paper) or 4-mil polyethylene film against the studs as protection against dampness. Then apply metal lath followed by the scratch coat.

Use painted or galvanized expanded metal lath 3.4 pounds per square yard, or sheet lath 4.5 pounds per square yard.

Scratch coat: For the scratch coat use portland cement (ASTM C-150 Type 1) and lime (ASTM C-206 Type S or ASTM C-207 Type S). Mix with clean water and sand (ASTM C-144). When mixing with lime use:

1 part portland cement

1/2 part lime

4 parts dry sand (5 parts if sand is damp)

If you don't mix with lime, use:

1 part portland cement

3 parts dry sand (4 parts if sand is damp)

If the mortar bed will be more than 3/4 inch thick or if variations in the scratch coat exceed 1/4 inch in 8 feet, apply a leveling coat.

Mortar bed: Apply the mortar bed on top of the scratch coat. Use the following proportions for mixing the mortar bed:

1 part portland cement

Special note to architects and specifiers:

On jobs where no plastering is required,
all of the items below to be included in the tile
section of the specifications.

A. Wood or steel stud construction with plaster above tile wainscot

Items by other trades	Items by tile contractor

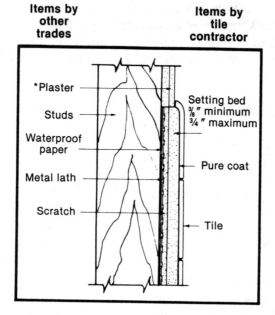

- *Plaster
- Studs
- Waterproof paper
- Metal lath
- Scratch

- Setting bed ⅜″ minimum ¾″ maximum
- Pure coat
- Tile

Items by other trades	Items by tile contractor

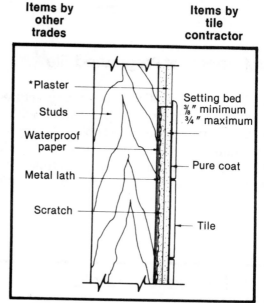

- *Plaster
- Studs
- Waterproof paper
- Metal lath
- Scratch

- Setting bed ⅜″ minimum ¾″ maximum
- Pure coat
- Tile

*This installation would be similar if wall finish above tile wainscot were of other material such as wallboard, plywood, etc.

Items by other trades	Items by tile contractor

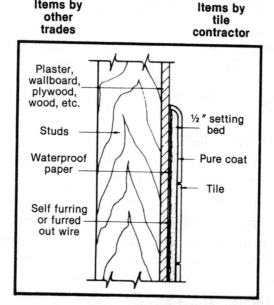

- Plaster, wallboard, plywood, wood, etc.
- Studs
- Waterproof paper
- Self furring or furred out wire

- ½″ setting bed
- Pure coat
- Tile

B. Wood or steel stud construction with solid covered backing

1. This is the "One Float Coat" method of applying tile and makes an excellent installation.

2. Backing should be specified to be a straight, firm and true surface. This should be specified in the proper section of the specifications for the trade that is to install the backing material.

Figure 10-2
Components needed in different tile installations
Courtesy: Ceramic Tile Institute

C. Solid type wall construction with plaster above wainscot

Items by other trades ▼ Items by tile contractor

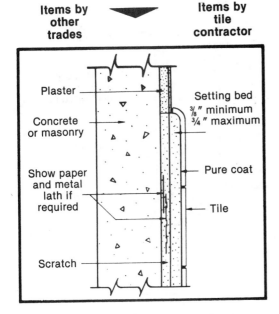

Plaster

Concrete or masonry

Show paper and metal lath if required

Scratch

Setting bed
3/8 " minimum
3/4 " maximum

Pure coat

Tile

D. Solid type wall construction without plaster above wainscot

Items by other trades ▼ Items by tile contractor

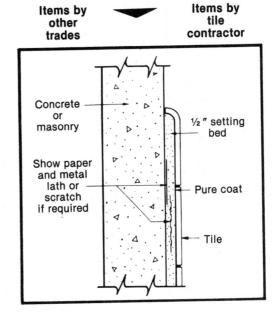

Concrete or masonry

Show paper and metal lath or scratch if required

1/2 " setting bed

Pure coat

Tile

E. Heavy gauge steel

1. Specify self-furring metal lath fastened with pan head metal screw 8" O.C.

2. "One Float Coat" method with 1/2" of mortar may be used or scratch coat may be specified.

CERAMIC TILE INSTITUTE

700 N. Virgil Ave.
Los Angeles, Calif. 90029
Phone (213) 660-1911

Items by other trades ► Items by tile contractor

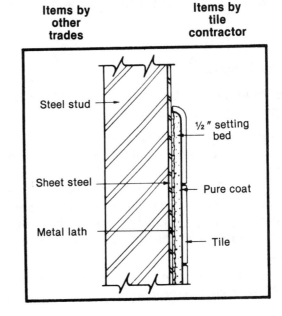

Steel stud

Sheet steel

Metal lath

1/2 " setting bed

Pure coat

Tile

Figure 10-2
Components needed in different tile installations (continued)
Courtesy: Ceramic Tile Institute

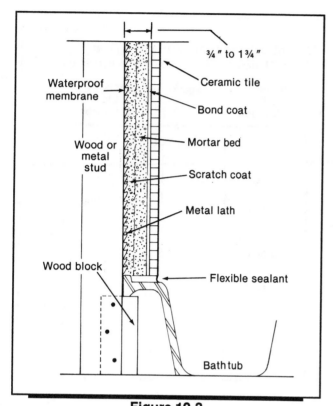

Figure 10-3
Cross section of bathtub wall using cement mortar

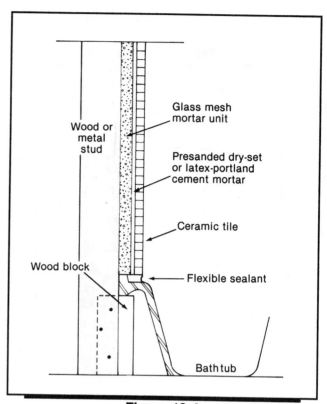

Figure 10-4
Cross section of bathtub wall using glass mesh
mortar units

1/2 part lime

5 parts damp sand

Bond coat: For the bond coat, use portland cement paste, dry-set, or latex-portland cement.

Tile and grout: Use the same procedures to lay out the tile as we discussed in Chapter 5. For bath wall grout, use a type that complies with ANSI A118.6. That includes commercial portland cement and dry-set, latex-portland cement, mastic, and silicone rubber grout. Make sure the grout you use is suitable for the tile and the area where it will be used.

After the tile and grout are dry, apply elastomeric (Type A silicone) caulking.

Hints

Here are some suggestions to help you make a professional tile installation.

- Make the tub recess no more than 1/2 inch longer than the length of the tub.

- Support and level the tub securely. Use wood blocks or approved metal hangers.

- Fireproof behind the tub when required.

- Protect the tub from scratches with padding or a blanket.

- When you use metal studs, be sure they meet ASTM C-645 requirements.

- Inspect the job progress daily to be sure all work is satisfactory.

Using Glass Mesh Mortar Units

Figure 10-4 shows a bathtub wall using glass mesh mortar units under the tile. Wood studs are recommended for this type of installation as well.

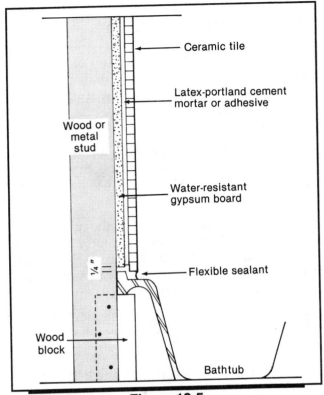

Figure 10-5
Bathtub wall using gypsum board

Again, they should be dry and braced, and spaced 16 inches on center. If you install metal studs, make sure they are minimum 20 gauge.

Install the units: Place the glass mesh mortar units against the studs, leaving a 1/8-inch spacing gap at all the joints and corners. Fill these spaces with latex-portland cement mortar or dry-set. Embed 2-inch wide glass fiber mesh tape in a thin coat of the same mortar and place it over the joints and corners. Always follow the manufacturer's instructions for installing the units. Figure 10-4 shows a cut-away of a glass mesh mortar unit installation.

Mortar: Apply a coat of latex-portland cement mortar or dry-set mortar to the unit.

Grout: Use a grout compatible with the materials used in the bond coat.

Caulk: Use silicone rubber caulking to complete the installation.

Make the tub recess no more than 1/2 inch longer than the length of the tub. Support and level the tub securely, using wood blocks or metal hangers.

Using Gypsum Board Backing

You can use water-resistant gypsum backing board satisfactorily on metal or wood studs in tub and shower enclosures.

Installation: Use 1/2-inch thick gypsum board over studs spaced 16 inches on center. Install the board horizontally, with the factory edge spaced 1/4 inch above the tub lip.

Seal and tape: Seal all openings cut in the board for plumbing, and all cut joints between pieces with adhesive. Tape board joints with a tape and joint compound bedding coat. Don't apply a finish coat. Cover nail heads with one coat of compound.

Tile and grout: Install ceramic tile with organic adhesive or latex-portland cement. See Figure 10-5 for this installation method.

Shower Walls and Receptors

You'll install shower wall tile just like bathtub wall tile. The difference is in the installation of the receptors or shower floor.

Using Cement Mortar

Figure 10-6 shows ceramic tile shower walls and receptor installed with cement mortar. Use this type of installation over wood or concrete subfloors.

Shower pan: Form the slope for the shower pan with cement mortar or preformed liners. Use crushed stone or broken pieces of tile around the drain to keep the mortar from blocking the weep

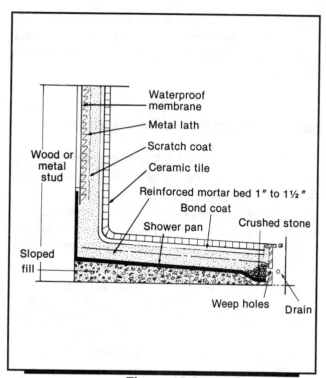

Figure 10-6
Shower walls and receptors using cement mortar

holes. Make the slope of the pan 1/4 inch per foot down to weep holes in the drain. Turn the pan up the shower wall at least 3 inches above the shower curb.

Mortar bed: Prepare the mortar bed by installing a waterproof membrane, metal lath, and scratch coat. Follow the procedures discussed for cement mortar bathtub walls. For mixing the mortar bed use:

1 part portland cement

4 parts damp sand by volume

Admixture to make mortar bed water resistant

Reinforce with 2-inch by 2-inch 16/16 gauge wire mesh.

Tile and grout: Lay out tile as discussed in Chapter 5. Select a grout meeting ANSI A118.6 specifications to complete the job.

Using Glass Mesh Mortar Units

Figure 10-7 shows the installation of a shower wall and receptor using glass mesh mortar units. You can use the units over metal studs, braced wood studs, and furring. Space the studs 16 inches on center.

Flush units to studs: To allow a flush fit with the face of the studs, you can notch the wood studs 1/4 inch to the height of the shower receptor.

Add 1/4-inch furring strips to the metal studs above the top of the shower receptor. Then the receptor will be flush with the face of the furring strips. Turn the receptor up the wall a minimum of 3 inches above the shower curb.

Prepare shower base: Form the slope for the receptor, 1/4 inch per foot to weep holes in the drain.

Install units: Use only glass mesh mortar units certified by the manufacturer as suitable for

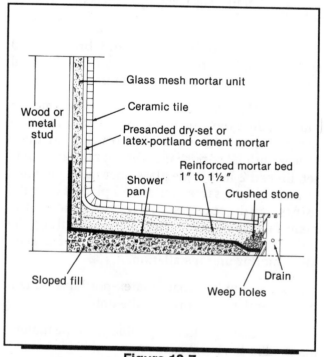

Figure 10-7
Shower walls and receptors using glass mesh mortar units

shower walls. Install the unit, leaving 1/8-inch spacing at all the joints and corners. Fill the spaces with dry-set or latex-portland cement. Embed 2-inch wide glass fiber mesh tape in a thin coat of the same mortar, and place it over joints and corners.

Mortar bed: Reinforce the mortar bed with 2-inch by 2-inch 16/16 gauge wire mesh. Use portland cement mortar. Place crushed stone or pieces of broken tile around the drain to prevent mortar from clogging the weep holes.

Tile and grout: Install the tile using dry-set mortar or latex-portland cement-mortar. Use grout that's compatible with bond and that is intended for use in showers. Complete your installation with silicone rubber caulking.

Using Gypsum Board Backing

Figure 10-8 shows a tile installation using water-resistant gypsum backing board over metal or wood studs. Install the gypsum board as we discussed in the installation of bathtub walls. Be sure you leave a 1/4-inch space between the gypsum board and the finished tile shower curb.

Shower receptor: The sloped fill, drain, and shower receptor in this installation are the same as in the cement mortar and glass mesh mortar unit installations already covered.

Tile and grout: Use an organic adhesive and install the tile following the adhesive manufacturer's instructions. Allow 24 hours after the tile is set before grouting.

The Finished Job

Figure 10-9 shows how elegant ceramic tile can look. Add mirrors to your design to give the bath an open feeling, especially in a room that has little natural light. In an installation of this type you'll

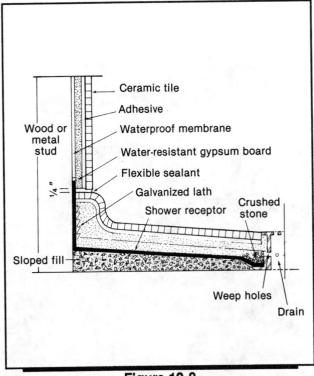

Figure 10-8
Shower walls and receptors using gypsum board

use many different types of tile trim. Figure 10-10 shows the types and placement of glazed tile trims in a bathroom.

We've covered some of the types of installations kitchen and bath remodelers do most often. Figure 10-11 is a typical architectural specifications (Section 09300) for tile installation which you can use as a helpful guide in preparing your specs. It can be modified to fit your job requirements.

Tilesetting is a specialist's field. When done properly, it's an art. Two good sources of information about ceramic tile are:

Ceramic Tile Institute of America
700 North Virgil Avenue
Los Angeles, CA 90029

Tile Council of America, Inc.
P.O. Box 326
Princeton, NJ 08540

Figure 10-9
An elegant tiled bathroom
Courtesy: Ceramic Tile Institute

Estimating Tile Manhours

As with all published labor tables, none are as good as the records you keep of your own crews' productivity. But until you have good records of your own, borrow mine. Figure 10-12 is my man-hour figures for installing ceramic tile. As usual, these figures include moving on and off the job, unloading materials and tools, and clean-up.

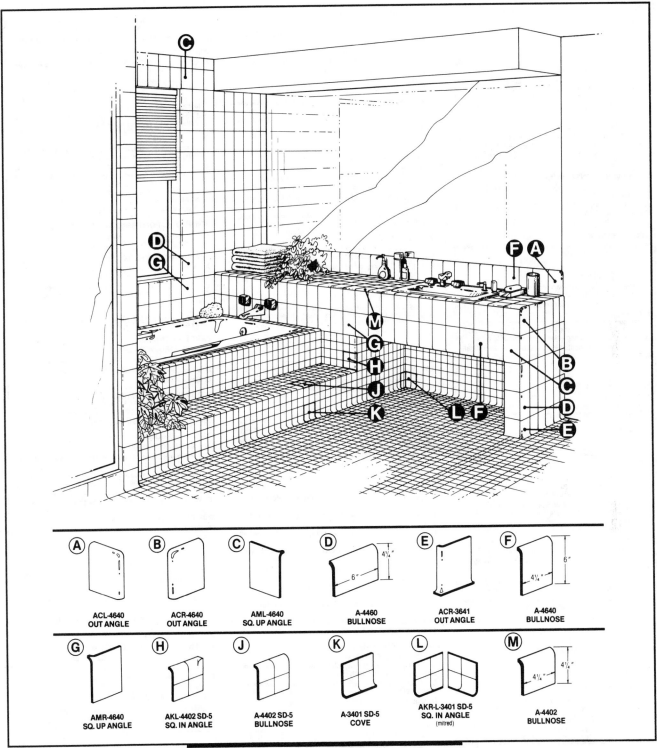

Figure 10-10
Glazed tile trim
Courtesy: American Olean Tile Co.

Ⓐ ACL-4640 OUT ANGLE	
Ⓑ ACR-4640 OUT ANGLE	
Ⓒ AML-4640 SQ. UP ANGLE	
Ⓓ A-4460 BULLNOSE 6" 4¼"	
Ⓔ ACR-3641 OUT ANGLE	
Ⓕ A-4640 BULLNOSE 6" 4¼"	
Ⓖ AMR-4640 SQ. UP ANGLE	
Ⓗ AKL-4402 SD-5 SQ. IN ANGLE	
Ⓙ A-4402 SD-5 BULLNOSE	
Ⓚ A-3401 SD-5 COVE	
Ⓛ AKR-L-3401 SD-5 SQ. IN ANGLE (mitred)	
Ⓜ A-4402 BULLNOSE 4¼" 4¼"	

Glazed Wall Tile   Section 09310

PART 1 — GENERAL

1.01 RELATED WORK SPECIFIED ELSEWHERE
A. Lathing and cement scratch coat   Section _____
B. Grab rails in tub areas   Section _____

1.02 SUBMITTALS
A. When applicable, furnish Master Grade Certificate signed by both tile manufacturer and tile subcontractor.
B. Submit one sample panel approximately 12″ square for each color, pattern and type of tile intended to be used. Obtain approval of job sample submittals before delivering any products to job site.

1.03 PRODUCT HANDLING
A. Deliver all products to job site in manufacturer's unopened containers with grade seals unbroken and labels intact.
B. Keep tile cartons dry.

1.04 ENVIRONMENTAL CONDITIONS
A. Maintain temperature at 50°F. minimum during tilework and for 7 days after completion.
B. Vent temporary heaters to outside to avoid carbon dioxide damage to new tilework.

1.05 EXTRA STOCK
A. Supply extra 2% of each tile used in clean marked cartons for owner's emergency use.

1.06 SUBSTITUTIONS
A. Where no brands or manufacturers are listed use any product which meets product specification.
B. Where brands or manufacturers are listed, use one of those listed.
C. Suggest substitution for brands or products listed only in writing, to be delivered to the architect at least 21 days prior to receipt of bids, and stating value of substitution to owner.
D. At least 14 days prior to bid date all bidders will be notified of any substitutions to be permitted in accordance with 1.06C.

PART 2 — PRODUCTS

2.01 CERAMIC TILE
A. Furnish only Standard Grade Glazed Wall Tile meeting ANSI A137.1, American Olean, _____ or, _____.

1. Supply _____
   size, shape, score, glaze
2. Use (Master-Set back-mounted sheets) (Redi-Set Systems 100 pregrouted sheets) (Redi-Set Systems 300 pregrouted sheets).
B. Glazed Wall Tile Trim
1. Furnish size, color and shade to match field tile.
2. Observe following requirements:
Wainscot Cap—Bullnose, except provide regular glazed flat tile where glazed tile wall surface is flush with plaster wall above.
Base — No cove required.
In-corners — Square or round.
Out-corners — Bullnose.
Jambs — Bullnose where tilework projects from jamb.
C. Accessories
1. Furnish vitreous china accessories, colors and size to (match) (coordinate with) glazed wall tile as follows:
   a. One soap holder at each shower and also at each tub.
   b. One roll paper holder at each water closet.

2.02 SETTING MATERIALS
A. Portland Cement: ASTM C150 Type 1, Gray or White.
B. Hydrated Lime: ASTM C206 or C207 Type S.
C. Sand: ASTM C144.
D. Water: Clean and drinkable.
E. Metal Lath:
1. Interior — ASTM C847.
   a. Most Uses — 2.5 lbs./sy., painted or galvanized.
   b. Metal Studs — 3.4 lbs./sy., painted or galvanized.
2. Exterior — ASTM C933, galvanized, 3.4 lbs./sy.
   a. Most Uses — 3.4 lbs./sy.

F. Concrete GMMU Backer Board: 7/16″ Wonder-Board®
G. Shrinkage Mesh: ASTM A82, A185, 2″ × 2″ 16/16.
H. Membrane:
   1. Roofing Felt: ASTM D226, asphalt.
   2. Reinforced Asphalt Paper: ASTM C171, duplex.
   3. Polyethylene: ASTM C171, 4 mil.
I. Dry-Set Mortars: ANSI A118.1, American Olean Sanded Thin-Set Mortar.
J. Latex Modified Thin-Set Mortars: ANSI A118.4.
   1. Interior: AO Latex Mortar Additive.
   2. Exterior: AO Acrylic Thin-Set Additive.
K. Organic Adhesives: ANSI A136.1 (Interiors).
   1. For walls in Non-Shower Areas — Type II, AO 1200.
   2. For walls in Shower Areas with Waterproof Joints (Silicone Rubber or Latex) — Type II, AO 1200.
   3. For walls in Shower Areas with Water-Permeable Joints (Dry Wall Grout) — Type I, AO 1200.
   4. For floors — Type I, AO 1700.
   5. For ceilings — Type I, AO 1700.
L. Silicone Rubber Adhesive: Dow Corning 784.
M. Epoxies:
   1. Floor & Wall Adhesive, AO 2000 Epoxy Adhesive.
   2. Light Duty Floor Mortar, AO 3000 Epoxy Mortar.
   3. Heavy Duty Floor Mortar: AO 4000 AAR-II Epoxy, ANSI A118.3.
   4. High Temperature Floor and Wall Mortar: AO 5000 HITOR II Epoxy ANSI A118.3.

2.03 GROUTING MATERIALS
A. For walls or floors: American Olean Dry Wall Grout _____ color ANSI A118.6.
B. For Redi-Set pregrouted glazed tile walls or floors: Dow Corning 784 White, fungicidal one-part, meeting Federal Specification TT-S-001543, Class A or B (COM-NBS).

2.04 SEALANTS
A. Tubs and Shower Receptors — Dow Corning 784 White, fungicidal one-part silicone rubber meeting Federal Specification TT-S-001543, Class A or B (COM-NBS).
B. Control Joints in Walls — Same as 2.04 A.

PART 3 — INSTALLATION

3.01 ACCEPTABILITY OF SURFACES
A. Before tiling, be sure variations of surface to be tiled fall within maximum variations shown below:

	Walls	Floors
Dry-Set Mortar	⅛″ in 8′	⅛″ in 10′
Epoxy	⅛″ in 8′	⅛″ in 10′
Organic Adhesive	⅛″ in 8′	1/16″ in 3′

Report all unacceptable surfaces to the architect and do not tile such surfaces until they are levelled enough to meet above requirements. Levelling coat (is) (is not) included in this section.
B. Before tiling, be sure surfaces to be tiled are free of curing membranes, oil, grease, wax and dust.

3.02 LAYOUT
A. Determine locations of all movement joints before starting tilework.
B. Determine locations of all porcelain accessories before starting tilework.
C. Lay out all tilework so as to minimize cuts less than one-half tile in size.
D. Locate tile cuts in both walls and floors so as to be least conspicuous.
E. Lay out tile wainscots to next full tile beyond dimensions shown.
F. Align all wall joints to give straight uniform grout lines, plumb and level.
G. Align all floor joints to give straight uniform grout lines, parallel with walls.
H. Make joints between tile sheets same width as joints within sheets so extent of each sheet is not apparent in finished work.

3.03 WORKMANSHIP
A. Supply first-class workmanship in all tilework.
B. Use all products in strict accordance with recommendations and directions of manufacturers.
C. Proportion all mixes in accordance with latest ANSI Standard Specifications.
D. Smooth all exposed cut tile edges.

E. Be sure cut tile edges are clean before installing.
F. Fit tile carefully against trim and porcelain accessories, also around pipes, electric boxes and other built-in fixtures so that escutcheons, plates and collars will completely overlap cut edges.
G. When using glazed tile sheets, minimize tearing sheets apart by drilling pipe holes as much as possible with a hole saw.
H. Be sure all tilework is free of grout film upon completion.

3.04 SETTING METHODS
A. GLAZED WALL TILE (Methods shown here are examples only. Specify one that is required.)
   1. Concrete Masonry Walls: ANSI A108.1 (Reference TCA Method W211, Cement Mortar, Bonded).
   2. On Wood Studs or Furring: ANSI A108.1 (Reference TCA Method W231, Cement Mortar).
   3. On Gypsum Wallboard: ANSI A108.4 (Reference TCA Method W242, Organic Adhesive).

3.05 GROUTING
A. Follow grout manufacturer's recommendations as to grouting procedures and precautions.
B. Remove all grout haze, observing both tile and grout manufacturers' recommendations as to use of acid and chemical cleaners.
C. Rinse tilework thoroughly with clean water before and after chemical cleaners.
D. Polish surface of tilework with soft cloth.

3.06 PROTECTION FROM CONSTRUCTION DIRT
A. Cover all tile floors with heavy-duty, non-staining construction paper, masked in place.

3.07 PROTECTION FROM TRAFFIC
A. Prohibit all foot and wheel traffic from using newly tiled floors for at least 3 days, preferably 7 days.
B. Place large, flat boards in walkways and wheelways for 7 days where use of newly tiled floors with cement type grout is unavoidable.

Ceramic Mosaics   Section 09320

PART 1 — GENERAL

1.01 RELATED WORK SPECIFIED ELSEWHERE
A. Waterproofing of shower floor.   Section _____
B. Lathing and cement scratch coat.   Section _____
C. Grab rails in tub areas.   Section _____

1.02 SUBMITTAL, 1.03 PRODUCT HANDLING, 1.04 ENVIRONMENTAL CONDITIONS, 1.05 EXTRA STOCK, 1.06 SUBSTITUTIONS.
Specification wording same as for Glazed Wall Tile.

PART 2 — PRODUCTS

2.01 CERAMIC MOSAICS
A. Furnish only Standard Grade ceramic mosaics conforming to ANSI A137.1, American Olean, _____ or _____.
B. Furnish porcelain type with all-purpose edges and patterns to be selected on basis of American Olean Price Range
C. Where shown, furnish tile with 7½% abrasive grain content.

2.02 CERAMIC MOSAIC TRIM
A. Furnish size, color and shade to match ceramic mosaic field tile.
B. Observe following requirements:
Walls — In-corners square.
Walls — Bullnose cap on wainscot except provide regular flat tile where ceramic mosaic wall surface is flush with plaster wall above.
Floors — Cove base required.
Curbs — Bullnose and cove are required for smooth rounded surface.
Jambs — Bullnose where tilework projects from jamb.

2.03 SETTING MATERIALS
A. Portland Cement: ASTM C150 Type 1, Gray or White.
B. Hydrated Lime: ASTM C206 or C207 Type S.
C. Sand: ASTM C144.
D. Water: Clean and drinkable.
E. Metal Lath:
   1. Interior — ASTM C847.
   a. Most Uses — 2.5 lbs./sy., painted or galvanized.
   b. Metal Studs — 3.4 lbs./sy., painted or galvanized.

Figure 10-11
Architectural specifications
Courtesy: American Olean Tile Co.

2. Exterior — ASTM C933, galvanized, 3.4 lbs./sy.
   a. Most Uses — 3.4 lbs./sy., painted or galvanized.
F. Concrete GMMU Backer Board: 7/16" Wonder-Board®
G. Shrinkage Mesh: ASTM A82, A185, 2" x 2" 16/16.
H. Membrane:
   1. Roofing Felt: ASTM D226, asphalt.
   2. Reinforced Asphalt Paper: ASTM C171, duplex.
   3. Polyethylene: ASTM C171, 4 mil.
I. Dry-Set Mortars: ANSI A118.1, American Olean Thin-Set Mortar (White) (Grey).
J. Latex Modified Thin-Set Mortars: ANSI A118.4.
   1. Interior: AO Latex Mortar Additive.
   2. Exterior: AO Acrylic Thin-Set Additive.
K. Organic Adhesives: ANSI A136.1 (Interiors).
   1. Walls, Floors, and Ceilings: AO 1700 Type I Adhesive.
L. Thin-Set Waterproofing: Tile Tite by Applied Polymers.
M. Epoxies:
   1. Floor & Wall Adhesive, AO 2000 Epoxy Adhesive.
   2. Light Duty Floor Mortar: AO 3000 Epoxy Mortar.
   3. Heavy Duty Floor Mortar: AO 4000 AAR-II Epoxy, ANSI A118.3.
   4. High Temperature Floor and Wall Mortar: AO 5000 HITOR II Epoxy ANSI A118.3.

2.04 GROUTING MATERIALS

A. Floors and Walls: American Olean Sanded Floor Grout, _____ color ANSI A118.6.
B. Floors and Walls: American Olean Sanded Floor Grout, _____ color, with AO Acrylic Grout Additive ANSI A118.6.
C. Special Floors: Epoxy grout meeting ANSI A118.3, TCA AAR-II Formulation, AO 4000 Epoxy _____ color.
D. High Temperature Resistant Floors: AO 5000 TCA Formulation HITOR II Epoxy Grout _____ color, ANSI A118.3.

PART 3 — INSTALLATION

3.01 ACCEPTABILITY OF SURFACES. Specification wording same as for Glazed Tile.

3.02 LAYOUT

A. Determine locations of all movement joints before starting tilework.
B. Lay out all tilework so as to minimize cuts less than one-half tile in size.
C. Locate tile cuts in both walls and floors so as to be least conspicuous.
D. Lay out tile wainscots to next full tile beyond dimension shown.
E. Align all wall joints to give straight uniform grout lines plumb and level.
F. Align all floor joints to give straight uniform grout lines.

3.03 WORKMANSHIP

A. Supply first-class workmanship in all tilework.
B. Use all products in strict accordance with recommendations and directions of manufacturers.
C. Proportion all mixes in accordance with latest ANSI Standard Specifications.
D. Smooth all exposed cut edges.
E. Be sure all tilework is clean of grout film upon completion.

3.04 SETTING METHODS (Methods shown are examples only. Specify one that is required.)
A. CERAMIC MOSAICS
   1. On Dimensionally Stable Concrete Subfloor: ANSI A108.1 (Reference TCA Method F112, Cement Mortar, Bonded).
   2. On Non-Dimensionally Stable Concrete Subfloor: ANSI A108.1 (Reference TCA Method F111, Cement Mortar, Cleavage Membrane).
   3. On Wood Subfloor: ANSI A108.1 (Reference TCA Method F141, Cement Mortar).
   4. On Dimensionally Stable Masonry Wall: ANSI A108.5 (Reference TCA Method W202, Dry-Set Mortar).

3.05 GROUTING
A. Follow grout manufacturer's recommendations as to grouting procedures and precautions.
B. Remove all grout haze, observing grout manufacturers' recommendations as to use of acid and chemical cleaners.
C. Rinse tilework thoroughly with clean water before and after using chemical cleaners.

3.06 PROTECTION FROM CONSTRUCTION DIRT
A. Cover all tile floors with heavy-duty, non-staining construction paper, masked in place.

3.07 PROTECTION FROM TRAFFIC
A. Prohibit all foot and wheel traffic from using newly tiled floors for at least 3 days, preferably 7 days.
B. Place large, flat boards in walkways and wheelways for 7 days where use of newly tiled floor with cement type grout is unavoidable.

Quarry Tile/ Quarry Naturals   Section 09330

PART 1 — GENERAL

1.01 RELATED WORK SPECIFIED ELSEWHERE
A. Sealants for movement joints.   Section _____
B. Waterproofing.   Section _____

1.02 SUBMITTALS
A. Furnish Master Grade Certificate signed by both tile manufacturer and tile subcontractor.
B. Submit one sample tile for each color, pattern and type to be used.

1.03 PRODUCT HANDLING
A. Deliver all products to job site in manufacturer's unopened containers with grade seals unbroken and labels intact.
B. Keep tile cartons dry.

1.04 ENVIRONMENTAL CONDITIONS
A. Maintain temperature at 50°F. minimum during tilework and for 7 days after completion.
B. Vent temporary heaters to outside to avoid carbon dioxide damage to new tilework.

1.05 EXTRA STOCK
A. Supply extra 2% of each tile used in clean marked cartons for owner's emergency use.

1.06 SUBSTITUTIONS
A. Where no brands or manufacturers are listed use any product which meets product specification.
B. Where brands or manufacturers are listed, use one of those listed.
C. Suggest substitution for brands or products listed only in writing to be delivered to the architect at least 21 days prior to receipt of bids, and stating value of substitution to owner.
D. At least 14 days prior to bid date all bidders will be notified of any substitutions to be permitted in accordance with 1.06C.

PART 2 — PRODUCTS

2.01 QUARRY TILE
A. Furnish only Standard Grade (Quarry Tile) (Quarry Naturals) conforming to ANSI A137.1, American Olean _____ or _____.
B. Supply _____ size, shape, color, flashing, abrasive grain
C. Quarry Tile trim.
   1. Furnish size, color and shade to match floor tile.
   2. Use (straight top) (round top) cove throughout.

2.02 SETTING MATERIALS
A. Portland Cement: ASTM C150 Type 1, Gray or White.
B. Hydrated Lime: ASTM C206 or C207 Type S.
C. Sand: ASTM C144.
D. Water: Clean and drinkable.
E. Metal Lath:
   1. Interior — ASTM C847.
   a. Most Uses — 2.5 lbs./sy., painted or galvanized.
   b. Metal Studs — 3.4 lbs./sy., painted or galvanized.
   2. Exterior — ASTM C933, galvanized, 3.4 lbs./sy.
   a. Most Uses — 3.4 lbs./sy., painted or galvanized.
F. Concrete GMMU Backer Board: 7/16" Wonder-Board®.
G. Shrinkage Mesh: ASTM A82, A185, 2" x 2" 16/16.
H. Membrane:
   1. Roofing Felt: ASTM D226, asphalt.
   2. Reinforced Asphalt Paper: ASTM C171, duplex.
   3. Polyethylene: ASTM C171, 4 mil.
I. Dry-Set Mortars: ANSI A118.1, American Olean Thin-Set Mortar (White) (Grey).
J. Latex Modified Thin-Set Mortars: ANSI A118.4.
   1. Interior: AO Latex Mortar Additive.
   2. Exterior: AO Acrylic Thin-Set Additive.

K. Organic Adhesives: ANSI A136.1 (Interiors).
   1. Walls, Floors, and Ceilings: AO 1700 Type I Adhesive.
L. Thin-Set Waterproofing: Tile Tite by Applied Polymers.
M. Epoxies:
   1. Floor & Wall Adhesive, AO 2000 Epoxy Adhesive.
   2. Light Duty Floor Mortar: AO 3000 Epoxy Mortar.
   3. Heavy Duty Floor Mortar: AO 4000 AAR-II Epoxy, ANSI A118.3.
   4. High Temperature Floor and Wall Mortar: AO 5000 HITOR II Epoxy ANSI A118.3.

2.03 GROUTING MATERIALS
A. Floors and Walls: American Olean Sanded Floor Grout, _____ color ANSI A118.6.
B. Special Floors: Epoxy grout meeting ANSI A118.3, TCA AAR-II Formulation, AO 4000 Epoxy _____ color.
C. High Temperature Resistant Floors: AO 5000 TCA Formulation HITOR II Epoxy Grout _____ color ANSI A118.3.
D. Special Chemical Resistance: Furan Grout: (Tiloment), (Black Furnane), (Furathane) as made by Atlas Minerals & Chemicals, Inc.

PART 3 — INSTALLATION

3.01 ACCEPTABILITY OF SURFACES
A. Before tiling, be sure variations of surface to be tiled fall within maximum variations shown below:

	Walls	Floors
Dry-Set Mortar	1/8" in 8'	1/4" in 10'
Epoxy Mortar	1/8" in 8'	1/4" in 10'
Organic Adhesive	1/8" in 8'	1/16" in 3'

Report all unacceptable surfaces to the architect and do not tile such surfaces until they are levelled enough to meet above requirements. Levelling coat (is) (is not) included in this section.
B. Before tiling, be sure surfaces to be tiled are free from coating, curing membranes, oil, grease, wax and dust.

3.02 LAYOUT
A. Determine locations of all movement joints before starting tilework.
B. Lay out all tilework so as to minimize cuts less than one-half tile in size.
C. Locate tile cuts in both walls and floors so as to be least conspicuous.
D. Align all floor joints to give straight uniform grout lines, parallel with walls.

3.03 WORKMANSHIP
A. Supply first-class workmanship in all tilework.
B. Use all products in strict accordance with recommendations and directions of manufacturer.
C. Proportion all mixes in accordance with latest ANSI Standard Specifications.
D. Be sure all tilework is free of grout film upon completion.

3.04 SETTING METHODS (Methods shown are examples only. Specify one that is required.)
A. On Dimensionally Stable Concrete, ANSI A108.1 (Reference TCA Method F112, Cement Mortar Bonded).
B. On Non-Dimensionally Stable Concrete Subfloor: ANSI A108.1 (Reference TCA Method F111, Cement Mortar, Cleavage Membrane).
C. On Wood Subfloor: ANSI A108.1 (Reference TCA Method F141, Cement Mortar).
D. On Wood Subfloor: ANSI A108.6 (Reference TCA Method F143, Epoxy Mortar).

3.05 GROUTING
A. Follow grout manufacturer's recommendations as to grouting procedures and precautions.
B. Remove all grout haze, observing grout manufacturers' recommendations as to use of acid and chemical cleaners.
C. Rinse tilework thoroughly with clean water before and after chemical cleaners.

3.06 PROTECTION FROM CONSTRUCTION DIRT
A. Cover all tile floors with heavy-duty, non-staining construction paper, masked in place.

3.07 PROTECTION FROM TRAFFIC
A. Prohibit all foot and wheel traffic from using newly tiled floors for at least 3 days, preferably 7 days.
B. Place large, flat boards in walkways and wheelways for 7 days where use of newly tiled floors with cement type grout is unavoidable.

Figure 10-11
Architectural specifications (continued)
Courtesy: American Olean Tile Co.

Work element	Unit	Manhours per unit
Floor tile in portland cement bed		
1" x 1", face mounted	100 SF	17.0
2" x 2", face mounted	100 SF	15.0
Floor tile in organic adhesive bed		
1" x 1", face mounted	100 SF	11.5
2" x 2", face mounted	100 SF	10.5
Wall tile and trim in portland cement bed		
4 1/4" x 4 1/4", unmounted	100 SF	19.0
6" x 6", unmounted	100 SF	18.0
Wall tile in organic adhesive bed		
4 1/4" x 4 1/4", unmounted	100 SF	15.0
6" x 6", unmounted	100 SF	14.0
Tile cap	100 LF	19.0
Tile base	100 LF	23.0
Shower walls and floor in portland cement bed		
4" x 4"	100 SF	19.0

Figure 10-12
Estimating tile manhours

Residential Wiring

If you remodel kitchen and baths, you'll have to deal with residential wiring. You'll add electrical circuits, add or relocate switches and receptacles, and install or replace light fixtures and appliances.

There are two very important items to remember when you work with electricity. First, make sure all the wiring you do complies with code, either national, state, or local. Second, *never work on a hot line*. Always disconnect the electricity *before* you begin work. Remove the fuse or trip the breaker in the main panel.

The Residential Electrical System

Most home electrical systems consist of a 120/240 volt power source. The power is delivered by three wires leading from a transformer through an electrical meter to the main service panel in the house. Circuits carry the electricity from the main panel to switches, receptacles, lights, and appliances throughout the home.

The main panel may be equipped with breakers or fuses. These are the brains that protect the system — and the house — from the hazards of overloads and shorts.

A modern, well-equipped home needs a 150-amp or 200-amp main panel to handle today's electrical demands. Many older homes have 60-amp or 100-amp panels. These provided adequate service when they were installed. But add a few appliances and an electric heater or air conditioner and your clients need larger panels. A 200-amp panel provides the same capacity as a 150-amp panel, except it will handle electrical heating loads as well. Electric heating puts a heavy demand on household systems.

Electrical Terms and Their Relationships

Volts, amperes, and watts are the terms you hear when people are talking about electricity. Not everyone understands what they mean. More important, not everyone knows how electricity works. Your clients just need to know that it works — but you need to know why and how.

Voltage is like the pressure in a garden hose. An ampere is the flow rate. In that garden hose, it would be the gallons per minute. The watt is the unit which measures current usage.

To continue the water hose analogy, suppose there's a small hole in the hose allowing water to spray out. This leak lowers the water pressure and rate of flow. In the same way, a current drain (wattage) in an electrical circuit affects the voltage (pressure) and amperage (rate of flow) of the current. Here's how it looks:

1 amp at 1 volt pressure equals 1 watt

1 watt used for 1 hour equals 1 watt-hour

1,000 watt-hours equal 1 kilowatt

Volts times amps equals watts. If you know the amps and voltage and want to find the watts, multiply volts by amps.

For example, your table saw is rated at 4.75 amps and you want to know the watts. Multiply the volts (most homes have a 120-volt power source) times the amps: 120 volts x 4.75 amps = 570 watts.

Watts divided by volts equals amps: If you know the watts and wish to know how many amps you're using, divide the watts by the voltage.

For example, your electric range uses 8,000 to 16,000 watts. You want to know amps. Divide your watts by volts (an electric range needs a 240-volt current):

8,000 watts divided by 240 volts = 33.33 amps

16,000 watts divided by 240 volts = 66.66 amps

Your range pulls 33.33 amps at 8,000 watts, and 66.66 amps at 16,000 watts.

Wire Size and Capacity

The chart shows the wire sizes used most in residential electrical systems. Notice that the smaller the wire size number, the larger the diameter of the wire and the greater its capacity.

Wire size (copper)	*Amps	**Watts
No. 14	15	1800
No. 12	20	2400
No. 10	30	3600
No. 8	40	4800
No. 6	50	8400
No. 4	70	9600
* Use same size fuse or circuit breaker **When using 120 volts		

Many electricians use nothing smaller than wire size No. 12 for 15-amp circuits. They use smaller wire sizes, like No. 18 and No. 16, for low-voltage systems such as door bells, thermostats, or intercoms.

Electric dryers, water heaters, and ranges all operate on 240-volt circuits. Use wire size Nos. 6, 8, and 10 for 240-volt appliance hook-ups. The amps rating of an appliance determines the wire size you'll need. Use the chart as a guide.

Many kitchen and bathroom remodelers prefer to install two 30-amp circuits in the kitchen instead of the two 20-amp circuits normally used. This gives homeowners a lot more capacity to handle future electrical needs. A 30-amp circuit requires wire size No. 10.

Cable Identification Markings

Romex is a trade name for a nonmetallic (NM) sheathed cable. BX or Greenfield are trade names for flexible armored cable. Plastic sheathed cable is a NM cable. It's available in indoor type and underground type for indoor or outdoor use.

Electrical cable is identified by special markings. A cable marked *10-2 G NM* tells you:

10 - wire size number

2 - number of conductor wires in cable

G - with ground wire (usually bare)

NM - nonmetallic

A cable marked *10-3 G NM* means: No. 10 wire size with 3 conductor wires, ground wire, nonmetallic.

Wire Color Coding

If you look inside the cables we just discussed, you'll find that the wires are different colors. The 10-2 G NM has a black wire (hot), a white wire (neutral), and a ground wire (bare). The 10-3 G NM has a black wire (hot), a red wire (hot), a white wire (neutral), and a ground wire (bare).

Color coding ensures the electrical system is properly wired. The color codes indicate the following:

- Black wire is *hot*

- Red wire is *hot*

- White wire is *neutral*

- Grounding wire is *bare*

Never connect a *black* wire to a *white* wire. Never connect a *red* wire to a *white* wire.

Always connect the black wire to the dark or copper-colored terminal on fuse boxes, switches, receptacles, and to the black wire of lights and fixtures.

Ground the white wire, also called the *continuous wire*, at the main panel ground bar. Connect the white wire to the light or silver-colored terminal of all receptacles, and to the white wire of lights and fixtures.

The grounding (or ground) wire is normally bare. Connect it to the green grounding hex screw or to the metal box. The ground wire carries an electrical short to the ground. It protects people from shock and electrical equipment from damage if there's a lightning strike.

Exception to the black-to-white wire rule. Where the electric source (power lead) enters the light fixture and the switch is at the end of the run, you can connect the white wire to the black lead to form a switch leg or loop. In a switch loop, always paint the white wire insulation black at both ends. (See *Switch Leg or Loop Connections* for details on how to wire this connection.)

Ground Fault Circuit Interrupters (GFCI)

The GFCI is a safety device that monitors the flow of electricity through the hot wire and the neutral wire. Normally, the same amount of electricity flows through both wires.

Here's how it works. Suppose someone touches a hot wire, creating a temporary electrical path to the ground. Some of the electricity passes through that person and into the ground. When less current returns through the white wire (because a portion of it is passing through the person), it results in an imbalance of electricity flowing through the hot and neutral leads. This is called a ground fault. The GFCI detects the imbalance and cuts off the current within about 25/1000 of a second. This can prevent an electrocution.

There are three types of GFCIs. One type plugs into a grounded receptacle. Any appliance plugged into the GFCI has ground fault protection. A second type replaces a regular receptacle. The third type replaces a circuit breaker, giving ground fault protection to the complete circuit.

Working with Residential Wiring

Here are guidelines for working with residential wiring:

Provide at least two 20-amp grounded circuits for the kitchen and laundry room, independent of lighting fixtures.

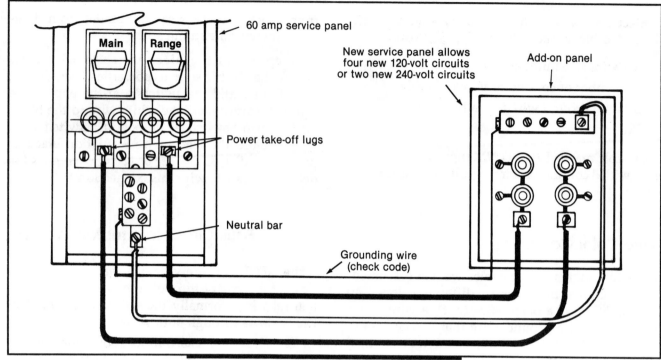

Figure 11-1
Add new circuits

- In your design, allow one outlet for each 12 feet of wall space. You can put eight receptacles on a convenience circuit, unless otherwise specified by your local code.

- Locate receptacles 12 inches up from the floor.

- Locate switches 48 inches up from the floor, on the swing side (door knob side) of the door.

- Locate receptacles 8 inches above countertops and 48 inches apart. It isn't a good idea to place receptacles over sinks or cooktops.

- Provide a separate 15-amp circuit for the refrigerator.

- Don't locate receptacles or switches near bathtubs or showers. Someone standing in the tub or shower shouldn't be able to touch an electrical source.

Adding on to the Household Electrical System

Adding new circuits, outlets, switches, and light fixtures is relatively easy when you're framing a new house or an addition. When you've already installed the finish wall and ceiling, however, adding them can be a real headache.

New Circuits

New circuits begin at the main service panel. Most fuse-type panels in older homes have two power take-off lugs located between the two left and two right plug fuses. You can add additional circuits by installing an add-on fuse panel or circuit breaker panel to the power take-off lugs. See Figure 11-1.

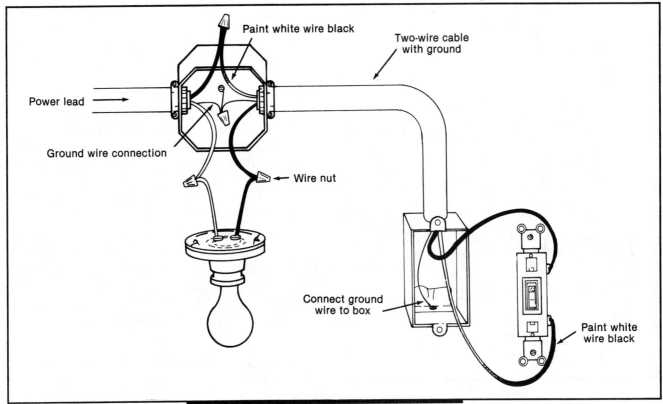

Figure 11-2
Switch loop

Use No. 6 wire or larger to connect the panels. Secure two black wires to the power take-off lugs. Attach a white wire to the neutral bar, and the ground wire to the grounding bar or strip (be sure to check your local code).

This hook-up provides 120 volts between the black and white wires, or a 240-volt circuit between the two black wires at the add-on panel. In most of these main fuse panels, the power take-off lugs are fused at 60 amps in the main disconnect. Any take-off from the lugs must be to a fused or breaker-type box.

The Switch Leg or Loop Connection

Before we cover adding new receptacles, switches or fixtures, let's discuss the switch leg or loop. It comes up in many situations where you're adding onto existing wiring. Figure 11-2 shows a switch loop. The two-wire cable power lead (with ground) runs from the power source to the ceiling box. The black (hot) wire loops from the ceiling box through the switch and back to the light fixture.

The only time you would connect a black wire to a white wire is in a switch loop. *The white wire is always neutral except when you use it in a loop. Then it becomes hot.* Paint the white wire black at the switch and at the ceiling box. Whenever you're working on wiring and you see a white wire painted black, it's a hot wire.

New Receptacles

A receptacle is a convenience outlet that allows you to plug in electrical items. You'll use 15-amp,

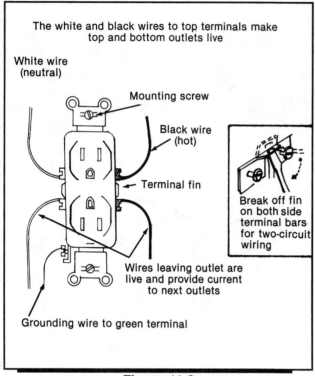

The white and black wires to top terminals make top and bottom outlets live

White wire (neutral)

Mounting screw

Black wire (hot)

Terminal fin

Break off fin on both side terminal bars for two-circuit wiring

Wires leaving outlet are live and provide current to next outlets

Grounding wire to green terminal

Figure 11-3
Duplex receptacle with single-circuit wiring

125-volt duplex outlets with grounding hex screws in most residential wiring. The outlets include two 6/32 threaded screws to secure them to the wall box.

Normally, you can have eight receptacles on one general purpose circuit. These circuits supply power to all the lights and outlets in a home except for the kitchen, dining area, and laundry or utility room. Usually, electrical codes require more circuits for kitchen and utility rooms. Be sure to check your local code for restrictions on kitchen and appliance circuits.

Use only grounded receptacles when you're adding outlets. Locate wall outlets 12 inches from the floor and no more than 12 feet apart. Over counter space, locate outlets no more than 4 feet apart and at least 8 inches above the countertop. Again, don't install outlets above a sink or stovetop surface.

The split-circuit outlet: The Leviton receptacle, No. 264B, has push-in terminals and side-wired terminals with a break-off fin for two-circuit wiring. Break off the terminal fin at the dark termi-

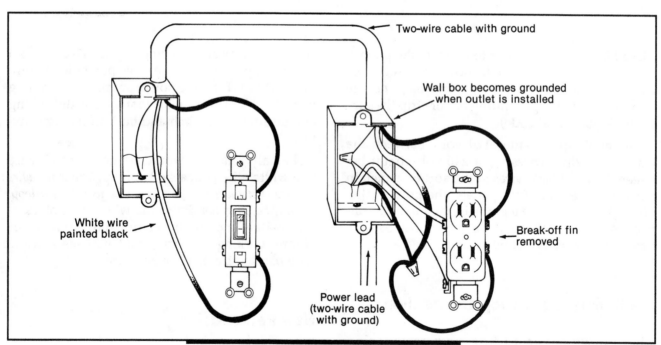

Two-wire cable with ground

Wall box becomes grounded when outlet is installed

White wire painted black

Break-off fin removed

Power lead (two-wire cable with ground)

Figure 11-4
Split-circuit outlet

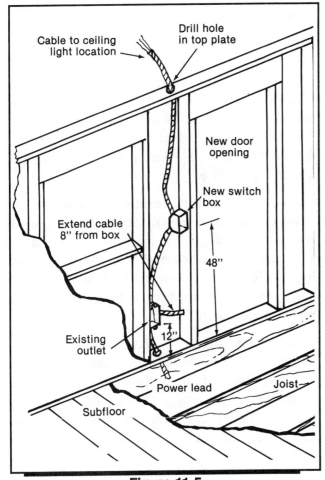

Figure 11-5
Add switch and light from an existing outlet

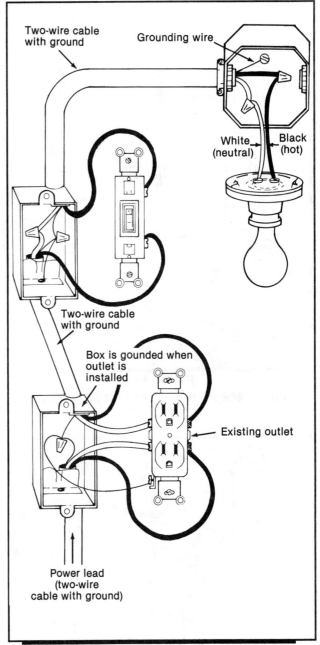

Figure 11-6
Adding switch and light to existing outlet

nals with a downward pry of a screwdriver. This interrupts the connection between the side terminals, permitting you to wire the duplex outlet to two separate circuits. You can have the top outlet on one circuit, and the bottom outlet on another. See Figure 11-3.

Figure 11-4 shows how to wire a split-circuit outlet. Notice that you have a switch loop and that the white wire is painted black, both at the switch and the outlet. The single pole switch controls the top half of the outlet. The bottom half is always hot.

Adding a switch and light fixture to an existing outlet: To add a switch and light fixture to an

existing outlet, cut an opening for a wall box at the new switch location. Locate the switch 48 inches up from the floor on the swing side of the door. Fish or snake a two-wire cable with a ground from the outlet box to the new switch box.

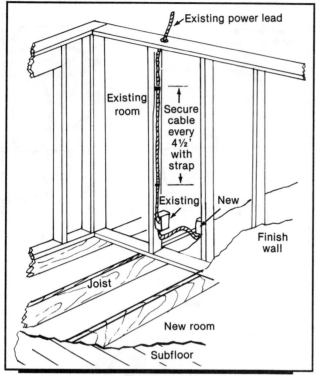

Figure 11-7
Add a receptacle from an existing outlet in adjacent room

Extend the cable about 8 inches out of the box so there's enough cable to make the connections.

From the attic area, drill a 3/4-inch hole in the top plate and run a cable down to the switch location. See Figure 11-5. Pull the other end of the cable to the light fixture location in the ceiling or wall. Drill a hole and run the wiring to the light fixture. To connect the wiring, follow the illustration in Figure 11-6.

Adding a receptacle to an existing outlet: The duplex outlet is the one most commonly used in residential wiring. In a finish wall installation you can use an existing outlet in an adjacent room to provide electricity to an add-on outlet. You can install the new outlet back-to-back with the old, or space them a stud apart.

Cut an opening in the finish wall for the new outlet box. If possible, locate the new outlet on the inside of the stud facing the existing outlet. See Figure 11-7. That way you don't have to drill a hole in the stud for the cable. Fish the cable from

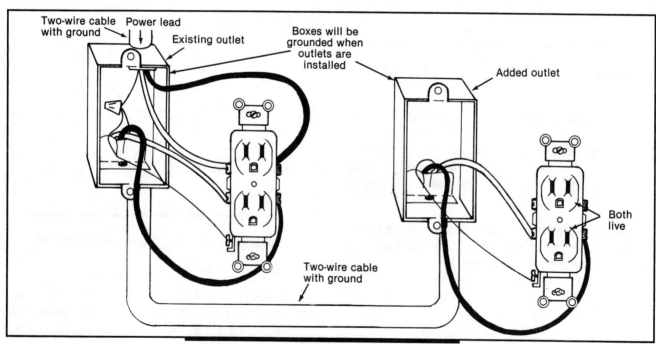

Figure 11-8
Adding new receptacle to existing outlet

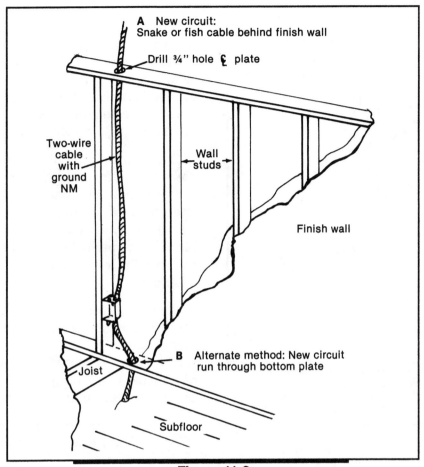

Figure 11-9
Add a receptacle by running a new cable
through top or bottom plate

the existing outlet to the add-on. Figure 11-8 shows you how to make the wiring connections.

Adding a receptacle on a new circuit: Sometimes you'll have to add a receptacle to a new circuit instead of using an existing outlet. Run the cable from a junction box or main panel through the top plate (See Figure 11-9, section A), or the bottom plate (section B). Drill a 3/4-inch hole in the center of the plate between studs and fish the wire into the add-on box.

New Fixtures

You can take current from an existing ceiling box or light fixture and add new wiring for a receptacle or fixture. Run the wiring direct or through a switch. Figure 11-10 shows how to make the connections.

Figure 11-11 shows how you can run current from an existing fixture to an add-on fixture and have them controlled by a common switch.

New Switches

There are three common types of residential switches. They are the single pole switch, the three-way switch, and the four-way switch. The three types are shown in Figure 11-12.

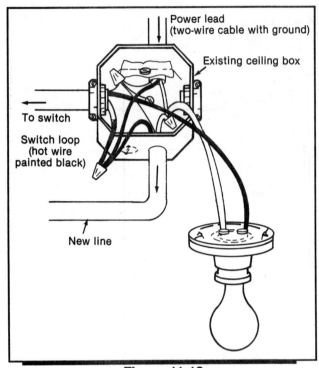

Figure 11-10
Take off new wiring from existing ceiling box

Single pole: A single pole switch controls a receptacle or light from one convenient location. It's usually immediately inside the room on the swing side of a door. The switch has two brass-colored terminals (screws) and *on* and *off* positions marked on the lever. Refer to Figure 11-11 to see the wiring for a single pole switch.

Three-way: A three-way switch must be used in pairs to control a receptacle or light from two different locations. You use this type of switch at either end of a hall or the top and bottom of stairwells. The switch has three terminals: one black, or copper-colored, and two brass or silver-colored. The lever has no markings for on and off positions.

Connecting three-way switches can be very confusing without a diagram to follow. Many remodeling projects in older homes require three-way switches. Figure 11-13 shows the connections of switches controlling a single light fixture with the power lead first going through the switches.

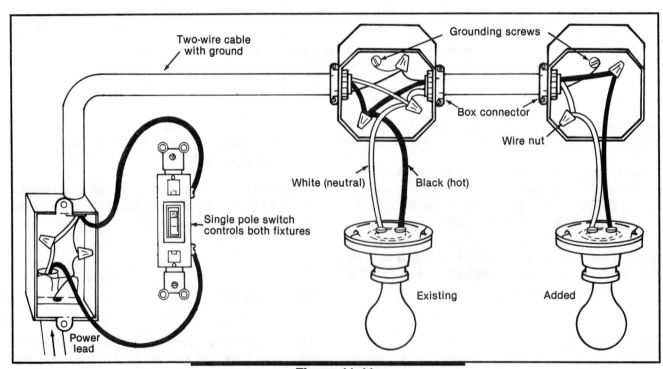

Figure 11-11
Adding light fixture to existing fixture

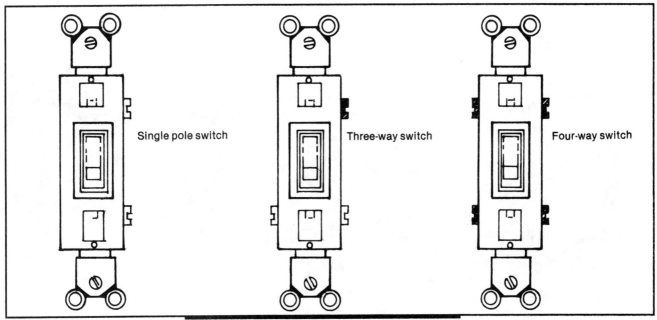

Figure 11-12
Three types of switches

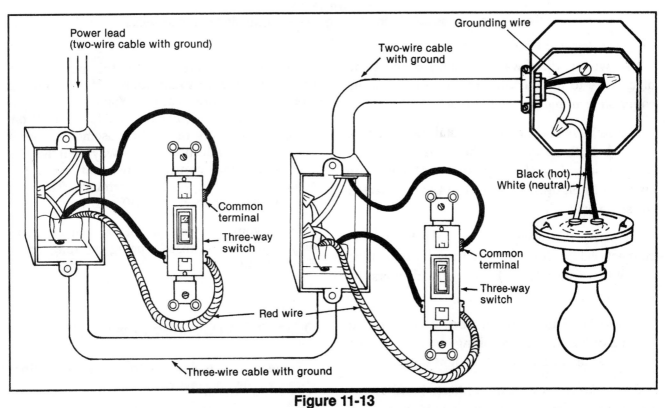

Figure 11-13
Three-way switches controlling one light — current first entering switches

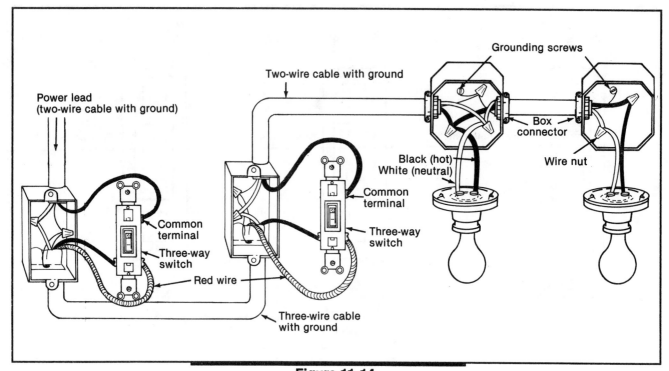

Figure 11-14
Three-way switches controlling two lights — current first entering switches

When wiring three-way switches, connect the black wire to the dark-colored terminal. It's the common terminal for the hot line.

Figure 11-14 shows how to install two lights at the end of three-way switches with the power lead first going through the switches. The switches in Figure 11-13 and 11-14 are connected the same way.

Figure 11-15 shows how to make the wiring connections for three-way switches located at the end of the circuit. Here the power lead enters the light fixture first.

Figure 11-16 illustrates a three-way switch at the end of the circuit controlling two lights, when the power lead first enters the light fixtures.

Figure 11-17 shows a light fixture installed between three-way switches with the power lead first entering the fixture.

Four-way: A four-way switch works with three-way switches to control receptacles or lights from three or more locations. You can use a four-way switch to turn lights on at the top and bottom of basement stairs or at the basement exterior entrance. Use additional four-way switches for each additional control point you need. The switch has four brass-colored terminals. The lever has no markings for on and off positions.

Make your connections for each of the four-way switches you install, using the diagram in Figure 11-18.

Other Switch Connections

There are several ways to make connections with a single pole switch.

Switch controlling two lights — power lead entering fixtures: Look carefully at Figure 11-19.

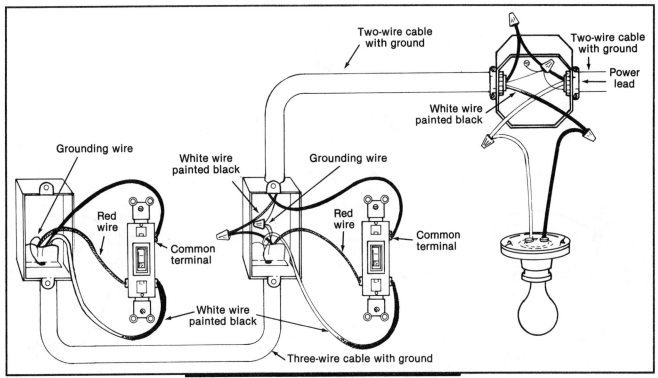

Figure 11-15
Three-way switches at end of circuit — current entering light fixture

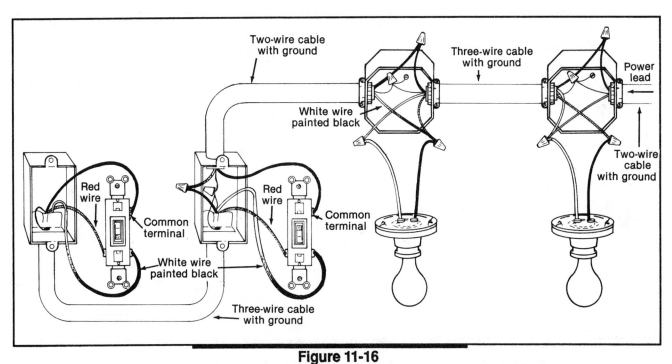

Figure 11-16
Three-way switches at end of circuit — current first entering light fixtures

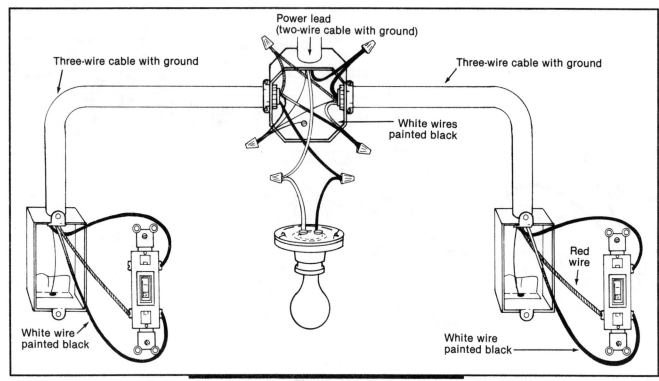

Figure 11-17
Fixture installed between three-way switches with current first entering light fixture

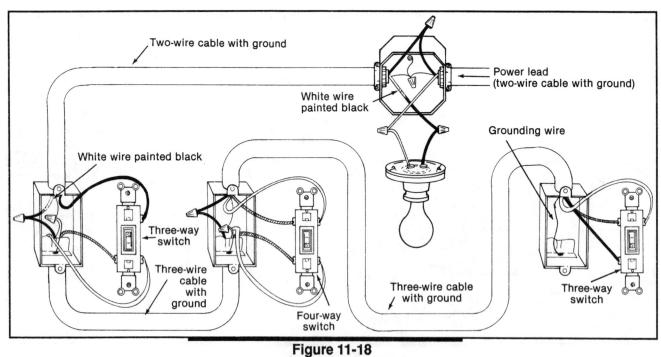

Figure 11-18
Connections using four-way switch — current first entering light fixture

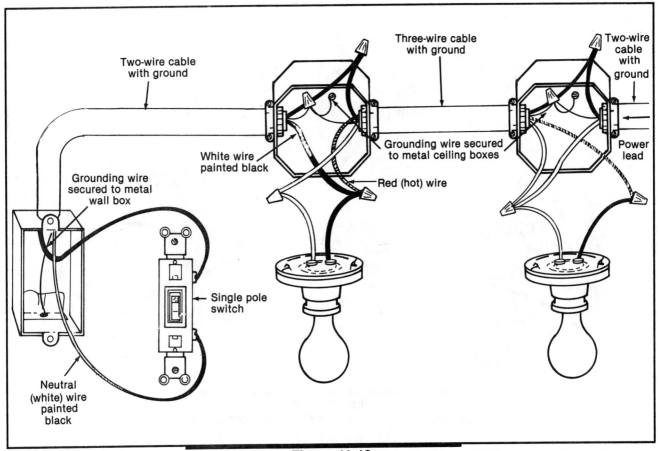

Figure 11-19
Connections with power lead first entering light fixture

This connection is similar to the one shown in Figure 11-16, except that you have only one switch. Figure 11-19 shows how to make a single switch connection when the power lead first enters through two light fixtures.

Wiring a single pole switch to light and outlet: Figure 11-20 shows how to wire a single pole switch to a light and outlet with the current first entering the switch. This connection makes the outlet always hot.

Figure 11-21 shows how to wire a single pole switch, outlet, and light with the current first entering the light fixture. Again, the outlet is always hot.

Switch-controlled outlet: A switch-controlled outlet is shown in Figure 11-22. In this connection the current first enters the outlet wall box.

Most remodeling jobs require that you add circuits, outlets, lights, or switches. You can do this work without complications if you plan carefully and take safety precautions.

- Never work on hot wiring. Always turn the electricity off *first*.

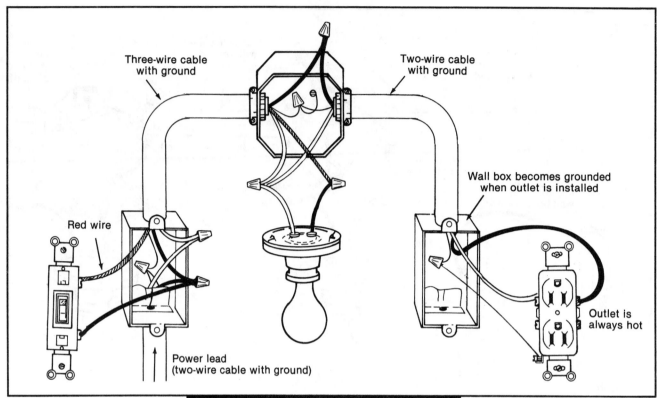

Figure 11-20
Connecting a single pole switch, light and outlet

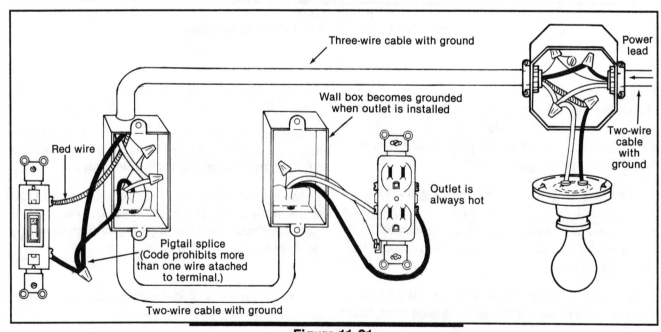

Figure 11-21
Connecting a single pole switch light and outlet with current entering light fixture

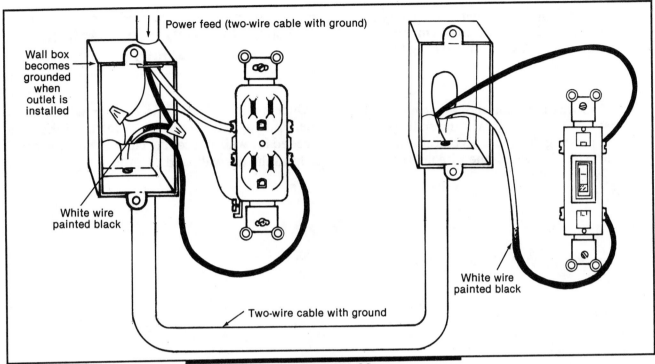

Figure 11-22
Switch-controlled outlet

Work element	Unit	Manhours per unit
Add 60-amp panel from power take-off lug	1	8.0
Run electrical circuit (non-metallic sheathed cable) with attic and crawl space access	50 LF	2.5
Install duplex wall outlet and cable in finished wall from existing outlet	each	2.5
Install 4" octagon ceiling box and cable in finished ceiling from junction box (attic access)	each	2.0
Install wall box, switch and cable in finished wall from existing ceiling box (attic access)	each	3.0
Install flush mounted ceiling light fixture	each	1.0
Install wall-mounted light fixture	each	0.7
Three-way switch hook-up	pair	1.0
Four-way switch hook-up with pair of three-way switches	set	1.5

Figure 11-23
Manhours for electrical wiring

- Don't overtighten the wire clamps on box connectors. Overtightening clamps can cause a short in the circuit. A snug fit is all that's necessary.

- Wrap wire nut connections with electrical tape. Wire nuts can crack and split open if you overtighten them. Electrical tape insulates the wires if the wire nuts crack.

Estimating Labor for Electrical Wiring

Once again, I'll end this chapter with typical manhour figures. Figure 11-23 includes the time needed for wall and ceiling cutouts, snaking cable behind the drywall, and clean-up.

Suspended and Luminous Ceilings

A suspended ceiling (also called a drop ceiling) might be the design idea that gets you the job for a kitchen or bath remodel. Suspended ceilings can be a good choice in an old kitchen or bath. You can use ceiling tile in combination with diffuser panels, or install all diffuser panels to produce a "ceiling of light." Either way, the added light will make the room brighter and larger in appearance.

Whether your clients choose ceiling tile or diffuser panels, the procedure for installing the gridwork is the same. There are many different types of tiles and panels to choose from. The most common are the 2- by 4-foot ceiling tile panels made of wood or mineral fiber, and the polystyrene light panels in the same size. The most important step in the installation is planning the job carefully. A proper layout will save you time and keep waste down to a minimum.

Determine Your Client's Lighting Needs

Plan to leave a minimum of 5-1/2 inches between the old ceiling and the suspended ceiling for the light fixtures. Some light fixtures may require even more space. Always check the fixture manufacturer's instructions. If your clients want a combination of ceiling tile and diffuser panels, be sure to line up your light fixtures so they're centered above the diffuser panels. If you're installing a luminous ceiling (using only diffuser panels), paint the old ceiling white to provide a light-reflective underneath surface.

For best results, use 40-watt, 4-foot fluorescent lamps. They give much more light per watt than incandescent bulbs. Allow at least 4 inches between the bottom of the tube and the light diffuser panel. Here are some suggestions to help you determine the number of fluorescent lamps needed for the area you're remodeling:

- High light - One 40-watt lamp for each 8 square feet of ceiling.

- Medium light - One 40-watt lamp for each 16 square feet of ceiling.

- Minimum light - One 40-watt lamp for each 24 square feet of ceiling.

A dimmer control switch is available if you want to offer varying light density.

Light Diffusers

Light diffusers come in many designs and textures. They're made of a high transmission, glare-free polystyrene. Flat and prismatic panels are the most popular, but your clients can also choose from other decorative styles. You can cut them to fit odd angles or ceilings that aren't quite square.

The texture and design as well as the type of lamp you're using determine how much light you'll have. The clear prism styles allow 80 to 85 percent of the light to penetrate the panel. The frosted or textured panels may allow only 60 to 65 percent light transmission. Louver type panels and cell type panels are also available. The less light you have coming through the panel itself, the more lamps you'll need to satisfy the lighting requirements. Keep that in mind when you're working on your plan.

The Gridwork

Aluminum is the most common material for suspended ceiling gridwork. Solid aluminum track is available in natural or a gold anodized finish. You can get painted rails as well, but they can peel, discolor, or rust. Steel track is available from some suppliers.

If you're installing ceiling tile and your client doesn't want the rails of the gridwork to show, you can use an interlocking tongue-and-flange type tile. They lock one into the other over the rail

as you install them. The Integrid Suspension System by Armstrong is a hidden grid system.

The Room Layout

Now let's look at a layout for a suspended ceiling. Assume that you're working with a kitchen that's 16 feet by 18 feet, with a cutout. Draw an outline of the room on a layout sheet. Use a printed grid sheet like the one shown in Figure 12-1 to do your drawing.

Indicate the main grid runners on the room layout sheet. They should be 4 feet apart and perpendicular to the ceiling joists. See Figure 12-2. Position the main runners so that the border panels along the room edges are equal in size and as large as possible.

Next, draw in the cross tees, keeping the border panels equal, and again, as large as possible. If you're installing 2- by 4-foot panels (whether they're luminous or tile), draw 4-foot cross tees every 2 feet between the main runners. For 2- by 2-foot ceiling tile, add another cross tee at the 2-foot midpoint of the cross tees. See Figure 12-3.

If you're installing ceiling tile with light fixtures above the ceiling, indicate the location of the diffuser panels on your drawing. For a luminous ceiling, all the panels are diffusers.

Use the same procedure for planning out simple square or rectangular rooms as you did for the rectangular cutout we used for our example.

Odd Dimensions

If you're planning a suspended ceiling for a room with odd dimensions, the layout is a little more complicated. Let's say the room is a rectangle, 9 feet by 20 feet 6 inches (see Figure 12-4). Draw the room layout on the grid just as we discussed above. Now you have to decide which way you want the panels to run. Usually, the

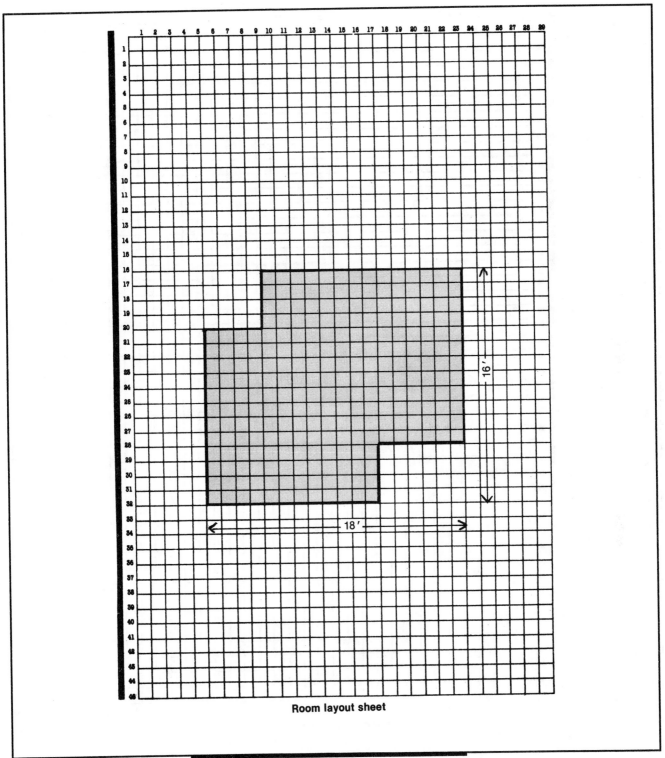

Figure 12-1
Show exact dimensions and shape

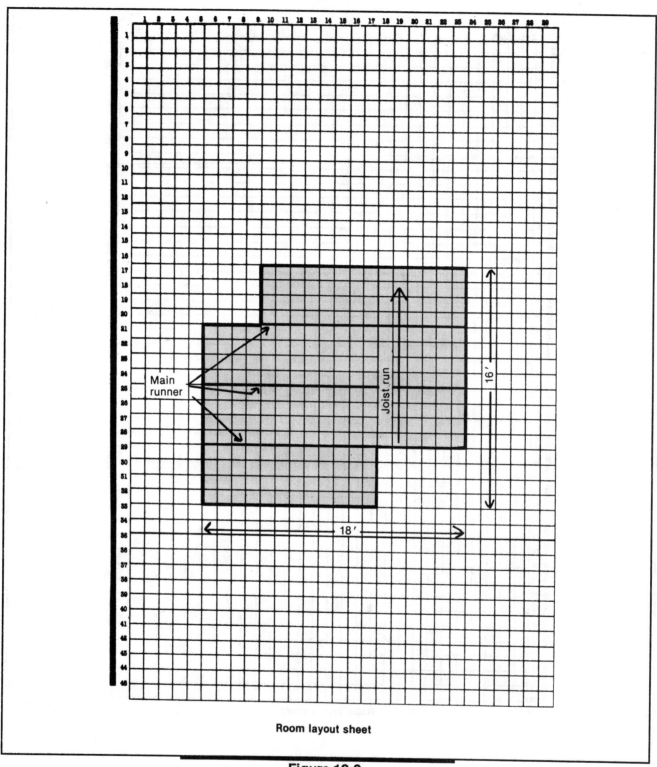

Room layout sheet

Figure 12-2
Main runners

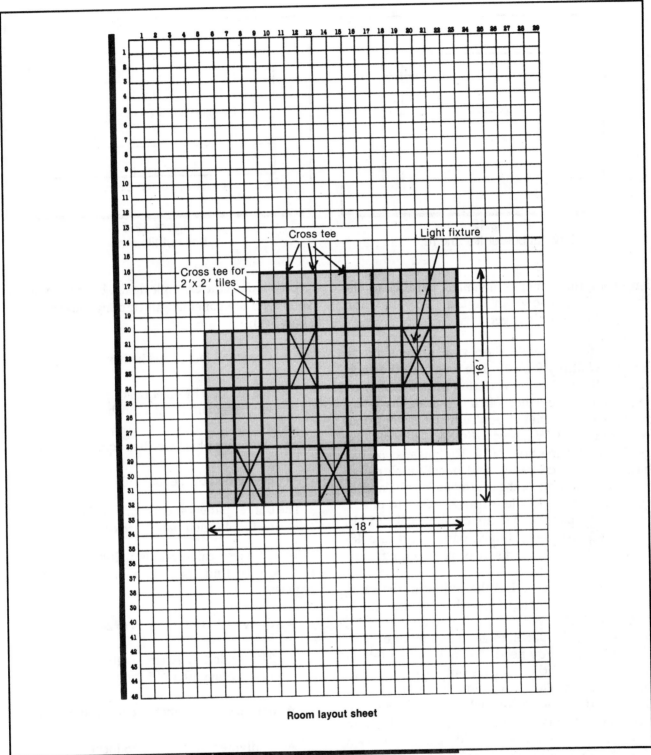

Figure 12-3
Draw in cross tees and light panels

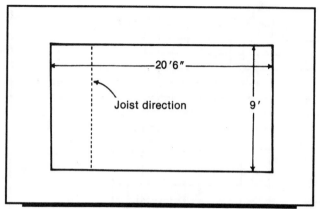

Figure 12-4
Lay out border tile and run

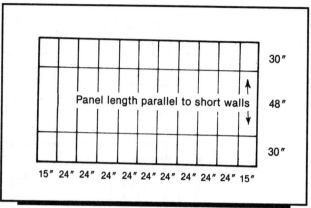

Figure 12-5
Lay out tile runs

length of the panel is installed parallel to the short wall, as shown in Figure 12-5. The short wall in the figure is 9 feet.

Convert the room's short-wall dimensions to inches. Multiply 9 by 12. The length of the short wall is 108 inches. Divide this measurement by the length of the panels (48 inches for 2- by 4-foot panels, or 24 inches if you're using 2- by 2-foot panels or tiles). When you divide 108 by 48, you get 2, with a remainder of 12. That means you can have two 48-inch panels and one 12-inch panel, but that would make the ceiling look unbalanced. To even it out, add the extra 12 inches to one of the 48-inch panels, and divide the total in half. That gives you two 30-inch panels and one 48-inch panel for the short side of your ceiling.

Figure the long wall of the ceiling in the same way. Convert the length to inches (12 times 20 is 240 plus 6 inches is 246 inches). Divide that by 24, the width of the panel, to get the number of panels you'll need. You need 10 panels, plus a 6-inch remainder. Add the 6 inches onto one of the ten 24-inch panels. That leaves you with nine 24-inch panels and one 30-inch panel. Divide the 30-inch panel in half to get two 15-inch panels. The long wall will take nine 24-inch wide panels and two 15-inch panels. Now you know the dimensions of all the border panels for the ceiling. See Figure 12-5. If your figures come out in fractions, round off to the closest whole number.

Let's look at the example again. For a room 9 feet wide with the panel length running parallel to the short wall:

- Convert 9 feet to 108 inches.

- 108 divided by 48 equals 2 panel lengths, with a remainder of 12 inches.

- 12 inches plus 48 inches equals 60 inches.

- 60 divided by 2 equals 30 inches.

The border panels at each side will be 30 inches, with one full 48-inch panel between.

Repeat these calculations using the length of the room to find the width of the end border panels:

- Convert 20 feet 6 inches to 246 inches.

- 246 divided by 24 equals 10 panel widths, with a remainder of 6 inches.

- 6 inches plus 24 inches equals 30 inches.

- 30 divided by 2 equals 15 inches.

The dimensions for the corner panels are 30 inches by 15 inches. Now you're ready to draw the gridwork pattern for your layout.

Plan your first and last main runners to coincide with the length of your border panels. Your main runners should be perpendicular (at a 90-degree angle) to the ceiling joists. Add the "in-between" runners at 48-inch intervals. (There are only two main runners in our example, so they're the first and last runners). Using a different-color pencil, draw in the cross tees. The end cross tees are equal to the width of the end panels. Add the "in-between" cross tees at 24-inch intervals. The cross tees intersect the main runners. (See Figure 12-6.)

Use your layout sheet to figure the number of grid components and materials you need for the job.

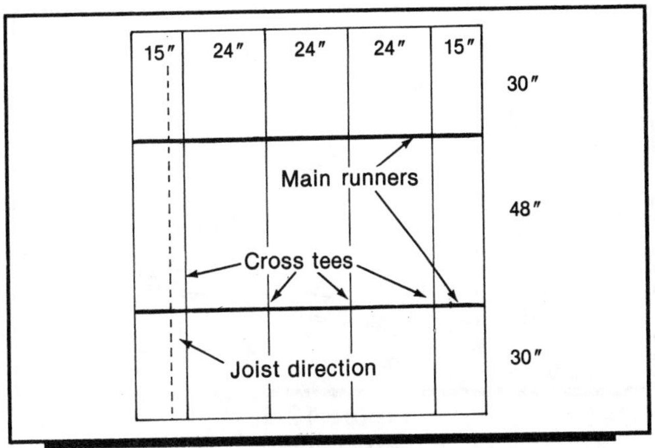

Figure 12-6
Main runner layout

Material Requirements

Wall Molding

You can buy wall molding (Figure 12-7) in 10-foot lengths. Measure the room's perimeter. Divide by 10 to find the number of molding pieces you'll need for the job.

Main Runners

Main runners (Figure 12-8) come in 12-foot lengths. There are tabs at each end of the main runners so you can join runners for lengths longer than 12 feet. Keep in mind when you're cutting runners that you can't cut more than two sections from each 12-foot main runner. You must have a tab-end to join the main runners. Use the cut end to fit against the wall at the wall molding. Using your layout, determine the number of main runner pieces you need for the job.

Cross Tees

Cross tees (Figure 12-9) have connecting tabs at each end. You can get them in 2-foot and 4-foot lengths. To cover odd lengths, cut two border cross tees from a standard-length cross tee. Again, you must have a tab or lock-end so you can connect the cross tee to the main runner. The cut end fits at the wall on the wall molding. Count the number of cross tees you show on your layout to determine the amount you need.

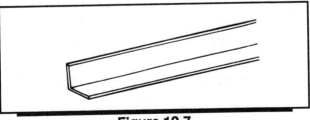

Figure 12-7
Wall molding

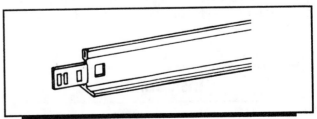

Figure 12-8
Main runner

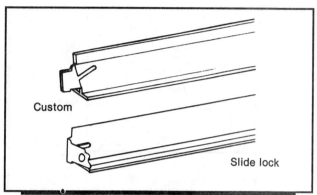

Figure 12-9
Cross tees

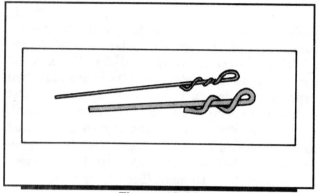

Figure 12-10
Hanger wire

Hanger Wire

You'll need enough hanger wire (Figure 12-10) to suspend the main runners every 4 feet. Make the wire at each suspension point 6 inches longer than the distance between the support point and the new ceiling. You can use 16-gauge wire or the heavier 12-gauge wire. For most residential jobs, the 16-gauge wire works well.

Wire Fasteners

You need wire fasteners (Figure 12-11) at each support point so you can attach wire to the existing ceiling or joist. Make sure your fasteners are long enough to provide strong support. Place them every 4 feet and on each side of each main runner joint. To find the number of fasteners you'll need, count the number of ceiling panels shown on your layout. Be sure to make allowances for the border panels you've cut down in size.

Figures 12-12A through 12-12D give you the material requirements you'll need for various room sizes.

Installation

To begin the installation, measure the new ceiling height in each corner of the room. Allow a mini-

mum of 5-1/2 inches below the level of the existing ceiling for the fixtures. Check the manufacturer's recommendations to make sure that you'll have adequate spacing for the light fixtures you're installing. Normally, if you're not using light fixtures *above* the suspended ceiling, you only need to allow 3-1/2 inches of space.

Wall Moldings

After you have all your corner measurements, snap a chalk line through the measurement marks. Check to make sure the chalk line is level. If the line isn't level, make adjustments. Next, nail wall molding to the wall along the chalk line mark. Figure 12-13 shows you how to cut both inside and outside corners for the molding.

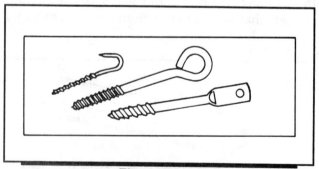

Figure 12-11
Wire fasteners

2' x 4' panel suspended system					
Room length (feet)	10' wall moldings	12' main runners	4' cross tees	# of panels	Square feet
6	4	1	6	9	72
8	4	2	9	12	96
10	4	2	12	15	120
12	5	2	15	18	144
14	5	3	18	21	168
16	6	3	21	24	192
18	6	3	24	27	216
20	6	4	27	30	240
22	7	4	30	33	264
24	7	4	33	36	288
26	8	5	36	39	312
28	8	5	39	42	336
30	8	5	42	45	360
32	9	6	45	48	384
34	9	6	48	51	408
36	10	6	51	54	432
38	10	7	54	57	456
40	10	7	57	60	480
42	11	7	60	63	504
44	11	8	63	66	528
46	12	8	66	69	552
48	12	8	69	72	576

Figure 12-12A
For a 10-foot wide room

2' x 4' panel suspended system					
Room length (feet)	10' wall moldings	12' main runners	4' cross tees	# of panels	Square feet
6	4	1	6	9	72
8	4	2	9	12	96
10	5	2	12	15	120
12	5	2	15	18	144
14	6	3	18	21	168
16	6	3	21	24	192
18	6	3	24	27	216
20	7	4	27	30	240
22	7	4	30	33	264
24	8	4	33	36	288
26	8	5	36	39	312
28	8	5	39	42	336
30	9	5	42	45	360
32	9	6	45	48	384
34	10	6	48	51	408
36	10	6	51	54	432
38	10	7	54	57	456
40	11	7	57	60	480
42	11	7	60	63	504
44	12	8	63	66	528
46	12	8	66	69	552
48	12	8	69	72	576

Figure 12-12B
For a 12-foot wide room

2' x 4' panel suspended system					
Room length (feet)	10' wall moldings	12' main runners	4' cross tees	# of panels	Square feet
6	4	2	8	12	96
8	5	2	12	16	128
10	5	3	16	20	160
12	6	3	20	24	192
14	6	4	24	28	224
16	6	4	28	32	256
18	7	5	32	36	288
20	7	5	36	40	320
22	8	6	40	44	352
24	8	6	44	48	384
26	8	7	48	52	416
28	9	7	52	56	448
30	9	8	56	60	480
32	10	8	60	64	512
34	10	9	64	68	544
36	10	9	68	72	576
38	11	10	72	76	608
40	11	10	76	80	640
42	12	11	80	84	672
44	12	11	84	88	704
46	12	12	88	92	736
48	13	12	92	96	768

Figure 12-12C
For a 14-foot wide room

2' x 4' panel suspended system					
Room length (feet)	10' wall moldings	12' main runners	4' cross tees	# of panels	Square feet
6	5	2	8	12	96
8	5	2	12	16	128
10	6	3	16	20	160
12	6	3	20	24	192
14	6	4	24	28	224
16	7	4	28	32	256
18	7	5	32	36	288
20	8	5	36	40	320
22	8	6	40	44	352
24	8	6	44	48	384
26	9	7	48	52	416
28	9	7	52	56	448
30	10	8	56	60	480
32	10	8	60	64	512
34	10	9	64	68	544
36	11	9	68	72	576
38	11	10	72	76	608
40	12	10	76	80	640
42	12	11	80	84	672
44	12	11	84	88	704
46	13	12	88	92	736
48	13	12	92	96	768

Figure 12-12D
For a 16-foot wide room

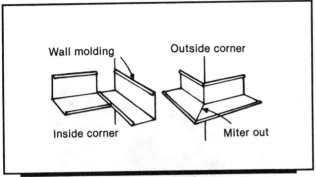

Figure 12-13
Corner treatment

Main Runners

Following your layout, locate the position of the first main runner. Starting at this point, snap a chalk line on the old ceiling perpendicular to the joists. Continue across the room, snapping main runner chalk lines every 4 feet, parallel to the first runner chalk line. Fasten wire fasteners (screw eye) into the joist every 4 feet where the ceiling joists intersect with the main-runner chalk line. Attach hanger wire to each screw eye. Securely wrap the wire around itself at least three times.

Pick the corner where you're going to start your installation. At the width of the border-panel from each wall, stretch two reference strings across the room. They should be at a perfect 90-

degree angle to each other. See Figure 12-14. Be sure to attach the strings right below the wall molding. These reference strings will serve as your guide for cutting main runners and cross tees.

Using reference string AB (Figure 12-14) as a guide, measure each main runner individually. *Don't use the first main runner as a pattern for cutting the others.* Cut each main runner so that the first reference string crosses it on a cross tee slot (Figure 12-15).

Locate the wire-support hole that's farthest from the starting end wall and closest to the last hanger wire. A wire-support hole is a small, round hole at the top of the main runner. Mark the hole on the first main runner (Figure 12-16).

Take the main runner to a sidewall and lay it against the wall molding with the cut end butting against the end wall. Make a mark on the sidewall through the top of the wire-support hole you've just identified. Remove the main runner and drive a nail into that point on the wall.

Repeat this measurement on the opposite wall of the room. Stretch a string from nail to nail, and align each hanger wire so it intersects with the string. See Figure 12-17. Bend the hanger wires at a 90-degree angle where they meet the string.

Now rest the cut end of the first main runner on the end-wall molding. Run the prebent hanger

Figure 12-14
Border tile layout

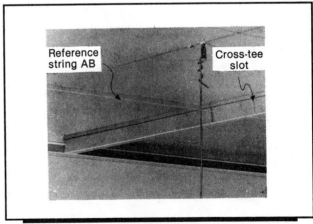

Figure 12-15
Use reference string as guide

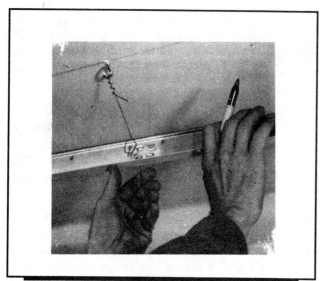

Figure 12-16
Locate wire support hole

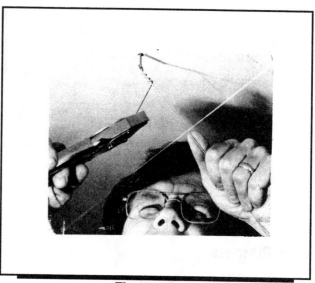

Figure 12-17
Make 90° turn in wire where it touches string

wire through the support hole. Secure it by bending it up sharply and twisting the wire around itself at least three times. Figure 12-18 shows how. Align the rest of the hanger wires to the appropriate support holes. Make a 90-degree bend in the wires where they intersect the top of the support holes, and attach each one in the same way.

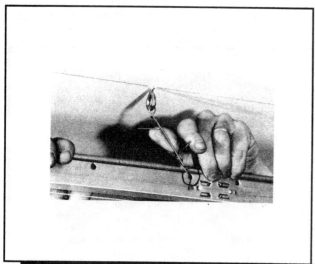

Figure 12-18
Secure the main runner

Connect as many main-runner sections together as you need to reach the other end of the room. Cut off any excess main runner section with snips, and use this piece to start the next row. Repeat this procedure for the remaining rows. Be sure to cut each main runner so that a cross tee slot aligns with reference string AB. For good support, place a hanger wire close to the point where you have connected two main runners. Position an additional hanger wire at the connection if necessary. Make sure that all main runners are level once they're in place.

Cross Tees

When you're ready to install the cross tees, begin by placing the full 4-foot cross tees in rows away from the borders. When you have them laid out, set in a few full panels. This helps to stabilize and square the entire grid system as you work.

Cut the first row of cross tees for the border panels. Measure each one individually using reference string CD as a guide. To measure the cross tees, line up the edge of the first main runner with the reference string under it. Measure from the sidewall to the near edge of the main runner. Cut

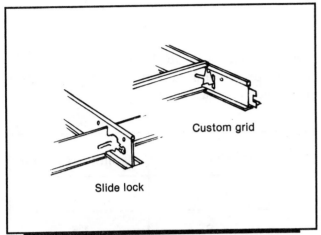

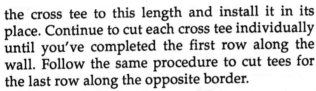

Figure 12-19
Connect cross tees to main runner
with either type of tee

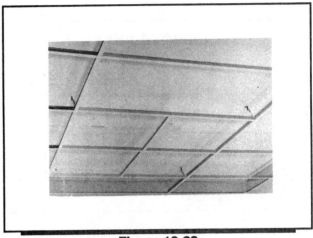

Figure 12-20
Cross tee connection for 2'x2' tiles

the cross tee to this length and install it in its place. Continue to cut each cross tee individually until you've completed the first row along the wall. Follow the same procedure to cut tees for the last row along the opposite border.

Attach the 4-foot cross tees to the main runners across the room at 2-foot intervals. Lock them in as shown in Figure 12-19. For 2- by 2-foot panels or tile, attach cross tees at the midpoints of 4-foot cross tees. (See Figure 12-20.)

Panels

Measure and cut the border panels individually. Use a leftover cross tee or main runner section as a straightedge and cut the ceiling tile panels face up, with a very sharp utility knife. With some plastic panels it's better to score them repeatedly with a sharp knife until the panel is completely cut through. If you're installing polystyrene light diffusers, you can cut the flat panels with tin snips. You'll need a saw to cut prismatic panels.

Set the panels into position by slightly tilting and lifting them above the framework. Gently rest the edge on the cross tee and main runner. Install the panels with the glossy or smooth side up. If you're installing fluorescent lighting fixtures above the

grid, be sure you center the tubes over the diffuser panel. Figure 12-21 shows the correct way to install surface-mounted fixtures.

Whatever panel design or lighting arrangement you install, you're sure to provide an eye-catching ceiling.

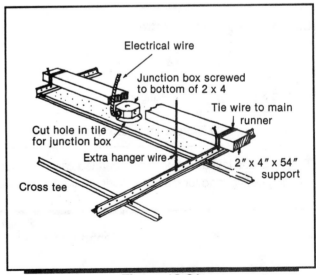

Figure 12-21
Method for installing surface-mounted
lighting fixtures

Estimating Manhours

After you've done a few suspended ceiling installations, you'll have good records of the time it takes your crews to do the job. Until you have those accurate manhour figures, use Figure 12-22 to help you estimate the time.

Work element	Unit	Manhours per unit
Wall molding	50 LF	1.0
Main runners, 4' o.c.	100 SF	1.5
Cross tees, 4'	100 SF	1.8
Cross tees, 2'	100 SF	1.8
Installing wire fasteners	100 SF	1.0
Installing hanger wire	100 SF	0.7
Placing whole diffuser panels 2'x4'	100 SF	1.0
Cutting & placing cut border diffuser panels	50 SF	1.5
Placing whole tile panels 2'x4'	100 SF	1.0
Cutting & placing cut border tile	50 SF	1.5
Ceiling tile laid in grid 2'x2'	100 SF	1.0
Cutting & placing border ceiling tile 2'x2'	50 SF	1.5
Installing one-bulb fluorescent fixture to existing ceiling	each	1.0

Time includes layout and fitting suspended ceiling components under existing ceiling. Add time for repairs, painting existing ceiling, and for electrical work required in installing additional circuits, ceiling boxes, and switches.

Figure 12-22
Manhours for installing suspended ceilings

Redoing Floors

Use the floor to add life to your remodeling design. The right floor can give vitality to the room. You might say that the floor is to a room as shoes are to your outfit. You wouldn't wear muddy brogans with a business suit, or tennis shoes with a tuxedo — not unless you want to draw attention to your nonconformity. The floor, like your shoes, must be appropriate for the whole look or the effect is spoiled.

No experienced kitchen and bath remodeler wants to do a project without redoing the floor. Floors *always* catch the eye. We involuntarily scan where we're walking and what we're walking on. So your remodeling plan should begin at the floor level. Unless, of course, the floor is in good condition. This may be the case if a ceramic tile, marble, or stone floor is already in place. Hard flooring often outlasts the rest of the room. If it's an attractive style that can be used to your advantage, be sure to tie the old floor into your new design.

Know Your Floors

Proper Inspection Pays Off

I've already talked about the importance of a thorough inspection of the condition of the floor, walls, ceilings, and structural members before you bid on a job. Be sure your inspection includes sills, floor joists, studs, and ceiling joists. If you contract to re-cover the floor and later find that there's damage to the floor joists and underlayment or subfloor, you could be in big trouble. Repairing or replacing them is a major cost item.

Beginners are sometimes surprised when they find that the subfloor must be replaced before the covering can be installed. The shock comes when they discover that they're doing it at their own expense and losing money on the job. You only need to learn this lesson once — and that's one time too many!

You should be surprised only when no repairs or replacements are needed. Don't leave it to chance. Inspect!

Occasionally, even the most experienced remodelers get caught by surprises. A good way to protect yourself is to include a provision in the contract that covers additional repair work that may be necessary. Structural repairs and anything you have to do to bring substandard construction up to code requirements should be done on a time and materials basis. Your contract should identify exactly what's to be removed and what's to be installed. If extra work is done, there will be extra costs. Make sure your clients understand that what is *not* listed in the estimate is *not* included in the price. Explain what repair work and materials your contract includes and what it doesn't. Homeowners shouldn't object to this kind of provision in the contract, as long as they are forewarned. After all, you're not a magician. What's beyond your control shouldn't be at your risk.

Resilient Floor Coverings

There are many different types of floor coverings for your clients to choose from. As a kitchen and bath remodeler you must be familiar with all the different materials that are available and how to install them. You may be subcontracting out some of the installations, but you'll still need to be able to help your clients choose the flooring that's right for their lifestyle.

Vinyl: Vinyl is a very popular and practical floor covering. It's made of polyvinyl chloride (PVC) mixed with resin binders and mineral fillers, plasticizers, stabilizers and pigments. Vinyl can be filled or clear.

The clear type consists of a layer of opaque particles or pigments. They're covered with a wearing surface of clear vinyl bonded to a vinyl or polymer-impregnated asbestos fiber or resin-saturated felt. It has a high resistance to wear. Filled vinyl is made of chips of vinyl having different colors and shapes, immersed in a clear vinyl base. It's bonded together by heat and pressure.

You can buy vinyl in sheet or tile form. *Sheet vinyl* is available in 6- and 12-foot widths and in any lengths you need. It's manufactured in 1/16 to 1/8-inch thicknesses. *Vinyl tile* is made of the same materials as sheet vinyl and is available in 1/16, 3/32, and 1/8-inch thicknesses.

Vinyl-composition tile: Vinyl composition tile is a blend of mineral fibers, vinyls, plasticizers, color pigments and fillers. The tiles come in 9- or 12-inch squares and are 1/16, 3/32 or 1/8-inch thick. Various patterns and textures are available. The tiles are semi-flexible, and offer good resistance to grease, alkaline substances, oils, and some acids.

Cork tile: Cork tile consists of granulated cork bark combined with a synthetic resin which acts as a binder. It's a natural material. The tile has good sound absorption qualities. When coated with a vinyl film, it's fairly easy to maintain. It comes in 12-inch squares and is available from 1/8 to 1/2 inch in thickness. Its major drawback for use as kitchen and bath flooring is that it can be damaged or stained by grease and alkaline substances.

Rubber tile: Rubber tile is made of natural or synthetic rubber. Mineral fillers and organic pigments are used to produce a limited range of patterns and colors. The tile comes in 9- and 12-inch squares. Rubber tile's indentation recovery is excellent. You can use epoxy adhesive for on-grade slab installation when there's no vapor barrier.

Hard Flooring

Hard flooring (non-resilient flooring) includes ceramic tile, terrazzo, stone, slate, and brick. You need to pay close attention to the requirements for proper framing and underlayment when you install hard flooring.

Terra cotta and glazed ceramic tile are both stain resistant. They do scratch easily however, and often form tiny cracks as they age.

You'll need to treat porous unglazed ceramic tile, flagstone, and slate with a special stain-resistant sealant. Clay or quarry tile, usually unglazed, has a long wear life. You can install tile in kitchens and bathrooms. If you seal it properly, it resists grease, oils and chemicals and provides a long-wearing attractive floor.

Terrazzo is made of marble chips mixed with portland cement mortar which is ground and polished to a smooth finish. It resists moisture and is easy to maintain.

Hard floors should be installed by a skilled tradesman. Unless you're skilled in this trade, it's best to sub out hard floor installation.

Carpet

Carpeting has a surface pile made of nylon, acrylic, polyester, polypropylene, wool, or cotton, and a backing. Wall-to-wall carpeting is sold by the square yard. To find the square yards of material needed to cover a room, multiply the length by the width in feet and divide by 9.

The padding or underlay extends the life of the carpet. Common types of padding are soft and hard-backed vinyl foams, sponge-rubber foams, latex (rubber), and felted cushions made either of animal hair or a combination of hair and jute. Latex and vinyl foams are probably the most practical. Their waffled surface helps to hold the carpet in position. Standard padding is 4-1/2 feet wide. "One-piece" and cushion-backed carpeting doesn't need padding or underlay.

Foam rubber-backed carpeting is popular. It's a good choice for basements and below grade. It's mildew proof and unaffected by water. You can lay it directly on unfinished concrete floors. It has a non-skid backing, and since it's a heavy material,

you don't need to use tacks or adhesives to hold it in place.

It's a good idea to recommend indoor/outdoor type carpeting in any area of the house where the carpet may be exposed to water. This is especially important if you're laying carpet over interior concrete or tile surfaces. The indoor/outdoor carpet backing is made of a closed-pore type of vinyl or latex foam which keeps out moisture. If you lay a regular indoor carpet over a surface which is exposed to dampness, you may have an unhappy customer. Floor tiles such as those made of vinyl and asbestos accumulate moisture when covered with carpet. The moisture soaks through into the carpet and will eventually produce a musty odor and mildew stains.

Carpeting may not be your first choice for kitchens, but I've had homeowners who request it. There are special carpets available for kitchen installation. Kitchen carpeting has a very close weave to prevent spills from penetrating the surface too quickly.

Many people like the warmth of carpeting in their bathrooms, and it works very well. If your clients request carpet for their bathroom floor, suggest an indoor/outdoor type designed to hold up under repeated wetting.

Removing Existing Flooring

Often it's necessary to remove the existing flooring before you install the new. For your health and safety, be sure to follow the correct procedures for the removal of each type of floor you work with.

Vinyl Sheet Floors

Do not sand existing resilient flooring, backing or lining felt. These products may contain asbestos fibers. Inhaling asbestos dust may cause asbestosis or other serious illness. The Resilient Floor Covering Institute has published a booklet, *Recommended Work Procedures for Resilient Floor Coverings,* that outlines safe procedures for working with and handling flooring containing asbestos fibers. Write the Institute for a free copy of the booklet at:

The Resilient Floor Covering Institute
966 Hungerford Drive
Rockville, MD 20850

To remove existing sheet vinyl flooring, cut the wear layer into narrow strips. Take care not to score the subfloor if it's a wood type. Peel up the strips from the backing by pulling or rolling around a core. This helps control the stripping angle and create a uniform and more constant tension.

After removing the wear layer, scrape off the remaining felt with a scraper. *Again, do not sand.* Level and smooth any unevenness in the subfloor with a latex underlayment mastic.

Resilient Tile

There are several good tile-removing machines and tools to use with resilient tile. They use vibration or blades to dislodge the tile. Such tools as hand scrapers, long-handled scrapers, ice chippers, and weighted scraping tools will also do the job.

The dry ice removal method involves placing dry ice inside a 2 by 2-foot wooden frame that doesn't have a bottom or top. Place a piece of carpet, burlap or some other insulating material over the frame. This prevents the dry ice from evaporating too quickly and directs the freezing action downward. Attach a rope to the frame to help you maneuver it over the floor.

Let the frame sit on an area of tile for five minutes. The tile will freeze and become brittle. You can then remove it easily with a scraper or brick chisel. If the tile doesn't snap loose readily, freeze

it some more. Freeze adjoining areas while you remove the already frozen tiles.

You can remove small areas of tile with heat. Use a blow torch or a small propane gas torch to provide the heat. Be careful when you work with torches; always have water available in case of fire.

Never use solvents for the removal of asphalt adhesive residue. The solvents carry the residue deep into the pores of the subfloor. The residue may rise or bleed to the surface later, damaging the new flooring.

A better method to remove asphalt adhesive residue is with a grinder, such as a concrete or a terrazzo grinder. Use wet sand with the grinder to prevent clogging the grinding stones. The sand also aids in removing the residue.

Whenever you find that you must remove a resilient floor covering, consider installing a thin underlayment instead. A 1/4-inch tempered hardboard installed over the existing flooring may be more economical and easier than removing the floor covering.

Keep in mind that you can install most sheet vinyl directly over any type of structurally sound subfloor whether it's above, on, or below grade. You can also install certain kinds of sheet vinyls over almost any type of existing floors. This includes asphalt tile, vinyl-composition tile, rubber tile, vinyl tile, linoleum, sheet vinyl, clay tile, marble, terrazzo, and unglazed ceramic tile.

You must roughen the perimeter on all nonporous surfaces before you install new sheet vinyl. You may also have to replace damaged tiles before installing sheet goods over a worn tile floor. To remove old damaged tiles, use a putty knife or a scraper. Take up the tile and the old adhesive. Apply new adhesive and a new (or used) piece of tile. The new tile doesn't have to match the old except in thickness. When you have a smooth, even surface, install the new sheet vinyl.

Never remove an entire existing floor covering unless it's absolutely necessary.

Use the Right Underlayment

Particleboard

Use care in selecting underlayment. Some resilient floor coverings can't be installed over just any particleboard underlayment — the adhesive won't hold. Choose a particleboard underlayment that's specifically approved for use with resilient floor coverings by the NPA (National Particleboard Association).

Plywood

Single-layer board floors that aren't tongued and grooved and that are not over 3 inches wide should be covered with 3/8-inch or heavier plywood in the following grades:

1) Underlayment INT-APA (Interior type)

2) Underlayment INT-APA (Exterior grade)

Where you anticipate excessive water spillage, such as in a bathroom or under a dishwasher and washing machine, use panels of exterior plywood or plywood bonded with exterior glues.

Some plugged plywood panels can stain sheet vinyl flooring. The stains are caused by certain urethane-based synthetic patching compounds which are incompatible with the plasticizers used in vinyl flooring. The type and color of the vinyl, its exposure to sunlight, and the temperature of the floor will influence how serious the stains are.

The American Plywood Association's (APA) laboratories and one of the major vinyl flooring manufacturers are working to solve this problem. Of course, they probably won't be able to solve the problem of stains already in place. The only solution is to replace the flooring and the plug in the plywood. One thing they have discovered however, is that as the patching compound ages, it becomes less volatile and less likely to cause stains in the vinyl laid over it. You may try covering plywood plugs with a small piece of sheet mylar to prevent stains, but the new vinyl may not adhere to the mylar.

Hardboard

Cover single-layer tongue and groove floorboards that are up to 3 inches wide with a tempered hardboard underlayment. You can also use the 1/4-inch grades of plywood recommended above.

Treat double-layer wood floors with boards 3 inches wide or more the same as single-layer floors — with an underlayment. If the double-layer boards are less than 3 inches wide, nail all loose boards and replace defective or badly worn boards with new ones. Fill cracks and holes with plastic wood or properly fitted wood pieces and then install the new floor covering.

A better method may be to install tempered hardboard over this floor as underlayment for a smooth floor covering job. A crack, bulge, protruding nail head or small hole will show through most resilient floor coverings. As a kitchen and bath specialist, you want to avoid potential problem situations. Put down a thin underlayment and save yourself some headaches. You want a smooth, firm base for any new floor covering.

Never install tempered hardboard or resilient flooring over sleeper-constructed subfloors on or below grade without a proper vapor barrier. If you install tempered hardboard over a crawl space, be sure the space is at least 18 inches high and ventilated.

Existing Resilient Floors

Sometimes you can install new resilient floor covering over an existing resilient surface. The surface must be firmly bonded to the floor, be free of dirt, grease and oil, and the finish not stripped. It's also important that the old vinyl isn't sharply or deeply embossed, or the pattern will show through. An old cushion type vinyl floor isn't a good underlayment either. The surface will be too soft and puncture or dent easily. If two resilient floors are already down, don't install a third on top.

Concrete Floors

A dry, dense, smooth concrete slab is an ideal surface for resilient flooring. It should also be free of expansion joints, depressions, scale and foreign deposits of any kind. Remove all paint, varnish, oil, or wax from the surface before you put down the new flooring.

Trisodium phosphate (TSP) in hot water makes a good paint remover for concrete subfloors. Oakite and climalene also do a good job.

TSP may not remove paints with a chlorinated rubber or resin base. If not, you'll have to remove them by grinding and sanding. Clean any cracks, expansion joints, or score marks in the concrete surface and fill them with a latex underlayment mastic.

Smooth rough concrete floors with clean, sharp white sand and a terrazzo grinder. Keep the sand and concrete wet while sanding to prevent dust. But don't soak the floor. It must be thoroughly dry before installing the flooring. If the floor is too rough for grinding, use a latex underlayment mastic to smooth it out.

Suspended concrete subfloors with a chalky or dusty surface will need to be swept clean and sized with one coat of primer. A dusty concrete floor on or below grade indicates that there's moisture coming through the floor.

You'll need to neutralize concrete floors that have been treated with alkali before installing floor tile. Use a mixture of one part muriatic acid and eight parts of water. Spread the solution over the floor and leave it for one hour. Rinse well with clear water. After the floor is thoroughly dry you can install the floor covering.

When you enclose concrete-floored porches to add space to a kitchen or bath, you may run into leveling problems. Porch floors are often pitched for water drainage. Also, exterior slabs that have frozen before setting up may be scaly and cracked. Sometimes you can add a top coat of concrete which will solve the surface problems and level the floor as well. Or you can add a top coat of concrete to bring the porch slab up flush to the adjacent room level. An alternative method is to install a sleeper joist system and put down a new subfloor, leveling the new room's floor with the rest of the house.

Sheet Vinyl Floor Installation

Room Preparation

To begin your installation, remove all the furniture and movable appliances from the room. This includes the bathroom toilet. The floor area must be clean, smooth and dry. Don't use resilient flooring for an area that's continually wet.

Remove any wax or floor finish from the existing floor. Use a heavy duty cleanser or other wax remover. Floor adhesives won't bond readily to wax or floor polish.

Carefully detach and remove the baseboard, shoe molding, or vinyl wall base. A thin screwdriver and wide putty knife work well. You'll need to replace the molding or wall base after the installation is complete to secure the edges of the floor covering. Use new material if the base and molding is damaged or no longer suitable.

You may need to trim the bottom of the doorway moldings so the flooring slips under easily. Use a cardboard scrap equal in thickness to the new flooring to determine how much molding to cut away. Hold a handsaw flat against the cardboard and cut. The inset in Figure 13-1 shows how.

Smooth and sweep the floor area. Drive down all protruding nail heads. Unroll the new floor covering in another room so you can plot your reference points.

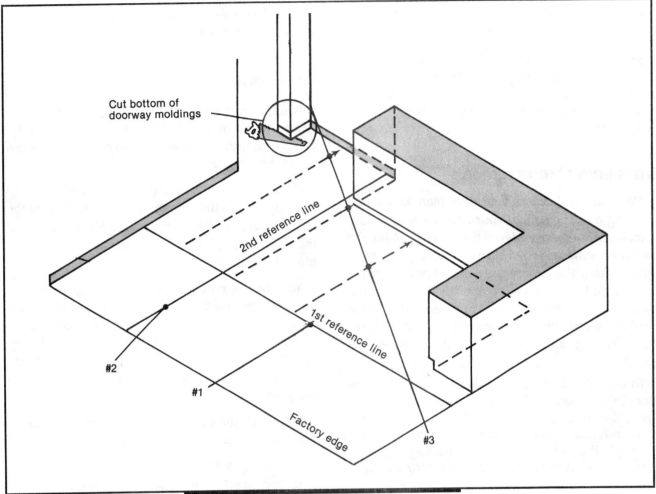

Figure 13-1
Establishing reference points

Establishing Reference Points

1) As a general rule, the factory edge of the new floor covering should run along the longest straight wall in the room. Factory edges run the entire length of the flooring, not the width of the roll. Select the wall where you'll put one of the factory edges, and begin your measurements from there.

2) At each end of the room, measure out from this wall a given distance — to about the center of the room. (See Figure 13-1, #1.)

3) Snap a chalk line through these two points.

4) Mark a second line, at a 90-degree angle to the first line. The two perpendicular lines should run the entire length and width of the room (as shown in Figure 13-1, #2). Make sure they are exactly perpendicular. They are the reference points that you'll use to determine how to *mark* and *cut* the vinyl sheet.

5) On a sheet of graph paper, draw the two reference lines you marked on the floor. Roughly sketch the room around the intersection of the two lines. Show all the cabinets and closets.

6) Measure from the reference lines on the floor out to the walls or cabinet every 2 feet around the room, including at least two measurements for every offset. Record these measurements on your paper layout. Be careful; walls are seldom straight. That's why you must measure every 2 feet. See Figure 13-1, #3.

Transferring Measurements

Position the sketch of your floor plan on the new flooring material so that your first reference line is parallel to the factory edge of the flooring. Using the measurements recorded on your floor plan, measure in from the factory edge on the new flooring. Mark your first reference point on the flooring equal to the distance from your first reference line to the wall. Measure out this distance at both ends on the new flooring, and snap a chalk line through the points.

To establish a second reference line on the new flooring, measure along the first reference line from the edges to where the floor plan indicates your reference lines intersect. Snap a chalk line through the points at an exact 90-degree angle. This second line should run the entire width of the floor.

You now have perpendicular reference lines on the new covering which correlate to those in the room. Measure out from these lines to all walls and cabinets at the same intervals as shown on the floor plans.

Connect these marks with a chalk line. Be as accurate as possible. These outside lines become your cut lines.

Cutting the Flooring

Don't make any cuts in the new flooring until you've transferred and rechecked all your room measurements. Place a scrap of plywood or cardboard beneath your cut line on the new flooring. Then make your cuts using a straight-blade utility knife with a metal straightedge as a guide. Cut

along all outside cut lines. You now have a single piece of sheet vinyl cut to the shape of the room.

One-Piece Installations

Before you take the new covering into the room where you'll install it, roll the sheet up, face in. When you unroll it, it should roll out into the room along the longest straight wall.

Place it in the room and unroll it enough to determine that it's in the correct position. Don't force the covering under offsets or cabinets. Now fold half of the covering back onto itself, being careful not to move the other half out of position.

You are now ready to spread the adhesive. Follow the exact instructions on the adhesive container. Spread the adhesive evenly onto the floor, using a trowel with notches 1/16 inch wide, 1/16 inch deep and 3/32 inch apart. Don't let the adhesive dry more than 15 minutes before placing the floor covering onto it.

Fold back the other half of the covering and repeat the process.

Use a heavy roller to press the covering to the floor and ensure a good bond. Roll from the center toward the edges to remove any air pockets.

Cap all doorways and openings with a metal threshold.

Two-Piece Installations

If any part of the room is more than 12 feet wide, you'll have to fit two pieces of flooring together with a seam. Add the following procedures to your one-piece installation instructions:

1) Before transferring measurements onto the new covering, overlap the two pieces at the seam area. Make certain that you match the pattern all along the seam area.

2) Place strips of masking tape across the overlap to hold the two pieces together.

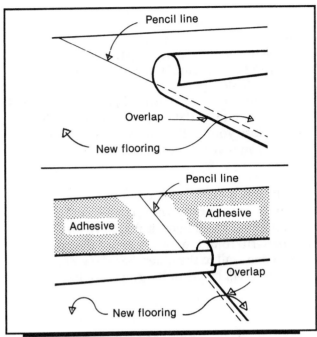

Figure 13-2
Procedures for two-piece installation

3) Transfer your measurements and cut the covering to the size and shape of the room. (Do not cut overlap seams.)

4) Untape the seams before you move the floor covering to the room where you'll be installing it.

5) Move and position one piece at a time.

6) Fold the top piece back halfway and draw a pencil line on the subfloor along the edge of the second piece (at the seam area).

7) Fold back the second piece and spread adhesive to within 12 inches of either side of the line. (See Figure 13-2.)

8) Place the first piece of flooring in the adhesive. Repeat Steps 6 and 7 for the other piece of flooring.

9) Using a straight-blade utility knife with a metal straightedge as a guide, cut through both pieces of flooring where they overlap.

10) Fold back both seam edges, spread adhesive, and place the covering into position.

The seam is the last edge you lay when installing most sheet vinyl. However, there are some coverings in which seam sealing is one of the first steps. Determine this from the supplier and follow the manufacturer's instructions. Follow the instructions on the seam sealer container.

An Alternative Installation Method

Some kitchen and bath remodelers prefer the cut-and-fit method of installing sheet vinyl. You can use this method when you need to match your connecting seam first. Prepare the room and subfloor as you would for the previous installation.

Two-Piece Installation

1) Unroll and position the first piece of the floor covering in the room where you're making the installation. Allow the excess flooring to extend up the walls and the front of the kitchen cabinets as shown in Figure 13-3. Be sure you allow enough material to cover the floor in every offset.

2) When the first piece is in position, draw a pencil line on the old floor (or underlayment) from one wall to the other along the factory edge of the new covering. This marks the position at which the two pieces will be seamed together. (See Figure 13-4.)

3) Place the second piece of flooring in position. Again, allow the excess to extend up the walls. Don't move the first piece which you have already positioned. (See Figure 13-5.)

4) Overlap the two pieces of flooring where the seam will be formed. Match up the pattern at the center (Figure 13-6), and cut off excess material at both ends of the overlay. Whenever possible, use one of the simulated grout lines (a straight recessed line in the surface design of the flooring) as your overlap matching point.

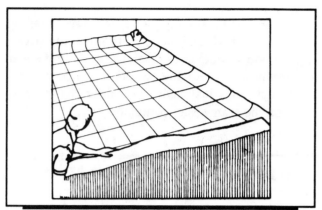

Figure 13-3
Extend excess up walls

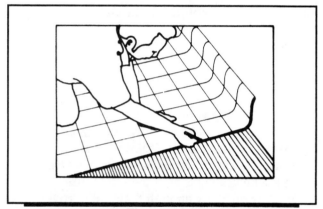

Figure 13-4
Mark the old floor

5) Cut and remove a wide-bottomed U-shaped piece of the flooring on each end of the seam where the excess extends up the wall. See Figure 13-7. The cutaway should allow a perfect fit along the wall base at the seam. This partial fitting of the flooring allows both ends of the seam to lie flat on the floor. Be careful not to lose your pattern match at the seam while you make these cuts.

6) Using a metal straightedge and a straight-blade utility knife, cut along the overlapped grout lines (if you have that kind of pattern) found in the flooring's design. Cut from one wall to the other. Be sure you cut through *both* layers of flooring. (See Figure 13-8.)

7) Remove both strips of flooring scrap created by the cut. (See Figure 13-9.) You now have the two pieces of flooring pattern-matched and cut to fit each other. Be careful not to move them out of position.

Seam edges may also be straightedged and butted if you prefer. Cut both seam edges using a sharp utility knife and straightedge. When the seam edges are butted together, the pattern should flow evenly and uniformly just

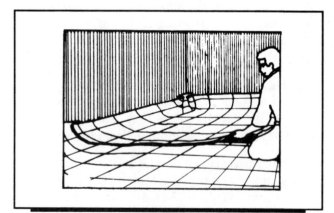

Figure 13-5
Place second piece into position

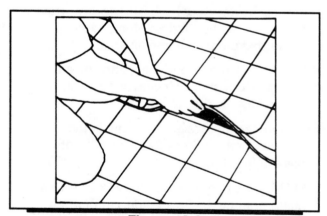

Figure 13-6
Match the pattern at overlap

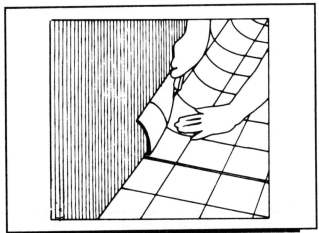

Figure 13-7
Remove part of the excess

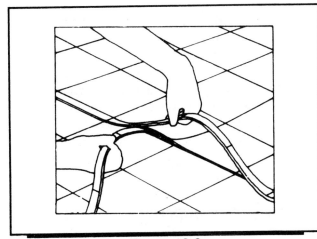

Figure 13-8
Cut the overlap

as they would if you had overlapped them to cut.

8) When you have your seam in place, gently fold back both edges and apply a 3-inch band of adhesive under the seam. (See Figure 13-10.) Lay one piece of material onto the adhesive, then slowly lay the second piece onto the adhesive, making sure that the seam is tight and the pattern matches.

9) Follow up by using a hand roller to press the flooring firmly into the fresh adhesive. (See Figure 13-11.)

10) Apply seam sealer with the applicator bottle, moving the bottle from one end of the seam to the other as the adhesive is squeezed out. (See Figure 13-12.) You don't need to worry about removing small amounts of excess sealer on the surface of the seam. They will gradually match the gloss level of the floor's surface. After sealing the seam, you can begin cutting and fitting the rest of the flooring.

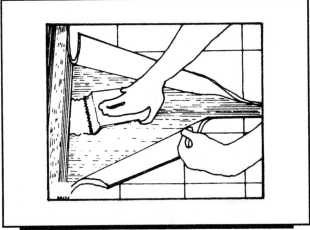

Figure 13-9
Remove both strips of scrap

Figure 13-10
Apply 3-inch band of adhesive under seam

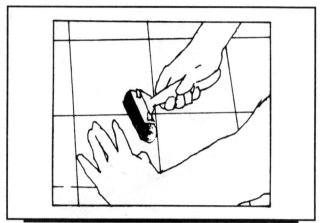

Figure 13-11
Press the flooring down

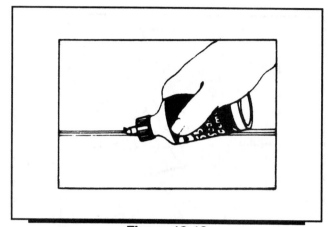

Figure 13-12
Apply sealer

Cutting and Fitting One-Piece Installations

If you only need one piece of flooring for your installation (no seam), use the following instructions:

1) Unroll and position the piece of flooring. Allow the excess to extend up the sides of the walls. Be sure you have enough material to cover the floor in every offset. Whenever possible, line up the floor's pattern with the longest unobstructed wall.

2) With this method of one-piece installation, you cut and fit the corners first. Fit inside corners by pressing the excess flooring into the corner's wall and floor juncture. Using a straight-blade utility knife, punch through the flooring at the base of the corner and cut upward through the excess material. See Figure 13-13.

3) Fit the outside corners by laying the flooring back at the base of the corner so the fold runs diagonally across it. Look at Figure 13-14. Holding the flooring against the corner, punch your knife through at the base and cut upward through the excess flooring. Any time you fold vinyl sheet flooring, be careful not to crimp the material.

4) Fit the flooring to the walls by firmly pressing the vinyl into the wall/floor juncture with a steel carpenter's square. Holding a utility knife at a 45-degree angle, cut off the excess material. (See Figure 13-15.) When you trim the flooring for a doorway, cut the edge so it will be directly under the closed door. Install a metal threshold molding over the exposed edge.

Adhering and Stapling

Once the flooring is trimmed to fit, you need to fasten it down. You should plan to complete the job

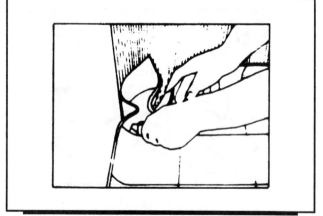

Figure 13-13
Fit and trim for corners

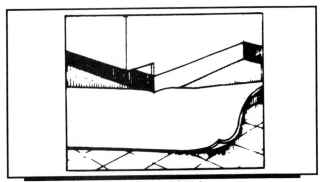

Figure 13-14
Fit and trim for outside corner

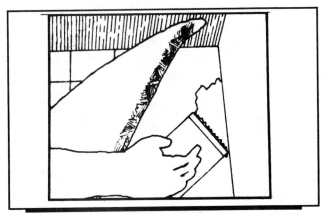

Figure 13-15
Trim at walls for fit

within two hours after cutting and fitting the vinyl. If you delay, the flooring will lose its elasticity, reducing its capacity to absorb any possible fitting mistakes. You can usually correct minor mistakes in fitting by stretching the flooring's edge when you fasten it down.

Depending on the type of subflooring, you can fasten the perimeter of the flooring with adhesive, staples, or a combination of the two. You have to use adhesive on concrete and some other hard surfaces. With some floor coverings it's best to use staples, although there are some areas you just can't reach with a staple gun. The toe-kick overhang on the front of cabinets is one place that always needs adhesive for a proper bond.

To fasten the perimeter of the floor with adhesive, apply a 3-inch band of adhesive around the perimeter and all fixtures. Don't get the adhesive on the face of the material and don't apply more than the recommended amount. You may notice a slight picture-frame effect right after installation, but this will disappear in about 24 hours.

Fold back the flooring along one wall. Starting 1 foot past the corner, trowel a 3-inch wide band of adhesive along the edge of the floor to within 1 foot of the next corner. You need to leave the adhesive off enough area to allow the flooring to be folded back from the next wall (Figure 13-16).

Use a hand roller to press the flooring firmly into the fresh adhesive (Figure 13-17).

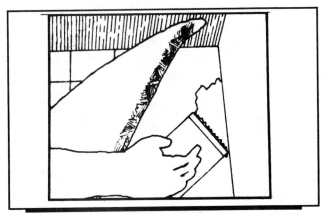

Figure 13-16
Apply adhesive at edges

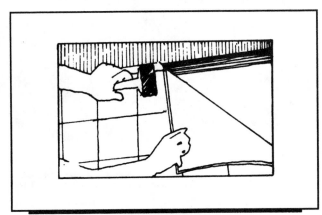

Figure 13-17
Press covering firmly in place

Fold back the flooring on the next wall and again spread a 3-inch band of adhesive along the edge, this time including the 1 foot left unspread at the corner. Continue spreading until you are within 1 foot of the next corner. Press this edge firmly into the adhesive with the roller. Repeat this process until the entire perimeter of the room has been fastened with adhesive.

Properly installed sheet vinyl makes an attractive, long-lasting and easily maintained floor. Figure 13-18 shows how your finished installation might look.

Installing Vinyl-Composition Tile

Vinyl-composition tile is a good choice for flooring above, on, or below grade level. The tiles don't require waxing and you can buy them with an easy-to-apply peel-and-stick backing. You must be aware, however, that you can only install vinyl-composition tile on a rigid subfloor.

Figure 13-18
Finished sheet vinyl floor installation
Courtesy: American Woodmark Corporation

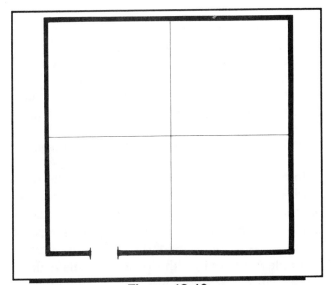

Figure 13-19
Lay room out into four equal parts, snap chalkline
on subfloor

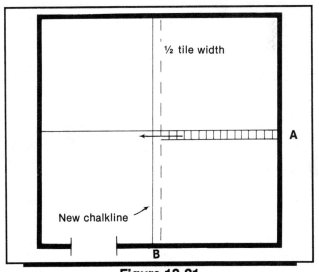

Figure 13-20
Lay a row of loose tiles

Plan Your Installation

If your clients choose vinyl-composition tile flooring, plan your installation out carefully. For a professional look, the border tiles on opposing sides of the room must be the same width. If the border tile on one side of the room is 7 inches, the border tile on the opposite side of the room should be 7 inches also. Likewise, the border tiles at one end of the room should be the same as the border tiles at the other end.

Lay out starter runs to help you determine the width of your border tiles. To lay the starter runs, locate the center of the room by finding the center of each wall. Snap one chalk line on the subfloor across the center of the room and another down the center length of the room. See Figure 13-19. This divides the room into four equal parts.

Now lay one row of loose tiles along the chalk line from the center point to one side wall and another from the center to one end wall. Figure 13-20 shows the pattern.

Measure the distance between the wall and the last full tile, shown at A in the figure. If this space is

less than a half of a tile wide, snap a new line half a tile width closer to the opposite wall. See Figure 13-21. This will ensure that your border tiles are not small pieces. They'll be half a tile plus whatever distance you measured between the last tile and the wall. If the measurement was greater than half a tile wide, lay your tiles using the original chalk line. Follow the same procedure for Row B.

Figure 13-21
Shift tiles to new chalkline, which is half a tile
width from old chalkline

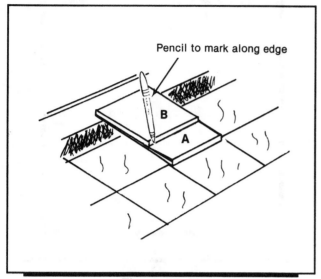

Figure 13-22
Measure wall border tile fit

Laying the Tile

Lay the A-B rows first, then the balance of this quarter section. Lay the next quarter, starting at the established chalk line and moving toward the walls.

Apply self-sticking tiles directly to the underlayment without adhesives. You'll need to apply a thin coat of adhesive for tiles that aren't self-sticking. Follow the adhesive manufacturer's instructions. You don't want to put too much adhesive on the floor. Set each tile flat and firmly in its place. Don't slide the tiles into place. Sliding them in causes the adhesive to pile up at the joint.

To cut and fit the border tiles next to the wall, place a loose tile (A, in Figure 13-22) squarely on top of the last full tile closest to the wall. Now place a third tile (B) on top of tile A and butting up against the wall. Using the edge of the top tile as a guide, mark tile A, under it, with a pencil. Cut tile A along the pencil line. It's now just the right size for the border space. Use the same procedure for marking and cutting border tile, corners and irregular shapes. See Figure 13-23.

If you have any doubts about your ability to install flooring, leave the installation to skilled craftsmen. A poorly-laid floor will spoil your whole job, no matter how well you did the rest of the work. A good installation will bring you more business.

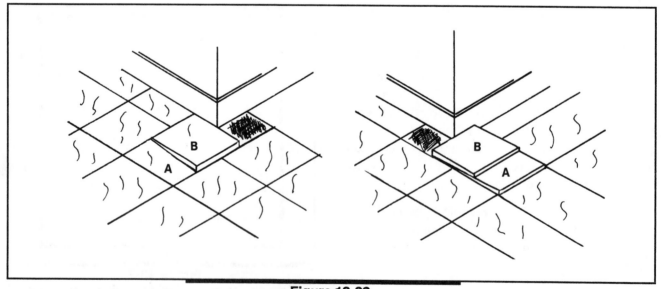

Figure 13-23
Measuring tile for corner fits

Work element	Unit	Manhours per unit
Removing existing resilient flooring	100 SF	8-12
Installing sheet vinyl	100 SF	3-6
Installing 9"x9" file	100 SF	5-8
Installing baseboard & molding	50 LF	2-3
Floor sanding	100 SF	1-2

Figure 3-24
Manhours for installing resilient flooring

Estimating Manhours

Remember, old floors can be profit robbers. A thorough inspection of the structure will minimize surprises and save you time and money. Repair work is time-consuming. Allow enough manhours for repairs when preparing your estimates.

Take the time to compile accurate records of your labor hours on every floor installation you do. They'll be your best guide to estimating future jobs. Remember that you have to figure in the time it takes to remove and replace furniture, appliances, fixtures, baseboard and shoe molding, and make floor and underlayment repairs.

The manhours in Figure 13-24 are only averages, at best. Add additional time for removal and reinstallation of toilets and other fixtures. And understand that these don't include repair work, whether minor or extensive. Add your estimate of the repair time to the times in the table.

Redoing Walls and Ceilings

Don't just think of walls and ceilings as the sides of a box. Use your imagination to create new and interesting ideas for the kitchens and baths you remodel. In Chapters 3 and 7 we discussed using many different materials — combinations of wallpaper, tile, wood paneling, gypsum board and masonry — for different decorating effects. You can also include a drop or luminous ceiling in your design.

The trend in kitchen design today is toward open styles. The kitchen in Figure 14-1 is a good example. It has a cathedral ceiling with an open-beam treatment and skylights to increase the natural light. The walls are gypsum board. Notice that there's little vacant wall space. This room was designed with beauty *and utility* in mind. The flooring is tile, but a similar pattern in a good quality sheet vinyl would also be appropriate for this room.

You can see from this example that painted gypsum board isn't too commonplace for an elegant kitchen or bathroom. In fact, gypsum board makes a long-lasting and smooth backing for wallpaper or paint. Adding a textured finish to a gypsum board ceiling also creates a nice effect.

Notice the clean simple lines of the rooms in Figures 14-2 and 14-3. The walls are made of gypsum wallboard. The cabinets are designed to be functional and easy to care for. So is the sheet vinyl flooring. With a pleasing color scheme, these are attractive and inviting rooms.

Don't allow conventional styling to restrict your treatment of walls and ceilings. Look at the kitchen in Figure 14-4. Walls and ceiling of plaster, old beams, decorative panels, and skylights combine to make an ordinary kitchen a showplace. Let this design remind you how unlimited your choices can be. Here the atmosphere set by the old beams and cathedral ceiling is continued in the "pegged" wood floor and random-plank cabinets.

Figure 14-1
Open styling in kitchen
Courtesy: Merillat Industries, Inc.

Figure 14-2
Clean, simple kitchen design
Courtesy: American Woodmark Co.

Figure 14-3
Gypsum wallboard creates a smooth wall surface
Courtesy: American Woodmark Corp.

Figure 14-4
Wall and ceiling treatments add variety to kitchen design
Courtesy: Merillat Industries, Inc.

Figure 14-5
Use paneling in kitchens for warm decor
Courtesy: Merillat Industries, Inc.

Wall and ceiling treatments are becoming increasingly important in remodeling as homeowners look for more pleasing and unique designs. Use wallpaper, brick, painted brick, stone or paneling to introduce a style or theme to the room. Light colors reflect more light and make rooms appear larger. Dark tones cut down on the amount of light and make rooms appear smaller. Wood paneling often adds warmth to a room. Try using plywood panels like the ones shown in Figure 14-5. They come in many woods and shades and they're easy to install directly to studs or over existing wallboard.

Figures 14-1 through 14-5 show what the right combination of materials can do. Give the walls and ceilings the attention they deserve right from the first planning stage of the job. Many remodelers make the mistake of slighting the walls and ceilings and concentrating on the showier features. But new cabinets, appliances, and bathroom fixtures won't look their best without the right backdrop. Of course, if a new coat of paint is all it takes to achieve the homeowner's goal, that's fine. But most of the time that's not enough.

New wall and ceiling finishes are something you'll have to consider if your plans include relocating walls or adding new partitions. Perhaps you're going to rob space from an existing closet, spare room, or porch to increase kitchen or bathroom space. If so, you can let your decorating skills go to work. In kitchen and bath remodeling, almost "anything goes" — as long as you do it right.

Working with Interior Walls

The interior walls of a house are generally referred to as partitions. If the house is built using roof trusses, the walls seldom carry weight. In stick construction, however, the center partition is almost always the one that bears the load. It's not easy to remove a load-bearing wall. You have to install beams to carry the weight before you can take the wall out. Exterior walls are always structural (load-bearing). If you're going to remove a section of exterior wall, support the weight during removal with a beam. Then install a header to carry the weight of the missing wall section.

Design and function dictate the placement of non-bearing interior partitions. You can remove or install them without too much concern for the structural requirements of the room.

Removing a Partition

The first step in removing a partition is to remove the finish material. If it's plaster, you're going to have a lot of dust. Open a window to bring in fresh air. Close off the rest of the house to keep the dust confined to your work area.

You can't salvage gypsum wallboard or plaster — it's strictly a demolition job. When removing paneling, however, you may need to reuse some. Take it off carefully, especially if you're going to patch or repair cavities left in the finish. Next remove the plaster lath or any furring strips between the finish and the framing.

When you get down to the framing, it's time to remove wiring or pipe in the partition. The wiring may be an end-run into a wall outlet or it may be a circuit run through an outlet.

If it's an end-run coming up through the sole plate beneath the floor or down through the overhead top plate, follow these steps. Cut off the electricity at the main panel. Remove the outlet and box, and push the wire back underneath the floor or into the attic. Run the end of the wire into a metal junction box. If there's a bare grounding wire in the cable, attach it to the junction box. Individually cap each remaining wire with a wire nut. Wrap plastic tape around each nut and wire, and install a metal cover over the box. Be sure you follow the electrical code.

If the wire is a circuit run, cut off the electricity at the main panel. Remove the wire from the partition. Rejoin it in at a junction box so that the circuit continues.

Disconnect the plumbing pipelines where they enter the wall. Cap them off or reroute them as necessary.

Before removing any wall, *be sure you know* whether it's load-bearing or non-bearing. Normally, non-bearing walls run parallel to the ceiling joists. A load-bearing wall runs perpendicular to the ceiling joists (though not all interior walls perpendicular to the run of ceiling joists are load-bearing). If the partition is non-bearing, removal is easy. Take out the studs, sole plate, and top plate. Don't worry, the ceiling won't sag. You can salvage the framing for reuse.

To remove a load-bearing partition, begin by supporting the ceiling joists. Where attic space above the partition allows you working room, install a supporting beam *above* the ceiling joists in the attic. The beam will support the joists. You then transfer support for the load to the foundation by resting the ends of the beam on an exterior wall, a bearing partition, or a post.

Secure the joists to the beam at the point of intersection, as shown in Figure 14-6. Keep in mind that getting the beam material up into the attic can be a problem. You'll need a suitable access hole or a removable vent in the attic. Install the beam and lock it together before you remove the partition. You won't need any temporary support.

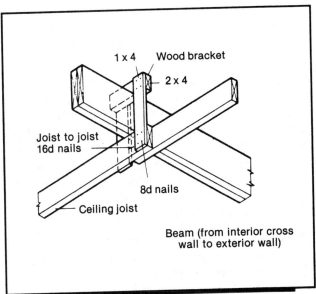

Figure 14-6
Framing for flush ceiling with wood brackets

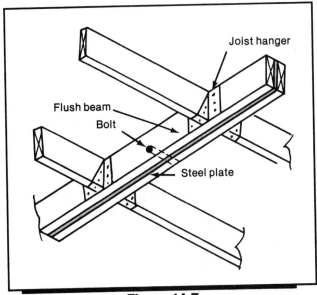

Figure 14-7
Flush beam steel reinforced

You may prefer to use the exposed beam approach. It ensures support, and you don't have to worry about space in the ceiling cavity or attic. Support the ceiling joists on each side of the partition with temporary jacks and blocking. Remove the partition and install the support beam. The bottom of the beam should be at least 6 feet 8 inches above the floor. Remove the jacks after you secure the beam. As long as the design of the kitchen is appropriate for the exposed-beam look, this method works well.

If the exposed-beam approach won't work, you can install a beam in the ceiling so that the ceiling joists butt into the beam. You'll need temporary jacks and blocking on each side of the partition while you install the beam.

Cut the joists to allow room for the beam. Use joist hangers to secure the joists to the beam, as shown in Figure 14-7. The beam span, the span of the joist framing, and the material you use for the beam will determine the size beam you need. Use a steel-reinforced beam to ensure adequate structural support. Make certain the steel is thick enough to do the job. Bolt the beam together. You can buy steel with pre-drilled bolt holes designed for this purpose.

This is a good way to provide support in lieu of a load-bearing partition when there isn't any attic space available. You can also use this method when you're removing a ground floor partition in a two-story house.

Repairs

Whenever you remove a partition, you're left with the problem of repairing the cavity left in the adjoining walls, ceiling, and floor. With plaster walls and ceilings, the problem is minor. Just spread plaster in the cavity and finish it smooth. For gypsum wallboard, fill in the space with a piece of material cut to the thickness and shape of the cavity. Finish and smooth the area with tape and joint compound.

When repairing wood flooring, you'll be fine as long as the repair runs parallel to the existing floor pattern. You can fill in the space with strips of new flooring and finish them to match. But if the run of the flooring is perpendicular to the wall you remove, you have a problem. Regardless of what you do, the patch will be obvious. A new floor covering is the best solution in this case.

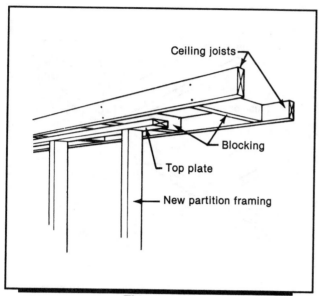

Figure 14-8
Add blocking between joists to secure
the new top plate

Adding a Partition

An added partition isn't load bearing — it just has to be strong enough to support itself. You can frame it with 2 x 4-inch material or make it a 2 x 3-inch partition, if the material is readily available. If it's a closet you're framing, 2 x 2-inch framing will do.

If you're adding a partition parallel to the floor joists, it's a good idea to place it over one of the joists. You can reinforce the joist from underneath by spiking a new framing member to it. Spiking the same size or smaller 2-inch member to another member (a 2 x 8 to a 2 x 10 joist) adds support.

If you have to build the partition between joists, you can provide extra support by installing a double joist. Of course, you can't do that if the partition is on the second story over a finished room. Partitions running perpendicular to the floor joists usually don't require additional support.

Begin your construction by marking off the partition on the floor. Snap a chalk line on the floor where the sole plate will go. With a level, draw a plumb line on each wall where the partition will intersect that wall. Mark the plumb line from floor to ceiling. Next, snap a chalk line on the ceiling from the plumb line of each wall.

Nail down the sole plate and the top plate. You need to secure the top plate to something solid in the ceiling. If the ceiling joists are parallel to the partition, and attic access is available, install solid blocking over the top plate area. Place the blocking at no more than 2-foot intervals (Figure 14-8) and nail the top plate to the blocking. If the ceiling and floor joists are perpendicular to the partition, nail the plates to each joist.

If you're adding on to a first floor room in a two-story home, you may have a problem securing the top plate unless the finish ceiling is wood. You'll have to install a double top plate to provide enough support.

Installing double top plates: Use this method to secure the double top plate. Nail the end studs in place. These are the two studs that go against the walls where you marked the plumb line. If you're lucky, there's an existing stud right where you need it. Just nail your new stud to the old one. But you're probably not that lucky.

If you're not, you'll have to cut the two end studs to fit on top of the sole plate and tight against the finished ceiling. Remove or notch out the crown molding so the stud fits snugly in the wall/ceiling juncture. Toenail the studs into the sole plate with 8d box nails. Then pre-drill for 16d (or longer) nails to go up through each of the end studs you just toenailed and catch the top plates of the intersecting walls. Two nails are sufficient to secure the studs at the top.

Now cut the new top plate (one continuous 2 x 4, or whatever size material you're using for framing) to fit snugly between the two end studs. Toenail it in place with 8d box nails. Cut two jack studs to fit against the end studs and under the new top plate. Nail these to the top plate and bottom plate with 8d box nails. Secure the jack studs to the end studs with 16d or 12d nails.

Cut another 2 x 4, 3 inches shorter than the top plate (one continuous piece). Use 12d nails to face nail it into the top plate and 8d nails to toenail it

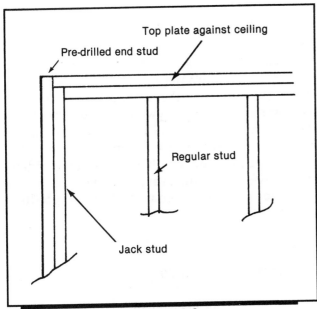

Figure 14-9
Double top plate framing for
non-bearing partitions

into the jack studs. Look at Figure 14-9. The double top plate will strengthen the wall span and eliminate any tendency for the wall to bow later.

Complete the framing by adding studs 16 or 24 inches on center. Fit the studs firmly between the plates. Check the required stud lengths at several points. There could be some variation.

Installing partially assembled partitions: If you have something solid to nail components to, you can sometimes raise a partially assembled wall partition. First nail the sole plate to the floor. Then nail the top plate to the studs and tilt the frame into place. When you have it properly seated, toenail the studs to the bottom plate.

You can't raise a fully assembled frame in a room unless the frame height is at least 1/2 inch shorter than the finished room height. Lifting the frame into place can damage the finish walls and ceiling. Even working a partially framed partition into place can cause some damage to the finish walls.

Special Framing

You may have to modify the standard framing for heating, plumbing, and electrical service. Heating ducts, water pipes, wires, plumbing stacks and drains need a place to run. You must strictly follow the local building codes where your renovations involve the structural components of the home.

Walls with utility runs: Walls containing plumbing stacks or vents often require special framing. You can't put 4-inch soil stacks in a standard 2 x 4-inch wall. Even a 3-inch plastic pipe stack is a tight squeeze. You have to cut out a section of the plate to make it fit.

At the time of this writing, the plumbing code was being changed to permit smaller pipe sizes and reduce the venting requirements. The Council of American Building Officials (CABO) recently published a national plumbing code for one- and two-family dwellings which allowed down-sizing building drains and sewers to 3 inches. It also allowed terminating vent stacks (3/4 inch to 1 inch depending on the number of fixtures served) through roof overhangs and side walls

These code changes will simplify things. But until they become effective in your area (check with your local authority), consider a thicker wall for utility runs. You'll need 2 x 6-inch or 2 x 8-inch bottom and top plates with 2 x 4's placed flat at the edge of the plates. See Figure 14-10. The center of the wall remains open so you can run supply and drain lines. You can also use 2 x 6 studs and plates with the studs notched or drilled for pipe runs.

Interior Wall Finishes

You're not finished with any job until the walls have a professional finish. The surface should be smooth and even. There shouldn't be any flaws such as waves, dips or humps in the plaster.

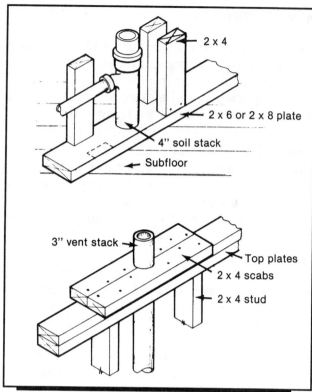

Figure 14-10
Framing for vents and pipes

Material	Minimum material thickness (inches) with framing spaced	
	Framing on 16" centers	**Framing on 24" centers**
Gypsum board	3/8	1/2
Hardboard	1/4	—
Wood paneling	1/4	1/2
Plywood	1/4	3/8
Fiberboard	1/2	3/4

Figure 14-11
Drywall thickness and spacing

Drywall should also be smooth, without any obvious seams.

You can easily repair most minor cracks in plaster or drywall with a plastic patching mix. Just fill the cracks and sand them smooth. To eliminate waviness in 1/4-inch plywood or hardboard, install it over a good base, like 3/8-inch gypsum board. An uneven wall in a remodeled house is like a dent in a new car. It *looks* like an accident and causes you pain every time you see it. In short, you are a professional and should produce professional results.

Working with Drywall

When you think of drywall, you usually think of gypsum board, hardboard, wood paneling, plywood and fiberboard. You can apply drywall to framing, or to furring strips over framing or masonry walls. It can also be glued to a smooth existing wall. The thickness of the drywall isn't as critical when you apply it to an existing wall. The wall provides a solid backing for the new material. Figure 14-11 shows the various thicknesses you need when applying drywall to framing or furring strips. The greater the space between framing studs, the thicker the material should be. If you're working on an exterior wall, don't forget the insulation between the furring strips.

Installing new material over old is a common practice. As long as the old surface is smooth, it works well. But sometimes it isn't. If the old wall is very irregular, you'll need furring and shims under the new drywall. See Figure 14-12.

Place a straightedge against the wall to see how much shimming you need. Locate the studs. They'll be on 16- or 24-inch centers. Some houses are built with the studs on non-bearing walls spaced from the outside wall toward the center. On load-bearing walls the studs are placed from right to left. Others are laid out just the opposite. Some homes are built with a combination of the two methods, with one room's studs measured one way and another room's another way. Each builder and carpenter works a little different.

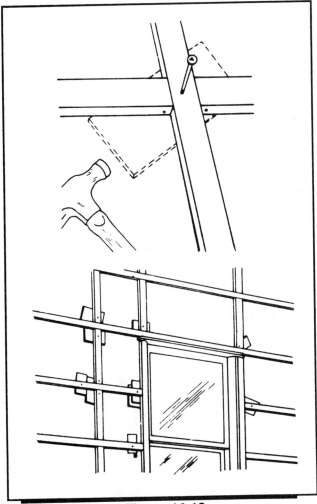

Figure 14-12
Place shingle shims behind furring for a smooth
vertical surface

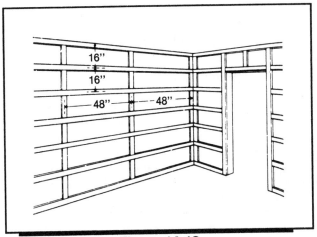

Figure 14-13
Apply horizontal furring to interior wall

Once you locate one stud, the next one will be easy to find. It should be 16 or 24 inches away.

Apply furring strips (1 x 2 or 1 x 4) horizontally on 16- or 24-inch centers, depending on the thickness of the new material. Remove all base moldings, ceiling moldings, and window and door casings. Fur out around all openings (Figure 14-13). Nail the furring strips to the studs with 8d or longer nails. You'll need to use nails that will penetrate the studs 1-1/2 inches. The thicker the existing finish wall, the longer the nails you'll need. Figure 14-14 shows nail sizes and penny conversions.

Gypsum Board

Gypsum board makes an attractive wall or ceiling, is easy to maintain, and lasts a long time. The gypsum filler is faced with paper. The side edges are recessed or tapered to make a flat surface after the tape and joint compound go on. Gypsum board is classified as a non-combustible material by building and fire insurance companies.

Choosing the Right Gypsum Board

Gypsum board sheets are 4 feet wide and available in lengths of 8, 10, and 12 feet. They come in 3/8-, 1/2-, and 5/8-inch thicknesses.

Use the 3/8-inch thickness over old walls and ceilings. Use the 1/2 or 5/8-inch thickness when you apply it to framing. If you apply it vertically over framing, the stud spacing should be a maximum of 16 inches o.c. When you install the length at right angles to the framing (horizontal application), the maximum frame spacing is 24 inches o.c. Use 1/2-inch horizontal sheets when the stud spacing is 16 inches or less, or 5/8-inch sheets with 16- to 24-inch framing.

If the ceiling will support insulation or have a spray-applied water-base texture coating, use the 5/8-inch thickness.

Size of nails	Length of nails (inches)	Gauge number	Approximate number to pound
2d	1	15	876
3d	1-1/4	14	568
4d	1-1/2	12-1/2	316
5d	1-3/4	12-1/2	271
6d	2	11-1/2	181
7d	2-1/4	11-1/2	161
8d	2-1/2	10-1/4	106
9d	2-3/4	10-1/4	96
10d	3	9	69
12d	3-1/4	9	63
16d	3-1/2	8	49
20d	4	6	31
30d	4-1/2	5	24
40d	5	4	18
50d	5-1/2	3	14
60d	6	2	11

Figure 14-14
Penny conversions

Protect gypsum wallboard from exposure to high humidity and moisture. For best results, apply gypsum wallboard finishes only when the temperature is above 55 degrees with continuous controlled heating provided at least 24 hours before starting. Provide adequate ventilation during periods of high humidity. Seal the wallboard with a pigmented primer before applying a texture material.

Framing

When you frame for gypsum wallboard, as for any other finish wall, space the framing members accurately on 16- or 24-inch centers. Set each member straight and true. Provide nailing members at all corners and junctures as shown in Figure 14-15. To ensure the gypsum wallboard fasteners work properly, use a good grade of 2 x 4's for your framing. They should be straight, dry, and uniform in dimension.

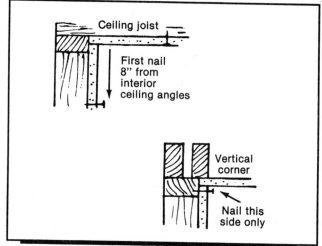

Figure 14-15
Nailing at corners

If the sheets are going to support insulation, the ceiling joists shouldn't be over 16 inches o.c. Apply the boards at right angles to the ceiling framing. Install a vapor barrier between the gypsum board and loose-fill insulation, or use fiberglass batts with a vapor barrier face. Provide adequate ventilation in any unheated spaces above gypsum board ceilings.

Floating Angle Installation

There are three operations involved in finishing a wall with gypsum board: hanging, taping and joint finishing, and painting.

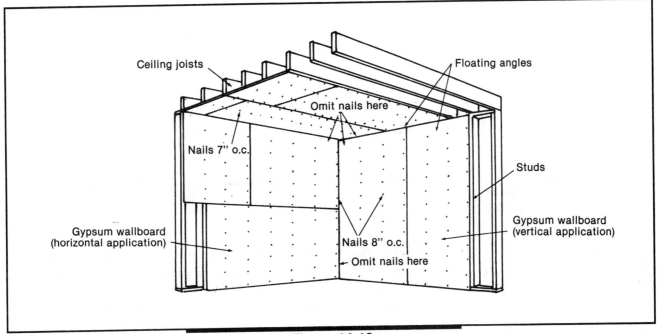

Figure 14-16
Sidewall application details

Use the floating angle installation to reduce stress and strain on the wallboard panels as the framing settles. With this method you eliminate certain nails or screws at the *interior* angles, where the ceiling and sidewalls meet and where sidewalls intersect. Figures 14-16 and 14-17 show floating angle installations. You use conventional fastening for the remaining ceiling or wall areas. Follow standard practices for framing.

Ceilings: Always install ceilings first. You can apply the gypsum board either parallel to the joists (as shown in Figure 14-16) or at right angles across the ceiling joists (Figure 14-17). When you apply it across the ceiling joists, use conventional nailing methods where the boards abut the wall intersection. At the long edges of the board running parallel to the intersection, drive the first nail about 7 inches from the wall joint.

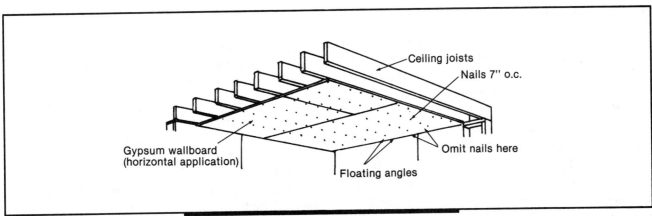

Figure 14-17
Ceiling application details

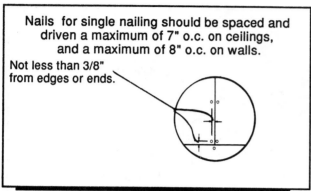

Figure 14-18
Single nailing

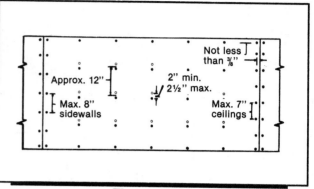

Figure 14-19
Double nailing

When you apply the wallboard parallel to the joists, nail the long edges of the board conventionally. At the wall intersections, where the ends of the boards meet, drive the first nail approximately 7 inches from the joint.

Walls: Fit wall panels snugly against the ceiling and square the first board with the adjacent wall. The wall panels must make firm contact at the ceiling line to support the ceiling panels. Along the ceiling intersections, *omit* the nails directly below the ceiling angle. Drive the first nail about 8 inches below the ceiling intersection. At all vertical interior angles, omit nailing the corner of the first board you apply. You will secure it at the angle by overlapping the adjacent corner board. Nail the overlapping board the usual way, 8 inches o.c. Refer again to Figures 14-15 and 14-16 for nailing at corners.

Install the square or beveled edge gypsum board vertically. You can install boards with tapered edges either vertically or horizontally. Bring the panels into moderate contact, but don't force them together. Stagger the joints. You don't want the corners of four boards meeting at one point. You should also avoid having perpendicular joints on opposite sides of a partition on the same stud. To reduce manhours, use the longest panels possible and apply them horizontally. This can cut your labor by about 10 percent on many jobs.

Fasteners: Fasten gypsum board panels by nailing from the center toward the ends and edges. For single nailing, space the nails 6 to 8 inches apart on intermediate and end wall supports. Intermediate and end ceiling boards should be secured every 5 to 7 inches. Keep nails 3/8 inches in from the ends and edges of panels. See Figure 14-18.

Double nailing minimizes the possibility of nail pops. Nail the field of the board 12 inches o.c., starting in the center. Drive the second nail 2 inches from each of the first nails as shown in Figure 14-19. Use conventional nailing around the perimeter of the panels.

You can also use an adhesive-nail-on application to attach the panels. Apply adhesive to studs, joists and gypsum boards, then place the boards in position. Fasten with nails no more than 24 inches o.c. for sidewalls, and 16 inches o.c. for ceilings. You can also use 1-1/2-inch Phillips head screws to fasten the panels to wood studs. Figure 14-20 shows fastener spacing for adhesive and supplemental fastening.

For applying single- or double-layer wallboard over wood furring, use the fasteners recommended in Figure 14-21. Space 1 x 3 or 1 x 4-inch furring strips no more than 24 inches o.c. In multi-layer construction, you can fasten the base layer of wallboard with flat staples. They should be 1/2-inch wide, 1-inch long 16-gauge galvanized wire. *Never use staples in single layer construction.*

Framing member spacing	Ceilings		Partitions (load-bearing)		Partitions (non-bearing)	
	Nail	Screw	Nail	Screw	Nail	Screw
16" o.c.	16"	16"	16"	24"	24"	24"
24" o.c.	12"	16"	12"	16"	16"	24"

Adhesive application patterns

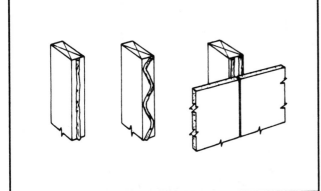

Figure 14-20
Fastener spacing with adhesive and
supplemental fastening

Cementing and Taping Joints

When installing gypsum board, drive the nails in so that heads are slightly below the panel surface. But don't use a nail set to drive the nails, use a hammer. You can see in Figure 14-22, Diagram A, that the head of the hammer will make a small dimple in the board. Be careful you don't break the paper face of the panel. Fill nail dimples with joint compound (often called *mud* or *cement* by sheetrockers). When the compound is dry, sand it smooth. Be careful not to sand the paper surface. Apply two coats of compound if necessary.

Cover the joints between panels with joint compound and paper tape. This helps smooth and level the wall surface. The compound comes in a powder form. Mix it with water to make a soft putty that can be spread with a putty knife. Or you can buy joint compound in a premixed form if you prefer.

Taping procedures for wall and ceiling joints: The procedures for taping and finishing are illustrated in Figure 14-22, Diagram B.

1) Starting at the top of the wall, use a 5-inch spackling knife and spread the compound into the tapered edges at the joint.

2) Using the same knife, press tape into the recess until the compound is forced through the perforations.

3) Cover the tape with additional compound. Feather the edges.

Nails (for application to wood framing)					
GWB-54 annular ring, .098 diameter. Maximum 19/64" head.		Smooth bright. 1/4" diameter head.		Coated 13 gauge. 1/4" cupped head.	
Wallboard thickness	Length of nail	Wallboard thickness	Length of nail	Wallboard thickness	Length of nail
1/4"	1-1/8"	1/4"	1-1/4"	1/4"	1-1/4"
3/8"	1-1/4"	3/8"	1-3/8" (4d)	3/8"	1-1/4"
1/2"	1-3/8"	1/2"	1-5/8" (5d)	1/2"	1-3/8"
5/8"	1-3/8"	5/8"	1-7/8" (6d)	5/8"	1-1/2"

Note: When Parkerhead-type nails are used, follow manufacturer's recommendations.

Figure 14-21
Recommended fasteners for single
and double layer wallboard

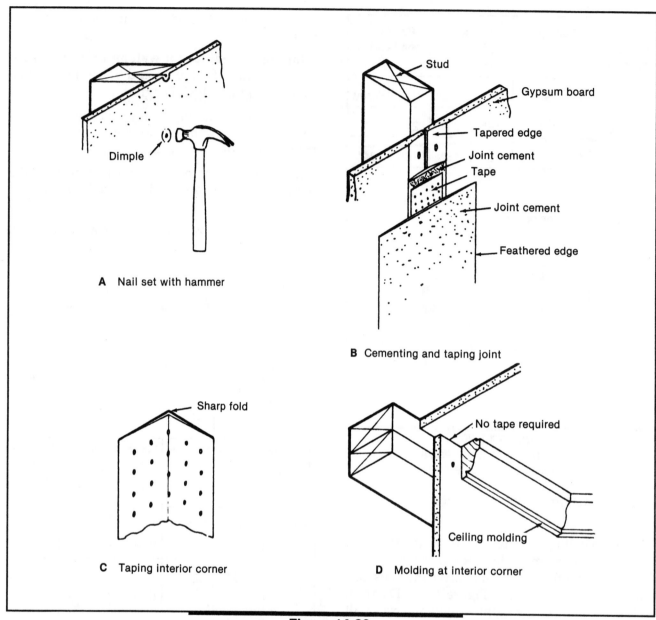

A   Nail set with hammer

B   Cementing and taping joint

C   Taping interior corner

D   Molding at interior corner

Figure 14-22
Gypsum board finishing details

4) Allow the compound to dry. Then apply a second coat, and feather the edges so they extend beyond the edges of the first coat. A steel trowel works best for the second coat. If you apply a third coat, feather it beyond the second coat.

5) After the joint is dry, sand it smooth.

6) Follow the same procedures for taping the ceiling joints.

Taping and finishing corners: Interior corner joints can be finished with either tape or molding. Tape's the most common. It makes a smooth, clean joint and it's less expensive to install.

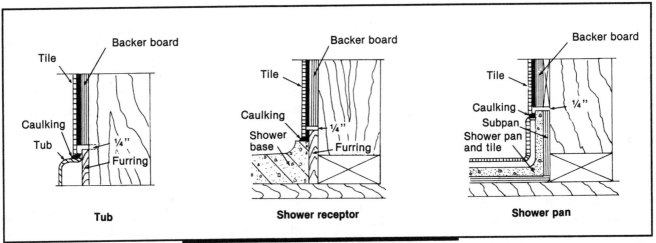

Figure 14-23
Backer board application details

1) Fold a strip of tape down the center so it forms a sharp angle, as shown in Figure 14-22, Diagram C.

2) Apply compound at the corner.

3) Press the tape into place.

4) Finish the corner with compound, feathering the edges.

5) When dry, sand smooth. Repeat the procedure with a second coat.

6) At outside corners, use corner beads to prevent damage to the corners. Fasten metal corner bead in place *over* the gypsum board and then cover it with joint compound. Sand and smooth the edges when the compound is dry.

Figure 14-22, Diagram D, shows an interior corner finished with molding. If you use molding, tape isn't necessary.

Installing Water-Resistant Gypsum Board

There's a specially-formulated backer board (B/B) available for use on walls in high moisture areas. It's designed for shower stalls and tub enclosures as a base for the adhesive application of ceramic tile, metal and plastic wall tile. But don't use backer board for ceilings, or as soffit material.

Backer board consists of an asphalt-treated core covered with a heavy water-repellent back paper and ivory face paper. You don't need to seal the surface or tape the joints before applying the tile.

B/B installation procedures: Figure 14-23 illustrates the details for backer board installation.

1) The wall studs should be spaced 16 inches o.c. Install one row of blocking approximately 1 inch above the top of the tub or shower receptor, and another midway between the fixture and the ceiling.

2) Use furring around the tub enclosure and shower stall so that the inside face of the fixture lip will be flush with the face of the backer board. The top of the furring should be about even with the upper edge of the tub or shower pan.

3) Provide appropriate headers or supports for the tub, plumbing fixtures, soap dishes, grab bars, and towel racks. Install the tub, shower receptor or pan before installing the backer board. Shower receptors or pans should have an upstanding lip or flange 1 inch higher than the water drain or threshold of the shower.

4) Apply the backer board horizontally to eliminate butt joints. Allow a 1/4-inch space between the lip of the fixture and the paper-bound edge of the board. Space nails 8 inches o.c. and screws 12 inches

o.c. If you're going to use ceramic tile thicker than 5/16 inch, space the nails 4 inches o.c. and screws 8 inches o.c. Dimple nail heads, but take care not to tear the face paper.

5) In areas where you'll be installing tile, treat the joints and angles with a waterproof tile adhesive. Don't use regular joint compound and tape. Caulk the openings around pipes and fixtures with a waterproof non-setting caulking compound.

6) Apply the tile down to the top edge of the shower floor surfacing material, or to the shower pan return, or over the tub lip, as shown in the figure.

7) Fill the space between fixtures and tile with non-setting caulking or tile grout compound.

Plywood and Hardboard

Plywood and hardboard panels are available in 4 x 8 foot sheets, usually 1/4 inch thick. The finished panels have the appearance of boards or planks cut in equal or random widths. Some have a durable plastic finish.

You can get plywood panels in a variety of colors and wood finishes. The price range (economy to quite expensive) depends on the type of wood finish and the quality of the panels. Hardboard imprinted with a wood-grain pattern is probably the least expensive. You can also get vinyl-coated hardboard surfaced in patterns and colors.

Preparations for Installation

Generally, the preparation necessary for plywood and hardboard application is the same as for gypsum board. The wall should be even, without dips, humps, or waves. If it isn't, you'll need to fur and shim to smooth it out. Space the furring the same as for gypsum board.

Always leave existing gypsum wallboard on the wall unless it, or the underneath framing, will prevent a good paneling job. Remove all the molding and trim from the walls and around doors and windows. Use care if you intend to reuse the molding and trim. In most cases, you'll have to insert a spacer strip in the door and window jambs to extend them out flush with the new panel surface.

When plywood panels are delivered to the job, you'll probably discover that the sheets vary in color and texture. Stand the panels up in the room and arrange them in the order that gives the best color or texture pattern for the room. You may have a panel that's too light or too dark to use. If it's obviously from a different mill run than the other panels, return it to the supplier. Make sure you have a good match-up before beginning your installation. Mark or stack the panels in the order that you want to install them.

Installation

First determine the stud run and wall centers in the room. Then decide on your method of installation. You can start around the center of the wall, nailing up whole sheets, and work your way to the corners. This way you may have to trim the sheets down at both ends of the wall. Or, you can start in one corner and go from there, completing each wall as you work around the room.

Plumb the first sheet and nail or glue it in place. Carefully butt the next sheet up to it. Hardboard paneling edges should touch very lightly. Sometimes the edge of a panel may not exactly fit the edge of the adjoining panel, leaving the stud or old wall showing through. Use a black felt marker and mark the spot on the stud or wall where the panels meet. Do this before you nail up the panel.

When you fasten the panels into place, space the nails 8 to 10 inches apart on the edges and at intermediate support points. Use color-matched nails. They're available for most paneling.

Carefully measure the spaces where you'll need partial sheets. Transfer your measurements to the panel. Use a hand or power saw to cut the panels.

When cutting with a hand saw, place the *finish* side up. If you use a power saw, use a hollow ground blade. Place the panel *back* side up on your workbench. Always cut into the panel face. If you must cut a panel with the face up, first score the saw line with a knife. This prevents splintering. Keep the blade on the waste side of the line.

When measuring for window and door openings, you can often hold the panel in position while your helper marks the opening on the back of the panel. You can then place the panel on your workbench and simply adjust the saw line to allow for the thickness of the jamb.

Cut-outs for wall outlets and switch boxes are simple to do. Mark the edges of the box with chalk. Place the panel in position and tap the panel against the box with your hand. This will mark the correct position of the box on the back of the panel. Return the panel to the workbench, back side up, and drill starter holes at each corner of the box. Be careful not to force the drill through or you may cause the panel face to splinter. Cut the piece out with a keyhole or saber saw.

If the corners of the room are true, you can complete the installation without inside corner molding. However you may want to use molding for the corners anyway. It gives the paneling a nice finished appearance.

Wood and Fiberboard Paneling

Tongue and groove wood and fiberboard paneling are available in various patterns. Wood is limited to 8-inch widths. Fiberboard is available in 12- and 16-inch widths. This "plank" paneling is usually applied vertically, but it can be applied horizontally for a special effect. If you install the paneling horizontally, you can nail it directly to the studs. When you install it vertically, use 1 x 4-inch nailing strips or 2 x 4-inch blocking at 24-inch intervals. You need to sand and finish wood paneling after installation.

Paneling, like gypsum board and plywood panels, cannot be installed directly over masonry. You need to install furring or nailing strips first. Secure the strips with concrete nails or a stud driver. Treat the furring material with a wood preservative to prevent moisture deterioration.

Blind nail tongue and groove panels through the tongue. Wider "planks" may need face nailing in addition to blind nailing. You can use an appropriate sized staple in the tongue of fiberboard in place of nails, if you prefer. If you use adhesive, only blind nailing is necessary.

Estimating Wallboard Materials and Labor Costs

To estimate wallboard requirements, figure the square feet of the walls and ceilings in each room you're covering. Figure 14-24 is a quick reference for finding square footage. It shows the total square feet for rooms with even wall lengths and standard 8-foot ceilings.

Figure 14-25 gives the square footage for standard size wallboard panels. It also has the figures for bundles of 3/8- and 1/2-inch lath, in case you're plastering the kitchen or bathroom. We'll cover that shortly.

Let's say you're estimating the wallboard for a 14 x 16-foot kitchen with an 8-foot ceiling. According to Figure 14-24, the wall and ceiling area totals 704 square feet. If you're using 4 x 8 panels, look under the 4 x 8 column on Figure 14-25. Go down the column until you come to 704, then follow that line to the left to find how many pieces of wallboard you need. For 704 square feet, you'll need 22 sheets of wallboard.

Room Areas Square feet — 4 Walls (W) and Ceilings (C)

LF/wall	6	8	10	12	14	16	18	20	22	24	26	28	30
6	C 36 / W 192	C 48 / W 224	C 60 / W 256	C 72 / W 288	C 84 / W 320	C 96 / W 352	C 108 / W 384	C 120 / W 416	C 132 / W 448	C 144 / W 480	C 156 / W 512	C 168 / W 544	C 180 / W 576
8	C 48 / W 224	C 64 / W 256	C 80 / W 288	C 96 / W 320	C 112 / W 352	C 128 / W 384	C 144 / W 416	C 160 / W 448	C 176 / W 480	C 182 / W 512	C 198 / W 544	C 224 / W 576	C 240 / W 608
10	C 60 / W 256	C 80 / W 288	C 100 / W 320	C 120 / W 352	C 140 / W 384	C 160 / W 416	C 180 / W 448	C 200 / W 480	C 220 / W 512	C 240 / W 544	C 260 / W 576	C 280 / W 608	C 300 / W 640
12	C 72 / W 288	C 96 / W 320	C 120 / W 352	C 144 / W 384	C 168 / W 416	C 192 / W 488	C 216 / W 480	C 240 / W 512	C 264 / W 544	C 288 / W 576	C 312 / W 608	C 336 / W 640	C 360 / W 672
14	C 84 / W 320	C 112 / W 352	C 140 / W 384	C 168 / W 416	C 196 / W 448	C 224 / W 480	C 252 / W 512	C 280 / W 544	C 308 / W 576	C 336 / W 608	C 364 / W 640	C 392 / W 672	C 420 / W 704
16	C 96 / W 352	C 128 / W 384	C 160 / W 416	C 192 / W 448	C 224 / W 480	C 256 / W 512	C 288 / W 544	C 320 / W 576	C 352 / W 608	C 384 / W 640	C 416 / W 672	C 448 / W 704	C 480 / W 736
18	C 108 / W 384	C 144 / W 416	C 180 / W 448	C 216 / W 480	C 252 / W 512	C 288 / W 544	C 324 / W 576	C 360 / W 608	C 396 / W 640	C 432 / W 672	C 468 / W 704	C 504 / W 736	C 540 / W 768
20	C 120 / W 416	C 160 / W 448	C 200 / W 480	C 240 / W 512	C 280 / W 544	C 320 / W 576	C 360 / W 608	C 400 / W 640	C 440 / W 672	C 480 / W 704	C 520 / W 736	C 560 / W 768	C 600 / W 800
22	C 132 / W 448	C 176 / W 480	C 220 / W 512	C 264 / W 544	C 308 / W 576	C 352 / W 608	C 396 / W 640	C 440 / W 672	C 484 / W 704	C 528 / W 736	C 572 / W 768	C 616 / W 800	C 660 / W 832
24	C 144 / W 480	C 182 / W 512	C 240 / W 544	C 288 / W 576	C 336 / W 608	C 384 / W 640	C 432 / W 672	C 480 / W 704	C 528 / W 736	C 576 / W 768	C 624 / W 800	C 672 / W 832	C 720 / W 864
26	C 156 / W 512	C 198 / W 544	C 260 / W 576	C 312 / W 608	C 364 / W 640	C 416 / W 672	C 468 / W 704	C 520 / W 736	C 572 / W 768	C 624 / W 800	C 676 / W 832	C 728 / W 864	C 780 / W 896
28	C 168 / W 544	C 224 / W 576	C 280 / W 608	C 336 / W 640	C 392 / W 672	C 448 / W 704	C 504 / W 736	C 560 / W 768	C 616 / W 800	C 672 / W 832	C 728 / W 864	C 784 / W 896	C 840 / W 928
30	C 180 / W 576	C 240 / W 608	C 300 / W 640	C 360 / W 672	C 420 / W 704	C 480 / W 736	C 540 / W 768	C 600 / W 800	C 660 / W 832	C 720 / W 864	C 780 / W896	C 840 / W 928	C 900 / W 960

Note: Based on wall height of 8'0''. C = Ceiling area. W = Wall area = 4 walls.

Figure 14-24
Room area chart

If you're figuring wallboard requirements for the walls only, use Figure 14-26 to find the number of 4 x 8 panels you'll need. Add the total of the four walls to find the perimeter of the room. For a 14 x 16-foot room, it's 60 feet. Look on the conversion table to find the number of panels you'll need. You'll see that you need 15 panels. Now check the deductions at the bottom of the figure. You have to subtract for doors, windows, and fireplaces.

Wallboard Finish Materials

Besides the wallboard, you'll need the following finish materials for your application:

- One roll of tape (250 feet) per 600 square feet of wallboard.

- Five gallons (one can) of joint compound per 1,000 square feet of wallboard.

- One 8-foot metal corner bead for each outside corner.

- With texture-finished ceilings using joint compound, five gallons per 400 square feet.

- With adhesive, one tube of adhesive per 500 square feet of wallboard and five pounds of 1-3/8-inch annular ring nails per 1,000 square feet of wallboard.

Board products — square feet   16" x 48" lath

Pieces	4' x 6'	4' x 7'	4' x 8'	4' x 9'	4' x 10'	4' x 12'	4' x 14'	4' x 16'	2' x 8'	2' x 10'	2' x 12'
2	48	56	64	72	80	96	112	128	32	40	48
4	96	112	128	144	160	192	224	256	64	80	96
6	144	168	192	216	240	288	336	384	96	120	144
8	192	224	256	288	320	384	448	512	128	160	192
10	240	280	320	360	400	480	560	640	160	200	240
12	288	336	384	432	480	576	672	768	192	240	288
14	336	392	448	504	560	672	784	896	224	280	336
16	384	448	512	576	640	768	896	1,024	256	320	384
18	432	504	576	648	720	864	1,008	1,152	288	360	432
20	480	560	640	720	800	960	1,120	1,280	320	400	480
22	528	616	704	792	880	1,056	1,232	1,408	352	440	528
24	576	672	768	864	960	1,152	1,344	1,536	384	480	576
26	624	728	832	936	1,040	1,248	1,456	1,664	416	520	624
28	672	784	896	1,008	1,120	1,344	1,568	1,792	448	560	672
30	720	840	960	1,080	1,200	1,440	1,680	1,920	480	600	720
32	768	896	1,024	1,152	1,280	1,536	1,792	2,048	512	640	768
34	816	952	1,088	1,224	1,360	1,632	1,904	2,176	544	680	816
36	864	1,008	1,152	1,296	1,440	1,728	2,016	2,304	576	720	864
38	912	1,064	1,216	1,368	1,520	1,824	2,128	2,432	608	760	912
40	960	1,120	1,280	1,440	1,600	1,920	2,240	2,560	640	800	960
42	1,008	1,176	1,344	1,512	1,680	2,016	2,352	2,688	672	840	1,008
44	1,056	1,232	1,408	1,584	1,760	2,112	2,464	2,816	704	880	1,056
46	1,104	1,288	1,472	1,656	1,840	2,208	2,576	2,944	736	920	1,104
48	1,152	1,344	1,536	1,728	1,920	2,304	2,688	3,072	768	960	1,152
50	1,200	1,400	1,600	1,800	2,000	2,400	2,800	3,200	800	1,000	1,200
52	1,248	1,456	1,664	1,872	2,080	2,496	2,912	3,328	832	1,040	1,248
54	1,296	1,512	1,728	1,944	2,160	2,592	3,024	3,456	864	1,080	1,296
56	1,344	1,568	1,792	2,016	2,240	2,688	3,136	3,584	896	1,120	1,344
58	1,392	1,624	1,856	2,088	2,320	2,784	3,248	3,712	928	1,160	1,392
60	1,440	1,680	1,920	2,160	2,400	2,880	3,360	3,840	960	1,200	1,440
62	1,488	1,736	1,984	2,232	2,480	2,976	3,472	3,968	992	1,240	1,488
64	1,536	1,792	2,048	2,304	2,560	3,072	3,584	4,096	1,024	1,280	1,536
66	1,584	1,848	2,112	2,376	2,640	3,168	3,696	4,224	1,056	1,320	1,584
68	1,632	1,904	2,176	2,448	2,720	3,264	3,808	4,352	1,088	1,360	1,632
70	1,680	1,960	2,240	2,520	2,800	3,360	3,920	4,480	1,120	1,400	1,680
72	1,728	2,016	2,304	2,592	2,880	3,456	4,032	4,608	1,152	1,440	1,728
74	1,776	2,072	2,368	2,664	2,960	3,552	4,144	4,736	1,184	1,480	1,776
76	1,824	2,128	2,432	2,736	3,040	3,648	4,256	4,864	1,216	1,520	1,824
78	1,872	2,184	2,496	2,808	3,120	3,744	4,368	4,992	1,248	1,560	1,872
80	1,920	2,240	2,560	2,880	3,200	3,840	4,480	5,120	1,280	1,600	1,920
82	1,968	2,296	2,624	2,952	3,280	3,936	4,592	5,248	1,312	1,640	1,968
84	2,016	2,352	2,688	3,024	3,360	4,032	4,704	5,376	1,344	1,680	2,016
86	2,064	2,408	2,752	3,096	3,440	4,128	4,816	5,504	1,376	1,720	2,064
88	2,112	2,464	2,816	3,168	3,520	4,224	4,928	5,632	1,408	1,760	2,112
90	2,160	2,520	2,880	3,240	3,600	4,320	5,040	5,760	1,440	1,800	2,160
92	2,208	2,576	2,944	3,312	3,680	4,416	5,152	5,888	1,472	1,840	2,208
94	2,256	2,632	3,008	3,384	3,760	4,512	5,264	6,016	1,504	1,880	2,256
96	2,304	2,688	3,072	3,456	3,840	4,608	5,376	6,144	1,536	1,920	2,304
98	2,352	2,744	3,136	3,528	3,920	4,704	5,488	6,272	1,568	1,960	2,352
100	2,400	2,800	3,200	3,600	4,000	4,800	5,600	6,400	1,600	2,000	2,400
200	4,800	5,600	6,400	7,200	8,000	9,600	11,200	12,800	3,200	4,000	4,800
300	7,200	8,400	9,600	10,800	12,000	14,400	16,800	19,200	4,800	6,000	7,200
400	9,600	11,200	12,800	14,400	16,000	19,200	22,400	25,600	6,400	8,000	9,600
500	12,000	14,000	16,000	18,000	20,000	24,000	28,000	32,000	8,000	10,000	12,000
600	14,400	16,800	19,200	21,600	24,000	28,800	33,600	38,400	9,600	12,000	14,400
700	16,800	19,600	22,400	25,200	28,000	33,600	39,200	44,800	11,200	14,000	16,800
800	19,200	22,400	25,600	28,800	32,000	38,400	44,800	51,200	12,800	16,000	19,200
900	21,600	25,200	28,800	32,400	36,000	43,200	50,400	57,600	14,400	18,000	21,600
1,000	24,000	28,000	32,000	36,000	40,000	48,000	56,000	64,000	16,000	20,000	24,000

16" x 48" lath

Bdls.	3/8"	1/2"
1	32	21.33
2	64	42.67
3	96	64.00
4	128	85.33
5	160	106.67
6	192	128.00
7	224	149.33
8	256	170.67
9	288	192.00
10	320	213.33
11	352	234.67
12	384	256.00
13	416	277.33
14	448	298.67
15	480	320.00
16	512	341.33
17	544	362.67
18	576	384.00
19	608	405.33
20	640	426.67
21	672	448.00
22	704	469.33
23	736	490.67
24	768	512.00
25	800	533.33
26	832	554.67
27	864	576.00
28	896	597.33
29	928	618.67
30	960	640.00
31	992	661.33
32	1,024	682.67
33	1,056	704.00
34	1,088	725.33
35	1,120	746.67
36	1,152	767.00
37	1,184	789.33
38	1,216	810.67
39	1,248	832.00
40	1,280	853.33
41	1,312	874.67
42	1,344	896.00
43	1,376	917.33
44	1,408	938.67
45	1,440	960.00
46	1,472	981.33
47	1,504	1,002.67
48	1,536	1,024.00
49	1,568	1,045.33
50	1,600	1,066.67
60	1,920	1,280.00
70	2,240	1,493.33
80	2,560	1,706.67
90	2,880	1,920.00
100	3,200	2,133.33
200	6,400	4,266.67
300	9,600	6,400.00
400	12,800	8,533.33
500	16,000	10,666.67

Figure 14-25
Wallboard area table

How to Figure a Room

Determine the perimeter of the room. This is merely the total of the widths of each wall in the room. Use the conversion table to figure the number of panels needed.

Perimeter	No. of 4' x 8' panels needed
36'	9
40'	10
44'	11
48'	12
52'	13
56'	14
60'	15
64'	16
68'	17
72'	18
92'	23

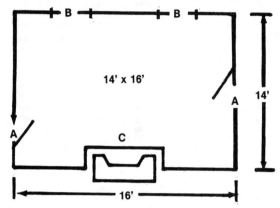

14' x 16'

14'

16'

Example: if your room walls measured 14' + 14' + 16' + 16', this would equal 60' and require 15 panels. Allow for areas such as windows, doors, fireplaces, etc. by using the deductions listed below:

Deductions:　Door　　1/2 panel each (A)
　　　　　　　Window　1/4 panel each (B)
　　　　　　　Fireplace　1/2 panel (C)

The actual number of panels needed for this room is 13 pieces (15 pieces minus 2 for the deductions.) If the perimeter of the room falls in between the figures in the table, use the next highest number to determine the panels required. These figures are only for rooms with 8' ceiling heights or less.

Figure 14-26
Figuring wallboard panels by room perimeter

Size of strips	O.C. spacing of furring	BF per SF of wall	Lbs nails per 1000 BF
1" x 2"	12"	.18	55
	16"	.14	
	20"	.11	
	24"	.10	
1" x 3"	12"	.28	37
	16"	.21	
	20"	.17	
	24"	.14	
1" x 4"	12"	.36	30
	16"	.28	
	20"	.22	
	24"	.20	

Figure 14-27
Materials required for furring

Furring Material

Use Figure 14-27 to help you figure furring materials needed to provide an even base for the drywall. The figure shows the board feet of furring strips and pounds of nails you'll use per square foot of wall.

Labor for Drywall Installation

Figure 14-28 breaks down the labor for installing gypsum wallboard. These are 25 to 35 percent higher than similar work in new construction. Use the low or high figure in the range given, based on the conditions of your particular job. Add extra manhours when working under conditions which involve carrying materials outside for measuring and sawing, working around fur-

Work element	Unit	Manhours per unit
Drywall on one face of metal or wood studs or furring		
1 layer, 3/8"	100 SF	2.2 - 2.4
1 layer, 1/2"	100 SF	2.3 - 2.6
1 layer, 5/8"	100 SF	2.6 - 2.8
2 layers, 3/8" (mastic)	100 SF	3.4 - 3.6
2 layers, 1/2" (mastic)	100 SF	3.7 - 4.0
2 layers, 5/8" (mastic)	100 SF	4.3 - 4.6
Drywall for columns, pipe chases or fire partitions		
1 layer, 3/8", nailed	100 SF	5.5 - 6.0
1 layer, 1/2", nailed	100 SF	5.6 - 6.1
1 layer, 5/8", nailed	100 SF	5.8 - 6.2
2 layers, 1/2", mastic	100 SF	10.6 - 11.5
2 layers, 5/8", mastic	100 SF	11.1 - 12.0
3 layers, 1/2", mastic	100 SF	15.6 - 16.9
3 layers, 5/8", mastic	100 SF	16.2 - 17.5
1 layer, 1-1/2", coreboard	100 SF	5.0 - 5.4
Drywall for beams or soffits		
1 layer, 1/2"	100 SF	5.0 - 5.4
1 layer, 5/8"	100 SF	4.9 - 5.3

Gypsum wallboard types

Regular is available in several thicknesses for both new and remodeling construction.

Fire rated is designed especially for fire resistance. Major additives are vermiculite and fiberglass.

Sound deadening board is usually applied in combination with other wallboard products to achieve higher sound and fire ratings.

Tile backer board is recommended as a base for adhesive application of ceramic, metal or plastic tile for interior areas where moisture and humidity are a problem. (Direct, continuous contact with moisture should be avoided.)

Sheathing is for exterior applications. Used as a substrate for siding, masonry, brick veneer and stucco.

Backer board is recommended for backing paneling and other multi-layered applications. Adds strength and fire protection. Also can be used effectively with ceiling tile.

Vinyl-surfaced wallboard resists scuffs, cracks and chips. Ideal for commercial and institutional use.

Tapered edge inclines into the board from the long edge. With joint finishing results in a smooth, monolithic wall.

Square edge is used where an exposed joint is desired.

Tapered round edge is for the same applications as tapered edge board. Designed to reduce beading and ridging problems often associated with poorly finished joints.

Beveled edge is used where a "panel" effect is desired. In this application the joints are left exposed.

Tongue and groove is available on 24" wide sheathing and backer boards.

Modified beveled edge needs no special joint finishing, though matching batten strips may be used if desired.

Thickness: 1/4", 3/8", 1/2", 5/8". (Not all products are available in all thicknesses.)

Width: 4'. **Length**: 6' through 16'

Figure 14-28
Manhours for installing gypsum wallboard

niture and appliances, or going up and down stairs, etc.

Figure 14-29 gives the labor for installing wall paneling. Use the low figure for simple jobs, and the high range for more complicated work.

When figuring your labor cost, don't forget to include additional costs for installing furring. In remodeling work, a carpenter should cut and install 250 to 300 linear feet of furring in eight hours.

Lath

Lath used to consist of rough (unplaned) wood strips nailed to wood framing members. If you've been in the home remodeling business a while, you've probably done work on older homes where plaster was applied over this type of lath. It made an excellent base, but it's seldom used in today's construction. Today, lath is either gypsum or metal.

Work element	Unit	Manhours per unit
Plastic faced hardboard, including molding and trim		
1/8"	100 SF	3.5 - 3.8
1/4"	100 SF	3.6 - 3.9
Plywood, 4' x 8' panels, including trim		
1/4"	100 SF	4.4 - 4.7
1/2"	100 SF	5.5 - 6.0
Plank paneling		
1/4"	100 SF	4.9 - 5.3
3/4"	100 SF	6.2 - 6.7
3/4", random width	100 SF	6.7 - 7.2
Cedar closet lining		
1" x 4" plank	100 SF	7.3 - 7.9
1/4" plywood	100 SF	5.6 - 6.1

Allow about 25% more time for ceiling installation. Deduct 5 to 15% when 9' or 12' high plywood panels are used. If installation is on metal studs, add 10% to the times listed.

Figure 14-29
Manhours for installing wall paneling

Gypsum Lath

Gypsum lath is made of paper bonded to a gypsum core. It's like gypsum wallboard, except that the long edges are generally rounded. It may be plain or perforated with 3/4-inch diameter holes spaced about 4 inches apart. It's available in 3/8-, 1/2-, 5/8-, and 1-inch thicknesses; 16-, 24-, and 48-inch widths; and 48- and 96-inch lengths.

Plain (unperforated) lath is available with aluminum foil backing for thermal insulation. Type X gypsum lath has special additives in the core to make it more fire resistant. Using perforated lath gives you a mechanical as well as a natural chemical bond with gypsum plaster.

Metal Lath

You can get expanded metal lath in galvanized steel or factory-painted copper-bearing steel. It's available in several forms.

The flat diamond mesh form is a uniformly expanded flat sheet that comes in two weights. Self-furring diamond mesh is similar to diamond mesh, except that it's indented at regular intervals to hold the body of the lath away from the sheathing.

Flat rib lath has 1/8-inch deep ribs evenly spaced along the *length* of the lath. There are deeper rib laths available, with 3/8- or 3/4-inch ribs. Each rib variety is made in two weights.

For exterior work, you'll usually use galvanized woven wire fabric with a hexagonal mesh pattern (sometimes called stucco netting, or poultry netting). It comes in sizes from 1- to 2-1/4-inch mesh with a maximum open area of 4 square inches per mesh. It may be dimpled at regular intervals to hold it away from the sheathing, or you can use special nails with fiber spacer washers on the shank to hold it out. For unsheathed framing, choose a woven wire fabric with a paper backing.

Lath made from welded wire fabric consists of a grid of 16 gauge wires, spaced not over 2 inches in either direction, and stiffened along its length with heavier wire. The wires are welded at all intersections. Most welded wire lath used today is galvanized and comes with a paper backing. Some welded wire lath is also crimped at regular intervals to hold the body of the lath away from the contact surface.

You can also use wire cloth as a plaster base. It's generally 19 gauge wires woven in a straight grid pattern and galvanized after weaving.

Fasteners

There are many types of fasteners available for you to use with lath and plaster. Some are designed for specific purposes, but most are used in a variety of common assemblies.

- Annealed galvanized steel wire is probably the most common fastener. It's used to support horizontal grid frames, to tie vertical and horizontal framing and furring members together, and to secure lath to supporting members.

- Several types of nails and staples are used to secure metal and gypsum lath to wood and metal supports. They come in various wire gauges, lengths, shank and head designs, and finishes. Choose from galvanized, zinc plated, blued, cement coated, or bright finishes. Shank designs are smooth, barbed, ringed, or threaded. Use hardened stub nails to secure metal or wood to concrete or masonry.

- You can use explosive-powder driven fasteners to secure metal runner tracks to concrete.

- Use self-drilling and thread-cutting or thread-forming fasteners to attach both metal and gypsum lath to metal supports, and to connect metal framing members. You can also use bolts for some framing member connections and to secure framing members to concrete or masonry.

- There are clips of various designs, made of spring wire or sheet metal, that you can use to attach furring channels to runner channels, gypsum lath to metal supports, and resilient furring to rigid supports. Clips are generally zinc plated.

Plaster

Plaster is a mixture of cement binders, inert aggregate fillers, and water. There are two types of plaster; one made from portland cement and the other from gypsum.

You can use portland cement plaster for both interior and exterior walls — but not over gypsum plaster, gypsum masonry, or gypsum lath. It doesn't finish up as smooth as gypsum plaster, or with the same intricate detail. It's also less stable, more susceptible to cracking, and less fire resistant than gypsum plaster. In some areas, portland cement plaster with integral color is called *stucco*.

Gypsum plaster's primary use is for interior surfaces. Unlike portland cement, it isn't suitable for exterior walls, except in well-protected areas. You can't use it in interior areas that are subject to dampness or extreme high humidity either. You can apply gypsum plaster over concrete masonry, cement plaster, and gypsum and metal laths.

Apply plaster with a trowel in one or more coats to form a durable wall or ceiling finish. You can also use it as a backing material for tile, or as fireproofing for structural framing. You can apply plaster directly to concrete or masonry, or support it with lath attached to concrete, masonry, sheathing, or wood or metal furring strips. Another method of support is attaching lath to a metal grid system suspended on wires from the structure.

Plaster Aggregate

Both cement and gypsum plasters are made with sand, various lightweight aggregates, organic and inorganic fibers, and a wide variety of admixtures. You can add other materials for color or workability, or to make the plaster harder or more fire resistant. Each coat in a multiple coat cement or gypsum plaster job is likely to have different ingredients or different proportions of the same ingredients.

The aggregates in plaster extend its coverage, reduce shrinkage, increase its strength, and lower the cost. Aggregates for plaster include wood fiber, sand, perlite and vermiculite.

Sand is the most common aggregate. It's dense, strong, and a good barrier against sound transmission. Vermiculite and perlite improve fire resistance, insulation value, sound absorption, and reduce the weight of the plaster.

Fiber aggregate, such as shredded wood or other fiber, is often used in combination with particle aggregates. The fiber increases the plaster's strength while reducing its overall weight. It also makes it easier to apply plaster with a gun.

Multiple Coat Application

You can apply single gypsum base coats, but it's more common to apply two coats. In two-coat work, the base coat is usually a factory mixture. You just need to mix it with water. Sometimes sand is added to the first (scratch) coat over gypsum lath or masonry bases. Additional aggregate is sometimes added to the second (brown) coat.

Job-mixed base coats contain neat gypsum plaster mixed with graded sand or vermiculite or perlite.

Gypsum Finish Coat

Gypsum finish coats can be made from several possible mixes for trowel, spray or float finish. They include gauging plaster, Keene's cement, and gypsum white coat. Each combination creates a particular quality that you may need on a job.

There are also special finishes you can use for integral coloring, special texturing, or a thin veneer or skin coat of plaster. You can apply a thin finish coat directly over any suitable base. It creates a smooth finish over an otherwise porous surface, adds texture, conceals joints, and camouflages defects in the wall.

Lime putty in a plaster mix produces whiteness, plasticity, and bulk. Lime, used alone, doesn't set hard, and it shrinks as it dries. Quicklime requires a long slaking (soaking) period at the job site to develop the plasticity needed for plastering. For these reasons, you need to blend lime with gypsum gauging plaster or Keene's cement to get the properties you want in a finish coat.

Hydrated lime is quicklime which has been partially slaked at the factory. Using hydrated lime reduces the slaking period needed in the field. There are two basic types of hydrated lime:

1) Normal (Type N, ASTM C-6) which requires 16 to 24 hours of soaking.

2) Special (Type S, ASTM C-206) which doesn't require soaking. You can use it immediately.

Gauging plasters are specially ground. When mixed with lime they give you a controlled set and strength with a minimum of shrinkage. Gauging plaster is available in slow and quick-set types. This allows you to control the hardening process without the use of retarders or accelerators.

Keene's cement provides a dense, harder-than-average finish with good resistance to moisture. It's available in Type I regular slow setting (3 to 6 hours), and Type II quick setting (1 to 2 hours).

Molding plaster is a finely-ground gypsum mix which produces a smooth, workable material suitable for intricate ornamental and decorative work.

There's also a specially-formulated plaster designed to fireproof the material it covers. It's a spray-applied material with mineral fibers or expanded mineral aggregates. You can apply it in one or more coats to structural members to retard the spread of fire.

Estimating Lath and Plaster

Lath and plaster work is almost always figured by the square yard. Unit costs are based on the square yard or 100 square yards. You only use linear foot measure when estimating moldings or continuous trim.

Figuring Wall Surfaces

Estimators don't always figure wall area the same way. Some will ignore a small window, treating it as a solid wall. The 4 or 5 square feet of wallboard or lath that's cut out for the window will almost certainly be wasted anyway. It's better to figure the quantity needed as though the window wasn't there. Doors are larger, but still won't offer much saving. You'll probably want to ignore most door openings when calculating wall surface. Some estimators deduct openings only if

Work element	Unit	Manhours per unit
Gypsum lath on wood studs and furring		
3/8" plain	100 SF	1.7
3/8" perforated	100 SF	1.5
Add for ceiling work	100 SY	2.5
2 coat plaster, with finish indicated, on wall		
Gypsum or lime finish	10 SY	5.2
Keene's cement finish	10 SY	6.4
Wood fiber finish	10 SY	5.7
Portland cement finish	10 SY	5.5
3 coat plaster, with finish indicated, on walls		
Gypsum or lime finish	10 SY	6.5
Keene's cement finish	10 SY	8.0
Wood fiber finish	10 SY	7.8
Portland cement finish	10 SY	7.6
Add for ceiling work	10 SY	5.5

Note: Plastering includes mixing plaster, application and finishing, and scaffolding.

Figure 14-30
Manhours for plastering

they exceed 100 square feet. Other estimators deduct one-half of all openings. The plasterer's union in your area may have certain rules for measuring. Use the method that works best for you.

A good way to figure the area of plaster work needed from your plans or your sketch is to find the inside dimensions of the room. Use these dimensions to calculate the actual surface area, as we did for figuring wallboard. This is the method

most lath and plaster subcontractors use to figure their contract prices.

Manhours

Estimating lath and plaster in kitchen and bathroom remodeling is more complicated than estimating for new construction. It's more difficult and takes considerably more time to do lath and plaster on a remodeling job. Use Figure 14-30 as a general guide.

The Trim

Moldings are strips of wood ripped from kiln-dried boards. They can be up to 16 feet long. There are about 30 different stock patterns or profiles of moldings, each designed for a specific purpose. Most of them can be used for more than one application, however. Standard molding patterns and the locations where they're commonly used are shown in Figure 14-31. You'll usually be working with soft wood moldings such as pine, fir, cedar, or hemlock.

Sloppy trim work can ruin an otherwise professional job. Don't rush your trim installation. Figure 14-32 shows how to cut ceiling moldings. You'll need to know how to miter, splice, and cope moldings for your installations.

Mitering

Most molding joints are cut on a 45-degree angle (see Figure 14-32, A). Set your miter box accordingly, and trim each of the two pieces to be mated at opposite angles. When you measure moldings for mitering, add the width of the molding to the length of each miter. If your molding is 1-1/2 inches wide and you have two miters, add 3 inches.

When mitering cove molding, put the molding in the miter box so that the molding is upside down and the end reversed from the way it will

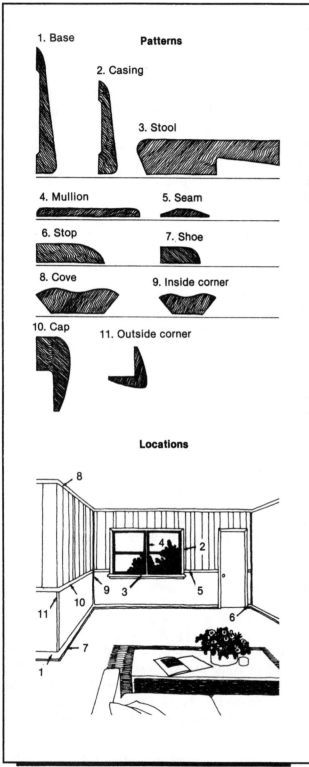

Figure 14-31
Molding patterns and locations

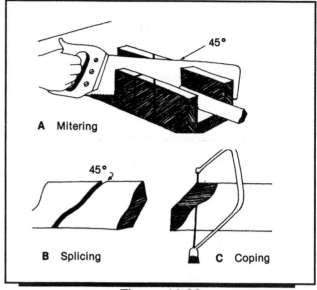

Figure 14-32
Cutting molding

be installed. For tight joints, use both glue and nails for installing the molding.

Splicing

When splicing two lengths of molding (as shown in Figure 14-32, B), place the molding flat on its backside in the miter box. Miter the ends to be joined at identical 45-degree angles. When you butt the ends together in their correct position, you'll have a neat match without unevenness.

Coping

Where two pieces of patterned molding meet in a corner, you'll have to match the joining pieces by coping. Place the molding in the miter box and position it upright against the backplate. Cut at a 45-degree angle. The cut exposes the profile of the molding. With the profile as a template, use the coping saw and follow along the profile. Trim away a wedge at another 45-degree angle. This duplicates the pattern so that it will fit over the face of the adjoining molding. See Figure 14-32, C.

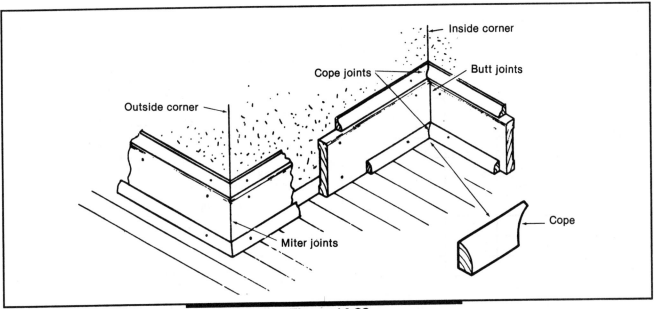

Figure 14-33
Base molding installation

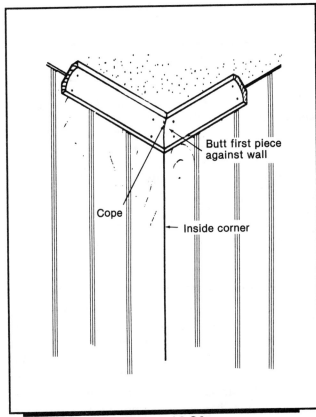

Figure 14-34
Ceiling molding installation

Work element	Unit	Manhours per unit
Baseboard		
2 member	100 LF	8-10
3 member	100 LF	9-11
Cove molding	100 LF	5-6

Figure 14-35
Manhours for installing trim

Trim Installation

Trimming out a room with molding is precise work. It takes a lot of practice to get it right. Have your most skilled carpenters do this work — and learn from them — if you're not already skilled at trim installation. Figure 14-33 shows joint cuts for base moldings. Ceiling molding installation is shown in Figure 14-34.

Use Figure 14-35 as a guide for estimating your labor costs for first class trim installation.

	Height of ceiling				
Size of room	8'	9'	10'	Yards of border	Rolls for ceiling
4 x 8	6	7	8	9	2
4 x 10	7	8	9	11	2
4 x 12	8	9	10	12	2
6 x 10	8	9	10	12	2
6 x 12	9	10	11	13	3
8 x 12	10	11	13	15	4
8 x 14	11	12	14	16	4
10 x 14	12	14	15	18	5
10 x 16	13	15	16	19	6
12 x 16	14	16	17	20	7
12 x 18	15	17	19	22	8
14 x 18	16	18	20	23	8
14 x 22	18	20	22	26	10
15 x 16	15	17	19	23	8
15 x 18	16	18	20	24	9
15 x 20	17	20	22	25	10
15 x 23	19	21	23	28	11
16 x 18	17	19	21	25	10
16 x 20	18	20	22	26	10
16 x 22	19	21	23	28	11
16 x 24	20	22	25	29	12
16 x 26	21	23	26	31	13
17 x 22	19	22	24	23	12
17 x 25	21	23	26	31	13
17 x 28	22	25	28	32	15
17 x 32	24	27	30	35	17
17 x 35	26	29	32	37	18
18 x 22	20	22	25	29	12
18 x 25	21	24	27	31	14
18 x 28	23	26	28	33	16

This chart assumes use of the standard roll of wallpaper, eight yards long and 18" wide. Deduct one roll of side wallpaper for every two doors or windows of ordinary dimensions, or for each 50 square feet of opening.

Figure 14-36
Single-roll wallpaper requirements

Work element	Unit	Manhours per unit
Wallpaper		
Light to medium weight, butt joint	100 SF	1.4
Heavy weight, butt joint	100 SF	1.5
Vinyl wall covering		
Light to medium weight, butt joint	100 SF	1.9
Heavy weight, butt joint	100 SF	2.1
Special wall coatings	100 SF	3.4
Flexwood	100 SF	7.1
Flexi-wall	100 SF	8.1

Time includes move on and off site, unloading, limited surface and material preparation, cleanup and repair as needed.

Suggested crew: 1 paper hanger, 1 laborer

Figure 14-37
Labor installing wall coverings

Wallpaper

Most of your kitchen and bathroom wall and ceiling projects will use the materials we've discussed in this chapter. And don't forget that you can use a combination of materials effectively. Almost all of the materials we covered work well in combinations, especially ceramic tile and wallpaper. The popularity of wallpaper as a wall finish in kitchens and bathrooms seems to come and go. It always makes an attractive wall covering, however, and it's easy to install.

Standard rolls of wallpaper are 18 inches wide. You need to estimate your surface area and adjust your figures for pattern match. Use the chart in Figure 14-36 to help you estimate the number of rolls you need for your room size. Apply wallpaper over a smooth wall surface. In remodeling work, a skilled paper hanger can generally apply 100 SF of standard width paper in 1-1/2 to 2 hours, depending on the type and weight of the paper. Figure 14-37 gives manhour estimates for installing wall coverings.

How to Install Skylights

Skylights add style and value to a home — and throw in free light as a bonus. A kitchen or bathroom is an ideal location for a skylight, especially if the room is small. Skylights open up small spaces. They also do more to modernize a room than almost any other improvement you can make. Homeowners are always pleased with the result

Properly installed skylights give long-lasting, trouble-free service. The money saved in energy-free lighting soon pays for the unit and the cost of installation. Could you ask for a better item to offer your customers?

Choose the Appropriate Skylight

Whatever type roof you're dealing with, there's a suitable skylight available. You can get slim low-profile models or the more complex venting type with built-in screens. There are self-flashing units and units having an extruded aluminum curb. Your best bet is a skylight with double acrylic glazing and a thermal break which eliminates condensation. Another good feature to look for is a shade or blind that permits the home-owner to regulate the light. Be ready to suggest just the right skylight to brighten up your client's gloomy kitchen or bathroom.

Skylights are available to fit roofs with trusses or rafters 16 and 24 inches on center. So rafter spacing is no problem. When you install the right width, it takes very little carpentry to do the job.

To determine the size your customer needs, figure that under most conditions you need about 1 square foot of skylight for each 20 square feet of floor space. A 24-inch by 24-inch skylight is 4 square feet. It will light about 80 square feet of floor space. Figure 15-1 shows the pattern of light distribution.

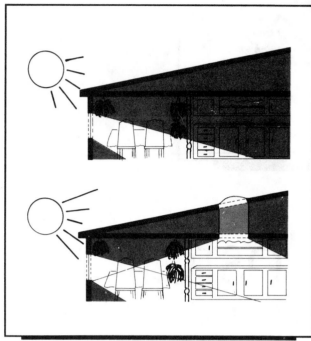

Figure 15-1
Light distribution

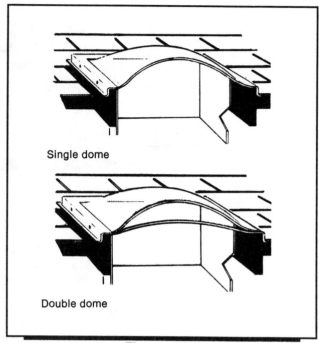

Figure 15-2
Single and double dome skylights

Double dome skylights provide insulation and guard against condensation. The dead air space between the dome and diffuser creates a thermal insulation barrier. It reduces the transfer of heat or cold through the skylight, without reducing the transmission of light. Use single dome skylights where insulation and condensation aren't a problem, such as in a patio or greenhouse. Figure 15-2 shows you the difference between single and double dome skylights. Triple dome units are also available.

Skylights are available with clear, frosted and bronze domes. You can also install combinations of these in multi-dome units. A clear dome, with or without a clear inner dome, gives maximum visibility and the most intense light. If you want to eliminate the harsh glare, install a clear dome with a white diffuser panel. This is the most popular model with homeowners. It lights a large area without glare.

A bronze skylight eliminates harsh glare and lends a slightly bronze tint to the area below. The advantage of a bronze dome is that it blends well with the existing roof cover.

If homeowners want extra ventilation, you can install hatch-type skylights. The installation is the same for hatch-type as curb-mounted units. Hatch-type units are usually equipped with a cranking mechanism for opening and closing. Some have extension rods that allow you to operate very high units. You can also purchase units that have automatic or remote controls for opening and closing.

Curb-Mounted Skylights

Curb-mounted skylights have an integral flashing which caps down over a supporting curb. You build the wood frame curb to the size recommended by the manufacturer, apply flashing, and secure the skylight to the curb (Figure 15-3). A continuous flange rests on top of the curb.

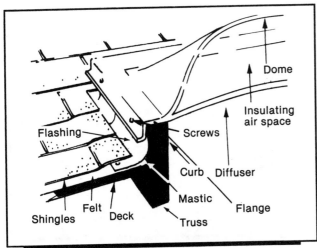

Figure 15-3
Curb mount

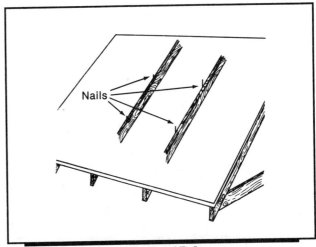

Figure 15-4
Locate rafter position

Placement of the skylight: When you install the skylight in a room with an open beam ceiling, begin by driving a 3-inch nail up through the roof at each corner of the proposed opening (Figure 15-4). If you're installing a unit in an attic access, you'll need to locate the skylight's position in relation to where you want it in the ceiling below. Drive the nails up through the roof once you've identified the proper location. Make sure there are no electrical wires, water pipes, vent pipes, or ductwork in the way.

Once you've positioned the nails, go up and locate them on the roof. Remove the roofing material back about 12 inches all around the skylight area. Take care in removing the material if you intend to reuse it. Cut a hole through the sheathing as shown in Figure 15-5.

Framing: Frame inside the roof opening at the top and bottom (Figure 15-6). If a rafter runs through the opening, cut it back. If you have to cut more than one rafter, double the headers so

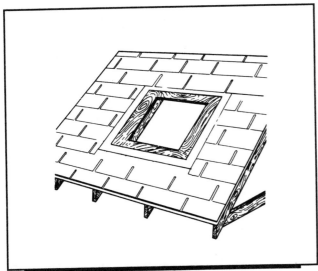

Figure 15-5
Cut through the roof

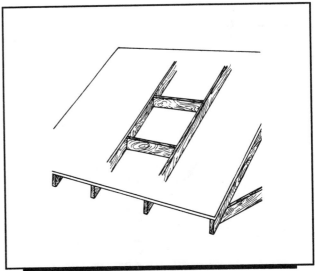

Figure 15-6
Frame the opening

329

Figure 15-7
Apply asphalt roofing cement

Figure 15-8
Construct the curb

you don't weaken the roof. You may have to do additional framing if the seams of the skylight don't line up with the rafters.

Apply asphalt plastic roofing cement around the opening, about 1/4 inch thick. Be sure you cover all the exposed wood and felt. See Figure 15-7.

Building the curb: Build the curb out of 2 x 6-inch lumber. Make the inside dimensions the same as the opening in the roof (Figure 15-8). Use roofing cement to seal all joints.

Apply roofing cement on the outside of the curb at the bottom and on all four sides. Nail the cant strip in place as shown in Figure 15-9.

Now look at Figure 15-10. Cover the entire outside of the curb with roofing cement. Apply roofing felt in the still soft roofing cement. Use 15-pound building paper. Place the bottom strip at the low side of the skylight first, then the sides. Finish the application with the strip at the top of the unit. Apply roofing cement at all joints where the felt overlaps. Cover the exposed seams with

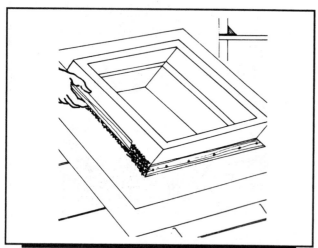

Figure 15-9
Seal outside curb

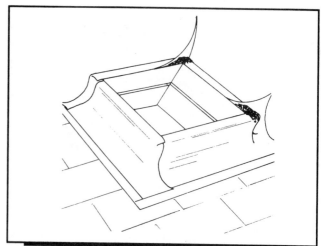

Figure 15-10
Apply roofing felt

Figure 15-11
Replace shingles

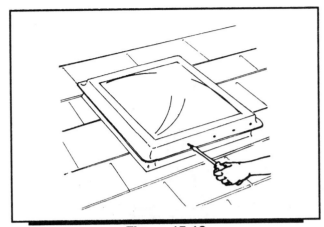

Figure 15-12
Install skylight

roofing cement. Replace the shingles as shown in Figure 15-11.

Installing the unit: Apply a bead of clear mastic weatherstripping around the tip edge of the curb. Press the skylight down into place. Drill small screw holes about every three inches and secure the flange around the edge of the curb. See Figure 15-12. Use corrosion-resistant screws with

rubber washers over the mounting holes. Figure 15-13 is a section view of the installed skylight.

After installing the unit, wash it with a non-abrasive soap and warm water. Don't use a petroleum-based cleaner. It'll damage the dome surface. You want to leave your client with a bright and shiny new skylight. The skylight should require no further maintenance. Normal rainfall will keep the dome reasonably clean. The finished installation should look like the example in Figure 15-14.

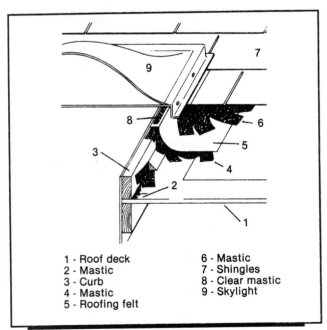

1 - Roof deck
2 - Mastic
3 - Curb
4 - Mastic
5 - Roofing felt
6 - Mastic
7 - Shingles
8 - Clear mastic
9 - Skylight

Figure 15-13
Section view of installation

Figure 15-14
The completed job

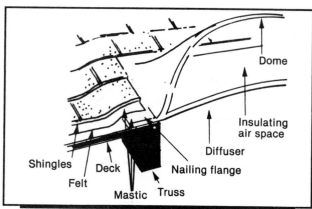

Figure 15-15
Self-flashing skylight

Figure 15-16
Install the unit

Figure 15-17
Apply cement and felt

Self-Flashing Skylights

Instead of building a curb, you install a self-flashing skylight directly on the roof. That gives it a lower profile so it's less conspicuous. Figure 15-15 shows this type of installation.

The installation: Locating, marking, and cutting for a self-flashing skylight are the same as for a curb-mounted skylight. Place the dome over the opening in a 1/4-inch-thick bead of roofing cement and nail it in place through pre-drilled holes (Figure 15-16). Most units come with special nails and rubber washers for securing the unit.

Apply a thick coat of roofing cement over the edge of the skylight up to the bubble. Cut strips of roofing felt wide enough to go from the bubble to the deck. Make sure it overlaps the felt on the deck. Put the side pieces on first. Apply more cement at the top of these strips and place a strip of felt across the top. You don't need a felt strip across the bottom. Look at Figure 15-17.

Apply mastic over the felt strips and replace the asphalt shingles. After the shingles are in place, apply roofing cement across the bottom of the skylight. Figure 15-18 shows a cross-section of the installation, and Figure 15-19 shows the finished project.

Framing dimensions for skylights of various sizes are shown in Figure 15-20.

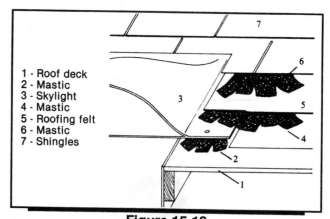

1 - Roof deck
2 - Mastic
3 - Skylight
4 - Mastic
5 - Roofing felt
6 - Mastic
7 - Shingles

Figure 15-18
Section view of installation

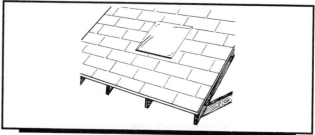

Figure 15-19
Finished installation

Roof opening size chart							
Size	**Maximum roof opening**	**Size**	**Maximum roof opening**	**Size**	**Maximum roof opening**	**Size**	**Maximum roof opening**
16 x 16	14-1/2 x 14-1/2	24 x 24	22-1/2 x 22-1/2	32 x 32	30-1/2 x 30-1/2	36 x 48	34-1/2 x 46-1/2
16 x 24	14-1/2 x 22-1/2	24 x 32	22-1/2 x 30-1/2	32 x 48	30-1/2 x 46-1/2	48 x 48	46-1/2 x 46-1/2
16 x 32	14-1/2 x 30-1/2	24 x 48	22-1/2 x 46-1/2	36 x 36	34-1/2 x 34-1/2	48 x 72	46-1/2 x 70-1/2

Framing dimension chart

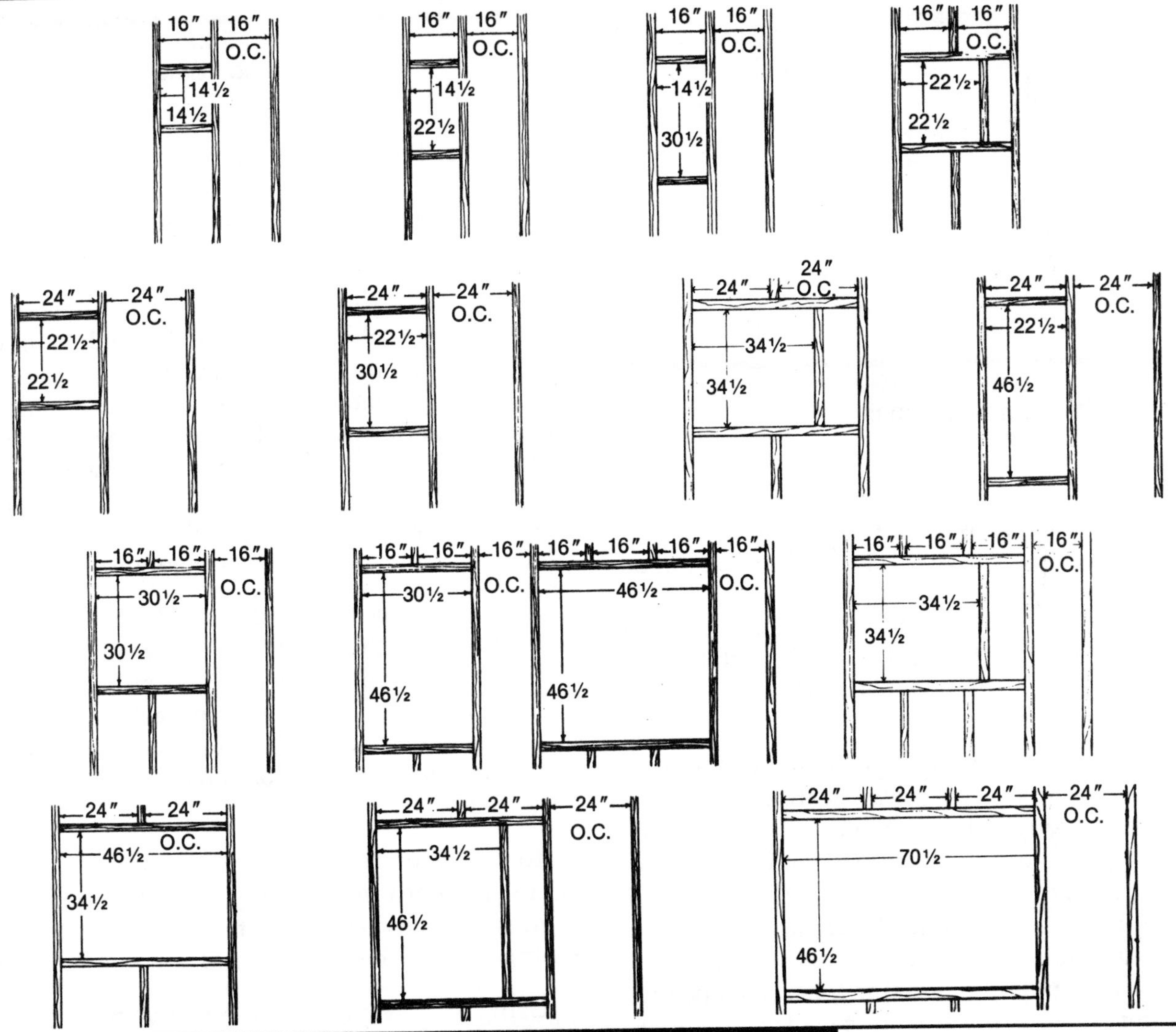

Figure 15-20
Roof opening size chart and framing dimension chart

Size	A	B	C
16 x 16	14-1/2	19	19
24 x 24	22-1/2	27	27
32 x 32	30-1/2	35	35
36 x 36	34-1/2	39	39
48 x 48	46-1/2	51	51

Figure 15-21
Opening requirements in inches

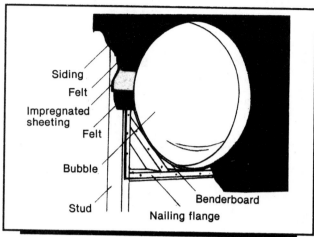

Figure 15-22
Install wood frame

The Bubble Skylight

You can install the round bubble skylight on a roof or in a vertical wall. For a roof installation, follow the same procedures that you'd use to install a self-flashing skylight.

Wall installation: Begin your wall installation by checking for any electrical, heating, or plumbing runs through the area where you want to place the bubble. Locate the wall studs and determine the size opening you need for the wood frame. The chart in Figure 15-21 shows standard opening requirements. You can use the information in the figure to determine the frame opening requirements for roof as well as wall installations.

Cut the opening in the outside and inside walls. Install the wood support frame as shown in Figure 15-21. Pre-drill nail or wood-screw holes in the flange of the bubble. Tack the unit to the outside surface of the frame. You nail the flange to the framing, not to the benderboard casing.

Using 1/4- to 1/2-inch-thick benderboard, shape the circular casing. You'll need 40 linear feet to make three overlapping layers for a window 4 feet in diameter. Before installing, soak the boards (exterior plywood) in water to make them pliable. The boards should be soft enough to bend easily. Install the casing from the interior side, making sure it will butt up tightly to the bubble. Bevel the ends to make smooth joints.

After you have the benderboard installed, align the bubble in the opening. For weather protection, slip building paper (15-pound felt) under the bottom flange of the bubble. Fasten the bubble securely, and caulk all the nail or screw heads. Overlap building paper on the top and sides (Figure 15-22).

To apply or reapply exterior siding, interior gypsum board or paneling, lay the material flat and scribe the diameter of the bubble on it with a compass. Cut the material and fasten it in place.

Using a sabre saw, cut the inside circular trim from particle board. Sand the edges to round them, and pre-paint the piece before you install it. Put the trim on last.

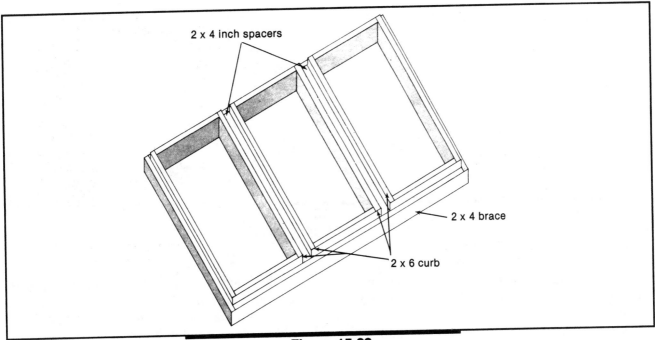

Figure 15-23
Framing for cluster installation on existing roofs

Clustering Skylights

You can install skylights in clusters to provide more light and create a very modern look. First, build individual curbs from 2 x 6-inch lumber. Put 2 x 4-inch spacers between the curbs. Then tie the curbs together by fastening 2 x 4-inch lumber around the outside of the frames (Figure 15-23).

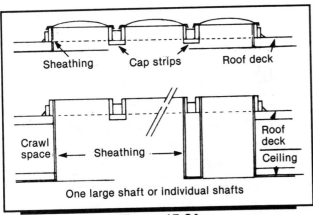

Figure 15-24
Optional shaft treatment for cluster installation

Cut the opening in the roof the total skylight width (from inside the first 2 x 6 to the last 2 x 6) by the total height (from inside the bottom 2 x 6 to inside the top 2 x 6). Be sure the roof is well braced inside. When installing cluster skylights, you can install one large light shaft or individual shafts for each skylight. Figure 15-24 shows both options.

The Light Shaft

In a conventional attic home, you have to install a light shaft below the skylight. A straight shaft works best for a direct, overhead highlight. To distribute the light over a broader area, increase the angle of the shaft. Use a slanted angle shaft to provide soft, diffused light. See Figure 15-25 for angle variations.

The shaft, from roof to interior ceiling, is just a frame box. Be sure you locate its position carefully before cutting into the finish ceiling. When you've established the location, saw out the ceil-

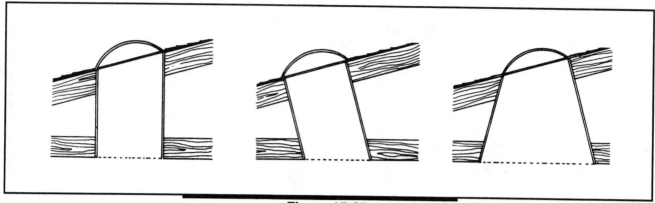

Figure 15-25
Shafts control light direction

ing joist and add headers. Use the same size material as the joists. Figure 15-26 shows plan and section views of the shaft framing.

Insulate the shaft with fiberglass batts. Staple the batts between the framing just like you do for exte-

rior walls, with the vapor barrier on the heated (shaft) side. Finish the shaft with gypsum board or with the same material you use to finish the ceiling. The shaft will reflect light best if you paint it a light color, preferably white.

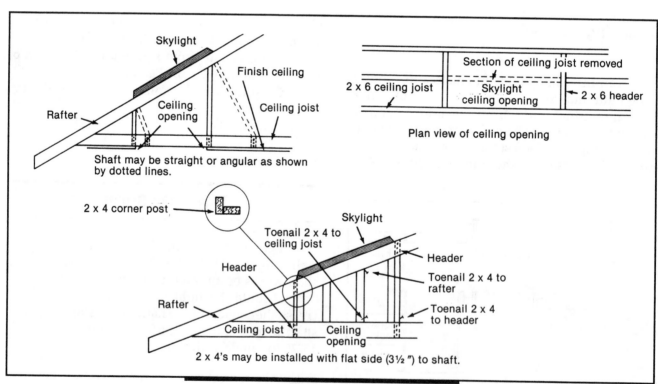

Figure 15-26
Framing the shaft

Work element	Unit	Manhours per unit	Work element	Unit	Manhours per unit
Ceiling cut-outs (in inches)			Framing openings		
14½" x 22½	each	1.5	22½ x 22½	each	0.7
22½ x 22½	each	1.6	22½ x 46½	each	1.0
22½ x 46½	each	2.0	30½ x 46½	each	1.2
30½ x 30½	each	2.3	Construct curb	4 SF	1.0
30½ x 46½	each	2.5	Install skylight		
Roof cut-outs (in inches)			Curb mount		
14½ x 14½	each	1.0	4 SF	each	2.0
14½ x 30½	each	1.5	Larger	each	3-4
22½ x 22½	each	1.8	Self flashing		
22½ x 46½	each	2.0	4 SF	each	1.5
30½ x 30½	each	2.0	Larger	each	2-3
30½ x 46½	each	2.5	For bubble installation add 50% to 75%		
Framing openings			Construct shaft		
14½ x 14½	each	0.5	Straight	4 SF	2.0
14½ x 30½	each	0.6	Angle	4 SF	3.0

Figure 15-27
Manhours for installing skylights

Estimating Installation Manhours

Estimating skylight installation labor is difficult because of the variations in attic access, roof pitch, roof covering, ceiling materials, and their cut-out problems. The manhour figures in Figure 15-27 are for gypsum board ceilings and asphalt shingled roofs with no more than a 5/12 rise. Add 25 to 75 percent for steep roofs and other ceiling finish materials.

The Use of Paint

Nothing does more for a room in less time and at a lower cost than a fresh coat of paint. Like the frosting on a cake, paint is the finishing touch on your remodeling job. Your work in designing, remodeling, installing lights, cabinets, sinks, and appliances will suffer if the paint isn't expertly applied using just the right type and color.

Often, paint is the accent that "makes" your design. The kitchen in Figure 16-1 is quite simple. It's the combination of colors in the walls and cabinetry that give it life. Paint accentuates the unusual ceiling work in the kitchen shown in Figure 16-2. This is a very compact and functional kitchen, with no wasted space. The soffit carries the duct runs, while the unique ceiling panel conceals the pipe runs. The wrong choice of colors would make this design awkward instead of interesting.

Like everything else in kitchen and bath remodeling, painting requires know-how. And since most of your jobs will require too small a volume of painting to subcontract out, you need to know the basic principles of painting, paints,

and their uses. You also need to know which colors and textures go together and how to use them in different situations for the best effect. You don't have to be an interior decorator to know how to use color. But you do need to understand the key points we're about to cover.

Texture and Color Sense

To provide some background for texture and color sense, we need to look at the *whole* house.

Home Interiors

Every home should have a coordinated, unified look. The floor covering, drapes, cabinetry, wall tile, and appliances should all complement each other and blend with the walls. The walls are especially important because they make up the largest color surface.

338

Figure 16-1
Use contrasting colors in cabinetry for design effect
Courtesy: Wood-Mode Cabinetry

Figure 16-2
Paint accentuates unusual ceiling work
Courtesy: Wood-Mode Cabinetry

Choose paint colors that complement other colors and textures in the room. Look at the style of the furnishings, fixtures and accessories in the room. Are you working with porcelain, brass, bronze, gold, silver, copper, wicker, rattan, or various types and textures of wood? How about the use of plants and flowers?

Is the design centered on a particular period? If so, use the colors complementing that era. For instance, Louis XIV and Louis XV styles call for soft greens, golds, and other delicate hues. Queen Anne and other 18th century styles use rich, subtle color combinations of crimson reds, blues, greens, and indigos.

And what about textures? They add dimension and interest to a room. Consider varying the paint finish for texture as well as color. Different textures say different things about a room.

Use a flat finish for formal settings. A high quality latex flat paint gives a room a quiet elegance. For a more casual look use a low luster finish to add softness and warmth to your comfortable rooms. A satin enamel with a soft sheen works well for these areas.

An eggshell finish works well in any setting, but is especially suitable for deep accent colors and for high traffic areas. Use textured paints for a Mediterranean, Early American, or the Southwest look. They're available in three finishes: sand, rough, and stucco.

A high gloss finish creates the wet look. High gloss is ideal for a contemporary room where "loud" is the effect that your client wants. Use enamel paint for this finish. It washes easily, making it a practical finish for trim, cabinets, doors, and children's rooms. A high gloss finish reflects light and may appear cold to some people. This may not be a problem in a warm climate, but it could make people feel uncomfortable in cold weather areas. That's something you want to consider when choosing paints.

Northern climates need warm colors to compensate for the intermittent sunlight. Cool pastel tones are perfect for southern climates. Be sure that the pastels are bright enough so the color won't look weak in intense sunlight.

How Color Affects Us

Color affects space, light, and mood. The smaller the space, the greater the effect colors seem to have on us.

Space

In a small home, you can create a feeling of more space and continuity between rooms by using similar colors. The total living space will appear larger if all rooms are color coordinated.

The smaller the room, the less contrast there should be within that room. The area will appear larger if the walls, ceiling, and woodwork are all the same color. Use a light shade of color and eliminate any breaks in the flow of the room. Coordinate the floor and window coverings to blend in, rather than using them to accent the color design. This will create a feeling of spaciousness.

You can be more generous with color when working with larger spaces. Square up a long, narrow room by painting the two end walls a deeper color. A room that's too large will seem better proportioned and more inviting if you paint it a darker tone. You can also lower a ceiling by painting it a slightly darker color than the adjacent walls.

Make a square room more interesting by painting one wall a dramatic, contrasting color — usually the wall directly opposite the entrance to the room. Choose a color based on a dominant shade in the furnishings, floor covering, upholstery, fixtures, or wall tile.

Light

Consider the location of the sun in relation to a room when you're choosing the color. Northern light is cold, and eastern light is harsh. Rooms facing either of these directions look their best when you use warm colors such as reds, oranges, yellows, and brown tones.

Light from the south and west is warm and bright. Use cool greens, blues, violets or gray tones in rooms facing these directions.

Varying light conditions can change the effect of the color in the room at different times of the day. Be sure you check your color selections under the various light sources in the room — sunlight, fluorescent light or incandescent bulbs. Study paint chips in the actual room under actual lighting conditions to see the real color.

Mood

The colors your clients choose for their kitchens and bathrooms will create a particular mood in the room. For example, a kitchen done in gay, cheerful colors will promote a happy outlook for each new day. You can help steer them towards the feeling they prefer by understanding how colors affect us.

According to the experts, here are the moods that colors can create.

Yellow and lime: bright and sunny

Gold and bronze: rich and friendly

Olive tones: somber and quiet

Greens: cheerful and open

Gray greens, aquas, and jades: calm and serene

Pinks and reds: lively and aggressive

Purples and violet blues: sophisticated and daring

Blues and turquoises: refreshing and tranquil

Orange and peaches: active and inviting

Spice tones: advancing and bold

Camels, beiges, and taupes: subtle and elegant

Earth tones: warm and cozy

Grays, charcoals, and neutrals: cool and receding

Paint Materials

Now that you know something about colors, let's look at paints. The base for most paints is a film former or binder dissolved in a solvent or emulsified in water. When applied, the paint cures to form a dry, tough coating. Paints are used for weather protection and decoration. Other types of binders dissolved in a solvent go by different names. They're called clear finishes or varnishes if they dry by oxidation, or lacquers if they dry by evaporation.

To produce the different paint colors, opaque pigments or tints are dispersed in the binder. Varying the pigment concentration produces a high gloss, a semi-gloss, or a lusterless (flat) finish. You can add special pigments such as red lead and zinc chromate to primers for corrosion resistance. Adding a metallic pigment to a varnish produces metallic coatings, like aluminum paints.

Binders

The type of binder used in the paint determines how a paint will perform.

Alkyd binders: Alkyd binders, for the most part, are oil modified phthalate resins which dry by reacting to oxygen in the surrounding air. Alkyd finishes are economical and available as clear or pigmented coatings. The finishes are available in flat, semi-gloss, and high gloss, in a wide range of colors. They are easy to apply, and you can use them on most clean surfaces, except for fresh (alkaline) concrete, masonry, and plaster. Alkyd finishes have good color and gloss, and they hold their color well in normal interior and exterior areas. Their durability is excellent in rural environments, but only fair in mildly corrosive areas.

Cement: Portland cement combines with several ingredients to make a good paint for special applications. It comes as a powder to which you add water. Use cement paints on rough surfaces such as concrete, masonry, and stucco. They dry to form a hard, flat, porous film that allows water to pass through without damaging the surface. Since cement paints are powders, you can mix them with masonry sand and less water to form filler coats to smooth rough masonry before applying other paints.

Most often, you'll be using cement paints on fresh masonry. They must be applied to a damp surface and kept damp a few days for curing. Good quality cement paints are very durable when properly cured. If you don't cure them properly however, they chalk heavily and soon need repainting.

Epoxy: Generally, epoxy binders come with two components, an epoxy resin and a polyamide hardening agent. Mix them just before use. When mixed, the two ingredients react to form a hard final coating. Anything left at the end of the day must be thrown out. You can apply epoxy paint in a thick coat to cover a textured surface. You can also use it to create a tile-like glaze coating for concrete and masonry. The cost per gallon is high, but you don't have to apply many coats to get good coverage.

Epoxy paints will chalk on exterior jobs. They lose their gloss and fade. Otherwise, their durability is excellent.

Latex: Latex paints dry by the evaporation of their water content. They have little odor, they're easy to apply, they dry very rapidly, and fade very little. They're also non-inflammable and inexpensive. You can use interior latex paints as a prime or finish coat on interior walls and ceilings whether they are plaster or wallboard. You can apply exterior latex paints directly on exterior masonry (including alkaline) or on primed wood. Also, the blistering caused by moisture vapor is less of a problem with latex paints than with solvent-thinned paints. When using latex paints, be sure to prepare the paint surface carefully. Latex doesn't stick very well to chalked, dirty, or glossy surfaces.

Oil: The major binder in oil house paint is linseed oil. The best use for oil paint is on exterior wood and metal surfaces. It dries too slowly for most interior uses and you can't apply it to masonry. Oil paints are easy to use and can be applied fairly thick. They also wet the surface very well, so surface preparation is less critical than with latex paints. Oil paints aren't particularly hard or resistant to abrasion, chemicals, or strong solvents. However, in normal environments they are durable.

Rubber-base: The so-called rubber-based paints are solvent thinned. They are not the same as latex paints, which have rubber-based emulsions.

They dry rapidly to form finishes which are highly resistant to water and mild chemicals. Rubber-based paints are available in a wide range of colors and levels of gloss. They're used for exterior masonry and for areas which are wet, humid or subject to frequent washing. That makes them a good choice for kitchens and baths.

Urethane: Two types of urethane finishes are oil-modified and oil-free moisture-curing. Both can be clear, but the oil-free type is also available pigmented.

Oil-modified urethanes are more expensive but have better color than varnishes. They also dry quicker, they're harder, and they resist scuffing better. You can use them on all surfaces, as exterior varnishes, or as tough floor finishes. However, like all clear finishes, they're not very durable.

Moisture-curing urethanes cure by reacting with moisture from the air. Keep the containers full to exclude moisture. Otherwise the contents will turn to gel.

Figure 16-3 shows the important properties of the major paint binders.

	Alkyd	Cement	Epoxy	Latex	Oil	Phenolic	Rubber	Moisture curing urethane	Vinyl
Ready for use	Yes	No	No	Yes	Yes	Yes	Yes	Yes	Yes
Brushability	A	A	A	+	+	A	A	A	—
Odor	+[1]	+	—	+	A	A	A	—	—
Cure normal temp.	A	A	A	+	—	A	+	+	+
Cure low temp.	A	A	—	—	—	A	+	+	+
Film build/coat	A	+	+	A	+	A	A	+	—
Safety	A	+	—	+	A	A	A	—	—
Use on wood	A	—	A	A	A	A	—	A	—
Use on fresh concrete	—	+	+	+	—	—	+	A	+
Use on metal	+	—	+	—	+	+	A	A	+
Corrosive service	A	—	+	—	—	A	A	A	+
Gloss, choice	+	—	+	—	A	+	+	A	A
Gloss, retention	+	X	—	X	—	+	A	A	+
Color, initial	+	A	A	+	A	—	+	+	+
Color, retention	+	—	A	+	A	—	A	—	+
Hardness	A	+	+	A	—	+	+	+	A
Adhesion	A	—	+	A	+	A	A	+	—
Flexibility	A	—	+	+	+	A	A	+	+
Resistance to:									
Abrasion	A	A	+	A	—	+	A	+	+
Water	A	A	A	A	A	+	+	+	+
Acid	A	—	A	A	—	+	+	+	+
Alkali	A	+	+	A	—	A	+	+	+
Strong solvent	—	+	+	A	—	A	—	+	A
Heat	A	A	A	A	A	A	+[2]	A	—
Moisture permeability	Mod.	V. High	Low	High	Mod.	Low	Low	Low	Low

+ = Among the best for this property   [1] Odorless type   A = Average
— = Among the poorest for this property   [2] Special types   X = Not applicable

Figure 16-3
Comparison of paint binder's principal properties

Paint Types

So far, we've discussed paint bases. You can also describe paint by the type. Most of us are more familiar with types of *paints* than types of *bases*.

Lacquer: All coatings which dry solely by evaporation of the solvents are lacquers, including rubber-base coatings and vinyl coatings. Lacquers dry rapidly even at low temperatures, making a smooth brush application difficult. Several coats may be needed to cover an area because of their relatively low solid content. You must recoat very carefully to avoid lifting the existing coat, especially if you're using a brush.

Varnishes: Varnishes are alkyds or resins in solvent with driers added so they'll dry by oxidation. Varnishes produce a clear or nearly clear film. They're available in a variety of types such as spar varnish, aluminum mixing varnish, sealer, and flat varnish.

Oil stain: Oil stains use a drying oil, such as linseed oil, thinned to a very low consistency for maximum penetration when you apply it to wood. Apply interior stains only to a sanded, dust-free surface. Allow them to dry for a short time, then wipe the excess off so that only the stain which penetrates the wood remains.

Paint and enamel: The main difference between paint and enamel is the way they're used. You can roll paints on, but you rarely apply enamels with a roller.

Enamels have a higher gloss created by a higher pigment content. You reduce the gloss in paints by adding non-opaque, lower cost pigments called extenders. Typical extenders are calcium carbonate (whiting), magnesium silicate (talc), aluminum silicate (clay), and silica. If there are no extenders, you get a highly durable and washable finish called *high gloss*.

Use water to thin acrylic latex enamels and mineral spirits or paint thinner for alkyd enamels.

Primer for paint and enamel: Often you need two types of paints to do a job. You need a first coat, called a primer. It seals porous or alkaline surfaces. The top coat, applied after the primer, produces the finish color and texture.

The primer-sealer prepares the surface so that the top coat doesn't lose its binder into the surface. Some paints, such as interior latex wall paints, are self-priming and usually don't need a special primer.

Enamel undercoater is a coating which dries to a smooth, hard finish that you can sand. Once sanded, the smooth surface is ideal for a top coat of smooth enamel.

House paint: That's a broad term which describes many paint formulations. It's the most widely used type of paint. There are formulas available for special household needs, such as chalk or mildew resistance. House paint comes in oil base and latex.

Surface Preparation

The amount of preparation required for painting depends on the material you're painting and the type of covering you're applying. For just about any job however, you'll need a clean, dry surface, free of peeling paint, holes, cracks and gouges. You can't do a proper job of painting without proper preparation. Never cut corners on surface preparation.

Preparing Wood Surfaces for Paint

New wood surfaces should be dry, sanded, smooth, and free of dirt, dust and grit. Seal knots and sappy spots with a sealer. Fill nail holes, cracks and blemishes with filler tinted to match the stain color, or the wood color if you're leaving it natural. Fill open-grained wood such as oak or walnut with a suitable wood filler. Seal the tops and bottoms of doors with a clear finish coating.

Surfaces	Primer selection	Binder type	Finish coatings selection	Finish	Binder type
Painted/enameled: doors, trim cabinets, ceilings, paneling, framing, sash	Alkyd enamel underbody or latex enamel underbody	Alkyd Latex	Wall satin Flat Optional Optional Optional Optional Enamel Q.D. industrial enamel	Flat Eggshell Satin Semi-gloss High gloss	Latex Alkyd Latex Alkyd
Fire retardant	Alkyd enamel underbody	Alkyd	Latex fire retardant paint	Flat	Latex

Figure 16-4
Wood painting specifications - interior

When restaining wood surfaces treated with wax or an oily furniture polish, first clean them with a solvent. Change wiping cloths often so you don't wipe the oil or wax back into the surface. Remove scaling paint by scraping and sanding the surface with fine grit paper. Use fine steel wool or sandpaper to make glossy surfaces dull enough to take paint well.

Wood surfaces that need complete restoration must have the finish removed by power sanding or with a paint and varnish remover. Sand and feather any chips or scars until they're smooth and flush to the surface. Remove and replace loose or split caulking. Use a commercial mildew remover before painting or staining if any sign of mildew is present. Figures 16-4 and 16-5 show specifications for the painting and staining of interior wood surfaces.

Plaster and Drywall

All new plaster surfaces must be dry and clean before you begin painting. Let the plaster cure for 30 days before painting. Fill any cracks or voids with plaster filler, and finish the filler to match the wall texture. Spot-prime the repaired surface with a latex quick-dry primer before you apply the overall coat of primer-sealer.

Make sure gypsum wallboard is free of sanding dust. Repair damaged or defective surfaces with joint compound. The joint compound must be thoroughly dry before you begin painting. Coat steel corner beading with sealer before applying water-thinned paints.

If you're repainting plaster and drywall, begin by removing any peeling or scaling paint. Sand these areas and feather the edges. Fill holes, cracks, and blemishes and sand them flush as well. Spot-prime to control residual bleeding. Wash greasy walls and ceilings with a strong detergent solution or TSP. Use a primer to seal ceilings with water stains. (Be sure you check first to see if repairs to the ceiling or roof are necessary before painting over the stains.) Figure 16-6 shows requirements for painting plaster and drywall.

Masonry

Figure 16-7 gives specifications for interior masonry painting. You must allow concrete and masonry to cure for 60 to 90 days before painting. Brush the surface to remove loose mortar or sandy particles. Form oil residues and salts on the surface of the masonry will cause the paint to flake off. Clean form oil off with a solvent and

Surfaces	Primer selection	Finish coatings selection	Finish	Binder type
Stain/clear finish: doors, trim cabinets, open roof decking, trusses, paneling, framing, floors	See product descriptions	Stain Penetrating stain**	Flat	Alkyd
		Coating finishes Urethane finishes	Gloss/low lustre/flat*	Urethane
		Satin finish varnish	Satin	Alkyd Vinyl-toluene alkyd
		One hour clear finishes	Gloss/low lustre*	Latex Vinyl-toluene
		Latex finishes *	Gloss/satin	
		Sealer finishes Q.D. sanding sealer*		Castor-rosin ester
		Oil finish	Satin	

** Fill open-grained wood before staining, if desired.
* Not recommended for floors.
Q.D. = quick drying.

Figure 16-5
Wood staining specifications - interior

Surfaces	Primer selection	Binder type	Finish coatings selection	Finish	Binder type
Keene's cement plaster, textured/sand finish plaster, drywall, composition/wood pulp board	Alkyd primer sealer* or latex Q.D. prime seal or latex enamel underbody	Alkyd Latex Latex	Wall satin Flat Optional Optional Optional Enamel Q.D. enamel Enamel Tile-like enamel	Flat Eggshell Satin Semi-gloss High gloss	Latex Alkyd Latex Alkyd Epoxy-ester Epoxy-polyester
Fire retardant	Latex enamel underbody	Latex	Latex fire retardant paint	Flat	Latex

*Not for new drywall/composition board
Q.D. = quick drying

Figure 16-6
Plaster/drywall painting specifications

Surfaces	Primer selection	Binder type	Finish coatings selection	Finish	Binder type
Poured/precast concrete, cement, and cinder block walls and ceilings	Block filler Latex,Q.D. prime seal* Waterproofing masonry paint†	Latex Latex Vinyl toluene-buta-diene	Wall satin Alkyd flat Optional Optional Satin Enamel Optional Enamel Q.D. enamel Enamel Tile-like enamel Ceilings: Sweep-up spray finishes Texture: Texture paint	Flat Eggshell Satin Semi-gloss High gloss Flat or eggshell Sand/rough/ Spanish	Latex Alkyd Latex Alkyd Alkyd Epoxy-ester Epoxy-polyester Alkyd Latex
Fire retardant (new unpainted block) New unpainted smooth surfaces or repaint	Block filler Latex enamel underbody	Latex	Latex fire retardant paint	Flat	Latex
Concrete floors, platforms, stairs	Same as finish coat. (1st coat thinned)		Porch & floor enamel Enamel Latex floor & patio finish	High gloss Satin	Alkyd Epoxy ester Latex-epoxy modified

* For smooth surfaces or repaint priming.
† For new/unpainted wall surfaces subject to excessive moisture. Particularly effective under solvent thinned coatings and primer for the tile-like enamel.

Figure 16-7
Masonry painting specifications - interior

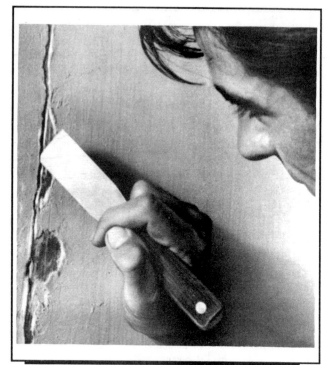

Figure 16-8
Clean out and fill cracks

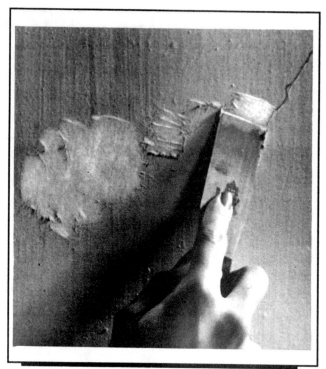

Figure 16-9
Smooth patching compound into crevices

remove salts with a wire brush. Fill cracks and voids by repointing and caulking.

Before repainting masonry surfaces that are peeling, scaling, or have started to chalk, you must scrape or brush them clean with a wire brush. Fill all the cracks with a patching compound. Remove and replace cracked and loose caulking. Treat and kill any mildew which has started to form on the surface.

New concrete floor slabs need to cure 60 to 90 days before coating. Etch steel-troweled concrete with a 10 percent solution of muriatic acid, then rinse thoroughly. Let the surface dry completely before you apply the paint. Remove cement spatters and fill holes and crevices. Sweep out any remaining dust and dirt.

To repaint masonry floors, first remove any scaling and peeling paint by scraping and sanding. Then wash the floor with a strong detergent or solvent to remove grease and oily residue. Treat an unpainted floor like a new floor, but be

sure you clean off oil and grease spots with a grease-dissolving compound before you paint.

Now You're Ready to Paint

After you've finished the surface prep, carefully examine the walls, ceilings, and trim. Make sure you've filled all the nail holes, cracks, and gouges in the surfaces. If you haven't, you still have work to do before the paint goes on.

Rake out any large plaster cracks in the walls and ceilings with a putty knife to remove loose particles (Figure 16-8). Dampen those cracks and any other large wall and ceiling holes with water before patching. Using a putty knife, firmly press latex patching compound into the crevices and smooth it until it's flush with the surface, as shown in Figure 16-9.

Figure 16-10
Remove loose and scaling paint

Press compound into the crevices of any joints which have opened, and door or window trim which has separated from the wall. Smooth with your finger. Allow them to dry and then sand lightly. Because patching compound shrinks as it dries, you'll probably need a second application of compound for large holes and cracks after the first has dried.

Remove loose or scaling paint with a putty knife. See Figure 16-10. Sand the edges smooth. If you remove paint from sash, trim, or doors, sand the entire surface with fine emery cloth or sandpaper. Spot-prime patched wall surfaces and wood surfaces where you've exposed the bare wood.

Begin painting in one corner of the room. With a brush, apply a strip about 4 inches wide along the joint where the ceiling and the walls meet.

Starting again in the corner, use a roller to blend the paint into the 4-inch strip you just completed. Paint across the width rather than the

length of the ceiling. Don't stop until you've covered the ceiling completely.

When the ceiling is dry, return to the spot where you began, and, using a trim brush, "cut in" the wall/ceiling line. Then coat along the baseboard and around the door and window trim. Now paint the walls, one at a time. Beginning at your starting place, use a roller to coat the first wall with slow even strokes to minimize spattering. Paint the remaining walls, following the same procedures.

Double-Hung Sash Windows

When painting a double-hung sash window, begin by removing the sash lock. Then lower the upper half of the window, and raise the bottom sash out of the way. Coat the window sash, then the rails. Don't paint the sash tracks. Return the top sash to a near closed position, lower the bottom sash and paint it the same way. To complete the window, coat the check rails, frame and sill.

Use a 2- or 2-1/2-inch angular sash brush, as shown in Figure 16-11. It's suitable for flat trim work as well. Leave the upper and lower sash slightly open until the paint is completely dry. Finally, use a razor blade to remove paint smears or spatters from the glass.

Doors

Remove all the hardware from the door before you begin painting. Open the door and place a block of wood on the floor between the door and its casing to brace it open. If it's a paneled door, first paint the panels, then the horizontal sections, and finally, the vertical sections.

If the door is the flush type, begin at the top and continue until it's completely covered. Keep the brush fully loaded and work rapidly, always brushing *into* the wet areas. Coat the door edges. Keep a rag handy to stop paint that might run onto the other side of the door.

Figure 16-11
Use angular sash brush for windows

Window and Door Trim

Using the edge of the sash brush, carefully coat the edge of the window trim nearest the wall. Then paint the facing of the trim. Coat the door trim the same way. Extend the color over the door casing to include the door stop.

Baseboards and Molding

These are the last trim surfaces painted. Protect the floor or carpet with a metal trim guard, a rigid piece of cardboard, or tape. Before painting the shoe molding, brush the baseboard surface a few times to remove any excess paint which might run between the trim guard and the molding. As you progress along the trim surfaces, be sure to wipe paint from the trim guard each time you move it to an adjacent location. If any paint should fall on the floor or carpet, remove it immediately with a rag dampened with the appropriate solvent — water if it's latex paint, mineral spirits if you're using oil-based paint.

Paint Estimating

Professional painters know their paints, colors, surface preparation, and painting techniques. Qualified painters don't work for minimum wage, contrary to what some homeowners think. Painting takes skill and painters have to be paid accordingly. If you're doing your own painting and you know your trade, charge the going rate, plus your overhead and profit.

If you don't know much about paints and painting, take the time to review this chapter. Know-how is important for success in the competitive remodeling business.

Estimating Paint Needs

Most paints will cover 400 to 450 square feet per gallon on smooth, sealed surfaces. Oil stain will cover 300 to 500 square feet per gallon depending on surface porosity. Figure 16-12 shows you how to calculate square-foot coverage of various shapes.

Estimating Paint Drying Times

Consider paint drying times in your estimate. Different coverings have different drying times, and individual products vary as well. Keep this in mind when choosing types of paint coverings and products. You have a schedule to keep. Use the chart in Figure 16-13 as a guide.

Triangle

To find the number of square feet in any shape triangle or 3 sided surface, multiply the height by the width and divide the total by 2.

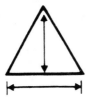

Square

Multiply the base measurement in feet times the height in feet.

Rectangle

Multiply the base measurement in feet times the height in feet.

Cylinder

When circumference (distance around cylinder) is known, multiply height by circumference.

When diameter (distance across) is known, multiply diameter by 3.1416. This gives circumference. Then multiply by height.

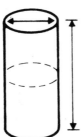

Circle

To find the number of square feet in a circle multiply the diameter (distance across) by itself and then multiply this total by .7854.

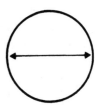

Arch Roof

Multiply length (B) by width (A) and add one-half the total.

Gambrel Roof

Multiply length (B) by width (A) and add one-third of the total.

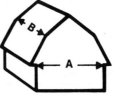

Cone

Determine area of base by multiplying 3.1416 times radius (A) in feet.

Determine the surface area of a cone by multiplying circumference of base (in feet) times one-half of the slant height (B) in feet.

Add the square foot area of the base to the square foot area of the cone side for total square foot area.

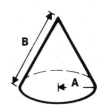

Figure 16-12
Calculating square foot coverage

Material	Touch	Recoat	Rub
Lacquer	1-10 min.	1-1/2 - 3 hrs.	16-24 hrs.
Lacquer sealer	1 - 10 min.	30 - 45 min.	1 hr. (sand)
Paste wood filler	—	24 - 48 hrs.	—
Paste wood filler (Q.D.)	—	3 - 4 hrs.	—
Water stain	1 hr.	12 hrs.	—
Oil stain	1 hr.	24 hrs.	—
Spirit stain	Zero	10 min.	—
Shading stain	Zero	Zero	—
Non-grain raising stain	15 min.	3 hrs.	—
NGR stain (quick-dry)	2 min.	15 min.	—
Pigment oil stain	1 hr.	12 hrs.	—
Pigment oil stain (Q.D.)	1 hr.	3 hrs.	—
Shellac	15 min.	2 hrs.	12 - 18 hrs.
Shellac (wash coat)	2 min.	30 min.	—
Varnish	1-1/2 hrs.	18 - 24 hrs.	24 - 48 hrs.
Varnish (Q.D. synthetic)	1/2 hr.	4 hrs.	12 - 24 hrs.
Heavy duty alkyd gloss enamel	5 hrs.	12 hrs. (floors - 24 hrs.)	
Semi-gloss alkyd enamel	1 hr.	18 hrs.	
Semi-gloss latex enamel	3 hrs.	3 hrs.	
Acrylic latex enamel	1 hr.	3 hrs.	
Latex porch and floor enamel	2 hrs.	2 hrs.	
Alkyd gloss porch and floor enamel	1 hr.	18 hrs.	
Alkyd gloss house paint	18 hrs.	36 hrs.	
Acrylic latex house paint	1 hr.	3 hrs.	
Flat latex house paint	1 hr.	3 hrs.	
Q.D. = quick drying			

Figure 16-13
Average drying times of coatings

Estimating Manhours

When you estimate labor for painting, give special attention to miscellaneous items such as moving furniture and appliances, and working around the occupants. Detail work, such as painting wood trim, is subject to many variables: the location, height, surface conditions, amount of masking and covering, quality specifications, and the type of material you use. All of these things affect your labor time. The manhour tables in Figure 16-14 will help you estimate your painting times. Figure 16-15 shows preparation manhours. However, your own experience is your best guide to estimating. On difficult jobs, your manhours may be up to three times higher than those given in the table.

Work element	Unit	Manhours per unit
Brush, per coat		
Wood flat work	500 SF	4.9
Doors & windows, interior side	each	1.0
Plaster, sand finish	500 SF	4.0
Plaster, smooth finish	500 SF	3.5
Wallboard	500 SF	3.3
Masonry	500 SF	4.0
Varnish flat work	500 SF	5.2
Enamel flat work	500 SF	3.8
Interior trim, 2 coats	100 LF	1.5
Kitchen cabinets, 2 coats	100 SF	1.5
Wood casework, 2 coats	100 SF	2.5
Roller, per coat		
Wood, flat work	500 SF	3.5
Plaster, sand finish	500 SF	1.5
Plaster, smooth finish	500 SF	1.7
Wallboard	500 SF	1.7
Masonry	500 SF	1.7
Time includes minor surface preparation and minor spot cleaning and sanding.		

Figure 16-14
Manhour estimates for painting

Work element	Unit	Manhours per unit
Caulking		
⅛" gap	50 LF	.8
¼" gap	50 LF	.9
⅜" gap	50 LF	1.1
½" gap	50 LF	1.3
Sanding (medium)		
Interior flat wall areas	100 SF	.3
Interior enamel areas	100 SF	.4
Sanding (light)		
Interior flat wall areas	100 SF	.3
Interior enamel areas	100 SF	.7
Sanding (extra fine, varnish)	100 SF	1.2
Spackle		
Surface in good condition	100 SF	1.1
Surface in average condition	100 SF	1.5
Surface in poor condition	100 SF	3.3

Figure 16-15
Manhours for paint preparation

You Need a Business Plan

Too many skilled craftsmen jump into kitchen and bath remodeling without a plan. But being a superb cabinetmaker, electrician, plumber, or tilesetter won't guarantee success as a remodeler. You also have to be a good businessperson. And that includes making — and following — a plan to guide your business to success and profitability.

Pause a minute. Ask yourself these questions:

- What business am I in?

- What do I sell?

- Who is my competition?

- What is my sales strategy?

- How much money do I need to operate my business?

- How will I get the work done?

- What management controls are needed?

- How can I carry them out?

- Where can I go for help?

Only you can answer these questions. Your banker, lawyer or accountant can't do it for you. And quick, glib answers aren't good enough. As the owner-manager, you have to search for the answers and draw up *your* business plan. You need a plan that lays out a logical progression from where you are to where you want to be a year from now.

How to Use This Chapter

Planning anything, even a fishing trip, requires some thinking. But a business plan takes more than an hour or so of thought. It takes your *active participation* to come up with a workable plan customized for your business. That's why I've packed this chapter with worksheets for you to fill out. When you've finished, you'll have a unique business plan, tailored specifically for *your* business.

Photocopy the pages and write on the copies if you don't want to write in the book. But whatever you do, keep the worksheets when you've finished the plan. No business plan is set in stone. You'll want to review these pages frequently and update the plan to fit changing conditions. And there's one thing you can bank on — conditions will change.

Use this chapter as a springboard. Get your ideas and supporting facts down on paper. As a kitchen and bath specialist, you have an excellent opportunity to earn a fair profit *if* your operations are based on an effective business plan.

As you're working on your business plan, never forget the importance of *cash planning*. Here's a guiding principle to keep in mind: *Cash in hand is the first demand.* You can't grow — or even stay in business — unless you have money available when you need it. That means you can't afford to omit any important cost items. Anything you leave out will be a cash drain you didn't expect. Too many of these and your business is headed for bad times.

And remember this: A plan isn't worth a crooked 2 x 4 unless you put it into action. Until *you do something*, nothing happens. We'll cover action steps at the end of this chapter.

What a Business Plan Will Do for You

You know how to use the tools of your craft. You've mastered the hammer, saw, trowel, and wrench. Think of management as another tool you must learn to use. Every job must be *planned* and *organized* if your company is going to run smoothly and efficiently. That's the goal of management — and the reason for planning.

When complete, your business plan will be a guide for each business decision you have to make. When you know where you want to go, it's easier to plan what you must do to get there. Also, the business plan can introduce your business to your employees, suppliers, bankers — anyone who needs to know about your goals and your operations.

Whether you're just starting as a kitchen and bath remodeler or have some experience under your belt, a business plan is an absolute necessity. It's the roadmap you'll follow from where you are to where you want to be — while avoiding the fast lane to disaster.

It will also point out some of the strengths you can draw on and the weaknesses to beware of. To be a successful remodeler, you must know your business thoroughly, and also know your limitations. It's O.K. if you don't know much about law or accounting. But it's a mistake if you don't get professional help when legal and accounting issues arise. Knowing the things you do well and the things you need help with will make you a better, more successful contractor.

The Business Plan Worksheet

Now look at Figure 17-1, your business plan worksheet. It's the first step in building your business plan. Take time to answer the questions thoughtfully and carefully. Let's consider the questions one at a time.

Why Am I in Business?

Most contractors are in business because they want to make money and be their own boss. But you're not likely to stay in business unless you also satisfy a consumer need at a competitive

Why am I in business? _____
_____
_____
_____
_____
_____
_____
_____
_____
_____
_____
_____
_____
_____
_____
_____
_____

What business am I in? _____
_____
_____
_____
_____
_____
_____
_____
_____
_____
_____
_____
_____
_____
_____
_____

Figure 17-1
Business plan worksheet

price. Profit is your reward for satisfying those needs.

In the first years of business, your profits may not compensate you for the long hours, hard work, and responsibility of being the boss. Few businesses earn big profits during their first years. So why *are* you in business instead of drawing a steady paycheck and letting someone else shoulder the burdens?

Be as specific as possible. What you're doing here is setting goals, for your business performance and for yourself. Do you want to grow to be the largest remodeler in your area? Or do you want to stay small and provide high-quality custom work to a few discriminating homeowners? Try to identify at least three goals, both short and long term, that will guide your business decisions.

What Business Am I In?

This is an easy question. You're in the kitchen and bathroom remodeling business. Right? But what else do you do? Do you also remodel other rooms or do repair work? Your planning depends on your definition of the kind of business you want to run. On Figure 17-1, state what business you're really in. Focus on the work you want to do, and can handle profitably.

Do you want to put limits on your growth by specializing in kitchen remodels, or accepting only bathroom updates? Are you considering branching out into room additions? Until you know what kind of work you want to do, you can't plan effectively for your business future.

How Will I Market My Business?

When you've decided what sort of remodeling business you're really in, you've just made your first marketing decision. Now, to sell your service, you face other marketing decisions.

Define Your Objective

Your marketing objective is to find enough jobs at the right times to provide a *profitable continuity* for your business. Your job starts must be coordinated to eliminate the down time between jobs. You want to get enough jobs, starting at the right times, to stay full-time in the remodeling business.

Unless you can come up with enough ideas to keep a crew working on kitchen and bath projects 12 months a year, you'll have to do other types of remodeling and repairs.

Where Is Your Market?

On Figure 17-2, describe your market in terms of customer profile (age, income and location) and price range of the projects you prefer. For example, if you don't want to do small jobs like repaints, you would eliminate this segment of the market from your plan.

Perhaps you want to limit your work to certain geographical areas. You might target tracts built after World War II, for example. Many of them may be ready for their second kitchen and bath remodel by now.

In most cases you can get your customer profile by just visiting the neighborhood. Most of us live in homes about as expensive as we can comfortably afford. So you can usually estimate your customer's income by the neighborhood. Is it upper middle class, average middle class, a lower income or high income area? How old are the homes? Is the neighborhood in transition — are the property values going up or down? Is it an area of mostly young families, retirees or a mixture? Do tradespeople or professionals live in the neighborhood? What businesses are nearby?

This kind of information will help you determine the income range of an area. Is this the income range you want to work in? If so, does the location offer remodeling possibilities? With the high cost of housing in many parts of the country, young professionals are moving into older homes

Customer income : _____

_____

_____

_____

_____

_____

_____

_____

Age range: _____

_____

_____

_____

_____

_____

_____

_____

_____

Location: _____

_____

_____

_____

_____

_____

_____

_____

Price range of preferred jobs: _____

_____

_____

_____

_____

_____

_____

Figure 17-2
Customer profile worksheet

and fixing them up. You have a great market potential right there.

Once you've defined your customer profile, it will help you narrow your advertising to those media that will reach the customers you've targeted.

Planning Effective Advertising

Now that you've described your ideal customers, what is it about your operation that will make these people want to buy your service? For instance, do you offer quality work, competitive prices, guaranteed completion dates, unique design, or other services that set you apart?

If, for example, you're experienced in redoing kitchens and bathrooms in turn-of-the-century homes, you might wish to capitalize on the experience by concentrating on that market. Use the top part of Figure 17-3 to describe your operation's selling points. You'll feature these qualities in all of your advertising.

What form should your advertising take? Ask the local media (newspaper, radio, yellow pages, etc.) for information about their services and the results they offer for your money. But proceed with caution. Don't throw away your advertising dollars. Get expert help in plotting out an effective program of advertising. In most cases, the sales staff of the media you're using can provide you with excellent advice at little or no cost. In large metropolitan areas, consider using the services of an advertising agency or a freelance ad agent, especially if you're trying to expand your market area.

Use the middle portion of Figure 17-3 to help you figure out which media are good values for the money. What you want to do, of course, is reach the largest number of people who meet your customer profile for the lowest cost per prospect. But start off slowly. You don't want to go into debt to advertise. Once the business starts coming in, plan on spending about 10 percent of your profits on advertising. When you reach your job-load objectives, you can cut back a little on your advertising costs.

Whipping the Competition

The intense competition in kitchen and bath remodeling can too easily result in low profit margins. But that may work to your advantage if you're just starting out, or if you're still a small business. A small firm with a low overhead can usually offer lower prices than the larger outfits. If your office is in your home, it doesn't cost you as much to do business.

Competition usually boils down to price competition, although a good reputation for quality and efficiency can lift you above some of the price wars. Because the remodeling industry is highly competitive, there's a high failure rate for poor planners and poor performers. I've been in the construction business for over 25 years, and I'd estimate that over 50 percent of the remodelers I've known performed below par. Naturally, many of them are no longer in business. Success requires careful planning, particularly in the areas of estimating, bidding, and designing.

Now let's assess your competition. Answer the following questions on Figure 17-3:

- Who are your major competitors?

- How will you compete against them?

Designing Your Sales Strategy

The kitchen and bath remodeling market is unique in many ways. It changes with changes in economic conditions, the local labor pool, labor relations, the availability of good subcontractors, and interest rates. Hard work is just one factor. It doesn't guarantee you success — but you can't succeed without it. You have to depend on others, such as clients or financial institutions for payment, and subcontractors for quality work.

What should my advertising tell prospective customers? _____

_____

_____

_____

_____

_____

Form of advertising	Size of audience	Frequency of use		Cost of a single ad		Estimated cost
			x		=	
			x		=	
			x		=	
			x		=	
			x		=	
			x		=	
				Total	$	

Who are my major competitors? _____

_____

_____

_____

_____

_____

How will I compete against them? _____

_____

_____

_____

_____

_____

Figure 17-3
Advertising worksheet

Personnel

Will I carry a permanent crew or hire workers as needed? _____

Will I use union or nonunion labor? _____

How many workers will I need? _____

What is the hourly rate I will pay? _____

What will fringe benefits cost? _____

Will I supervise the work myself or hire a foreman? _____

If I hire a foreman, what will the salary be? _____

Will I need clerical help? _____ What will it cost? _____

Equipment	Rent	Buy	My cost
			$
			$
			$
			$
			$

Will I need an office or use my home? _____

If I will need an office, what will the rent and other expenses be? _____

_____

_____

Figure 17-4
Personnel and equipment requirements

What Personnel and Equipment Do You Need?

You'll have to decide whether to carry a permanent crew or hire workers as needed. Will you use union or nonunion labor? How many workers will you need? What will they cost in wages and fringe benefits? What about a foreman? Will you need clerical help? Answer these questions on Figure 17-4.

What Equipment Do You Need?

What special equipment will you need? Will employees supply their own hand tools? Will you rent or buy? What about office space? Put your answers on Figure 17-4.

Put Your Plan Into Dollars

An important part of good business management is *financial management*. The financial part of the job has to be planned as carefully as the actual remodeling. Your contract price must cover the direct and indirect construction costs, a share of overhead, and if you've planned well, a little profit.

Your accountant will help you set up an accounting system that meets your needs. But you have to do most of the financial planning yourself. It's up to you to establish the goals and set your own limits.

In your financial planning, the first consideration is where the dollars will come from. In dollars, how much business will you be able to do in the next 12 months? Fill in the top line of Figure 17-5, the income and expenses worksheet, with the amount of cash you expect to take in for each of the months in the next year. Try to be as realistic as possible. When you've projected 12 months of income, total them for the annual sales volume.

Expenses

Now you need to think about expenses. If you plan to do $100,000 worth of work, how much will it cost you? And even more important, what will be left over as profit at the end of the year?

Profit is your payoff. Even after you pay yourself a salary, your business must make a profit if it's to survive and pay back the money and time you invest in it. Profit helps your firm grow strong, and that means having a financial reserve for the inevitable lean periods.

Use Figure 17-5 to figure your yearly expenses and estimated net profit. You've already filled in the top line, estimated income. Now start calculating the rest of the information. The second line is cost of sales. That's your direct labor and material costs for each job. Now estimate your controllable and fixed expenses for each month. Finally, calculate your net profit.

Matching Money and Expenses

After you've forecast your month-to-month income and expenses, here's the next question: Will there be enough money coming in to meet these expenses and to keep you going if there's any down time between jobs? You may discover periods when you expect to be short of cash. For example, you need materials and supplies to start a new job, even though it'll be a few weeks before you're paid. What do you do in the interim if your supplier won't credit you?

Your bank may be able to help with a short-term loan. But any banker you approach will want to know your company's financial condition before even discussing a loan. The first thing the bank will ask for is a balance sheet.

Even if you don't need to borrow, you should have a current balance sheet for your business. It's like an X-ray that reveals your company's financial health. You could do it yourself, but it's best to have your accountant draw up a balance sheet. Figure 17-6 shows the balance sheet format you can follow.

It's never too early to build good relations with your banker. There may come a time when you'll need a quick loan. So even if you won't need to borrow anytime soon, you may want to share your balance sheet and your business plan with your banker. If you do need money for unexpected expenses, having laid the foundation can speed up the loan process.

Many kitchen and bath remodelers are able to finance their own operations, since most jobs are completed quickly and payment is usually prompt. If you can operate without borrowing, the money you save on interest charges goes straight to your bottom line.

	% of your sales	Your annual sales $	Jan	Feb	Mar	Apr	May	Jun	Jul	Aug	Sep	Oct	Nov	Dec
Sales														
Cost of sales														
Gross profit														
Controllable expenses														
Outside labor														
Operating supplies														
Gross wages														
Repairs and maintenance														
Advertising														
Car and delivery														
Bad debts														
Administrative and legal														
Miscellaneous expenses														
Total controllable expenses														
Fixed expenses														
Rent														
Utilities														
Insurance														
Taxes and licenses														
Depreciation														
Total fixed expenses														
Total expenses														
Net profit (before income tax)														

Figure 17-5
Income and expenses worksheet

Is Your Plan Workable?

Now that you've planned this far, step back and take a look at your plan. Is it realistic? Can you do enough business to make a living?

Now's the time to revise your plan if it isn't workable — not after you've committed time and money. If you feel some revisions are needed before you start implementing your plan, make them now. Go back to the cash flow and expenses forecasts and adjust the figures. Better yet, show your plan to someone who hasn't had a hand in making it. You may need fresh ideas. Your banker, or an experienced contractor, will be able to point out strong points and weaknesses in the plan.

Put Your Plan Into Action

Action is the difference between dreamers and doers. When your plan is as good as you can make it, you're ready to put it into motion. If you're just starting a business, the first action step would probably be acquiring enough capital to get started. Do you really have the money? Will you borrow it from friends, relatives, or a bank? Where and when will you hire your employees?

What else needs to be done? Look for positive action steps that will get your business rolling. For example, where and how will you get the licenses you need to be a contractor? The regulations for businesses may vary for different kinds of business and certainly will vary from state to state. You can find out by contacting the various levels of government, including the IRS for federal tax regulations. Also contact your local SBA (Small Business Administration) office. They can give you specific information for all levels of government. Your local Chamber of Commerce may also be able to advise you.

Current Balance Sheet	
As of (date) _____	
	Assets
Current assets	$
Cash	$
Receivables	$
Inventories of supplies and tools	$
Total current assets	$
Fixed assets	$
Other assets	$
Total assets	$
	Liabilities
Current liabilities	$
Notes payable	$
Accounts payable	$
Misc. current liabilities	$
Total current liabilities	$
Equipment contracts	$
Owner's equity	$
Total liabilities	$

Figure 17-6
Balance sheet

Use Figure 17-7 to list the actions you must take to implement your business plan. Give each item a date — then follow up to make sure they're completed on time. If your business is already established, use the action worksheet to plan the steps you'll take to meet the goals you established in Figure 17-1.

Action	Completion date

Figure 17-7
Action worksheet

Keep Your Plan up to Date

No one can predict the future with accuracy. Things change. That's only natural. The difference between successful and unsuccessful planning is often only the ability to keep alert and watch for changes. Stay on top of changing conditions and adjust your plan accordingly.

In order to adjust your plan to account for changes, you must:

1) Be alert to the changes occurring in your industry, your market, and in your clients.

2) Check your plan against these changes.

3) Determine what revisions, if any, your plan needs.

About once a month or so, go over your plan. See whether it needs adjusting. If revisions are needed, make them and put them in action. If you're not making a profit, just getting more jobs probably won't solve the problem. Chances are you'll just work harder, and still won't have anything left over after the work is done. Analyze your plan. Find out why profits are eluding you. Check your estimating and scheduling to keep your business on track *and* in the money.

Planning the Work

If your marketing efforts are successful, you have a job to do, at the right time and the right price. Now how will you plan the work so that the job gets done on time?

In planning the work, keep two things in mind; the timing of starts, and the timing of the various steps in remodeling. If you have enough help and dependable supervisory personnel, you can take on as many projects as you can *control*.

Effective planning helps you two ways: First, it helps you maintain your production schedule. Second, it gives flexibility to meet changed conditions. What if you had to delay work because of a death or some other emergency in the homeowner's family? Or cope with a bad-weather delay?

The work schedule will show the various operations in sequence, and show how many days each operation should take. It also has space for the calendar dates. Several operations may be in progress simultaneously. For example, the bathroom floor can be repaired while the cabinetmaker installs kitchen cabinets. A work schedule will show at a glance whether the work is on schedule. Remember, you need to get in the kitchen and bathroom, do the work, and get out in the time planned. If your job takes longer than it should, you'll face unhappy homeowners and mini profits.

Figure 17-8 is a simple work schedule that you can use as a guide. It has columns for working days (start and finish) and calendar days. And there's a column that you mark with an X — or part of an X — to indicate if the work is done as scheduled. An empty box shows that the job's behind schedule. A box with an X in it means that you're up to date. A partial X, like the one on line 3, indicates that the job scheduled for that day is partially done. The X has three of its four segments drawn in, so the job is three-quarters done. The job on line 4 can't be started until line 3 is completed.

You fill in the start, finish and calendar day columns as the work progresses. If you estimated the completion of this project in ten working days, you can quickly see where you are in relation to where your estimate says you should be. This is an easy way to spot trouble while there's still time to take corrective action.

Always save your work schedules. They're the basis for future estimates. Old work schedules can help you plan the job, order the materials, schedule the subs, and anticipate problems. When you consider all these things, you'll be more likely to submit an accurate bid.

Business planning is an important subject. It's also a big subject. It would take a whole book to cover it in depth. If you want more information, the Small Business Administration offers many guides and aids at reasonable prices. There are SBA offices in many larger cities. Or you can order *Contractor's Growth and Profit Guide* from this publisher. There's an order form at the back of the book.

Smith project - estimated completion: 4/23/89				
Activity	Working day		Calendar day	Completed
	Start	Finish		
1. Remove kitchen cabinets & install wallboard	1	1	4/15	☒
2. Install luminous ceiling	2	3	4/17	☒
3. Remove bathroom fixtures & repair floor	4	5	4/19	◩
4. Install bathroom fixtures	6	7	4/21	☐
5. Install new kitchen cabinets	8	10	4/24	☐
6. Paint	11	13	4/27	☐

Figure 17-8
Typical work schedule

Managing for Profits

Management means getting the right things done at the right time. In kitchen and bath remodeling it's also getting the good jobs at a good price. In short, effective management can mean making a profit while your competitors go broke.

Successful management takes hard work, good organization and careful attention to paperwork. And it takes paying as much attention to running your business as you do to completing your jobs. You can't survive as a remodeler without both remodeling and business skills.

While it doesn't take a college education to run a remodeling business, every professional remodeler has to master both administrative and technical tasks. Every job requires planning and scheduling of resources: equipment, workers, and materials. You have to reorganize your field work for each job while maintaining payroll, accounting, insurance, and tax records.

When you sell a kitchen and bathroom remodeling job, what's the homeowner actually buying? The materials you use are about the same throughout the industry. Your equipment isn't unique. Neither are your tradesmen. There are skilled workers available in every community. So why did the customers choose *you*? Because you convinced them that you can get the job done right. They're buying your skill as a manager, and your business know-how.

The Function of Management

Some of these management functions would be your responsibility no matter what business you were in. Others are unique to the remodeling industry. They require specific technical knowledge and experience.

If you don't have this experience and knowledge, there are three choices. The first is to get out of the business while you're still solvent. The second is to learn enough to handle your responsibilities as soon as possible. And learn you can. Management skills aren't inherited — they're learned. The third way is to bring in a partner who has the skills you lack. But most remodelers can't find or afford a full-time business pro to organize and run the construction office.

One kitchen and bath specialist I know was skilled in several trades. He could transform any kitchen or bathroom into a showplace that would bring shouts of delight from the pickiest of homeowners. But he absolutely hated government regulations and other "aggravating" paperwork. If he couldn't keep it all on the back of an envelope, he didn't bother with it. But he knew he was headed for trouble. So he took in as partner a school teacher with a flair for paperwork and scheduling. The teacher did the work in his spare time, freeing the owner to concentrate on the things he was good at. It was a profitable solution for both of them.

The business functions you have to perform, or hire someone to perform, fall into several broad areas. They are:

1) General administration

2) Legal matters

3) Personnel

4) Designing

5) Purchasing

6) Subcontracting

7) Financial control

8) Planning

9) Sales

A growing business can often hire clerical and supervisory personnel, and even skilled specialists, to tackle some of the business problems. But in the beginning, you've got to be able to do it all yourself. Here's a look at some of the skills you need to master.

Making Decisions

Your primary job as manager is deciding how to allocate your resources. You'll find yourself asking:

- What types of work do we want?

- How are we going to get it?

- What profit margin do we require?

- What crew do we put on what job today?

- Who gets paid today and who gets to wait?

Whether you succeed or fail will depend primarily on the quality of your decisions. And the validity of your decisions will depend to a great extent on the accuracy and completeness of the information you base them on.

Information will come to you from many sources, both inside and outside the company. Sources within the company include your own experience and observations, input from employees, cost records and financial reports.

Every remodeling business needs a simple but complete reporting system. A system that's too complex or detailed takes too much time. The information may not be ready when you need it. But a system that's too sketchy misses too much. Good records allow you to stay informed on all the important facts and satisfy the requirements of federal, state, and local governments. That's all you need. Later in this chapter, we'll talk about the kind of record keeping you need for a successful remodeling company.

No matter how complete your company records, however, you need some information from outside the company. You'll get it from contacts with clients and suppliers, newspapers and magazines, and your observations of local conditions. You should also consult with professionals when you need the information they can provide.

Using the information you gather, you'll make both short-range and long-range decisions: choosing designs, estimating costs, purchasing, subcontracting, scheduling jobs, hiring and guiding personnel, and planning sales programs, to name a few.

Always Think Ahead

Take time to look ahead and decide where you want your business to go, and how you're going to get there. Start with a well-defined goal instead of drifting in whatever direction circumstances carry you. The business plan we did in the last chapter puts you way ahead here. Kitchen and bath remodeling is here to stay. As new home prices rise, more and more homeowners will choose to stay put and remodel. The specialist who sticks to a defined goal will be there to collect the profits.

How to Build Your Management Ability

There's no magic involved in acquiring management ability. You just need ordinary skills developed by everyday experience and, of course, effort. Here are some of the characteristics that successful builders have in common.

Integrity

In kitchen and bath remodeling, the homeowners' only real protection is their confidence in the integrity of the remodeler. That makes it especially important for you to be open and aboveboard in all your transactions. This doesn't mean you have to tell everyone all about your business. Simply treat customers with frankness and fairness. Remember that a list of satisfied clients is about the best advertisement you can have. Your happy customers help convince prospects that you can be trusted. This reputation for square dealing may be one of your most valuable business assets.

It's just as important to treat your employees fairly. Insist on professionalism. Assign workers to tasks they're trained to do. Provide fair and just reward for work done, unbiased settlement of all disputes between employees, and prompt and friendly adjustment of mistakes in time and wages. Make sure no person loses their job without a fair hearing.

You want workers to arrive to work on time, confine breaks and lunch periods to the specified times, and dress appropriately. Provide (and enforce) a dress code, work code, and behavior code. Make sure your employees know what you expect of them. Provide incentives to meet your expectations.

These are methods which develop a well-organized, well-disciplined work crew. Handling personnel matters fairly and consistently results in a satisfied group of workers who produce high-quality work and represent your business well. Resentful employees cost you more than you can afford.

Creativity

You can also create confidence and goodwill by offering good suggestions. Point out any potential problems you spot. Offer suggestions for improvements. As a specialist in the field, you owe your client the full benefit of your knowledge and experience to ensure the project is well-designed and well-built.

Perseverance

Every successful remodeler needs the ability to see ahead and devise ways to cut costs and circumvent obstacles. You also must have the initiative to overcome problems, and to start and complete a project. Perseverance keeps it all going. If you're not persistent, you're in the wrong business.

There was the old carpenter who fell with the scaffold and viewed the twisted pile from his backside. He cursed his stupidity: "If I'd driven that last nail, I'd still be on my feet!" That's the problem with a lot of us. We quit when all it takes is one more nail — one final effort.

Building a Strong Company

When you start your business, you'll be thinking and planning two or three months ahead. Later, as your company grows, you may be planning ahead for a year or more. The size and success of your company in the future depend on how well you:

- Adjust to technical and economic changes

- Build a management team

- Plan and achieve short-term goals

- Build for long-term growth

Everyone who's tried to run a one-person remodeling company has been discouraged about the heavy workload and the variety of skills needed to get the job done. Many have wondered if it's worth all the time and effort.

What can you do to ease the burden a little? Consider putting your lead carpenter on salary while you teach him to take over as foreman or superintendent.

What do you look for in a potential foreman? First, choose a good craftsman who knows (or can learn) the technical details of kitchen and bath remodeling. Second, look for a self-starter. Pick someone who shows initiative — who finds a way to get the work done without bringing you all the details and complaints. Third, look for the ability to become a manager. Remember, this person will be responsible for important aspects of *your* business. If he can't manage his own time, he won't be able to manage the crews. Rate your candidate on these points. Then ask yourself if he could, with training, run the company in your absence.

It's also important to choose someone who can get along with people. Can he supervise workers without stirring up conflict? Can he negotiate with subcontractors? Is he considerate and patient with demanding clients who don't understand a remodeler's problems?

You don't want a carbon copy of yourself. What you need is someone who complements your personality and skills. Try to select someone whose strong points balance your weak points. For instance, if you're good at paperwork, pick someone who's good out in the field supervising a job.

Train your foreman by delegating work to him. While he's learning, coach him and check his work. As soon as he's shown he can handle certain tasks well, back away and let him handle them. Give him the authority, material, equipment, and labor he needs to do the job, and turn him loose. If you've trained him properly, he'll know when to ask for help.

Record Keeping

Good records are the foundation for building a profitable business. Sloppy or nonexistent records will ruin you. Even if you're working out of your home or truck, with no help except family members willing to pitch in, some things just have to be done. There are phones to answer, routine correspondence to take care of, and records to update — including the bookkeeping and accounting.

If you don't know bookkeeping, have a public bookkeeping service set up your books. They'll install whatever system you need and train you to keep the necessary daily records. The accountant will spend only one or two days a month bringing your books up to date.

Regardless of how you do it, keep adequate records. Both state and federal tax laws require it, and good sense demands it. You must maintain a record of money passing in and out of your business or you'll never be able to grow into a profitable company.

What Kind of Records?

Your accountant will tell you that you should have a record of every dime earned, where it came from, and where it went. You also have to know what materials and labor cost before you can set fair prices for your services.

The key to record keeping is to spend the minimum time needed to keep records that are just adequate for your needs. Start with the records you need to make up annual profit and loss statements and balance sheets. You'll need these to file tax returns.

You'll also need these statements when you want to borrow money. No bank or S&L is going to lend you money without seeing your business records. Suppose you want to bid on a job remodeling the bathrooms in an apartment complex. You'll need a bank loan to complete the job. Your banker will demand a current financial statement. Among other things, your lender will want to know the *ratio* of your company's outstanding debts to its net worth. We'll get into that a little later. Without a current financial statement, that ratio is only speculation.

Your Cash Schedule

Cash in hand is the first demand. Remember that from the last chapter? One of your chief responsibilities as manager is to see that your company has the cash it needs when bills are due. Have your accountant set up a system that will track your cash flow, so you can anticipate problems before they become a crisis.

You must record all cash received and all cash paid out in your business by posting the items to the appropriate journal. You might be able to get by with a single combined journal or cash book. Ask your accountant about simplified record-keeping systems.

Regardless of how you set up your books, remember that keeping records is like keeping score in a ball game. If you don't collect those numbers

and take the time to understand what they mean, you don't know who's winning and who's losing.

Remember also that records become more important as your company grows. You have to rely more and more on what the numbers say and less and less on first-hand observation. Don't wait until the cabinet shop calls to scream that your check bounced. Have your accountant set up a simple but efficient bookkeeping system — and then faithfully keep the system up to date.

Act on Your Records

Records must be used, not just kept. Study and understand what those numbers mean. Compare this month's results with last month's results and the results from this month a year ago. If the trend is positive, understand why. Do more of what you've been doing. If it's negative, figure out why while there's still time to make changes. When the reports show unexpected gains, figure some way to make these improvements a permanent part of your operation.

Problems arise daily in the remodeling business. The larger your company, the larger the problems can be. You'll have to make decisions like these:

- What markup percentage do you require? How do you allocate overhead expense among the jobs in progress so you can tell where you're making or losing money?

- How much work in progress can you carry without running out of working capital? Should you replace the two old trucks?

- There's only so much money available. Where should you invest it? Should you build and equip a cabinet shop to manufacture your own kitchen cabinets?

Your current balance sheet and profit and loss statement are a good guide when decisions like this have to be made — *if* you know how to interpret them. A balance sheet tells how your business stands at one given moment. The profit and loss statement sums up your operations over a period of time. In themselves, these two financial documents are a collection of lifeless figures. To make them valuable, you have to interpret and evaluate them.

Take your month-end balance sheets for 12 consecutive months. Arrange the figures in 12 vertical columns across a page so you can compare asset and liability account totals for each month in the year. You'll begin to see trends in the figures. Then compare the month of March for this year and last year. See how things are changing. Compare August for both years. What do you see? That's important information for anyone running a business.

Comparing profit and loss statements will show changes in expense categories and the profit margin. Did you cut prices to meet competition? Then look for a lower gross profit, unless you cut construction costs proportionately. Did sales go up? If so, what about expenses? Did they remain proportionate? Was more money spent on office help? How about fixed overhead? Where did the money come from? By comparing operating income and cost account items from one period to another, you'll find the answers.

Compare Operating Ratios

Operating ratios (your balance sheet and expense ratios) have many uses. You can use them to analyze collections, check the condition of finances, and pinpoint potential or actual problems in expense categories. Even better, compare ratios for your company with ratios for other companies, or the construction industry as a whole. The figures that follow let you do exactly that: compare your company with industry averages.

When dealing with balance sheet ratios, you want to be better than average, of course. But you'll be reassured to know that the averages represent a margin of safety. If your organization's key ratios are close to the propor-

tions reflected by standard ratios, you're not likely to get into trouble.

But take the averages I'll give you here as guidelines, not as a map of how your business should operate. Your company is unique. Only you can say if your ratios make sense. Compare your ratios at set intervals to spot the trends. There's no better way to evaluate your company's financial health.

Interpreting Expense Ratios

The expense ratios in Figure 18-1 are based on figures compiled and published by the Internal Revenue Service, U.S. Treasury Department, and major lending institutions. They show the net profit before taxes for small contractors with sales less than a million dollars per year. Expense ratios are always taken as a percentage of total revenue (sales). Use these average ratios to evaluate the condition of your company.

Make a worksheet with the average ratios, and space for your ratios for comparison. Note any items that are seriously out of line. But don't take drastic steps to bring your ratios in line with the averages. Instead, think about why your ratios are different. Your expense ratios might be higher than average, for instance, because you provide special services to clients, compensated for by higher prices. Or a good sales program might bring a better-than-average margin of gross profit. So consider each item in the context of your business.

Once you've analyzed these comparisons, make corrections that will bring expenses into balance with sales. These don't necessarily have to be negative steps. You may see a way to improve your numbers by *adding* expenses, for example. Perhaps your advertising budget is too low. An increase might bring in more income.

	General contractors	Subcontractors
Sales (contract revenues)	100%	100%
Material & subcont. work	44	44
On-site wages (excl. owner)	19	23
Gross profit	37	33
Controllable expenses		
Off-site labor	2	1
Operating supplies	3	2
Repairs and maintenance	1	1
Advertising	1	1
Auto and truck	3	2
Bad debts	Under .5	Under .5
Administrative and legal	.5	.5
Miscellaneous expense	2	1
Total controllable expense	13	9
Fixed expenses		
Rent	1	1
Utilities	1	1.5
Insurance	1	1
Taxes and licenses	.5	1
Interest	Under .5	Under .5
Depreciation	2	2
Total fixed expenses	6	7
Total expenses	19	16
Net profit	18	17

Figure 18-1
Typical expense ratios for small contractors

Your gross profit will fluctuate with cost variables in material, labor and subcontracted work. But if it's seriously out of line with construction industry averages, it's a good idea to examine your labor and material costs and bidding practices.

Interpreting Balance Sheet Ratios

If you're like most remodelers, you probably focus on your income account when you're trying to increase profits or reduce losses. But a careful review of your balance sheet may show other areas that need your attention. Compare the distribution of assets and liabilities in your company with the way assets and liabilities are distributed in other companies. That may suggest ways to change the financial structure of your company and improve operating performance. Figure 18-2 shows a typical balance sheet and income statement.

A cash shortage isn't always the result of poor sales. It may point to an unhealthy situation that threatens the business. No matter how little cash and working capital you have available, there's some level of business you can maintain with a reasonable cushion of safety.

A careful study of your balance sheet may show slow collections, an ill-thought-out expansion program, or even too much money tied up in vehicles. These are things you can change to improve your company's performance. Don't just rationalize a bad situation and hope it goes away. Do something to correct it.

All remodeling companies experience peaks and valleys in business activity. Your business should be able to adapt to changes in prices and sales. There's always a chance of trouble developing from some unforeseen event like a material shortage or labor dispute. If your liabilities are too heavy, you may not be able to ride it out.

Here are brief descriptions of the key balance sheet ratios, including average ratios for general and subcontractors.

Kitchen and Bath Remodelers, Inc.
December 31, 19___
BALANCE SHEET

Cash	$ 948	Notes payable, bank	$ 7,000
Notes receivable	2,438	Notes receivable, discounted	2,421
Accounts receivable	48,728	Accounts payable	76,120
Work in progress and inventory	78,411	Accruals	2,720
Total current assets	$130,525	Total current liabilities	$ 88,261
Depreciation, land and buildings	23,129	Mortgage	5,000
Equipment and fixtures	5,729	Total liabilities	$93,261
Prepaid expenses	639	Net worth	66,761
Total assets	$160,022	Total liabilities and net worth	$160,022

INCOME STATEMENT

	Dollars		Percent
Net sales		$363,558	100.00
Cost of production		298,852	82.22
Gross profit on sales		64,706	17.79
Operating expenses:			
Wages	$30,689		8.44
Delivery	4,698		1.29
Bad debts allowance	1,807		0.49
Depreciation allowance	3,600		0.99
Total expenses		$ 40,794	11.21
Net profit before other charges		23,912	6.58
Other charges:			
Interest	$ 350		0.09
Nonoperating charges	500		0.13
Drawings	7,490		2.06
Provisions for taxes	4,328		1.19
Total other charges		$12,668	3.47
Net profit for period		$11,244	3.10

Figure 18-2
Typical balance sheet and income statement

Current Assets to Current Liabilities

Widely known as the *current ratio,* this is one test of solvency. It measures the liquid assets available to meet all debts falling due within a year's time.

For each ratio, I'll give the formula for working it out, and an example based on the typical balance sheet and income statement in Figure 18-2. Of course, you need to substitute your own figures from your records. Here's the first one:

$$\frac{\text{Current assets}}{\text{Current liabilities}} = \frac{\$130,525}{\$\ 88,261} = 1.48 \text{ to } 1$$

Current assets are those normally expected to flow into cash in the course of one year. They usually include cash, notes and accounts receivable, and the value of work in progress. Some firms consider items such as the cash surrender value of life insurance as current, but I don't recommend it.

Current liabilities are short-term obligations due for payment within a year: notes and accounts payable for materials, loans payable, short-term installment loans, taxes, and contract advances received but not earned.

Most small general contractors have a current ratio ranging from 1.1 to 1 through 1.5 to 1. More solvent firms have about twice as much in current assets as current debts. Current assets are normally 50 to 60 percent of total assets. Cash should be about 6 percent of assets.

Subcontractors should have a current ratio of 1.5 (assets) to 1 (liabilities). Even 2.5 to 1 wouldn't be excessive. Current assets should be 60 to 80 percent of total assets, and cash should be about 10 percent of total assets for subcontractors.

Current Liabilities to Tangible Net Worth

Like the current ratio, this is another means of evaluating financial condition by comparing what you *own* to what you *owe.* The formula looks like this:

$$\frac{\text{Current liabilities}}{\text{Tangible net worth}} = \frac{\$88,261}{\$66,761} = 132\%$$

Tangible net worth is the total asset value of a business, minus any *intangible* items such as goodwill, trademarks, patents, copyrights, and leaseholds. In a corporation, the tangible net worth would consist of the sum of all outstanding capital stock, preferred and common, and surplus, minus intangibles. In a partnership or proprietorship, it could include the capital account, or accounts, less the intangibles.

In a going business, the *intangibles* may have a substantial — but undeterminable — value. Until they're actually liquidated by sale, it's difficult to evaluate what they might bring. In a profitable business up for sale, the goodwill conceivably could represent the potential earning power over a period of years. It might even bring in more than the assets themselves. But most small businesses have no way to cash in on their goodwill.

Many general contractors have current liabilities which are 140 percent of tangible net worth. A more reasonable figure would be about 80 percent. General contractors who subcontract less of their work, and most subcontractors, usually have current liabilities of about 70 percent of net worth.

Turnover of Tangible Net Worth

Sometimes called *net revenues to tangible net worth,* this ratio shows how actively-invested capital is working by measuring its turnover during a certain period. It helps measure the profitability of the investment. The formula uses net sales for a year and the tangible net worth:

$$\frac{\text{Net sales (year)}}{\text{Tangible net worth}} = \frac{\$363,558}{\$\ 66,761} = 5.4 \text{ turnovers}$$

Find the turnover of tangible net worth by dividing the average tangible net worth into net revenues for the same periods. The ratio is expressed as the number of turnovers in the period. General contractors should "turn" their net worth about 5 to 5-1/2 times a year, and subcontractors should average 6 to 6-1/2 times.

Turnover of Working Capital

Also known as the ratio of *net sales to net working capital*, this ratio measures how hard your working cash is working in terms of sales. Working capital is assets that can readily be converted into operating funds within a year. It doesn't include invested capital. A low ratio shows unprofitable use of working capital; a high one, vulnerability to creditors.

Here's the formula:

$$\frac{\text{Net sales (year)}}{\text{Working capital}} = \frac{\$363,558}{\$42,264} = 8.6 \text{ times}$$

To find the working capital, deduct the sum of the current liabilities from the total current assets. It includes the business assets that you can readily convert into operating funds. A builder with $100,000 cash, receivables, and work in progress, and no unpaid obligations, would have $100,000 in working capital. A business with $200,000 in current assets and $100,000 in current liabilities also would have $100,000 working capital. Obviously, however, items like receivables can't be turned into cash overnight.

Most businesses need a margin of current assets over and above current liabilities to provide for stock and work in progress, and to carry receivables until they're collected. General contractors should "turn" their working capital about 14 times a year, while subcontractors average 6 to 8 times a year.

Net Profits to Tangible Net Worth

This measures your return on investment. It's one of the best indicators of profitability, often the key yardstick of management ability. Profits after taxes are the final source of growth. If this return on capital is too low, the capital involved could be better used elsewhere.

You divide net profits for a given period by tangible net worth for that period:

$$\frac{\text{Net profit (after taxes)}}{\text{Tangible net worth}} = \frac{\$11,244}{\$66,761} = 16.8\%$$

The ratio is expressed as a percentage. It relates profits earned in a given length of time to the average net worth during that time. *Net profit* means the revenue left over from sales income after all costs have been paid. These include costs of goods sold, writedowns and chargeoffs, federal and other taxes, and miscellaneous adjustments needed to reduce assets to current, going values.

General contractors should show a profit after taxes of at least 12 percent of net worth. A 20 percent profit is a reasonable expectation. The top 10 percent of the industry shows about a 40 percent profit on net worth. Subcontractors should show a profit of at least 15 percent of net worth, although some reach 35 percent or more. Small concrete and electrical contractors can average about 20 percent, but contractors in the mechanical trades usually average less than a 15 percent profit on net worth.

Fixed Assets to Tangible Net Worth

This ratio shows the relationship between investment in land, buildings and equipment, and the owner's capital. It indicates how liquid the net worth is. The higher this ratio, the less of the owner's capital is available for use as working capital, or to meet debts.

To find the ratio:

$$\frac{\text{Fixed assets}}{\text{Tangible net worth}} = \frac{\$23,076}{\$66,761} = 34.6\%$$

Fixed assets include land, buildings, leasehold improvements, fixtures, furniture, machinery, tools, and equipment, less depreciation. General contractors should not have more than 25 percent of their tangible net worth invested in fixed assets. Of course, contractors who need heavy equipment on a daily basis may have 50 percent or more of their net worth invested in fixed assets.

Subcontractors who don't need expensive equipment should have no more than 25 percent of their tangible net worth invested in fixed assets.

Net Profit on Net Sales

This ratio measures the rate of return on net sales. It's expressed as a percentage which indicates the number of cents of each sales dollar remaining after deducting all income statement items and income taxes. It reveals the profitability of sales — that is, the profit realized on the regular operations of a business.

Many people think a high rate of return on net sales is necessary for a business to be successful. But this isn't always true. To evaluate the significance of the ratio, consider such factors as the value of sales and the total capital employed. A low rate of return compared with rapid turnover and large sales volume, for example, may result in satisfactory earnings.

Here's an example:

$$\frac{\text{Net profit}}{\text{Net sales}} = \frac{\$ 11,244}{\$363,558} = 3.1\%$$

Most general contractors and subcontractors show a net profit on sales of between 1 and 2 percent, after taxes and overhead. An exceptionally profitable operation would show about a 4 percent profit. These figures may be misleading because "profit" in a small company often disappears into the owner's pocket before the final figures are prepared for each year.

Overhead

As you know, your cost for every job is more than just what you pay for materials and labor.

You carry an overhead that includes several kinds of taxes, insurance, and miscellaneous expenses. When estimating a job, don't forget to include these costs in your estimate:

Taxes and Insurance

Most states impose an unemployment insurance tax on employers. This tax is based on the total payroll for each calendar quarter. The actual tax percentage, based on the employer's history of unemployment claims, may be from 1 to 4 percent or more.

The federal government also imposes an unemployment insurance tax based on payroll (FUTA). This tax runs about 0.7 percent. And the federal government collects Social Security taxes (FICA) and Medicare taxes. These two taxes come to about 7-1/2 percent of payroll. They're collected from the employer each calendar quarter.

States generally require employers to carry worker's compensation insurance to cover their employees for job-related injuries. The cost of the insurance is a percentage of payroll based on the type of work each employee performs. Most light construction trades have a rate between 5 and 15 percent. The cost varies from one period to the next, depending on the history of injuries.

You should also carry liability insurance to protect yourself in case of an accident. Liability insurance usually costs about 2 percent of payroll. The higher the liability limits, the higher your costs.

Here are your approximate total costs for taxes and insurance:

State Unemployment Insurance	4.0%
FICA and Medicare	7.51%
FUTA	0.7%
Worker's Compensation Insurance	5.0 to 15.0%
Liability Insurance	2.0%
Total	19.21 to 29.21%

Miscellaneous Expenses

Other important "cost-of-doing-business" expenses include:

- Supervision

- Payroll and reports

- Interest on borrowed money

- Licenses

- Office expenses

- Car and truck expenses

- Advertising

- Legal and accounting fees

- Sales commissions

These additional expenses will vary from job to job. To cover these expenses, some remodelers add 22 to 28 percent to the estimated payroll. Others prefer to list them separately. Just be sure you account for these expenses, or they'll come straight out of your profit.

In remodeling, labor is always an estimate. Inflation can increase material costs weekly. And some costs can't be foreseen, even with the most careful estimate. But your actual cost should be within 5 percent of your estimate.

To allow for the difference between the estimate cost and the actual cost, some remodelers add a contingency percentage to the estimated cost of the job before profit. Your experience from previous jobs is your best guide to the appropriate percentages.

Summary

Understanding and using the management techniques in this chapter will help you control your remodeling business, instead of being controlled by it. Skilled workers and the finest materials don't necessarily make a success. You have to manage these resources to keep them working for you.

Know where your business stands in comparison with others in the same field. Search for ways to improve your profits. Is your expense ratio too high? Find out why and take steps to bring it into line. If your balance sheet shows high labor costs, correct the problem or suffer loss of profits.

Organizing, planning, and careful record keeping are absolutely essential if you want to keep your company thriving. Although you probably get great satisfaction from the actual remodeling, don't let it lure you away from your management responsibilities. Successful management is a continuing process. You'll never complete the job, but treat it as though your business depended on it. It probably does.

If you don't feel you have the necessary management skills, find someone who can help. At the very least, get a copy of *Running Your Remodeling Business*. An order form is bound into the back of this book. It may help keep you off the list of skilled remodelers who failed because they didn't know how to run a business. Remember, running a remodeling company is a highly competitive task. In the long run, your management ability probably counts for more than your trade skills.

index

Abbreviations
base cabinets, 58
blind corner cabinets, 58
dimension, 51
ABS plastic wall surround, 147
Action worksheet, 366
Adjusting block, drain, 182
Adding
decorative edge, 117
new circuits, 252
receptacle, 256
switch and light, 255
Adhering and stapling, flooring, 292
Adhesive application, gypsum board, 311
Adhesive spreading, 288
Advertising, 10-13
Advertising worksheet, 361
Aggregate, plaster, 321
Agreement, memorandum, 19
Air cap, whirlpool, 179
Air gap, dishwasher, 132
Alternate installation method, 289-294
Aluminum tape, 114
American Olean Tile Co., 15
American Woodmark Corp., 15
Amperes, 249
Annealed galvanized steel wire, 320
Appliance installation, 74
manhours, 141-142
Approach (selling), 17
Architectural specifications, tile, 246, 247
Area table, wallboard, 317
Assembly parts, Eurostyle cabinets, S60, 61
Assets, 365
Average drying times of coatings, 352

Backer board installation procedures, 313
Backsplash
ceramic tile, 116
Corian, 115-116
Balance sheet, 365
income statement, 375
ratios, 374
Ball and retainer assemblies, 179-180
Base cabinets, 51, 54
abbreviations, 58
Basic kitchen layouts, 33
Base molding installation, 325
Bathroom
checklist, 165-168
design and layout, 143, 144
divided, 163
floor coverings, 156
layout, 160-164
lighting, 154
locations, 164
minimum space, 163
plans and specifications, 165
preference form, 23
storage, 154, 157
vanity cabinetry, 158, 159
wall coverings, 156
Bathroom fixtures
choices, 147-149
installation, 162, 170
manhours, 209, 210
Bathtub
framing, 171
installation, 171
surround kits, 233

wall kit installation, 212
walls, 237
Bathtubs, 147-150
Batten style shower surrounds, 222
Beam construction, 303
Bender board, skylight, 334
Bidets, 153
Billboards, advertising, 11
Binders, 341
Blind corner cabinets, 52, 58
abbreviations, 58
Board, ironing, 138
Board products, square feet, 317
Bond coat, 240
Border tile layout, 272, 277
Bowl specifications, ITB, 199
Bringing in customers, 8
Bubble skylight, 334
Builder Magazine, 31, 145
Built-in
cooktops, 123
double oven, 130
ironing center, 138
ovens, 127, 128
Bullnose and cap thin-set trim, 90
Bus stop benches, 11
Business plan, 355-357
Butcher block maple, 85

Cabinet
accessories, 57
layout, Eurostyle, 59-61
shelving system, 56
soffits, 68
space, 43
types and specifications, 49-57
Cabinet, dimensions
abbreviations, 51
dishwasher, 131
standard, 50
Cabinet installation
installation tools, 70
kitchen, 69, 71, 72
manhours, 78, 83
steps, 70
Cabinets
base, 51, 54
bathroom, 154
blind corner, 52, 58
corner, 73
corner treatment, 45
double door, 52, 53
double faced, 52-54
Eurostyle, 59
kitchen, installing, 49
lazy susan, 54
linen, 158
medicine, 155
microwave, 53
oven, 54
sink, 53
special, 51
utility, 55
vanity, 158, 159
wall, 50, 51, 52
Cable identification markings, 250
Calculating SF coverage, 351
Cancellation notice, 30
Carousel cabinet, 73
Carpet, 283
Carpeted step-up, 149
Cash schedule, 372
Cast-iron tubs, 147
Ceiling
application details, 309
framing, 303
height problems, 64
molding installation, 325

Ceiling-hung wall cabinets, 73
Ceilings, 309
redoing, 298
suspended and luminous, 267
suspended, material, 274-276
Cement
mortar, 237, 241
paints, 342
plaster, 321
Cementing, gypsum board, 311, 312
Centers
ironing, 138
meal planning, 41
serving or eating, 41
Ceramic mosaic trim, 91
Ceramic tile, 85, 157
backsplash, 116
choices, 157, 159
countertops, 86, 88, 94-99
glazed trim, 245
glazed/unglazed, 86
installation components, 238-239
installed on Wonder-Board, 101
shower floor, 224
step-up, 149
tub and shower wall, 235
tub surround, 230
types, 235
Ceramic Tile Institute of America, 243
Chart, room area, 316
Checklist, bathroom, 165-168
Circuits, 249
Clean-up center, 38
Clean-up sink, 33, 38, 40
Cleats, 207
Clips, spring wire, 321
Close-coupled toilets, 153
Closet flange, 190
Closing the sale, 19
Clustering sky lights, 335
Color coding, electrical, 251
Color, how to use, 42
Colors, choosing, 41
Common wall plumbing, 160
Comparing operating ratios, 373
Comparison, paint binders, 343
Components, tile installation, 238, 239
Compound, joint, 311
Compression nut, 190
Concrete floors, 286
Connections
4-way switches, 262
3-way switches, 258
Contract and proposal, 28
Cooking center, 33, 37, 39
Cooktops, 81, 82, 123
Coping molding, 324
Corian, 85, 198, 199, 212
backsplash installation, 115
care of, 119
countertops and work island, 118
countertops, installation, 110
integral countertops and sinks, 107-109
integral tops and bowls, 198
sheets, 105
Corner
installation, dishwasher, 131
lavatory installation, 153
measurement, floor tile, 296
nailing, 308
Correcting irregular walls, 307
Corridor kitchen, 33, 35
Cork tile, 282
Cost estimate form, 25
Cost of doing business, 379

Counter leg, 34
Countertop
glass cooktop, 124
installation, ceramic tile, 88
installation, Corian, 110
installation manhours, 119
materials, 84
storage space, 44
work island, 118
Countertops, 84-87, 105
Covering damaged flooring, 285
Coves, shower, 147,148
Creativity, 370
Cross sections, tile installation, 106
Cross tees, 273, 278, 279
Cross tees and light panels, 271
Crystalline ceramic tile, 157
Curb mount, 329
Curb-mounted skylights, 328
Current
assets, 376
balance sheet, 365
liabilities, 376
Custom bathrooms, 143
Customer profile worksheet, 359
Customer's cancellation notice, 30
Cut out measurement, sink, 122
Cutting
ceiling panels, 279
flooring, 288
molding, 324
Cutting and fitting
one-piece installations, 292
sheet flooring, 289-294

Dal-Tile Corporation, 15
Decorative edge, Corian, 117
Design, 33, 145
bathroom, 143,144
dimension standards, 42,43
kitchen, 32
Desk drawer units, 158
Diagonal corner wall cabinets, 73
Diagrams, wiring, 252-265
Dial assembly, drain, 181
Diffuser panels, 267-268
Dimensions
bathrooms fixtures, 161
built-in oven, 128
Corian, 109
kitchen cabinet, 43
standard cabinet, 50
Direct mail letters, 11
Dishwasher
air gap, 133
cabinet dimensions, 131
drain line, 132
high loop, 133
installation, 131, 133-136
Divided bathroom, 163
Door knob hangers, 11, 12
Door removal, oven, 129
Double-dome skylights, 328
Double-door skylights, 52,53
Double-faced cabinets, 52-54
Double nailing, 310
Drain
bathtub, 173, 174
shower cove, 185
Drain line, dishwasher, 132
Drain linkage, installation, 181, 182
Drawer units, 158
Drawing, shower surround, 225
Drying times, paint, 352
Dry-set mortar, 101-104
Drywall, 306
installation, labor 318
painting specifications, 346

Duplex receptacle, 254
DuPont Company, Inc, 15

Eating center, 41
Elastomeric caulking, 240
Electric cooktops, 82
Electric ranges
  drop-in, 78
  freestanding, 76
  slide-in, 75
Electric panels, 249
Electric wall heaters, 199-202
Electric wall ovens, 77
Electrical
  connections, whirlpool, 177-178
  outlets, bathroom, 154
  system, 252
Electrical terms, 249
Electrical wiring
  diagrams, 252-265
  manhours, 265
  residential, 249
Elevation, 18
Epoxy binders, 342
Equipment requirements, 362
Establishing reference points, 287
Estimating manhours
  appliances, 141, 142
  bathroom fixtures, 209-210
  cabinets, 74, 83
  countertops, 119
  flooring, 297
  gypsum wallboard, 315, 319
  painting, 353, 354
  plastering, 322
  skylights, 337
  suspended ceilings, 280
  tile setting, 244, 248
  trim, 325
  tub/shower surround, 233, 234
  wall coverings, 326
  wall paneling, 320
Estimating paint materials, 350-351
Eurostyle cabinetry, 59
Exhaust fan installation, 202-207
Existing resilient floors, 285
Expense ratios, 374
Expenses, 363, 379

Fan
  hanger bars, 204
  installation, 202-207
  switch connections, 206
Fasteners
  gypsum board, 310, 311
  lath and plaster, 320
  wire, 274
Faucets, 154
Federal law requirements, 30
Fiberboard paneling, 315
Fiberglass shower
  base, 183
  cove installation, 181
  framing, 183, 184
Fiberglass tub/shower, 146, 147
  installation, 187-188
FICA, 378
Finish materials, wallboard, 316
Finish sheet vinyl installation, 294
Finish wall installation, 177
Fire-rated gypsum drywall, 183
First reference line, 288
Fixed assets, 377
Fixtures, bathroom, 147
Flange, closet, 190
Flexible duct, 207
Flexible supply hook-up, 192
Floating angle installation, 308
Floor covering
  installation manhours, 297
  removal, 283
  resilient, 282
Floor plan and elevation, 18
Floor reference points, 287
Floor, sheet vinyl, 283
  fitting, 289-292
  installation, 286
Floor stapling, 292
Floor tile, 282
  corner measurements, 296

installation, 294-296
  layout, 295
Floors
  concrete, 286
  hard, 282
  inspecting, 281
  redoing, 281
Fluorescent lamps, 267
Flush-beam, steel reinforced, 303
Flyers and doorknob hangers, 11, 12
Food preparation center, 33, 37, 39
Food storage, 33, 36
Forms
  bathroom preference, 23
  cost estimate, 25
  kitchen preference, 21
Formed vanity top and bowl, 197-200
Four-inch soil stack, 306
Four-way switches, connecting, 260-262
Framing
  bathtub, 171
  ceiling, 303
  fiberglass shower, 183, 184
  fiberglass tub/shower, 188
  skylight, 329, 332-335
  skylight shaft, 336
  standard tub, 173
  vents and pipes, 306
  whirlpool tub, 178
Framing centers, 306
Furring materials, 318
FUTA, 378

Gas
  cooktops, 81
  freestanding ranges, 79
  slide-in ranges, 80
Gauging plaster, 322
Glass mesh mortar units, 240, 242
Glass mesh mortar units, 240, 242
Glazed tile, 86
  A-type trim, 89
  trim, 245
  trim, installation usage, 87
Gridwork, ceiling, 267-268
Ground fault circuit interrupters, (GFCI), 251
Grout, 236
Gypsum board, 307
  backing, 241, 243
  finishing details, 312
  installation labor, 319
  types, 319
  walls, 298-300
  water resistant, 313
Gypsum finish coat, 322
Gypsum lath, 320
Gypsum plaster, 321
Gypsum white coat, 322

Hair dryer, 207
Hamper, vanity, 158
Hanger wire, 274
Hard flooring, 282
Hardboard and plywood installation, 314
Hardboard, underlayment, 285
Heater
  assembly, 201
  electric, wall, 199
  operation, 202
High loop, dishwasher, 133
Hold-down screws, 117
Home interiors, 338
Hood, range, installation, 125
Horizontal furring, 307
Hot water supply pipe location, 132
House paint, 344
Hydrated lime, 322

Income and expenses worksheet, 364
Income statement/balance sheet, 375
Indoor/outdoor carpet, 283
Inspecting floors, 281
Installation
  appliance units, 74
  base molding, 325
  bathroom fixtures, 170, 209
  bathtub wall kit, 212
  built-in ovens, 127, 128
  ceiling molding, 325
  ceilings, suspended, 274

ceramic tile countertops, 88
ceramic tile, tub/shower walls, 235
Corian backsplash, 115
Corian bathtub wall kit, 214-217
Corian countertop, 110-113
details, tile, 237
dishwasher, 131, 133-136
drain linkage, 181, 182
electric wall heater, 199-202
exhaust fan, 202-207
fan duct, 204
fiberglass shower cove, 181
fiberglass tub/shower units, 187, 188
finish wall material, 177
floating angle, 308
gypsum board backing, 241
gypsum board, water-resistant, 313
hair dryer, 207
ironing center, 138
kitchen cabinets, 49
lavatory, 192-194
pedestal lavatory, 195-197
plywood and hardboard, 314
range hood, 125
self-flashing skylights, 332
sheet vinyl, 286
shower wall, 221, 227-230
sink, 122, 124
skylight, 331
standard cabinets, 69
surface-mounted lighting fixtures, 279
tile-adhesive on laminate, 94
tiling-in bead, 175
toilet, 189-191
trim strip, 219
tub drain, 171, 173, 174
tub/shower surrounds, 211
tub surround over tile, 230
vinyl composition tile, 294-296
wallboard labor, 319
whirlpool tub, 177
Insurance and taxes, 378
Integral vanity tops and bowls, 197-200
Integrity, 370
Interior walls, 302, 305
Interiors, home, 338
Ironing center, 138
Island clean-up center, 40

Job specifications, 25
Joint compound, 311

Keene's cement, 322
Keeping records, 371
Kit
  bathtub surround, 233
  presentation, 14
Kitchen
  appliances, 121
  cabinet dimensions, 43
  cabinetry, 14
  cabinets, installing, 49
  centers, 40, 41
  design and layout, 32-33
  hood, 121
  preference form, 21
  sink, 121
  storage area dimensions, 44
  work island, 35, 36
Kitchens, 34-37
Kohler Company, 14, 16

Lacquer, 344
Laminated plastic, 84
Lap style shower surround, 223
Latex paints, 342
Latex portland cement and mortar, 240
Lath, 319-320
Lavatories, 152, 153
Lavatory installation, 192-194
Laying floor tile, 296
Layout
  bathroom, 143, 144, 160-164
  border tile, 272, 277
  floor tile, 295-296
  kitchen, 32

main ceiling runners, 270
  room, 268
  sheet, suspended ceiling, 269
Lazy susan cabinet, 54
Lead pan, 224
Letters, direct mail, 11
Leveling and setting tub, 176
Liabilities, 365
Liability insurance, 378
Lift assembly drain, 181
Light
  conditions, 341
  diffusers, 268
  distribution, 328
  shaft, 335, 336
Lighting, 42, 154
Lime, 322
Linen cabinet, 158
Load-bearing partition, removal, 302
L-shape kitchen, 33, 34
Luminous ceilings, 267

Main electric panels, 249
Main ceiling runners, 270, 273, 277
Making decisions, 369
Management
  ability, 370
  function, 368
Managing for profits, 368
Manhour estimates
  appliances, 141, 142
  bathroom fixtures, 209-210
  cabinets, 83
  countertops, 119
  electrical wiring, 265
  flooring, 297
  gypsum wallboard, 319
  painting, 353, 354
  plastering, 323
  resilient flooring, 297
  skylights, 337
  suspended ceilings, 280
  tile setting, 244
  trim, 325
  tub/shower surround, 233, 234
  wall coverings, 326
  wall paneling, 320
Marble, 85
Masonry, 345
Masonry painting specifications, 347
Material reference drawing, 225
Meal planning center, 41
Measuring the room, 65, 67
Medicare, 378
Medicine cabinet, 155, 159, 162
Melamine overlay, 84
Memorandum of agreement, 19
Merillat Industries, Inc. 14
Metal corner bead, 316
Metal lath, 320
Microwave cabinet, 53, 56
Minimum dimensions, bathroom fixtures, 161
Miscellaneous expenses, 379
Mitering, 323
Modular fiberglass tub/shower, 147
Molded
  countertops, 85
  shower pan, 222
Molding
  cutting, 324
  patterns and locations, 324
  plaster, 322
  wall, 273
Mortar, 101-104, 237
Mosaics, ceramic tile, 86
Mottled ceramic tile, 157
Mounting heater housing, 199
Multiple coats, plaster, 322

Nail sizes, 308
Nailing at corners, 308
National Association of Home Builders, 31
Net
  profit, 377-378
  revenues, 376
  sales, 377
  working capital, 377
Newspapers, advertising in, 11
NM cable, 250
Notice to customers, 30
NuTone Inc., 16

*O*il paint binders, 342
Oil stain, 344
One-piece toilets, 153
Open styling, kitchen, 299
Operating ratios, 373
Outlets
  bathroom, 154
  split-circuit, 254
  switch controlled, 263-265
  wall, 254
Oven cabinets, 54
Ovens, 77
  built-in, 127-128
Overflow ell, 174
Overhead, 378
Overlay, vinyl sheet flooring,
  289-294

*P*adding, carpet, 283
Paint
  drying times, 350, 352
  materials, 341
  types, 344
Paint estimating
  manhours, 350, 353
  preparation, 354
Painting
  baseboard and molding, 350
  doors, 349
  window and door trim, 350
  windows, 349
Painting specifications
  interior masonry, 347
  interior wood, 345
  plaster/drywall, 346
Panel installation, 214
Paneling, 301, 315
Panels, ceiling, 279
Particleboard underlayment, 285
Partition
  removal, 302, 303
  repairs, 303
Pedestal lavatory, 153, 195-197
Penny conversions, nail, 308
Perlite, 321
Personnel requirements, 362
Plan, business, 355
Planning
  effective advertising, 360
  job, 366
Plans and specs, bathroom, 165
Plaster
  aggregate, 321
  fasteners, 320
  gauging, 322
Plaster painting specifications, 346
Plastering manhours, 323
Plastic
  laminate, 84
  pipe, 146
Plumbing access wall, 182
Plywood underlayment, 285, 314
Posters, advertising, 11
Postformed countertop, 85
Precast terrazzo shower pan, 223
Prefabricated countertops, 85
Pregrouted tile, 237
Preparation for
  installing kitchen cabinets, 64
  painting wood surfaces, 344
Presanded dry-set mortar, 240
Presentation
  kit, 14
  selling, 17
Pressure-sensitive tape, 175
Primer for paint and enamel, 344
Professional attitude, 31
Profit, managing, 368
Properties, paint binders, 343
Proposal and contract, 28
Prospect list, 12

*Q*uarry tile, 236
Quick lime, 322

*R*adio advertising, 11
Range hoods, 56, 125
Ranges, 75-76, 78-80
  countertop, 44
Ratios
  balance sheet, 374
  expense, 374
  operating, 373

Rear outlet toilets, 153
Receptacles, bathroom, 154
Record keeping, 371
Rectangular metal tubs, 147
Redi-Set tile, 237
Redoing
  floors, 281
  walls, 298
Reference lines, 288
Reference string, 277
Refrigeration center, 33, 36
Refrigerator, countertop, 44
Reinforced mortar bed, 242
Remodeling bathrooms, 146
Removal
  baseboard, 286
  ceramic tile, 231
  flooring, 283-284
  partitions, 302, 303
Repairs, wall, 303
Residential electrical systems, 249
Resilient Floor Covering Institute,
  284
Resilient floor coverings, 282, 284
  manhours, 297
Retainer plate tub, 174
Romex, 250
Roof opening skylights, 333
Room
  layout, 268-269
  perimeter, 318
  preparation, 286
  size, 147
Room area chart, 316
RTV sealant, 175
Rubber-base paints, 342
Rubber tile, 282
Runners, main, 273, 277
Running new cable, 257

*S*ales, 13
Scalloped trim, 232
Scraping, old flooring, 284
Scratch coat, plaster, 237
Seam matching, 288, 289
Second reference line, 288
Self-flashing skylights, 332
Selling steps, 16
Sheetrock application, 308-312
Sheet vinyl installation, 286, 287
Shims, 307
Shower
  receptors, 241
  surround with tile, 224
  wall installation, 221, 227-230
  walls, 241
Shower cove
  drain, 185
  installation, 181, 184-186
  modules, 147, 151
Shower pan
  installation, 241, 242
  molded, 222
  precast terrazzo, 223
Sidewall application details, 309
Single nailing, 310
Single-pole switch, 257
Sink
  base cabinets, 53
  clean-up, 33, 38, 40
  cutout measurements, 122
  fronts, 53
  installation, 122, 124
  size, 44
Skid boards, 173
Skylights
  bubble, 334
  clustering, 335
  double-dome, 328
  framing, 329, 332-334
  installation, 327
  light shaft, 335-336
  self-flashing, 332
  shaft framing, 336
  single-dome, 328
Solid-material countertops, 105
Special cabinets, 51
Special framing, 305
Specifications
  architectural, 246, 247
  bathroom, 165
  cabinets, 52-57
  job, 25
  tub, 172

Splicing molding, 324
Split-circuit outlet, 254
Spreading adhesive, 288
Staining interior wood, 346
Standard dimensions
  bathtub, 147
  cabinet, 50
  design, 42-43
Stapling, flooring, 292
State Unemployment Insurance, 378
Steel
  reinforced beam, 303
  tubs, 147
Step-down tub design, 150
Stopper, drain, 182
Storage
  bathroom, 154
  kitchen 43-44
Straight-wall kitchen, 33, 35-37
Strainer, tub, 174
Suction assembly, whirlpool, 181
Surface preparation, painting, 344
Suspended ceilings, 267
  installation, 274
  manhours, 280
  material requirements, 274-276
Switch-controlled outlet, 263, 265
Switch leg, 253
Switch loop, 253
Switches
  four-way, 260
  four-way connections, 262
  single pole, 257
  three-way, 258-260

*T*ail piece, tub, 174
Tangible net worth, 376
Taping, gypsum board, 311-312
Taxes, 378
Teak wood tubs, 147
Tees, cross, 273
Television advertising, 11
Template, lavatory, 193
Texture and color sense, 338
Three-way switch, 258
  connections, 259-262
Three-wire cable, 251
Tile
  ceramic, 85
  hints, 240
  mottled or crystalline, 157
  Redi-Set, 237
  resilient, 284
  run layout, 272
  wainscot, 238
Tile Council of America, Inc., 243
Tile installation
  adhesive, 92, 93
  conventional mortar, 94-99,
   237-239
  cross section, 106
  dry-set mortar, 101
  manhours, 244, 248
Toilet installation, 189-192
Toilets, 153
Tongue & groove paneling, 315
Tools and materials
  cabinet installation, 70
  Corian installation, 108, 109, 212
  lavatory installation, 192
  toilet installation, 189
  tub installation, 171
Towel bar spacing, 162
Transferring measurements, 288
Trash compactor, 39
Trim
  Corian, 219
  glazed tile, 245
  installation, 325
  scalloped, 232
  wood, 323
Trim cap, whirlpool, 179
Twenty amp circuits, 251
Two-wire cable with ground, 251
Tub
  drain installation, 173-174
  framing, 173, 178
  leveling and setting, 176
  specifications, 172
  whirlpool installation, 177
Tub/shower combination, 147, 148
Tubs, bath, 147-150

Turnover
  tangible net-worth, 376
  working capital, 377

*U*nderlayment, floor, 285
Uneven areas, cabinet installation,
  68
Unglazed tile, 86
Urethane, 342
U-shape kitchen, 33, 34
Utility cabinets, 55

*V*anity cabinets, 154, 158, 159
Varnishes, 344
Vent stacks, 305
Ventilation, kitchen, 46
Vermiculite, 321
Vinyl
  composition tile installation,
   294-296
  floor fitting, 289-292
  sheet floors, 283
  tiling-in bead, 175
Void corner base cabinet, 73
Volts, 249

*W*all
  finishes, 305
  heaters, electric, 199-202
  installation, skylight, 334
  kit, bathtub surround, 212
  molding, 273-274
  mounted hair dryer, 207
  outlet, 254
  paneling installation manhours,
   320
  surfaces, figuring, 322
  surround, ABS plastic, 147
Wall cabinets, 50-52, 68, 69
  vanity, 158
Wall coverings
  choices, 156
  manhours, 326
  wallpaper, 326
Wallboard, gypsum
  area table, 317
  finish materials, 316
  labor costs, 315
  tape, 316
Walls
  gypsum board, 298-300, 310
  interior, 302
  redoing, 298
Water damage, 170
Water-resistant sealer, 177
Watts, 249
Whirlpool tub
  ball and retainer assembly, 180
  electrical connection, 178
  framing, 178
  installation, 149, 177
  specifications, 172
  trim and assemblies, 179
Wire
  color coding, 251
  fasteners, 274
  hanger, 274
  size and capacity, 250
Wire connection
  heater, 201
  ironing center, 140
  whirlpool tub, 178
Wiring
  diagrams, 252-265
  residential, 249
Wonder-Board, 101
Wood
  brackets, 303
  painting specifications, 345
  paneling, 315
  staining specification, 346
  trim, 323
Wood-Metal Industries, Inc., 14
Work
  centers, 36
  island, 35, 36, 37
  schedule, 367
  triangle, 33
Workers' Compensation Insurance,
  378

*Y*ellow pages, 11

Practical References for Builders

Painter's Handbook
Loaded with "how-to" information you'll use every day to get professional results on any job: The best way to prepare a surface for painting or repainting. Selecting and using the right materials and tools (including airless spray). Tips for repainting kitchens, bathrooms, cabinets, eaves and porches. How to match and blend colors. Why coatings fail and what to do about it. Thirty profitable specialties that could be your gravy train in the painting business. Every professional painter needs this practical handbook. **320 pages, 8½ x 11, $21.25**

Remodeler's Handbook
The complete manual of home improvement contracting: Planning the job, estimating costs, doing the work, running your company and making profits. Pages of sample forms, contracts, documents, clear illustrations and examples. Chapters on evaluating the work, rehabilitation, kitchens, bathrooms, adding living area, re-flooring, re-siding, re-roofing, replacing windows and doors, installing new wall and ceiling cover, re-painting, upgrading insulation, combating moisture damage, estimating, selling your services, and bookkeeping for remodelers. **416 pages, 8½ x 11, $23.00**

Kitchen Designer
Create the perfect kitchen for your customers with this ¼" scale isometric kitchen planner. Includes symbols for virtually every size cabinet and appliance plus tables, chairs, doors, windows, and every element that goes into planning a kitchen remodel. With these stick-down and movable scale objects you can create a 3-dimensional kitchen plan that really brings your remodeling ideas to life and gets you the job. **$23.00**

Rough Carpentry
All rough carpentry is covered in detail: sills, girders, columns, joists, sheathing, ceiling, roof and wall framing, roof trusses, dormers, bay windows, furring and grounds, stairs and insulation. Many of the 24 chapters explain practical code approved methods for saving lumber and time without sacrificing quality. Chapters on columns, headers, rafters, joists and girders show how to use simple engineering principles to select the right lumber dimension for whatever species and grade you are using. **288 pages, 8½ x 11, $16.00**

Video: Designing Your Kitchen
This videotape, put together by a kitchen designer with over 25 years' experience, can help you create kitchen designs to impress your customers and get you the job. Here you'll see how to create your own sample book, how to use a color board to coordinate color and material; how to improve dark kitchens with minimum expense, how to replace appliances, sinks and tile, add bay windows, granite countertops, and utilize storage space. You'll see how to use scale models in kitchen planning to allow your clients to visualize the completed job. **1 hr. and 15 minutes, VHS, $32.00**

Estimating Painting Costs
An accurate, step-by-step estimating system, based on a set of easy-to-use formulas. You'll find complete manhour and material tables for every painting operation, from simple residential repaints to the most complicated commercial job -- even heavy industrial and government work. There are valuable estimating tips, tables, take-off forms and checklists you can copy and use, and sample estimates that show exactly how to use this reliable estimating system. **8½ x 11, 448 pages, $28.00**

National Construction Estimator
Current building costs in dollars and cents for residential, commercial and industrial construction. Prices for every commonly used building material, and the proper labor cost associated with installation of the material. Everything figured out to give you the "in place" cost in seconds. Many time-saving rules of thumb, waste and coverage factors and estimating tables are included. **544 pages, 8½ x 11, $19.50. Revised annually.**

Manual of Professional Remodeling
This is the practical manual of professional remodeling written by an experienced and successful remodeling contractor. Shows how to evaluate a job and avoid 30-minute jobs that take all day, what to fix and what to leave alone, and what to watch for in dealing with subcontractors. Includes chapters on calculating space requirements, repairing structural defects, remodeling kitchens, baths, walls and ceilings, doors and windows, floors, roofs, installing fireplaces and chimneys (including built-ins), skylights, and exterior siding. Includes blank forms, checklists, sample contracts, and proposals you can copy and use. **400 pages, 8½ x 11, $19.75**

Contractor's Guide to the Building Code
Explains in plain English exactly what the Uniform Building Code requires and shows how to design and construct residential and light commercial buildings that will pass inspection the first time. Suggests how to work with the inspector to minimize construction costs, what common building short cuts are likely to be cited, and where exceptions are granted. **312 pages, 5½ x 8½, $16.25**

How to Sell Remodeling
Proven, effective sales methods for repair and remodeling contractors: finding qualified leads, making the sales call, identifying what your prospects really need, pricing the job, arranging financing, and closing the sale. Explains how to organize and staff a sales team, how to bring in the work to keep your crews busy and your business growing, and much more. Includes blank forms, tables, and charts. **240 pages, 8½ x 11, $17.50**

Residential Electrical Design
Explains what every builder needs to know about designing electrical systems for residential construction. Shows how to draw up an electrical plan from the blueprints, including the service entrance, grounding, lighting requirements for kitchen, bedroom and bath and how to lay them out. Explains how to plan electrical heating systems and what equipment you'll need, how to plan outdoor lighting, and much more. If you are a builder who ever has to plan an electrical system, you should have this book. **194 pages, 8½ x 11, $11.50**

Basic Plumbing with Illustrations
The journeyman's and apprentice's guide to installing plumbing, piping and fixtures in residential and light commercial buildings: how to select the right materials, lay out the job and do professional quality plumbing work. Explains the use of essential tools and materials, how to make repairs, maintain plumbing systems, install fixtures and add to existing systems. **320 pages, 8½ x 11, $22.00**

Spec Builder's Guide
Explains how to plan and build a home, control your construction costs, and then sell the house at a price that earns a decent return on the time and money you've invested. Includes professional tips to ensure success as a spec builder: how government statistics help you judge the housing market, cutting costs at every opportunity without sacrificing quality, and taking advantage of construction cycles. Every chapter includes checklists, diagrams, charts, figures, and estimating tables. **448 pages, 8½ x 11, $24.00**

Paint Contractor's Manual
How to start and run a profitable paint contracting company: getting set up and organized to handle volume work, avoiding the mistakes most painters make, getting top production from your crews and the most value from your advertising dollar. Shows how to estimate all prep and painting. Loaded with manhour estimates, sample forms, contracts, charts, tables and examples you can use. **224 pages, 8½ x 11, $19.25**

Stair Builders Handbook

If you know the floor to floor rise, this handbook will give you everything else: the number and dimension of treads and risers, the total run, the correct well hole opening, the angle of incline, the quantity of materials and settings for your framing square for over 3,500 code approved rise and run combinations—several for every 1/8 inch interval from a 3 foot to a 12 foot floor to floor rise. **416 pages, 8½ x 5½, $13.75**

Carpentry for Residential Construction

How to do professional quality carpentry work in homes and apartments. Illustrated instructions show you everything from setting batter boards to framing floors and walls, installing floor, wall and roof sheathing, and applying roofing. Covers finish carpentry, also: How to install each type of cornice, frieze, lookout, ledger, fascia and soffit; how to hang windows and doors; how to install siding, drywall and trim. Each job description includes the tools and materials needed, the estimated manhours required, and a step-by-step guide to each part of the task. **400 pages, 5½ x 8½, $19.75**

Video: Kitchens

How to best layout and design a kitchen, how to install upper wall, base, peninsula, pantry, and island cabinets. It also covers how to install and scribe countertops for an island cabinet, a kitchen passthrough, and 90 and 45 degree angles. You'll see how to install a kitchen sink, disposal, and dishwasher. Also explains how to wire and install a cooktop, oven, and overhead cooktop hood. **60 minutes, VHS, $15.50**

Roof Framing

Frame any type of roof in common use today, even if you've never framed a roof before. Shows how to use a pocket calculator to figure any common, hip, valley, and jack rafter length in seconds. Over 400 illustrations take you through every measurement and every cut on each type of roof: gable, hip, Dutch, Tudor, gambrel, shed, gazebo and more. **480 pages, 5½ x 8½, $22.00**

Video: Roof Framing 1

A complete step-by step training video on the basics of roof cutting by Marshall Gross, the author of the book **Roof Framing**. Shows and explains calculating rise, run, and pitch, and laying out and cutting common rafters. **90 minutes, VHS, $80.00.**

Video: Roof Framing 2

A complete training video on the more advanced techniques of roof framing by Marshall Gross, the author of **Roof Framing**, shows and explains layout and framing an irregular roof, and making tie-ins to an existing roof. **90 minutes, VHS, $80.00.**

Bookkeeping for Builders

This book will show you simple, practical instructions for setting up and keeping accurate records — with a minimum of effort and frustration. Shows how to set up the essentials of a record keeping system: the payment journal, income journal, general journal, records for fixed assets, accounts receivable, payables and purchases, petty cash, and job costs. You'll be able to keep the records required by the I.R.S., as well as accurate and organized business records for your own use. **208 pages, 8½ x 11, $19.75**

 Craftsman Book Company
6058 Corte del Cedro, P.O. Box 6500
Carlsbad, CA 92008 · 0992
FAX No. (619) 438-0398

 In a hurry?
We accept phone orders charged to your MasterCard, Visa or American Express
Call (619) 438-7828

Name (Please print clearly)

Company

Address

City/State/Zip

Send check or money order
Total enclosed _____ (In California add 6% tax)
If you prefer, use your ☐ Visa or ☐ MasterCard
Card no. _____
Expiration date _____ Initials _____

We ship within 48 hours of receiving your order. If you prefer, we can ship U.P.S. For the fastest service available call in your order with your Visa or MasterCard number. We will ship within 24 hours.

These books are tax deductible when used to improve or maintain your professional skill.

10 Day Money Back GUARANTEE

☐ 22.00 Basic Plumbing with Illustrations
☐ 19.75 Bookkeeping For Builders
☐ 19.75 Carpentry for Residential Construction
☐ 16.25 Contractor's Guide to the Building Code
☐ 28.00 Estimating Painting Costs
☐ 17.50 How to Sell Remodeling
☐ 23.00 Kitchen Designer
☐ 19.75 Manual of Professional Remodeling
☐ 19.50 National Construction Estimator
☐ 19.25 Paint Contractor's Manual
☐ 21.25 Painter's Handbook
☐ 23.00 Remodeler's Handbook
☐ 11.50 Residential Electrical Design
☐ 22.00 Roof Framing
☐ 16.00 Rough Carpentry
☐ 24.00 Spec Builder's Guide
☐ 13.75 Stair Builder's Handbook
☐ 32.00 Video: Designing Your Kitchen
☐ 15.50 Video: Kitchens
☐ 80.00 Video: Roof Framing 1
☐ 80.00 Video: Roof Framing 2
☐ 26.25 Remodeling Kitchens & Baths

Craftsman Book Company
6058 Corte del Cedro
Carlsbad, CA 92009

10 Day Money Back GUARANTEE

In a hurry?
We accept phone orders charged to your MasterCard, Visa or Am. Ex. Call (619) 438-7828

Name (Please print clearly)
_____

Company
_____

Address
_____

City/State/Zip
_____

Total Enclosed _____
(In California add 6% tax)

Use your ☐ Visa ☐ MasterCard ☐ Am. Ex.
Card # _____
Exp. date _____ Initials _____

☐ 95.00 Audio: Construction Field Sup.
☐ 19.95 Audio: Plumbers Exam
☐ 22.00 Basic Plumbing with Illust.
☐ 30.00 Berger Building Cost File
☐ 11.25 Blprt Read. for Blding Trades
☐ 19.75 Bookkeeping for Builders
☐ 17.25 Builder's Guide to Accting. Rev.
☐ 15.25 Blder's Guide to Const. Fin.
☐ 15.50 Builder's Office Manual Revised
☐ 14.00 Building Cost Manual
☐ 11.75 Building Layout
☐ 25.50 Carpentry Estimating
☐ 19.75 Carp. for Residential Const.
☐ 19.00 Carp. in Commercial Const.
☐ 16.25 Carpentry Layout
☐ 17.75 Computers: Blder's New Tool
☐ 14.50 Concrete and Formwork
☐ 20.50 Concrete Const. & Estimating
☐ 26.00 Const. Estimating Ref. Data
☐ 22.00 Construction Superintending
☐ 19.25 Const. Surveying & Layout
☐ 19.00 Cont. Growth & Profit Guide
☐ 16.25 Cont. Guide to the Blding Code
☐ 16.75 Contractor's Survival Manual
☐ 16.50 Cont. Year-Round Tax Guide
☐ 15.75 Cost Rec. for Const. Est.
☐ 9.50 Dial-A-Length Rafterule
☐ 18.25 Drywall Contracting
☐ 13.75 Electrical Blueprint Reading
☐ 25.00 Electrical Const. Estimator
☐ 19.00 Estimating Electrical Const.

☐ 17.00 Estimating Home Blding Costs
☐ 28.00 Estimating Painting Costs
☐ 17.25 Estimating Plumbing Costs
☐ 21.50 Esti. Tables for Home Building
☐ 22.75 Exca. & Grading Handbook, Rev.
☐ 9.25 E-Z Square
☐ 10.50 Finish Carpentry
☐ 23.00 Kitchen Designer
☐ 24.75 Hdbk of Const. Cont. Vol. 1
☐ 24.75 Hdbk of Const. Cont. Vol. 2
☐ 15.00 Home Wiring: Imp., Ext., Repairs
☐ 17.50 How to Sell Remodeling
☐ 24.50 HVAC Contracting
☐ 20.25 Manual of Elect. Contracting
☐ 19.75 Manual of Prof. Remodeling
☐ 13.50 Masonry & Concrete Const.
☐ 26.50 Masonry Estimating
☐ 19.50 National Const. Estimator
☐ 23.75 Op. the Tractor-Loader-Backhoe
☐ 19.25 Paint Contractor's Manual
☐ 21.25 Painter's Handbook
☐ 23.50 Pipe & Excavation Contracting
☐ 13.00 Plan. and Design. Plumbing Sys.
☐ 19.95 Plumber's Exam Audiotape
☐ 21.00 Plumber's Exam Prep. Guide
☐ 18.00 Plumber's Handbook Revised
☐ 14.25 Rafter Length Manual
☐ 23.00 Remodeler's Handbook
☐ 26.25 Remodeling Kitchens & Baths
☐ 11.50 Residential Electrical Design
☐ 16.75 Residential Electrician's Hdbk.

☐ 18.25 Residential Wiring
☐ 22.00 Roof Framing
☐ 14.00 Roofers Handbook
☐ 16.00 Rough Carpentry
☐ 21.00 Running Your Remodeling Bus.
☐ 24.00 Spec Builder's Guide
☐ 13.75 Stair Builder's Handbook
☐ 15.50 Video: Asphalt Shingle Roofing
☐ 15.50 Video: Bathroom Tile
☐ 15.50 Video: Contracting a Home 1
☐ 15.50 Video: Contracting a Home 2
☐ 32.00 Video: Designing Your Kitchen
☐ 24.75 Video: Drywall Contracting 1
☐ 24.75 Video: Drywall Contracting 2
☐ 15.50 Video: Electrical Wiring
☐ 15.50 Video: Exterior Painting
☐ 15.50 Video: Finish Carpentry
☐ 15.50 Video: Hanging An Exterior Door
☐ 15.50 Video: Int. Paint & Wallpaper
☐ 15.50 Video: Kitchen Renovation
☐ 24.75 Video: Paint Contractor's 1
☐ 24.75 Video: Paint Contractor's 2
☐ 15.50 Video: Plumbing
☐ 80.00 Video: Roof Framing 1
☐ 80.00 Video: Roof Framing 2
☐ 15.50 Video: Rough Carpentry
☐ 15.50 Video: Windows & Doors
☐ 15.50 Video: Wood Siding
☐ 7.50 Visual Stairule
☐ 14.25 Wood-Frame House Const.

rkb card

Craftsman Book Company
6058 Corte del Cedro
Carlsbad, CA 92009

10 Day Money Back GUARANTEE

In a hurry?
We accept phone orders charged to your MasterCard, Visa or Am. Ex. Call (619) 438-7828

Name (Please print clearly)
_____

Company
_____

Address
_____

City/State/Zip
_____

Total Enclosed _____
(In California add 6% tax)

Use your ☐ Visa ☐ MasterCard ☐ Am. Ex.
Card # _____
Exp. date _____ Initials _____

☐ 95.00 Audio: Construction Field Sup.
☐ 19.95 Audio: Plumbers Exam
☐ 22.00 Basic Plumbing with Illust.
☐ 30.00 Berger Building Cost File
☐ 11.25 Blprt Read. for Blding Trades
☐ 19.75 Bookkeeping for Builders
☐ 17.25 Builder's Guide to Accting. Rev.
☐ 15.25 Blder's Guide to Const. Fin.
☐ 15.50 Builder's Office Manual Revised
☐ 14.00 Building Cost Manual
☐ 11.75 Building Layout
☐ 25.50 Carpentry Estimating
☐ 19.75 Carp. for Residential Const.
☐ 19.00 Carp. in Commercial Const.
☐ 16.25 Carpentry Layout
☐ 17.75 Computers: Blder's New Tool
☐ 14.50 Concrete and Formwork
☐ 20.50 Concrete Const. & Estimating
☐ 26.00 Const. Estimating Ref. Data
☐ 22.00 Construction Superintending
☐ 19.25 Const. Surveying & Layout
☐ 19.00 Cont. Growth & Profit Guide
☐ 16.25 Cont. Guide to the Blding Code
☐ 16.75 Contractor's Survival Manual
☐ 16.50 Cont. Year-Round Tax Guide
☐ 15.75 Cost Rec. for Const. Est.
☐ 9.50 Dial-A-Length Rafterule
☐ 18.25 Drywall Contracting
☐ 13.75 Electrical Blueprint Reading
☐ 25.00 Electrical Const. Estimator
☐ 19.00 Estimating Electrical Const.

☐ 17.00 Estimating Home Blding Costs
☐ 28.00 Estimating Painting Costs
☐ 17.25 Estimating Plumbing Costs
☐ 21.50 Esti. Tables for Home Building
☐ 22.75 Exca. & Grading Handbook, Rev.
☐ 9.25 E-Z Square
☐ 10.50 Finish Carpentry
☐ 23.00 Kitchen Designer
☐ 24.75 Hdbk of Const. Cont. Vol. 1
☐ 24.75 Hdbk of Const. Cont. Vol. 2
☐ 15.00 Home Wiring: Imp., Ext., Repairs
☐ 17.50 How to Sell Remodeling
☐ 24.50 HVAC Contracting
☐ 20.25 Manual of Elect. Contracting
☐ 19.75 Manual of Prof. Remodeling
☐ 13.50 Masonry & Concrete Const.
☐ 26.50 Masonry Estimating
☐ 19.50 National Const. Estimator
☐ 23.75 Op. the Tractor-Loader-Backhoe
☐ 19.25 Paint Contractor's Manual
☐ 21.25 Painter's Handbook
☐ 23.50 Pipe & Excavation Contracting
☐ 13.00 Plan. and Design. Plumbing Sys.
☐ 19.95 Plumber's Exam Audiotape
☐ 21.00 Plumber's Exam Prep. Guide
☐ 18.00 Plumber's Handbook Revised
☐ 14.25 Rafter Length Manual
☐ 23.00 Remodeler's Handbook
☐ 26.25 Remodeling Kitchens & Baths
☐ 11.50 Residential Electrical Design
☐ 16.75 Residential Electrician's Hdbk.

☐ 18.25 Residential Wiring
☐ 22.00 Roof Framing
☐ 14.00 Roofers Handbook
☐ 16.00 Rough Carpentry
☐ 21.00 Running Your Remodeling Bus.
☐ 24.00 Spec Builder's Guide
☐ 13.75 Stair Builder's Handbook
☐ 15.50 Video: Asphalt Shingle Roofing
☐ 15.50 Video: Bathroom Tile
☐ 15.50 Video: Contracting a Home 1
☐ 15.50 Video: Contracting a Home 2
☐ 32.00 Video: Designing Your Kitchen
☐ 24.75 Video: Drywall Contracting 1
☐ 24.75 Video: Drywall Contracting 2
☐ 15.50 Video: Electrical Wiring
☐ 15.50 Video: Exterior Painting
☐ 15.50 Video: Finish Carpentry
☐ 15.50 Video: Hanging An Exterior Door
☐ 15.50 Video: Int. Paint & Wallpaper
☐ 15.50 Video: Kitchen Renovation
☐ 24.75 Video: Paint Contractor's 1
☐ 24.75 Video: Paint Contractor's 2
☐ 15.50 Video: Plumbing
☐ 80.00 Video: Roof Framing 1
☐ 80.00 Video: Roof Framing 2
☐ 15.50 Video: Rough Carpentry
☐ 15.50 Video: Windows & Doors
☐ 15.50 Video: Wood Siding
☐ 7.50 Visual Stairule
☐ 14.25 Wood-Frame House Const.

rkb card

BUSINESS REPLY MAIL

FIRST CLASS   PERMIT NO. 271   CARLSBAD, CA

POSTAGE WILL BE PAID BY ADDRESSEE

Craftsman Book Company
6058 Corte Del Cedro
P. O. Box 6500
Carlsbad, CA 92008 — 0992

BUSINESS REPLY MAIL

FIRST CLASS   PERMIT NO. 271   CARLSBAD, CA

POSTAGE WILL BE PAID BY ADDRESSEE

Craftsman Book Company
6058 Corte Del Cedro
P. O. Box 6500
Carlsbad, CA 92008 — 0992

BUSINESS REPLY MAIL

FIRST CLASS   PERMIT NO. 271   CARLSBAD, CA

POSTAGE WILL BE PAID BY ADDRESSEE

Craftsman Book Company
6058 Corte Del Cedro
P. O. Box 6500
Carlsbad, CA 92008 — 0992